Visual C++ Templates

PRENTICE HALL PTR MICROSOFT® TECHNOLOGIES SERIES

- Tuning and Sizing NT Server
  Aubley
- Windows NT Device Driver Book
  Baker
- Building Microsoft SQL Server 7 Web Sites
  Byrne
- Building SQL Server Web Sites
  Byrne
- COM-CORBA Interoperability
  Geraghty/Joyce/Moriarty/Noone
- Windows NT 4.0 Server: Security Guide
  Goncalves
- Web Database Development for Windows Platforms
  Gutierrez
- Visual Basic 6: Design, Specification, and Objects
  Hollis
- Architecting and Admistering a Microsoft Backoffice
  Kemp/Goncalves/Kemp
- Windows NT Cluster Server Guidebook
  Libertone
- Microsoft Site Server 3.0 Commerce Edition
  Libertone/Scoppa
- Building COM Applications with Internet Explorer
  Loveman
- Distributed COM Application Development Using Visual C++ 6.0
  Maloney
- Windows NT Security
  McInerney
- Zero Administration Kit for Windows
  McInerney
- NT Network Programming Toolkit
  Murphy
- Introduction to Windows 98 Programming
  Murray/Pappas
- Visual C++ Templates
  Murray/Pappas
- Understanding DCOM
  Rubin/Brain
- Internetworking with Microsoft TCP/IP on Microsoft Windows NT 4.0
  Ryvkin
- Windows NT Server: Management and Control, 2nd ed.
  Spencer/Goncalves
- Microsoft Technology: Networking, Concepts, Tools
  Woodard/Gattuccio/Brain

PRENTICE HALL PTR MICROSOFT® TECHNOLOGIES SERIES

William H. Murray/Chris H. Pappas

Visual C++ Templates

Prentice Hall, Upper Saddle River, NJ 07458
www.phptr.com

Editorial/Production Supervision: *Mary Sudul*
Acquisitions Editor: *Jeffrey Pepper*
Marketing Manager: *Dan Rush*
Manufacturing Manager: *Maura Goldstaub*
Copy Editor: *Christa Carroll*
Cover Design Direction: *Jerry Votta*
Series Design: *Gail Cocker-Bogusz*

Prentice-Hall, Inc.
Upper Saddle River, NJ 07458

Prentice Hall books are widely used by corporations and government agencies for training, marketing, and resale.

The publisher offers discounts on this book when ordered in bulk quantities. For more information, contact Corporate Sales Department, Phone: 800-382-3419; fax: 201-236-7141; email: corpsales@prenhall.com or write Corporate Sales Department, Prentice Hall PTR, One Lake Street, Upper Saddle River, NJ 07458.

Printed in the United States of America

10 9 8 7 6 5 4 3 2 1

ISBN 0-13-022487-1

Prentice-Hall International (UK) Limited, *London*
Prentice-Hall of Australia Pty. Limited, *Sydney*
Prentice-Hall Canada Inc., *Toronto*
Prentice-Hall Hispanoamericana, S.A., *Mexico*
Prentice-Hall of India Private Limited, *New Delhi*
Prentice-Hall of Japan, Inc., *Tokyo*
Prentice-Hall(Singapore) Pte. Ltd., *Singapore*
Editora Prentice-Hall do Brasil, Ltda., *Rio de Janeiro*

DEDICATED TO OUR FRIEND

Teresa Pendergrass

CONTENTS

PREFACE

Programming with the STL and Windows MFC

This is an exciting time to be a programmer—exciting, but sometimes a little scary. The knowledge base for C and C++ programmers has grown tremendously in the past few years. The first hurtle included procedure-oriented Windows programming, but has now grown to include object-oriented MFC Windows programming, OLE, STL and more!

This book assumes a knowledge of object-oriented C++ programming at the beginner/intermediate level. You'll quickly apply your programming knowledge to these new programming concepts.

In this book, Murray and Pappas will guide you through a solid integrated understanding of the latest STL (Standard Template Library) concepts couple with MFC's (Microsoft Foundation Class library) programming concepts that apply to both Windows 98 and Windows 2000.

The first six chapters deal exclusively with the STL. You'll learn terms, definitions and reasons for using the STL. Many command line examples will teach new programming concepts in simple applications.

In the next six chapters, you'll learn how to develop object-oriented MFC Windows applications. It's all here—wizards, icons, cursors, menus, dialog boxes and more. When you complete this group of chapters, you'll have a solid understanding of object-oriented programming under Windows.

In the final four chapters, STL concepts from the first six chapters are integrated with MFC Windows applications, from the second six chapters, to build robust MFC Windows applications using the STL. When you complete these four chapters, you understand how well both the STL and MFC integrate together to produce powerful new applications.

O N E

What Is the Standard Template Library?

From a programming point of view, today's development environment is a hundred times more complex than a decade ago. Instead of PC application development targeting a standalone DOS text-mode environment, it must now deal with hundreds of PC clones and other popular competing platforms.

The Complexity of Multiplatform Target Environments

These new architectures have their own evolving operating systems and multitasking, multimedia capabilities. Add to these the typical Internet presence. In other words, today's programming environment, programmed by a single developer, was once the domain of systems, communications, security, networking, utility, etc. specialists all working as a team to keep the "mother ship," or mainframe, up and running!

Something had to come along to enable application developers to keep pace with this ever-increasing resource management nightmare. Voilà, enter C and C++. These new languages incorporated brand-new programming capabilities to melt through this hidden iceberg of programming demands.

Unintentional Misuse or Ignorance of C/C++ Features

The biggest stumbling block to accessing these incredibly powerful C/C++ features is ignorance of their existence. In the real world, most experienced FORTRAN, COBOL, Pascal, PL/I, and Assembly Language programmers, when asked by their bosses to use a new language, taught themselves the new language! Why? Because of course, the company wouldn't give them the time off. They diligently studied nights and weekends, on their own, and mapped their understanding of whatever language they knew well, to the new language's syntax.

This approach worked for decades as long as a programmer went from one "older high-level language" to the next. Unfortunately, this approach, when it comes to C/C++, leaves the diligent self-motivated, learn-on-his/her-own employee, *fired* and wondering what went wrong *this time?*

Here's a very small example to illustrate the point. In COBOL, for instance, to increment a variable by 1, you would write:

```
accumulator = accumulator + 1;
```

Then one day the boss says that you need to write the program in FORTRAN. You learn FORTRAN and rewrite the statement:

```
accumulator = accumulator + 1;
```

No problem. Then your company migrates to Pascal and once again you teach yourself the new syntax:

```
accumulator := accumulator + 1;
```

Ta da! Then your boss says that your million dollar code needs to be ported over to Microsoft Windows in C/C++. After a divorce, heart attack, and alcohol addiction, you emerge feeling that you have mastered Microsoft Windows/C/C++ logic and syntax and finally rewrite the statement:

```
iaccumulator = iaccumulator + 1; //i for integer in
Hungarian notation
```

and you get fired! The senior programmer, hired from a local two-year college, looks at your code and scoffs at your inept translation. Oh, sure you got the idea behind Hungarian Notation (a C/C++ naming convention that precedes every variable's name with an abbreviation of its data type), but you created a literal statement *translation* instead of incorporating the efficiency alternatives available in C/C++.

Your senior programmer, green, twenty years younger than you, only knowing Microsoft Windows, C and C++ syntax, knew that the statement should have been written:

```
iaccumulator++;
```

This statement, using the C/C++ increment operator, efficiently instructs the compiler to delete the double fetch/decode of the incorrectly written *translation* and to treat the variable *iaccumulator*, as its name implies, as an accumulator within a register, a much more efficient machine language encoding.

This extremely simple code example is only the beginning of hundreds of C/C++ language features waiting, like quicksand, to catch the unwary programmer.

Data Structures—The Course to Separate Hackers from Pros!

In a programmer's formal educational path stands a course typically called Data Structures, which statistically has an attrition rate of 50%. Why? Because it deals with two extremely efficient concepts, pointers, and dynamic memory allocation/deallocation, which when combined generate a geometric complexity in program development and debugging requirements. These concepts typically present such a steep learning curve that many programmers either avoid the course altogether, or lop along getting by, and then *never* using the concepts in the real world.

This result is unfortunate, since pointers and dynamic memory allocation present some of the most powerful and efficient algorithms available to a programmer. Enter the Standard Template Library!

So, Just What Is the Standard Template Library?

In a nutshell, STL (the Standard Template Library) encapsulates the pure raw horsepower of the C/C++ languages, plus the advanced efficient algorithms engendered within a good Data Structures course, all bundled into a simple-to-use form! It is similar in a way to having struggled with years of pre-Calc and Calculus courses, only to be given an advanced portable calculator that does all the work for you.

You may view the Standard Template Library as an extensible framework that contains components for language support, diagnostics, general utilities, strings, locales, standard template library (containers, iterators, algorithms, numerics), and input/output.

The Origins of STL

With the ever-increasing popularity of C/C++ and Microsoft Windows controlled environments, many third-party vendors evolved into extremely profitable commodities by providing libraries of routines designed to handle the storage and processing of data. In an ongoing attempt to maintain C/C++'s viability as a programming language of choice and to keep the ball rolling by maintaining a strict control of the language's formal definition, the ANSI/ISO C++ added a new approach to defining these libraries called the Standard Template Library or STL.

STL was developed by Alexander Stepanov and Meng Lee of Hewlett Packard. STL is expected to become the standard approach to storing and processing data. Major compiler vendors are beginning to incorporate the STL into their products. The Standard Template Library is more than just a minor addition to the world's most popular programming language; it represents a revolutionary new capability. STL brings a surprisingly mature set of generic containers and algorithms to the C++ programming language, adding a dimension to the language that simply did not exist before.

What Do I Need to Know to Take Advantage of STL?

You have all you need to know right now, simply by picking up this book. Unlike many other STL books, which simply enumerate endless lists of STL template names, functions, constants, etc., this book will begin by first teaching you the advanced C/C++ language fundamentals that make the Standard Template Library syntactically possible.

Along the way, this instructional section will show you the syntax that allows an algorithm to be generic, in other words, how C/C++ syntactically separates *what* a program does, from the *data type(s)* it uses. You will learn about generic **void** * pointer's strengths and weaknesses, the "a better way" with generic types, and the "an even better way" using templates, and finally the "best way" with cross-platform, portable Standard Templates!

The section on template development begins with simple C/C++ structures used syntactically to create *objects* (yes, you can create an object with this keyword; however, it is a very bad idea—you'll have to wait till Chapter 2 to see why). The **struct** object definition is then evolved over, logically and syntactically, into the C++ **class**. Finally, the **class** object is mutated into a generic **template**. This progressive approach allows you to easily assimilate the new features of C/C++ and paves the way to technically correct use of STL. With this under your belt, you will both logically and syntactically understand how STL works and begin to immediately incorporate this technology into your application development.

Generic programming is going to provide you with the power and expressiveness of languages like SmallTalk while retaining the efficiency and compatibility of C++. STL is guaranteed to increase the productivity of any programmer who uses it.

A High-Level View of STL

Although STL is large and its syntax can be initially intimidating, it is actually quite easy to use once you understand how it is constructed and what elements it employs. At the core of STL are three foundational items called *containers, algorithms*, and *iterators*. These libraries work together allowing you to generate, in a portable format, frequently employed algorithmic solutions, such as array creation, element insertion/deletion, sorting, and element output. But STL goes even further by providing internally clean, seamless and efficient integration of iostreams and exception handling.

Kudos to the ANSI/ISO C++ Committee

Multi-vendor implementations of C/C++ compilers would have long ago died on the vine were it not for the ANSI C/C++ Committees. They are responsible for giving us *portable* C and C++ code by filling in the *missing* details for the formal language descriptions of both C and C++ as presented by their authors, Dennis Ritchie and Bjarne Stroustrup, respectively. And to this day, the ANSI/ISO C++ Committee continues to guarantee C++'s portability into the next millennium.

While on the subject of language authorship, Alexander Stepanov and Meng Lee of Hewlett Packard developed the concept and coding behind the Standard Template Library. The industry anticipates that STL will become *the* standard approach to storing and processing data.

The ANSI/ISO C++ Committee's current standards exceed their past recommendations, which historically decided only to codify existing practice and resolve ambiguities and contradictions among existing translator implementations. The C++ committee's changes are innovations. In most cases, the changes implement features that committee members admired in other languages, features that they view as deficiencies in traditional C++, or simply features that they've always wanted in a programming language. A *great* deal of thought and discussion have been invested in each change, and consequently the committee feels that the new C++ definition, along with the evolutionary definition of STL, is the best definition of C++ possible today.

Most of these recommended changes consist of language additions that should not affect existing code. Old programs should still compile with newer compilers as long as the old code does not coincidentally use any of the new keywords as identifiers. However, even experienced C++ programmers may be surprised by how much of C++ has evolved even without discussing STL—for example, the use of namespaces, new-style type casting, and runtime type information (discussed in detail in Chapter 2).

STL's Tri-Component Nature

Conceptually, STL encompasses three separate algorithmic problem solvers. The three most important are containers, algorithms, and iterators. A *container* is a way that stored data is organized in memory, for example an array, stack, queue, linked list, or binary-tree. However, many other kinds of containers exist, and STL includes the most useful. The STL containers are implemented by template classes so they can be easily customized to hold different data types.

All the containers have common management member functions defined in their template definitions: insert(), erase(), begin(), end(), size(), capacity(), and so on. Individual containers have member functions that support their unique requirements.

Algorithms are behaviors or functionality applied to containers to process their contents in various ways. For example, some algorithms sort, copy, search, and merge container contents. In STL, algorithms are represented by template functions. These functions are not member functions of the container classes. Instead, they are standalone functions. Indeed, one of the surprising characteristics of STL is that its algorithms are so general. You can use them not only on STL containers, but also on ordinary C++ arrays or any other application-specific container.

A standard suite of algorithms provides for searching for, copying, reordering, transforming, and performing numeric operations on the objects in the containers. The same algorithm is used to perform a particular operation for all containers of all object types!

Once you have decided on a container type and data behaviors, the only thing left is to interact the two with *iterators*. You can think of iterators as a generalized pointer that points to elements within a container. You can increment an iterator, as you can a pointer, so that it points in turn to each successive element in the container. Iterators are a key part of the STL because they connect algorithms with containers.

Containers

All STL library syntax incorporates the full use of C++ templates (data type independent syntax). As we discuss the container types, remember that they are implemented as templates; the types of objects they contain are determined by the template arguments given when the program instantiates the containers. Three major types of containers, vectors (or dynamic arrays), deques (or double-ended queues), and linear lists exist: bitset, map, and multimap.

Sequence containers store finite sets of objects of the same type in a linear organization. An array of names is a sequence. You use one of the sequence types—vector, list, or deque—for a particular application, depending on its retrieval requirements.

VECTOR CLASS

Vector sequences allow random data access. A vector is an array of contiguous homogeneous objects with an instance counter or pointer to indicate the end of the vector sequence. Random access is facilitated through the use of a subscript operation. Vector sequences allow you to append entries to and remove entries from the end of the dynamic structure without undue overhead. Inserts and deletes from the middle, however, naturally take longer, due to the time involved in shifting the remaining entries to make room for the new or deleted item.

LIST CLASS

A list sequence provides bidirectional access; it allows you to perform inserts and deletes anywhere without undue performance penalties. Random access is simulated by forward or backward iteration to the target object. A list consists of noncontiguous objects linked with forward and backward pointers.

DEQUE CLASS

A deque sequence is similar to a vector sequence, except that a deque sequence allows fast inserts and deletes at the beginning as well as the end of the container. Random inserts and deletes are less efficient.

BITSET CLASS

The bitset class supports operations on a set of bits, such as flip(), reset(), set(), size(), to_string, etc.

MAP CLASS

The map class provides associative containers with unique keys mapped to specific values.

MULTIMAP CLASS

The multimap class is very similar to the map class in raw horsepower, except for one minor difference, the availability of a nonunique key mapped to specific values.

Container Adapters

STL supports three adapter containers, which you can combine with one of the sequence containers listed above. The scenario goes like this: First you select the appropriate application-specific container. Next you instantiate a container adapter class by naming the existing container in the declaration:

```
queue< list< bank_customer_struct > >TellerOneQueue;
```

The example instantiates a queue container, one of the three adapter containers supported by STL—by using the list container as the underlying data structure built around a hypothetical bank customer waiting for an available teller.

Container adapters hide the public interface of the underlying container and implement their own. A queue data structure, for example, resembles a list but has its own requirements for its user interface. STL incorporates three standard adapter containers: stack, queue, and priority_queue.

STACK CLASS

The stack adapter provides the logical operations of push() and pop(), enabling the standard Last In First Out, or LIFO solution. Stacks are great for certain types of problem solutions, like evaluating an Infix arithmetic expression that has been translated into Postfix for the purposes of unambiguous evaluation.

QUEUE CLASS

Regardless of whether or not the storage sequence container is a vector, or linked list, the queue adapter uses this underlying scheme to add items to the end of the list, using the push() method, and to delete or remove items from the front of the list, using pop(). The acronym for a queue algorithm is First In First Out, or FIFO.

PRIORITY_QUEUE CLASS

A priority_queue is similar to a queue adapter in that all items added to the queue are at the end of the list. However, unlike a queue adapter, which *only* removes items from the front of the list, a priority_queue adapter removes the highest priority item within the list first!

Algorithms

Similar to container adapters, algorithms also act on containers. Algorithms provide for container initializations, sorting, searching, and data transformations. Interestingly, algorithms are implemented *not* as class methods, but rather as standalone template functions. For this reason, they work not only on STL containers, but also on standard C++ arrays or with container classes you create yourself.

Typical algorithmic behaviors include find(), to locate a specific item; count(), letting you know how many items are in the list; equal(), for comparisons; search(); copy(); swap(); fill(); sort(); and so on.

Iterators

Whenever an application needs to move through the elements of a container, it uses an iterator. Iterators are similar to pointers used to access individual data items. In STL, an iterator is represented by an object of an iterator class. You can increment an iterator with the C/C++ increment operator ++, moving it to the address of the next element. You can also use the dereference operator * to access individual members within the selected item. Special iterators are capable of remembering the location of specific container elements.

There are different classes of iterators that must be used with specific container types. The three major classes of iterators are forward, bidirectional, and random access:

- Forward iterators can only advance forward through the container one item at a time. They cannot move backward, nor can they be updated to point to any location in the middle of the container.
- Backward iterators work like the forward iterator counterparts, except backwards.
- Bidirectional iterators can move forward as well as backward and cannot be assigned or updated to point to any element in the middle of the container.
- Random-access iterators go one step further than bidirectional iterators in that they do allow the application to perform arbitrary location jumps within the container.

In addition, STL defines two specialized categories known as input and output iterators. Input and output iterators can point to specific devices; for example, an input iterator may point to a user-defined input file, or cin, and be used to perform sequential reads into the container. Likewise, an output iterator may point to a user-defined output file or cout, performing the logical inverse operation of sequentially outputting container elements.

Unlike forward, backward, bidirectional, and random-access iterators, input and output iterators cannot store their current values. The first four iterators must hold their values in order for them to know where they are within the container. The last two, input and output, since they are pointers to devices, do not structurally represent the same type of information and therefore have no memory capabilities.

Additional Elements

Beyond containers, algorithms, and iterators, STL defines:

- *allocators* for managing memory allocation for an individual container.
- *predicates*, which are unary or binary in nature, meaning that they work on either one operand or two and always return either true or false.
- *comparison function*, a unique binary predicate comparing two elements and returning true only if the first argument is less than the second.
- *function objects*, including plus, minus, multiply, divide, modulus, negate, equal_to, not_equal_to, greater, greater_equal, less, less_equal, logical_and, logical_or, logical_not, and so on.

STL Review

The following review is included to help you formalize the structural components of the Standard Template Library. You can logically divide the Standard Template Library into the following categories:

A. STL headers, grouped into three major organizing concepts:

1. Containers, template classes that support common ways to organize data: <deque>, <list>, <map>, <multimap>, <queue>, <set>, <stack>, and <vector>.
2. Algorithms, template functions for performing common operations on sequences of objects including <algorithm>, <functional>, and <numeric>.
3. Iterators, the glue that pastes together algorithms and containers and include <iterator>, <memory>, and <utility>.

B. Input Output includes components for:

1. forward declarations of iostreams <iosfwd>
2. predefined iostreams objects <iostream>
3. base iostreams classes <ios>
4. stream buffering <streambuf>
5. stream formatting and manipulators: <iosmanip>, <istream>, and <ostream>
6. string streams <sstream>
7. file streams <fstream>

C. Other Standard C++ headers include:

1. Language Support includes:
   - **a.** components for common type definitions used throughout the library <cstddef>
   - **b.** characteristics of the predefined types <limits>, <cfloat>, and <climits>

c. functions supporting start and termination of a C++ program <cstdlib>
d. support for dynamic memory management <new>
e. support for dynamic type identification <typeinfo>
f. support for exception processing <exception>
g. other run-time support <cstdarg>, <ctime>, <csetlmp>, and <csignal>

2. Diagnostics includes components for:
   a. reporting several kinds of exceptional conditions <stdexcept>
   b. documenting program assertions <cassert>
   c. a global variable for error number codes <cerrno>
3. Strings includes components for:
   a. string classes <string>
   b. null-terminated sequence utilities: <cctype>, <cwctype>, and <cwchar>
4. Cultural Language components includes internationalization support for character classification and string collation, numeric, monetary, and date/time formatting and parsing, and message retrieval using <locale>and <clocale>.

In the Following Chapters

This chapter presented the nuts 'n' bolts of this newest addition to C++, the ANSI/ISO Standard Template Library. You now know:

- what the STL concept entails,
- how it evolved into existence,
- who is credited for inventing it,
- what it gives you as an application developer
- a logical overview of STL's underlying data structures
- their predefined behaviors
- directional container processing
- and finally element comparison and translation capabilities.

Chapter 2, which does *not* use or *teach* any individual component of STL, is designed to take a beginning to intermediate C/C++ programmer and with both a logical and a C++ syntactical approach, demonstrate how the *standard* features of C++ are bundled together to make STL possible.

Chapter 2 is unquestionably *the* most important chapter of the book if you are new to C/C++ pointers, void pointers, templates, and classes (class is the keyword that C++ uses to implement the generic concept of an object).

Even "experienced" C/C++ programmers, wishing to dive directly into the later chapters, may be surprised to see just how much C++ has changed within this past year, even without the topic of STL. Therefore, we highly recommend that every reader, regardless of C/C++ programming experience, read this most informational second chapter.

TWO

Understanding Template Syntax

Chaos! The world of C/C++ programming is a mess. You have "Historic C," ANSI C, C++, ANSI C++, ANSI/ISO C++, Borland International's C/C++, Microsoft's C/C++, your senior programmer's version of C/C++, maybe even a version of C/C++ created by an ego-centric, self-taught university professor, not to mention next year's state-of-the-art C/C++ bell 'n' whistle standard.

The biggest problem to learning C/C++ is finding a reputable source. With few exceptions, many programmers have taught themselves C/C++. They were professionally degreed programmers, with many years of experience, who evolved from some institutional training language, to whatever language was in vogue that day. So typically the scenario went from COBOL, to FORTRAN, to PL/I, to Pascal, to Modula-2, and on and on.

This scenario actually worked out quite well in the past, because all the older high-level languages had basically the same features, just different syntax. Now take this previously successful self-taught, highly motivated programmer and thrust him/her into the world of multitasking application development, in a GUI (graphical user interface) environment, using C/C++ and object-oriented technology. Result? "Chaos!"

C and C++ provide so many new language features, design philosophies, and sophisticated syntax, that mapping over your understanding from some other language just will not do. This book is all about you learning to fly a stealth bomber called STL and quite possibly the only thing you've ever gotten off the ground was a Piper Cub.

The great news is that with a few instructional tips, you can take what you currently know about any programming language and get up-to-speed on this latest technology. That goal is what this chapter is all about. So let's get started.

Chapter Overview

This chapter assumes only a minimum comfort level with C/C++. It begins with a review of the pivotal fundamentals provided by C/C++ that make STL possible and ends with the highest level C++ syntax that actually creates STL's generic algorithms.

Although you may think that you are an experienced enough C/C++ programmer to skip this chapter and begin immediately using STL, you may be surprised to find out just how much C++ has evolved. Even if you had an intro and advanced C/C++ course, you may again be surprised to find out just how much your professor *didn't* know or tell you. Or even worse, the C/C++ you currently know, well quite frankly, is just plain incorrect. For all these reasons, we strongly suggest that you sit down with a nice cup of coffee and read this chapter, and *Chapter 3*, all the way through.

Dynamic Memory Allocation and Pointers

The code contained within the Standard Template Libraries is extremely efficient. One means to this efficiency is that the objects created use dynamically allocated memory, tracked by pointers. This section reviews the C/C++ building blocks making this possible.

(2)Static vs. Dynamic

First, you need to understand that the word "static" used in this section is *not* the C/C++ keyword **static**. Instead, static is used to describe a category of memory allocation. Since most programmers understand code more clearly than verbiage, here's an example:

```
void main( void )
{
  int ivalue;// i(nt)value
.
.
.
}
```

This code segment declares an integer variable *ivalue*. Now if you think about it, *ivalue*'s storage location is allocated when the program loads, and this memory allocation persists until the program exits. This is an example of static memory allocation.

Static memory allocation is *not* under the control of the programmer at run-time, but instead, is under load-time control. The programmer cannot get more *ivalues*, nor can the programmer delete *ivalue*'s memory allocation at run-time. And that impossibility is the downfall to this storage class.

Dynamic memory allocation has the advantage of being under run-time control. Unfortunately, its syntax is not as straightforward and entails the use of pointers (note: this example only highlights the difference between static and dynamic memory allocation and is not intended as a real-world example):

```
void main( void )
  int *pivalue;    // p(ointer to)i(nt)value;
  int iLoopControl, iAsManyAsUserWants;
  cout << "How many integer's would you like to create at run-time?";
  cin >> iAsManyAsUserWants;
  for( iLoopControl = 0, iLoopControl < iAsManyAsUserWants, iLoopControl++)
    pivalue = new int; // pivalue set to address of
                       // run-time dynamically allocated RAM
```

In this example, the variable *pivalue* is not an integer, but instead is a *pointer variable* that can hold the address to a RAM location big enough to store an integer. Actual integer-sized RAM allocation is accomplished with the C++ **new** keyword. C programmers might recognize the equivalent to **new** as malloc() or calloc().

Most importantly, notice that the end user, at run-time, can select just how many integers s/he would like to store. Also, at run-time, the user can chose how many to delete by simply using the C++ keyword **delete**, as in:

```
delete pivalue;
```

You can easily see that run-time control of memory allocation/deallocation has tremendous efficiency benefits. Your program is never grabbing system resources beyond its current needs. STL makes heavy use of this fundamental.

Typed Pointers

Unlike normal variables of the type **int**, **float**, **char**, and so on, pointer variables do not hold data per se; instead they hold addresses to data. In the last section, you saw just how efficient this concept can be when combined with dynamic memory allocation. However, one problem is generated by these sibling concepts: type checking!

By design, C and C++ are not strongly typed languages. So both compilers will accept statements like:

```
char cvalue = 65;// initializing a character variable with an integer
```

and

```
int ivalue = 'A';// initializing an integer variable with a character
```

However, when it comes to pointers, both C and C++ become strongly typed languages. So for example, a float-sized dynamically allocated memory location's address may not be assigned to a pointer of type int, as in:

```
int *pivalue;          // p(ointer to) i(nt)value;
pivalue = new float;   // illegal attempt to
                       // assign a float address to int pointer
```

From their inceptions, C and C++ have had a syntatical way around type-checking by using the standard type **void**.

Void Pointers

The C/C++ void data type, when combined with pointer variable definitions, tells the compilers that the defined variable does not hold data per se, but rather an address; but it does *not* tell the compilers to what data type! The C/C++ void data type can lead to very powerful code solutions.

In the following example, one subroutine is used to output one of three dynamically allocated data types:

```
#include <iostream>
using namespace std;

void printit ( void *pData, char cRunTimeChoice );

void main ( void )
{
  char  *pchar, cRunTimeChoice;
  int   *pivalue;
  float *pfvalue;

  cout << "Please enter the dynamic data type you want to create\n"
       << " press c for char, i for int, or f for float: ";

  cin  >> cRunTimeChoice;

  switch ( cRunTimeChoice ) {

    case 'c': pchar = new char;
              cout << "\nEnter a character: ";
                  cin  >> *pchar;
                  printit ( pchar, cRunTimeChoice );
                  break;

    case 'i': pivalue = new int;
```

```
                cout << "\nEnter an integer: ";
                cin  >> *pivalue;
                printit ( pivalue, cRunTimeChoice );
                break;

    default:  pfvalue = new float;
                cout << "\nEnter a float: ";
                cin  >> *pfvalue;
                printit ( pfvalue, cRunTimeChoice );

  }
}

void printit ( void *pData, char cRunTimeChoice )
{
  cout << "\nThe Dynamic Data type entered was ";

  switch ( cRunTimeChoice ) {

   case 'c': cout << "char and a value of: "
                  << *(char *)pData;
                 break;

   case 'i': cout << "int and a value of: "
                  << *(int *)pData;
                 break;
   default:  cout << "float and a value of: "
                  << *(float *)pData;

  }
  delete pData;
}
```

The key statements to understanding void pointers are the *printit()* prototype:

```
void printit ( void *pData, char cRunTimeChoice );
```

and the three calls to *printit()*:

```
printit ( pchar,   cRunTimeChoice );
printit ( pivalue, cRunTimeChoice );
printit ( pfvalue, cRunTimeChoice );
```

Notice how officially you have told the compiler that *printit()*'s first formal argument type is a **void** pointer (**void** *). This suspends normal type checking between a function's formal argument list, and the calling statement's actual arguments—the only reason the program works.

However, unlike **int** *, definitions, or **float** *, syntax using

```
void * pToWhoKnowsWhat;
```

doesn't specify to *what* the address points. This is both good and bad. It's good because the compiler can't do any type checking when an actual address is assigned, and bad because the compiler can't do any type checking! Even worse, a program can not point with a **void** * type. This explains the three cast statements within *printit()*'s **switch-case** statement converting a pointer to nothing (**void** *) to a specific pointer type:

```
*(char *)pData;
    *(int *)pData;
    *(float *)pData;
```

Without type checking, if your code accidentally assigns the wrong address type, the code compiles:

```
void * pivalue;  // variable name indicates it will hold an int type 61
address
...
pivalue = new float;// incorrect assignment of RAM float precision!
```

The previous code section declares *pivalue* as a **void** * pointer; however, the variable's name implies that it will hold the address to an integer *p*(ointer to)*i*(nt). The pointer is then initialzed to the address of a float-sized memory location. Still, perfectly legal code may be even logically okay for some applications, but look at these next two statements:

```
some_function( pivalue );            // call to some function
...
void some_function( int * pivalue );  // function prototype
```

First, the code will not compile, because the compilers (C/C++) recognize that *pivalue*'s formal declaration - **void** * does not match the function's first formal argument type of - **int** *. Remember, by default, pointers are typed and the compiler at compile-time recognizes the mismatch. But a clever C/C++ programmer could rewrite the call statement to:

```
some_function( (int *) pivalue );           // working call statement!
...
void some_function( int * pivalue )
{
  //   sample function body code...
  cout << "The integer value is: " << *pivalue;  // outputs garbage
```

Executing a program of this nature causes *some_function()* to output garbage, since the memory location contains an IEEE floating-point encrypted value and the function instructs the compiler to decode a four-byte integer!

The sad news is that the code compiles! No warnings and no errors. The point is (no pun intended) that **void** pointers can create debugging and run-time nightmares. The solution is the C++ template.

What's the i in iValue?

Test question: Is anything wrong with the following code segment?

```
int operandA = 1, operandB = 2;
float result;
...
result = operandA / operandB
```

If you answered yes, great! However, if you think the equation is fine, well, let's just say that it's a good thing that we have Hungarian Notation, invented by Charles Simony.

The initial problem begins with the C/C++ divide operator /, which is overloaded for different data types. In many other programming languages, two separate operators distinguish integral division from floating-point division. Pascal, for example, uses the divide operator / for floating-point precision and the **div** operator for integral results. Obviously, a Pascal programmer can easily see which operator an equation employs. Unfortunately for unwary C/C++ programmers, no visual clue similarities exist. Instead, the C/C++ divide operator itself examines each operand's formal data type and then decides whether or not to perform integer/integer division with an integer result, or floating-point/floating-point with a floating-point result. The previous equation assigns a 0 to the variable *result* instead of the logically intended 0.5 (since *result*'s type is float) because *operandA*'s and *operandB*'s data types are integer.

Now, imagine that the equation is nested in a large program that is miscalculating values and you, *not* the author of the code must track down the problem. Enter Hungarian Notation. In Hungarian Notation, each identifier's name (your name for variables, constants, etc). begins with an abbreviation of its data type. Here are some examples:

```
char           cMenuSelection;
int            iValue;
float          fValue;
char           szLastName[ MAX_LETTERS + NULL_STRING_TERMINATOR ];
int            *piValue;
float          *pfValue;
char           *pszLastName = szLastName;
double         dValue, *pdValue = &pValue;
long double     ldValue, *pldValue = &pldValue;
```

Now imagine the rewrite of the original code segment:

```
int iOperandA = 1, iOperandB = 2;
float fResult;
...
fResult = iOperandA / iOperandB
```

In this version, an experienced C/C++ programmer, seeing the divide operator employed on two *i*(nt tagged) variable names and then a *f*(loat tagged)*Result* storage precision, would immediately suspect the equation as possibly generating the beginnings of a numeric miscalculation.

With the hundreds of thousands of lines of code given to you in the Microsoft Windows objects or IBM's OS/2 objects, and so on, Hungarian Notation goes a long way to helping a programmer intimately understand the data types involved in an algorithm. This directly translates into a time savings, whether in digesting a program's logic or in flagging starting points for a debugging session.

Function Overloading

Many C++ object-oriented concepts have procedural underpinnings. Function overloading is a procedural concept that allows a programmer to define several functions by the same name. The syntax requires only that each function's formal argument list be unique. Unique is defined by the number of formal arguments and/or their order, and/or their data type(s). Look at the following example function prototypes:

```
int averageArray(int iarray[]);
float averageArray(float farray[]);
double averageArray(double darray[]);
```

Beyond the straightforward syntax, you have the proper logical use of function overloading. Typically, this involves a repetition of function body algorithms that do the same thing, but very often on different data types. Case in point: the averaging of array elements. One subroutine performs this array element processing on integer array elements, another on float array elements, and the third on double array elements. However, all three functions *average array elements!*

Note: An overloaded function's return type does not play any role in defining uniqueness. For this reason, the following overloaded function prototypes are illegal:

```
void averageArray(int iarray[]);
int averageArray(int iarray[]);
float averageArray(int iarray[]);
```

Although function overloading is a powerful procedural problem-solving tool, it is also the building block concept behind overloaded class member functions (classes are reviewed later in this chapter).

Pointers to Functions

All the examples so far have shown you how various items of data can be referenced by a pointer. As it turns out, you can also access *portions of code* by using a pointer to a function. Pointers to functions serve the same purpose as do pointers to data; that is, they allow the function to be referenced indirectly, just as a pointer to a data item allows the data item to be referenced indirectly.

A pointer to a function can have a number of important uses. For example, consider the qsort( ) function. The qsort( ) function has as one of its parameters a pointer to a function. The referenced function contains the necessary comparison that is to be performed between the array elements being sorted. qsort( ) has been written to require a function pointer because the comparison process between two elements can be a complex process beyond the scope of a single control flag. You cannot pass a function by value, that is, pass the code itself. C/C++, however, does support passing a pointer to the code or a pointer to the function.

The concept of function pointers is frequently illustrated by using the qsort( ) function supplied with the compiler. Unfortunately, in many cases, the function pointer is declared to be of a type that points to other built-in functions. The following C and C++ programs demonstrate how to define a pointer to a function and how to "roll your own" function to be passed to the STDLIB function qsort( ). Here is the C program:

```
/*
*   fncptr.c
*   A C program illustrating how to declare your own
*   function and function pointer to be used with qsort( )
*   Chris H. Pappas and William H. Murray, 1999
*/

#include <stdio>
#include <stdlib>
using namespace std;

#define IMAXVALUES 10

int icompare_funct(const void *iresult_a, const void *iresult_b);
int (*ifunct_ptr)(const void *, const void *);

void main( )
{
  int i;
  int iarray[IMAXVALUES]={0,5,3,2,8,7,9,1,4,6};

  ifunct_ptr=icompare_funct;
  qsort(iarray,IMAXVALUES,sizeof(int),ifunct_ptr);
```

```
  for(i = 0; i < IMAXVALUES; i++)
    printf("%d ",iarray[i]);
}

int icompare_funct(const void *iresult_a, const void *iresult_b)
{
  return((*(int *)iresult_a) - (*(int *) iresult_b));
}
```

The function icompare_funct( ) (which will be called the *reference function*) was prototyped to match the requirements for the fourth parameter to the function qsort( ) (which will be called the *invoking function*).

To digress slightly, the fourth parameter to the function qsort( ) must be a function pointer. This reference function must be passed two const void * parameters and it must return a type int. (Note: Remember that the position of the const keyword, in the formal parameter list, *locks* the data pointed to, not the address used to point. So even if you write your compare routine so that it *does not* sort properly, it can in *no way* destroy the contents of your array!) The reason is that qsort( ) uses the reference function for the sort comparison algorithm. Now that you understand the prototype of the reference function icompare_funct( ), take a minute to study the body of the reference function.

If the reference function returns a value < 0, then the reference function's first parameter value is less than the second parameter's value. A return value of zero indicates parameter value equality, with a return value > 0 indicating that the second parameter's value was greater than the first's. Calculating the appropriate return value is accomplished by the single statement in icompare_funct( ):

```
return((*(int *)iresult_a) - (*(int *) iresult_b));
```

Since both of the pointers were passed as type void *, they were cast to their appropriate pointer type int * and then dereferenced (*). The result of the subtraction of the two values pointed to returns an appropriate value to satisfy qsort( )'s comparison criterion.

Although the prototype requirements for icompare_funct( ) are interesting, the meat of the program begins with the pointer function declaration below the icompare_funct( ) function prototype:

```
int icompare_funct(const void *iresult_a, const void *iresult_b);
int (*ifunct_ptr)(const void *, const void *);
```

A function's type is determined by its return value and argument list signature. A pointer to icompare_funct( ) must specify the same signature and return type. You might therefore think that the following statement would accomplish this:

```
int *ifunct_ptr(const void *, const void *);
```

The code statement is almost correct. The problem is that the compiler interprets the statement as the definition of a function ifunct_ptr( ) taking two arguments and returning a pointer of type int *. The dereference operator unfortunately is associated with the type specifier, not ifunct_ptr( ). Parentheses are necessary to associate the dereference operator with ifunct_ptr( ).

The corrected statement declares ifunct_ptr( ) to be a pointer to a function taking two arguments and with a return type int—that is, a pointer of the same type required by the fourth parameter to qsort( ).

In the body of main( ), the only thing left to do is to initialize ifunct_ptr( ) to the address of the function icompare_funct( ). The parameters to qsort( ) are the address to the base or zeroth element of the table to be sorted (*iarray*), the number of entries in the table (*IMAXVALUES*), the size of each table element (sizeof(int)), and a function pointer to the comparison function (ifunct_ptr( )).

The C++ equivalent follows:

```
//  qsort.cpp
//  A C program illustrating how to declare your own
//  function and function pointer to be used with qsort( )
//  Chris H. Pappas and William H. Murray, 1998

#include <iostream>
#include <stdlib>

#define IMAXVALUES 10

int icompare_funct(const void *iresult_a, const void *iresult_b);
int (*ifunct_ptr)(const void *,const void *);

void main( )
{
  int i;
  int iarray[IMAXVALUES]={0,5,3,2,8,7,9,1,4,6};

  ifunct_ptr=icompare_funct;
  qsort(iarray,IMAXVALUES,sizeof(int),ifunct_ptr);
  for(i = 0; i < IMAXVALUES; i++)
    cout <<[{|"|}]" << iarray[i];
}

int icompare_funct(const void *iresult_a, const void *iresult_b)
{
  return((*(int *)iresult_a) - (*(int *)iresult_b));
}
```

Learning to understand the syntax of a function pointer can be challenging. Let's look at just a few examples. Here is the first one:

```
int *(*(*ifunct_ptr)(int))[5];
float (*(*ffunct_ptr)(int,int))(float);
typedef double (*(*(*dfunct_ptr)( ))[5])( );
  dfunct_ptr A_dfunct_ptr;
(*(*function_ary_ptrs( ))[5])( );
```

The first statement defines ifunct_ptr( ) to be a function pointer to a function that is passed an integer argument and returns a pointer to an array of five int pointers.

The second statement defines ffunct_ptr( ) to be a function pointer to a function that takes two integer arguments and returns a pointer to a function taking a float argument and returning a float.

By using the typedef declaration, you can avoid the unnecessary repetition of complicated declarations. The typedef declaration is read as follows: dfunct_ptr( ) is defined as a pointer to a function that is passed nothing and returns a pointer (to an array of five pointers that point to functions) that is passed nothing and returns a double.

The last statement is a function declaration, not a variable declaration. The statement defines function_ary_ptrs( ) to be a function taking no arguments and returning a pointer to an array of five pointers that point to functions taking no arguments and returning integers. The outer functions return the default C and C++ type int.

The good news is that you will rarely encounter complicated declarations and definitions like these. However, by making certain you understand these declarations, you will be able to confidently parse the everyday variety.

Structures as Objects

Many C/C++ programmers are surprised to discover that the C++ **class** type is an extension of the standard type **struct.** In this section, you learn how you can use the **struct** type in C++ to form a primitive class, complete with data and members. Next, you examine the formal syntax for defining a class and see several simple examples of its implementation. The section discusses the differences between a primitive **struct** class type and an actual C++ class and presents several simple examples to illustrate class concepts.

A Structure as a Primitive Class

In many respects, the structure in C++ is an elementary form of a class. You use the keyword **struct** to define a structure. Examine the following code:

```
//  sqroot.cpp
//  C++ program using the keyword "struct" to illustrate a
//  primitive form of class. Here several member functions
//  are defined within the structure.
//  Chris H. Pappas and William H. Murray, 1999

#include <iostream>
#include <math>

using namespace std;
```

```
struct math_operations {
  double data_value;

  void set_value(double ang) {data_value=ang;}
  double get_square(void) {double answer;
                           answer=data_value*data_value;
                           return (answer);}
  double get_square_root(void) {double answer;
                                answer=sqrt(data_value);
                                return (answer);}
} math;

main()
{
  // set numeric value to 35.63
  math.set_value(35.63);

  cout << "The square of the number is: "
       << math.get_square() << endl;
  cout << "The square root of the number is: "
       << math.get_square_root() << endl;
  return (0);
}
```

The first thing to notice in this code is that the structure definition contains member data and functions. Although you are used to seeing data declarations as part of a structure, this is probably the first time you have seen member functions defined within the structure definition. These member functions can act upon the data contained in the structure (or class) itself.

Recall that a class can contain member data and functions. By default, in a **struct** declaration in C++, member data and functions are public. (A public section is one in which the data and functions are available outside the structure.)

In this example, the structure definition contains a single data value:

```
double data_value;
```

Next, three member functions are defined. Actually, the code for each function is contained within the structure:

```
void set_value(double ang) {data_value=ang;}
double get_square(void) {double answer;
                         answer=data_value*data_value;
                         return (answer);}
double get_square_root(void) {double answer;
                              answer=sqrt(data_value);
                              return (answer);}
```

The first member function is responsible for initializing the variable, *data_value*. The remaining two member functions return the square and square root of *data_value*. Notice that the member functions are not passed a value; *data_value* is available to them as members of the structure. Both member functions return a **double**.

The program's main() function sets the value of *data_value* to 35.63 with a call to the member function, set_value():

```
math.set_value(35.63);
```

Notice that the name *math* has been associated with the structure *math_operations*.

The remaining two member functions return values to the **cout** stream:

```
cout << "The square of the number is: "
     << math.get_square() << endl;
cout << "The square root of the number is: "
     << math.get_square_root() << endl;
```

This example contains a structure with member data and functions. The functions are contained within the structure definition. You won't find an example simpler than this one.

In the next program, the **struct** keyword is still used to develop a primitive class, but this time the member functions are written outside the structure. This is the way you will most commonly see structures and classes defined.

This example contains a structure definition with one data member, *data_value,* and seven member functions. The member functions return information for various trigonometric values.

```
//  tstruc.cpp
//  C++ program using the keyword "struct" to illustrate a
//  primitive form of class. This program uses a structure
//  to obtain trigonometric values for an angle.
//  Chris H. Pappas and William H. Murray, 1999

#include <iostream>
#include <math>

using namespace std;

const double DEG_TO_RAD=0.0174532925;

struct degree {
  double data_value;

  void set_value(double);
  double get_sine(void);
  double get_cosine(void);
  double get_tangent(void);
  double get_secant(void);
  double get_cosecant(void);
  double get_cotangent(void);
```

```
} deg;

void degree::set_value(double ang)
{
  data_value=ang;
}

double degree::get_sine(void)
{
  double answer;

  answer=sin(DEG_TO_RAD*data_value);
  return (answer);
}

double degree::get_cosine(void)
{
  double answer;

  answer=cos(DEG_TO_RAD*data_value);
  return (answer);
}

double degree::get_tangent(void)
{
  double answer;

  answer=tan(DEG_TO_RAD*data_value);
  return (answer);
}

double degree::get_secant(void)
{
  double answer;

  answer=1.0/sin(DEG_TO_RAD*data_value);
  return (answer);
}

double degree::get_cosecant(void)
{
  double answer;

  answer=1.0/cos(DEG_TO_RAD*data_value);
  return (answer);
}

double degree::get_cotangent(void)
{
  double answer;
```

```
  answer=1.0/tan(DEG_TO_RAD*data_value);
  return (answer);
}

main()
{
  // set angle to 25.0 degrees
  deg.set_value(25.0);

  cout << "The sine of the angle is: "
       << deg.get_sine() << endl;
  cout << "The cosine of the angle is: "
       << deg.get_cosine() << endl;
  cout << "The tangent of the angle is: "
       << deg.get_tangent() << endl;
  cout << "The secant of the angle is: "
       << deg.get_secant() << endl;
  cout << "The cosecant of the angle is: "
       << deg.get_cosecant() << endl;
  cout << "The cotangent of the angle is: "
       << deg.get_cotangent() << endl;
  return (0);
}
```

Notice that the structure definition contains the prototypes for the member functions. The variable, *deg*, is associated with the ***degree*** structure type.

```
struct degree {
  double data_value;

  void set_value(double);
  double get_sine(void);
  double get_cosine(void);
  double get_tangent(void);
  double get_secant(void);
  double get_cosecant(void);
  double get_cotangent(void);
} deg;
```

Immediately after the structure is defined, the various member functions are developed and listed. The member functions are associated with the structure or class by means of the scope operator (::). Other than the use of the scope operator, the member functions take on the appearance of normal functions.

Examine the first part of the main() function:

```
// set angle to 25.0 degrees
deg.set_data(25.0);
```

Here the value 25.0 is being passed as an argument to the set_value() function. Observe the syntax for this operation. The set_value() function itself is very simple:

```
void degree::set_value(double ang)
{
  data_value=ang;
}
```

The function accepts the argument and assigns the value to the class variable, *data_value*. This approach is one way of initializing class variables. From this point forward, in the class, *data_value* is accessible by each of the six member functions. The job of the member functions is to calculate the sine, cosine, tangent, secant, cosecant, and cotangent of the given angle. The respective values are printed to the screen from the main() function with statements similar to the following:

```
cout << "The sine of the angle is: "
     << deg.get_sine() << endl;
```

You can use the dot notation commonly used for structures to access the member functions. Pointer variables can also be assigned to a structure or class, in which case the arrow operator is used.

The Syntax and Rules for C++ Classes

The definition of a C++ class begins with the keyword class. The class name (tag type) immediately follows the keyword. The framework of the class is very similar to the **struct** type definition you have already seen.

```
class type {
  type var1
  type var2
  type var3
       .
       .
       .
public:
  member function 1
  member function 2
  member function 3
  member function 4
       .
       .
       .
} name associated with class type;
```

Member variables immediately follow the class declaration. These variables are, by default, private to the class and can be accessed only by the member functions that follow. Member functions typically follow a public declaration, allowing access to the member functions from calling routines external to the class. All class member functions have access to public, private, and protected parts of a class.

The following is an example of a class that is used in the next programming example:

```
class degree {
  double data_value;

public:
  void set_value(double);
  double get_sine(void);
  double get_cosine(void);
  double get_tangent(void);
  double get_secant(void);
  double get_cosecant(void);
  double get_cotangent(void);
} deg;
```

This class has a type (tag name) *degree*. A private variable, *data_value*, will share degree values among the various member functions. Seven functions make up the function members of the class. They are *set_value()*, *get_sine()*, *get_cosine()*, *get_tangent()*, *get_secant()*, *get_cosecant()*, and *get_cotangent()*. The name that is associated with this class type is *deg*. Unlike this example, the association of a variable name with the class name is most frequently made in the main() function.

Does this class definition look familiar? It is basically the structure definition from the previous example converted to a true class.

A Simple C++ Class

In a C++ class, the visibility of class members is private by default. That is, member variables are accessible only to member functions of the class. If the member functions are to have visibility beyond the class, you must explicitly specify that visibility.

The conversion of the last program's structure to a true C++ class is simple and straightforward. First, the **struct** keyword is replaced by the **class** keyword. Second, the member functions that are to have public visibility are separated from the private variable of the class with the use of a public declaration. Examine the complete program:

```
//  tclass.cpp
//  C++ program illustrates a simple but true class and
//  introduces the concept of private and public.
//  This program uses a class to obtain the trigonometric
//  value for given angle.
//  Chris H. Pappas and William H. Murray, 1999

#include <iostream>
#include <math>
```

```
using namespace std;

const double DEG_TO_RAD=0.0174532925;

class degree {
  double data_value;

public:
  void set_value(double);
  double get_sine(void);
  double get_cosine(void);
  double get_tangent(void);
  double get_secant(void);
  double get_cosecant(void);
  double get_cotangent(void);
} deg;

void degree::set_value(double ang)
{
  data_value=ang;
}

double degree::get_sine(void)
{
  double answer;

  answer=sin(DEG_TO_RAD*data_value);
  return (answer);
}

double degree::get_cosine(void)
{
  double answer;

  answer=cos(DEG_TO_RAD*data_value);
  return (answer);
}

double degree::get_tangent(void)
{
  double answer;

  answer=tan(DEG_TO_RAD*data_value);
  return (answer);
}

double degree::get_secant(void)
{
  double answer;
```

```
  answer=1.0/sin(DEG_TO_RAD*data_value);
  return (answer);
}

double degree::get_cosecant(void)
{
  double answer;

  answer=1.0/cos(DEG_TO_RAD*data_value);
  return (answer);
}

double degree::get_cotangent(void)
{
  double answer;

  answer=1.0/tan(DEG_TO_RAD*data_value);
  return (answer);
}

main()
{
  // set angle to 25.0 degrees
  deg.set_value(25.0);

  cout << "The sine of the angle is: "
       << deg.get_sine() << endl;
  cout << "The cosine of the angle is: "
       << deg.get_cosine() << endl;
  cout << "The tangent of the angle is: "
       << deg.get_tangent() << endl;
  cout << "The secant of the angle is: "
       << deg.get_secant() << endl;
  cout << "The cosecant of the angle is: "
       << deg.get_cosecant() << endl;
  cout << "The cotangent of the angle is: "
       << deg.get_cotangent() << endl;
  return (0);
}
```

In this example, the body of the program remains the same. The structure definition has been converted to a true, but elementary, class definition with **private** and **public** parts.

Note that the variable, *data_value*, is private to the class (by default) and as a result is accessible only by the member functions of the class. The member functions themselves have been declared public in visibility and are accessible from outside the class. Each class member, however, whether public or private, has access to all other class members, public or private.

Again, class member functions are usually defined immediately after the class has been defined and before the main() function of the program. Non-member class functions are still defined after the function main() and are prototyped in the normal fashion.

C++ Class Objects

From the previous discussion, you learned that you could create a primitive C++ class by using the **struct** keyword. Next, several elementary C++ classes were created by using the **class** keyword. Both types of examples illustrated the simple fact that classes can contain member data and member functions that act on that data. In this section, you learn more details about C++ classes. The section details the nesting of classes and structures, the use of constructors and destructors, overloading member functions, friend functions, operator overloading, derived classes, virtual functions, and other miscellaneous topics. These class structures create objects that form the foundation of object-oriented programs.

Much of the programming flexibility offered to the C++ programmer is a result of the various data types discussed in earlier chapters. The C++ class gives you another advantage: the benefits of a structure along with the ability to limit access to specific data to functions that are also members of the class. As a result, classes are one of the greatest contributions made by C++ to programming. The added features of the class, over earlier structures, include the ability to initialize and protect sensitive functions and data.

In studying C and C++ programming, consider the increase in programming power you have gained with each new data type. Vectors or one-dimensional arrays allow a group of like data types to be held together. Next, structures allow related items of different data types to be combined in a group. Finally, the C++ class concept takes you one step further with abstract data types. A class allows you to implement a member data type and associate member functions with the data. Using classes gives you the storage concept associated with a structure along with the member functions to operate on the member variables.

Additional Class Features

In the previous discussions, you learned the syntax for creating an elementary C++ class. Classes have extended capabilities that go far beyond this simple syntax. This section is devoted to exploring these capabilities with an eye toward object-oriented programming.

A SIMPLE CLASS

Remember that a class starts with the keyword class followed by a class name (tag). In the following example, the class tag name is *car.* If the class contains member variables, they are defined at the start of the class. Their declaration type is private, by default. This example defines three member variables: *mileage, tire_pressure*, and *speed*. Class member functions follow the member variable list. Typically, the member functions are declared public. A private declaration limits the member variables to member functions within the class. This is often referred to as *data hiding*. A public declaration makes the member functions available outside the class:

```
class car {
  int   mileage;
  int   tire_pressure;
  float speed;

public:
  int maintenance(int);
  int wear_record(int);
  int air_resistance(float);
} mycar;
```

Here, three member functions are prototyped within the class definition. They are *maintenance(), wear_record(),* and *air_resistance()*. All three return an **int** type. Typically, however, the contents of the member functions are defined outside the class definition—usually, immediately after the class itself.

Let's continue the study of classes with a look at additional class features.

Nesting Classes

Recall from an earlier discussion that structures can be nested. This possibility also turns out to be true for C++ classes. When using nested classes, you must take care not to make the resulting declaration more complicated than necessary. The following examples illustrate the nesting concept.

NESTING STRUCTURES WITHIN A CLASS

The following is a simple example of how two structures can be nested within a class definition. Using nesting in this fashion is both common and practical. You can also use the class keyword in this manner.

```
//  wages.cpp
//  C++ program illustrates the use of nesting concepts
//  in classes. This program calculates the wages for
//  the named employee.
//  Chris H. Pappas and William H. Murray, 1999
```

```
#include <iostream>
using namespace std;

char newline;

class employee {
  struct emp_name {
    char firstname[20];
    char middlename[20];
    char lastname[20];
  } name;
  struct emp_hours {
    double hours;
    double base_sal;
    double overtime_sal;
  } hours;

public:
  void emp_input(void);
  void emp_output(void);
};

void employee::emp_input()
{
  cout << "Enter first name of employee: ";
  cin >> name.firstname;
  cin.get(newline);    // flush carriage return
  cout << "Enter middle name of employee: ";
  cin >> name.middlename;
  cin.get(newline);
  cout << "Enter last name of employee:  ";
  cin >> name.lastname;
  cin.get(newline);

  cout << "Enter total hours worked:  ";
  cin >> hours.hours;
  cout << "Enter hourly wage (base rate):   ";
  cin >> hours.base_sal;
  cout << "Enter overtime wage (overtime rate): ";
  cin >> hours.overtime_sal;
  cout << "\n\n";
}

void employee::emp_output()
{
  cout << name.firstname << " " << name.middlename
       << " " << name.lastname << endl;
  if (hours.hours <= 40)
    cout << "Base Pay:  $"
         << hours.hours * hours.base_sal << endl;
```

```
      else {
        cout << "Base Pay:  $"
             << 40 * hours.base_sal << endl;
        cout << "Overtime Pay: $"
             << (hours.hours-40) * hours.overtime_sal
             << endl;
      }
}

main()
{
  employee acme_corp;     // associate acme_corp with class

  acme_corp.emp_input();
  acme_corp.emp_output();
  return (0);
}
```

In the next example, two classes are nested within the ***employee*** class definition. As you can see, the use of nesting can be quite straightforward.

```
class employee {
  class emp_name {
    char firstname[20];
    char middlename[20];
    char lastname[20];
  } name;
  class emp_hours {
    double hours;
    double base_salary;
    double overtime_sal;
  } hours;

public:
  void emp_input(void);
  void emp_output(void);
};
```

The *employee* class includes two nested classes, *emp_name* and *emp_hours*. The nested classes, while part of the private section of the *employee* class, are actually available outside the class. In other words, the visibility of the nested classes is the same as if they were defined outside the *employee* class. The individual member variables, for this example, are accessed through the member functions (public, by default) emp_input() and emp_output().

Both member functions, emp_input() and emp_output(), are of type **void** and do not accept arguments. The emp_input() function prompts the user for employee data that will be passed to the nested structures (classes). The data collected includes the employee's full name, the total hours worked, the regular pay rate, and the overtime pay rate. Output is generated when the emp_output() function is called. The employee's name, base pay, and overtime pay will be printed to the screen.

The main() function in this program is fairly short because most of the work is being done by the member functions of the class:

```
employee acme_corp;     // associate acme_corp with class

acme_corp.emp_input();
acme_corp.emp_output();
```

First, the variable *acme_corp*, representing the Acme Computer Corporation, is associated with the *employee* class. To request a member function, the dot operator is used. Next, acme_corp.emp_input() is called to collect the employee information, and then acme_corp.emp_output() is used to calculate and print the payroll results.

AN ALTERNATE NESTING FORM

The following form of nesting is also considered acceptable syntax:

```
class cars {
  int mileage;
public:
  void trip(int t);
  int speed(float s);
};

class contents {
  int count;
public:
  cars mileage;
  void rating(void);
{
```

Here, *cars* becomes nested within the *contents* class. Nested classes, whether inside or outside, have the same scope.

Constructors and Destructors

A *constructor* is a class member function. Constructors are useful for initializing class variables or allocating memory storage. The constructor always has the same name as the class within which it is defined. Constructors have additional versatility: they can accept arguments and be overloaded. A constructor is executed automatically when an object of the **class** type is created. *Free store objects* are objects created with the **new** operator and serve to allocate memory for the objects created. Constructors are generated by Microsoft's Visual C/C++ compiler if they are not explicitly defined.

A *destructor* is a class member function typically used to return memory allocated from free store memory. The destructor, like the constructor, has the same name as the class it is defined in, preceded by the tilde character (~). Destructors are the complement to their constructor counterparts. A destructor is automatically called when the **delete** operator is applied to a class pointer or when a program passes beyond the scope of a class object. Destructors, unlike their constructor counterparts, cannot accept an argument and may not be overloaded. Destructors are also generated by Microsoft's Visual C/C++ compiler if they are not explicitly defined.

CREATING A SIMPLE CONSTRUCTOR AND DESTRUCTOR

In the first example involving the use of constructors and destructors, a constructor and destructor are used to signal the start and end of a coin conversion example. This program illustrates that constructors and destructors are called automatically:

```
//  coins.cpp
//  C++ program illustrates the use of constructors and
//  destructors in a simple program.
//  This program converts cents into appropriate coins:
//  (quarters, dimes, nickels, and pennies).
//  Chris H. Pappas and William H. Murray, 1999
//

#include <iostream.h>
using namespace std;

const int QUARTER=25;
const int DIME=10;
const int NICKEL=5;

class coins {
  int number;

public:
  coins() {cout << "Begin Conversion!\n";}       // constructor
  ~coins() {cout << "\nFinished Conversion!";}  // destructor
  void get_cents(int);
  int quarter_conversion(void);
  int dime_conversion(int);
  int nickel_conversion(int);
};

void coins::get_cents(int cents)
{
  number=cents;
  cout << number << " cents, converts to:"
       << endl;
}
```

```
int coins::quarter_conversion()
{
  cout << number/QUARTER << " quarter(s), ";
  return(number%QUARTER);
}

int coins::dime_conversion(int d)
{
  cout << d/DIME << " dime(s), ";
  return(d%DIME);
}

int coins::nickel_conversion(int n)
{
  cout << n/NICKEL << " nickel(s), and ";
  return(n%NICKEL);
}

main()
{
  int c,d,n,p;

  cout << "Enter the cash, in cents, to convert: ";
  cin >> c;

  // associate cash_in_cents with coins class.
  coins cash_in_cents;

  cash_in_cents.get_cents(c);
  d=cash_in_cents.quarter_conversion();
  n=cash_in_cents.dime_conversion(d);
  p=cash_in_cents.nickel_conversion(n);
  cout << p << " penny(ies).";
  return (0);
}
```

This program uses four member functions. The first function passes the number of pennies to the private class variable *number*. The remaining three functions convert cash, given in cents, to the equivalent cash in quarters, dimes, nickels, and pennies. Notice in particular the placement of the constructor and destructor in the class definition. The constructor and destructor function descriptions contain nothing more than a message that will be printed to the screen. Constructors are not specifically called by a program. Their appearance on the screen is your key that the constructor and destructor were automatically called when the object was created and destroyed.

```
class coins {
  int number;

public:
```

```
  coins() {cout << "Begin Conversion!\n";}       // constructor
  ~coins() {cout << "\nFinished Conversion!";}   // destructor
  void get_cents(int);
  int quarter_conversion(void);
  int dime_conversion(int);
  int nickel_conversion(int);
};
```

Here is an example of the output from this program:

```
Enter the cash, in cents, to convert: 157
Begin Conversion!
157 cents, converts to:
6 quarter(s), 0 dime(s), 1 nickel(s), and 2 penny(ies).
Finished Conversion!
```

In this example, the function definition is actually included within the constructor and destructor. When the function definition is included with member functions, it is said to be *implicitly defined*. Member functions can be defined in the typical manner or declared explicitly as inline functions.

You can expand this example to include dollars and half-dollars.

USING CONSTRUCTORS TO INITIALIZE MEMBER VARIABLES

Another practical use for constructors is for initialization of private class variables. In the previous examples, class variables were set by utilizing separate member functions. In the next example, the original class of the previous program is modified slightly to eliminate the need for user input. In this case, the variable *number* will be initialized to 431 pennies.

```
class coins {
  int number;

public:
  coins() {number=431;}                          // constructor
  ~coins() {cout << "\nFinished Conversion!";}   // destructor
  int quarter_conversion(void);
  int dime_conversion(int);
  int nickel_conversion(int);
};
```

The route to class variables is always through class member functions. Remember that the constructor is considered a member function.

USING CONSTRUCTORS AND DESTRUCTORS FOR CREATING AND DELETING FREE STORE MEMORY

Perhaps the most significant reason for using a constructor is in utilizing free store memory. In the next example, a constructor is used to allocate memory for the *string1* pointer with the **new** operator. A destructor is also used to release the allocated memory back to the system, when the object is destroyed. This is accomplished with the use of the **delete** operator.

```
class string_operation {
  char *string1;
  int  string_len;

public:
  string_operation(char *) {string1=new char[string_len];}
  ~string_operation() {delete string1;}
  void input_data(char *);
  void output_data(char *);
};
```

The memory allocated by **new** to the pointer *string1* can be deallocated only with a subsequent call to **delete**. For this reason, you will usually see memory allocated to pointers in constructors and deallocated in destructors. This approach also ensures that if the variable assigned to the class passes out of its scope, the allocated memory will be returned to the system. These operations make memory allocation dynamic and are most useful in programs that utilize linked lists.

The memory used by data types, such as **int** and **float**, is automatically restored to the system.

Overloading Class Member Functions

Class member functions, like ordinary C++ functions, can be overloaded. *Overloading* functions means that more than one function can have the same function name in the current scope. The compiler's responsibility becomes to select the correct function based upon the number and type of arguments used during the function call. The first example in this section illustrates the overloading of a class function named number(). This overloaded function will return the absolute value of an integer or double with the use of the math functions abs(), which accepts and returns integer values, and fabs(), which accepts and returns double values. With an overloaded function, the argument types determine which member function will actually be used.

```
//  absol.cpp
//  C++ program illustrates member function overloading.
//  Program determines the absolute value of an integer
//  and a double.
//  Chris H. Pappas and William H. Murray, 1999

#include <iostream>
#include <math>
#include <stdlib>

using namespace std;
```

```
class absolute_value {
public:
  int number(int);
  double number(double);
};

int absolute_value::number(int test_data)
{
  int answer;

  answer=abs(test_data);
  return (answer);
}

double absolute_value::number(double test_data)
{
  double answer;

  answer=fabs(test_data);
  return (answer);
}

main()
{
  absolute_value neg_number;

  cout << "The absolute value is "
       << neg_number.number(-583) 8<< endl;
  cout << "The absolute value is "
       << neg_number.number(-583.1749) << endl;
  return (0);
}
```

Notice that the dot operator is used in conjunction with the member function name to pass a negative integer and negative double values. The program selects the proper member function based upon the type of argument (integer or double) passed along with the function name. The positive value returned by each function is printed to the screen:

```
the absolute value is 583
the absolute value is 583.1749
```

In another example, angle information is passed to member functions in one of two formats—a double or a string. With member function overloading, you can process both types.

```
//  overld.cpp
//  C++ program illustrates overloading two class member
//  functions. The program allows an angle to be entered
//  in decimal or deg/min/sec format. One member function
//  accepts data as a double, the other as a string. The
```

```
//  program returns the sine, cosine, and tangent.
//  Chris H. Pappas and William H. Murray, 1999

#include <iostream>
#include <math>
#include <string>
using namespace std;

const double DEG_TO_RAD=0.0174532925;

class trigonometric {
  double angle;
  double answer_sine;
  double answer_cosine;
  double answer_tangent;

p8ublic:
  void trig_calc(double);
  void trig_calc(char *);
};

void trigonometric::trig_calc(double degrees)
{
  angle=degrees;
  answer_sine=sin(angle * DEG_TO_RAD);
  answer_cosine=cos(angle * DEG_TO_RAD);
  answer_tangent=tan(angle * DEG_TO_RAD);
  cout << "\nFor an angle of " << angle
       << " degrees." << endl;
  cout << "The sine is " << answer_sine << endl;
  cout << "The cosine is " << answer_cosine << endl;
  cout << "The tangent is " << answer_tangent << endl;
}

void trigonometric::trig_calc(char *dat)
{
  char *deg,*min,*sec;

  deg=strtok(dat,"° ");  //make ° with alt-248
  min=strtok(0,"' ");
  sec=strtok(0,"\"");
  angle=atof(deg)+((atof(min))/60.0)+((atof(sec))/360.0);
  answer_sine=sin(angle * DEG_TO_RAD);
  answer_cosine=cos(angle * DEG_TO_RAD);
  answer_tangent=tan(angle * DEG_TO_RAD);
  cout << "\nFor an angle of " << angle
       << " degrees." << endl;
  cout << "The sine is " << answer_sine << endl;
  cout << "The cosine is " << answer_cosine << endl;
  cout << "The tangent is " << answer_tangent << endl;
```

```
}

main()
{
  trigonometric data;

  data.trig_calc(75.0);
  data.trig_calc("35° 75' 20\"");
  data.trig_calc(145.72);
  data.trig_calc("65° 45' 30\"");
  return (0);
}
```

This program makes use of a very powerful built-in function, strtok(), prototyped in string. The syntax for using strtok() is straightforward:

```
char *strtok(string10,string20);  //locates token in string1
char *string10;                      //string that has token(s)

const char *string20;                //string with delimiter chars
```

The strtok() function will scan the first string, *string1,* looking for a series of character tokens. For this example, the tokens representing degrees, minutes, and seconds are used. The actual length of the tokens can vary. The second string, *string2*, contains a set of delimiters. Spaces, commas, or other special characters can be used for delimiters. The tokens in *string1* are separated by the delimiters in *string2*. Therefore, all the tokens in *string1* can be retrieved with a series of calls to the strtok() function. strtok() alters *string1* by inserting a null character after each token is retrieved. The function returns a pointer to the first token the first time it is called. Subsequent calls return a pointer to the next token, and so on. When there are no more tokens in the string, a null pointer is returned.

This example permits angle readings formatted as decimal values, or in degrees, minutes, and seconds of arc. For the latter case, strtok() uses the degree symbol (°) to find the first token. For minutes, a minute symbol (') will pull out the token containing the number of minutes. Finally, \" symbol is used to retrieve seconds. The last delimiter uses two symbols because the double quote by itself is used for terminating strings.

Class member function overloading gives programs and programmers flexibility when dealing with different data formats. If you are not into math or engineering programs, can you think of any applications that interest you where this feature might be helpful? Consider this possibility: if you are the cook in your household, you could develop an application that modifies recipes. You could write a program that would accept data as a decimal value or in mixed units. For example, the program might allow you to enter "3.75 cups, 1 pint 1.75 cups" or "1 pint 1 cup 12 tbs."

Using Friend Functions to Access Private Class Variables

One important feature of classes is their ability to hide data. Recall that member data is private by default in classes—that is, sharable only with member functions of the class. Almost ironic, then, is the fact that a category of functions exist specifically designed to override this feature. Functions of this type are called *friend functions*. Friend functions allow the sharing of private class information with nonmember functions. Friend functions, not defined in the class itself, can share the same class resources as member functions.

Friend functions offer the advantage that they are external to the class definition, as shown here:

```
//  secs.cpp
//  C++ program illustrates the use of friend functions.
//  Program will collect a string of date and time
//  information from system. Time information will
//  be processed and converted into seconds.
//  Chris H. Pappas and William H. Murray, 1999

#include <iostream>
#include <time>     // for tm & time_t structure
#include <string>   // for strtok function prototype
#include <stdlib>   // for atol function prototype
using namespace std;

class time_class {
  long secs;
  friend char * present_time(time_class);  //friend
public:
  time_class(char *);
};

time_class::time_class(char *tm)
{
  char *hours,*minutes,*seconds;

  // data returned in the following string format:
  // (day month date hours:minutes:seconds year)
  // Thus, need to skip over three tokens, ie.
  // skip day, month and date
  hours=strtok(tm," ");
  hours=strtok(0," ");
  hours=strtok(0," ");

  // collect time information from string
  hours=strtok(0,":");
  minutes=strtok(0,":");
  seconds=strtok(0," ");
```

```
    // convert data to long type and accumulate seconds.
    secs=atol(hours)*3600;
    secs+=atol(minutes)*60;
    secs+=atol(seconds);
  }

char * present_time(time_class);  // prototype

main()
{
  // get the string of time & date information
  struct tm *ptr;
  time_t ltime;
  ltime=time(NULL);
  ptr=localtime(&ltime);

  time_class tz(asctime(ptr));

  cout << "The date/time string information: "
       << asctime(ptr) << endl;
  cout << "The time converted to seconds: "
       << present_time(tz) << endl;
  return (0);
}

char * present_time(time_class tz)
{
  char *ctbuf;
  ctbuf=new char[40];
  long int seconds_total;

  seconds_total=tz.secs;
  ltoa(seconds_total,ctbuf,10);
  return (ctbuf);
}
```

Notice in the class definition the use of the keyword **friend** along with the description of the present_time() function. When you examine the program listing, you will notice that this function, external to the class, appears after the main() function description. In other words, it is written as a traditional C++ function, external to member functions of the defined class.

This program has a number of additional interesting features. In the function main(), the system's time is obtained with the use of time_t and its associated structure *tm*. In this program, *ltime* is the name of the variable associated with *time_t*. Local time is initialized and retrieved into the pointer, *ptr*, with the next two lines of code. By using ***asctime(ptr)***, the pointer will point to an ASCII string of date and time information.

```
struct tm *ptr;
time_t ltime;
ltime=time(NULL);
ptr=localtime(&ltime);

time_class tz(asctime(ptr));
```

The date and time string is formatted in this manner:

day month date hours:minutes:seconds year \n \0

For example:

```
Mon Sep 17  13:12:21 1999
```

A more detailed discussion of built-in functions occurs throughout the remainder of the chapter, including those prototyped in *time*.

The string information that is retrieved is sent to the class by associating *tz* with the class **time_class**:

```
time_class tz(asctime(ptr));
```

A constructor, **time_class(char** *), is used to define the code required to convert the string information into integer data. This conversion is accomplished by using the strtok() function.

The date/time information is returned in a rather strange format. To process this information, strtok() must use a space as the delimiter in order to skip over the day, month, and date information in the string. In this program, the variable hours initially serves as a junk collector for unwanted tokens. The next delimiter is a colon (:), which is used in collecting both hour and minute tokens from the string. Finally, the number of seconds can be retrieved by reading the string until another space is encountered. The string information is then converted to a **long** type and converted to the appropriate number of seconds. The variable *secs* is private to the class but accessible to the friend function.

The friend function takes the number of accumulated seconds, *tz.seconds,* and converts it back to a character string. The memory for storing the string is allocated with the **new** operator. This newly created string is a result of using the friend function.

The program prints two pieces of information:

```
The date/time string information: Mon May 25 16:01:55 1992

The time converted to seconds: 57715
```

First, **cout** sends the string produced by asctime() to the screen. This information is obtainable from the time_t() function and is available to the main() function. Second, the system time is printed by passing *present_time* to the **cout** stream.

Although friend functions offer some interesting programming possibilities when programming with C++ classes, they should be used with caution.

Using the this Pointer

The keyword **this** is used to identify a self-referential pointer that is implicitly declared in C++, as follows:

```
class_name *this;    //class_name is class type.
```

The **this** pointer is used to point to the object for which the member function is invoked. Here is an example, used in a class definition:

```
class class_name {
  char chr;

public:
  void begin_conv(char k) {chr=k;}
  char conv_chr(void) {return (this -> chr);}
};
```

In this case, the pointer **this** is used to access the private class variable member 20*chr*.

Additional uses exist for the **this** pointer. You can use it to include a link on a doubly linked list or when writing constructors and destructors involving memory allocations. Examine the following example:

```
class class_name {
  int x,y,z;
  char chr;

public:
  class_name(size) {this=new(size);}
  ~class_name(void) {delete(this);}
};
```

Using Operator Overloading

Earlier in this chapter, you learned that you can overload member functions in a class. In this section, you will learn that you can also overload C++ operators. In C++, new definitions can be applied to such familiar operators as +, -, *, and / in a given class.

The idea of operator overloading is common in numerous programming languages, even if it is not specifically implemented. For example, all compiled languages allow you to add two integers, two floats, or two doubles (or their equivalent types) with the + operator. This capability is the essence of operator overloading—using the same operator on different data types. In C++, you can extend this simple concept even further. In most compiled languages, you cannot, for example, to take a complex number, matrix, or character string and add them together with the + operator.

These operations are valid in all programming languages:

3 + 8
3.3 + 7.2

These operations are typically not valid operations:

(4 - j4) + (5 + j10)
(15° 20' 15") + (53° 57' 40")
"combine " + "strings"

If the last three operations were possible with the + operator, the workload of the programmer would be greatly reduced when designing new applications. The good news is that in C++, the + operator can be overloaded and the previous three operations can be made valid. Many additional operators can also be overloaded. Operator overloading is used extensively in C++. You will find examples throughout the various Microsoft C++ libraries.

OVERLOADING OPERATORS AND FUNCTION CALLS

In C++, the following operators can be overloaded.

```
+       -       *       /       =       <       >       +=      -=
*=      /=      <<      >>      >>=     <<=     = =     !=      <=
>=      ++      -       -%      &       ^^      !       |       ~
&=      ^=      |=      &&      ||      %=      []      ()      new
delete
```

The main restrictions are that the syntax and precedence of the operator must remain unchanged from its originally defined meaning. Another important point is that operator overloading is valid only within the scope of the class in which overloading occurs.

THE SYNTAX OF OVERLOADING

In order to overload an operator, the **operator** keyword is followed by the operator itself:

```
type operator opr(param list)
```

For example:

```
angle_value operator +(angle_argument);
```

Here, *angle_value* is the name of the class type, followed by the **operator** keyword, then the operator itself (+), and a parameter to be passed to the overloaded operator.

Within the scope of a properly defined class, several angles specified in degrees/minutes/seconds could be directly added together:

```
angle_value angle1("37°15' 56\"");
angle_value angle2("10° 44' 44\"");
angle_value angle3("75° 17' 59\"");
angle_value angle4("130° 32' 54\"");
angle_value sum_of_angles;

sum_of_angles=angle1+angle2+angle3+angle4;
```

As you know from earlier examples, the symbol for seconds is the double quote mark ("). This symbol is also used to signal the beginning and ending of a character string. The quote symbol can be printed to the screen if it is preceded with a backslash. This book uses this format for data input.

Another problem must be taken into account in programs such as this: the carrying of information from seconds to minutes and from minutes to hours must be handled properly. A carry occurs in both cases when the total number of seconds or minutes exceeds 59. This doesn't have anything to do with operator overloading directly, but the program must take this fact into account if a correct total is to be produced, as shown here:

```
//  opover.cpp
//  C++ program illustrates operator overloading.
//  Program will overload the "+" operator so that
//  several angles, in the format degrees minutes seconds,
//  can be added directly.
//  Chris H. Pappas and William H. Murray, 1999


#include <strstrea>
#include <stdlib>
#include <string>

using namespace std;

class angle_value {
  int degrees,minutes,seconds;

  public:
  angle_value() {degrees=0,
                 minutes=0,
                 seconds=0;}  // constructor
  angle_value(char *);
  angle_value operator +(angle_value);
  char * info_display(void);
};

angle_value::angle_value(char *angle_sum)
{
  degrees=atoi(strtok(angle_sum,"°"));
```

```
  minutes=atoi(strtok(0,"' "));
  seconds=atoi(strtok(0,"\""));
}

angle_value angle_value::operator+(angle_value angle_sum)
{
  angle_value ang;
  ang.seconds=(seconds+angle_sum.seconds)%60;
  ang.minutes=((seconds+angle_sum.seconds)/60+
              minutes+angle_sum.minutes)%60;
  ang.degrees=((seconds+angle_sum.seconds)/60+
              minutes+angle_sum.minutes)/60;
  ang.degrees+=degrees+angle_sum.degrees;
  return ang;
}

char * angle_value::info_display()
{
  char *ang[15];
  // strstream required for incore formatting
  ostrstream(*ang,sizeof(ang)) << degrees << "°"
                               << minutes << "' "
                               << seconds << "\""
                               << ends;
  return *ang;
}

main()
{
  angle_value angle1("37° 15' 56\"");   //make with alt-248
  angle_value angle2("10° 44' 44\"");
  angle_value angle3("75° 17' 59\"");
  angle_value angle4("130° 32' 54\"");
  angle_value sum_of_angles;

  sum_of_angles=angle1+angle2+angle3+angle4;
  cout << "the sum of the angles is "
       << sum_of_angles.info_display() << endl;
  return (0);
}
```

The details of how the mixed units are added together are included in the small piece of code that declares that the + operator is to be overloaded:

```
angle_value angle_value::operator+(angle_value angle_sum)
{
  angle_value ang;
  ang.seconds=(seconds+angle_sum.seconds)%60;
  ang.minutes=((seconds+angle_sum.seconds)/60+
              minutes+angle_sum.minutes)%60;
  ang.degrees=((seconds+angle_sum.seconds)/60+
```

```
                minutes+angle_sum.minutes)/60;
  ang.degrees+=degrees+angle_sum.degrees;
  return ang;
}
```

Here, divide and modulus operations are performed on the sums to ensure correct carry information.

Further details of the program's operation are omitted, since you have seen most of the functions and modules in earlier examples. However, be sure to remember that when you overload operators, proper operator syntax and precedence must be maintained.

The output from this program shows the sum of the four angles to be as follows:

```
the sum of the angles is 253° 51' 33"
```

Is this answer correct?

Derived Classes

A derived class can be considered an extension or inheritance of an existing class. The original class is known as a *base* or *parent class*, and the derived class as a *subclass* or *child class*. As such, a derived class provides a simple means for expanding or customizing the capabilities of a parent class, without the need for re-creating the parent class itself. With a parent class in place, a common interface is possible to one or more of the derived classes.

Any C++ class can serve as a parent class, and any derived class will reflect its description. The derived class can add additional features to those of the parent class. For example, the derived class can modify access privileges, add new members, or overload existing ones. When a derived class overloads a function declared in the parent class, it is said to be a *virtual member function*. You will see that virtual member functions are very important to the concept of object-oriented programming.

THE SYNTAX OF A DERIVED CLASS

You describe a derived class by using the following syntax:

```
  class derived-class-type :(public/private/protected) . . .
       parent-class-type { . . . .};
```

For example, in creating a derived class, you might write

```
class retirement:public consumer { . . . .};
```

In this case, the derived class tag is **retirement**. The parent class has public visibility, and its tag is **consumer**.

A third visibility specifier is often used with derived classes—protected. A protected specifier is the same as a private specifier with the added feature that class member functions and friends of derived classes are given access to the class.

CREATING DERIVED CLASSES

The next program depicts the concept of a derived class. The parent class collects and reports information on a consumer's name, address, city, state, and ZIP code. Two similar child classes are derived. One child class maintains information on a consumer's accumulated airline mileage, while the second derived child class reports information on a consumer's accumulated rental car mileage. Both derived child classes inherit information from the parent class. Study the listing and see what you can discern about these derived classes.

```
//  dercls.cpp
//  C++ program illustrates derived classes.
//  The parent class contains name, street, city,
//  state, and zip information. Derived classes add
//  either airline or rental car mileage information
//  to parent class information.
//  Chris H. Pappas and William H. Murray, 1999

#include <iostream>
#include <string>

using namespace std;

char newline;

class consumer {
  char name[60],
       street[60],
       city[20],
       state[15],
       zip[10];
public:
  void data_output(void);
  void data_input(void);
};

void consumer::data_output()
{
  cout << "Name: " << name << endl;
  cout << "Street: " << street << endl;
  cout << "City: " << city << endl;
  cout << "State: " << state << endl;
  cout << "Zip: " << zip << endl;
}

void consumer::data_input()
```

```
{
  cout << "Enter The Consumer's Full Name: ";
  cin.get(name,59,'\n');
  cin.get(newline);       //flush carriage return
  cout << "Enter The Street Address: ";
  cin.get(street,59,'\n');
  cin.get(newline);
  cout << "Enter The City: ";
  cin.get(city,19,'\n');
  cin.get(newline);
  cout << "Enter The State: ";
  cin.get(state,14,'\n');
  cin.get(newline);
  cout << "Enter The Five Digit Zip Code: ";
  cin.get(zip,9,'\n');
  cin.get(newline);
}

class airline:public consumer {
  char airline_type[20];
  float acc_air_miles;
public:
  void airline_consumer();
  void disp_air_mileage();
};

void airline::airline_consumer()
{
  data_input();
  cout << "Enter Airline Type: ";
  cin.get(airline_type,19,'\n');
  cin.get(newline);
  cout << "Enter Accumulated Air Mileage: ";
  cin >> acc_air_miles;
  cin.get(newline);       //flush carriage return
}

void airline::disp_air_mileage()
{
  data_output();

  cout << "Airline Type: " << airline_type
       << endl;
  cout << "Accumulated Air Mileage: "
       << acc_air_miles << endl;
}

class rental_car:public consumer {
  char rental_car_type[20];
  float acc_road_miles;
```

```
public:
  void rental_car_consumer();
  void disp_road_mileage();
};

void rental_car::rental_car_consumer()
{
  data_input();
  cout << "Enter Rental_car Type: ";
  cin.get(rental_car_type,19,'\n');
  cin.get(newline);      //flush carriage return
  cout << "Enter Accumulated Road Mileage: ";
  cin >> acc_road_miles;
  cin.get(newline);
}

void rental_car::disp_road_mileage()
{
  data_output();

  cout << "Rental Car Type: "
       << rental_car_type << endl;
  cout << "Accumulated Mileage: "
       << acc_road_miles << endl;
}

main()
{
  //associate variable names with classes
  airline jetaway;
  rental_car varooom;

  //get airline information
  cout << "\n--Airline Consumer--\n";
  jetaway.airline_consumer();


  //get rental_car information
  cout << "\n--Rental Car Consumer--\n";
  varooom.rental_car_consumer();

  //now display all consumer information
  cout << "\n--Airline Consumer--\n";
  jetaway.disp_air_mileage();
  cout << "\n--Rental Car Consumer--\n";
  varooom.disp_road_mileage();

  return (0);
}
```

In the example, the parent class is type *consumer*. The private part of this class accepts consumer information for name, address, city, state, and ZIP code. The public part describes two functions, data_output() and data_input(). You have seen functions similar to these to gather class information in earlier programs. The first derived child class is *airline*.

```
class airline:public consumer {
  char airline_type[20];
  float acc_air_miles;
public:
  void airline_consumer(void);
  void disp_air_mileage(void);
};
```

This derived child class contains two functions, airline_consumer() and disp_air_mileage(). The first function, airline_consumer(), uses the parent class to obtain name, address, city, state, and ZIP code, and *attaches* the airline type and accumulated mileage.

```
void airline::airline_consumer()
{
  data_input();
  cout << "Enter Airline Type: ";
  cin.get(airline_type,19,'\n');
  cin.get(newline);
  cout << "Enter Accumulated Air Mileage: ";
  cin >> acc_air_miles;
  cin.get(newline);      //flush carriage return
}
```

Do you understand how the derived class is being used? A call to the function data_input() is a call to a member function that is part of the parent class. The remainder of the derived class is involved with obtaining the additional airline type and accumulated mileage.

The information on accumulated air mileage can be displayed for a consumer in a similar manner. The parent class function, data_output(), prints the information gathered by the parent class (name, address, and so on), whereas disp_air_mileage() attaches the derived child class's information (airline type and mileage) to the output. The process is repeated for the rental car consumer. Thus, one parent class serves as the data-gathering base for two derived child classes, each obtaining its own specific information.

Experiment with this program by entering your own database of information. You might also consider adding additional member functions to the ***consumer*** class.

Templates in C!

Once again, C and C++'s flexible and extensible language constructs allowed clever programmers to generate very esoteric code solutions. These advanced code solutions got the job done with three down sides. First, the average programmer got lost in deciphering the code. Secondly, debugging was like trying do your first recursive call trace. Thirdly, the solutions were not necessarily as portable as today's environments demand.

Structures as Simple Templates

Take, for example, the following C code section that uses the **#define** and concatenation (##) preprocessor statements to define a binary tree node.

```
C Example
#define BINARY_TREE( t )
typedef struct _tree_##t {
  t data;
  struct _tree_##t *left;
  struct _tree_##t *right;
} BINARY_TREE_##;
```

Notice how the preprocessor would substitute the argument *t* with whichever data type the user chose, as in:

```
BINARY_TREE( int );

BINARY_TREE( float );

BINARY_TREE( my_structure );
```

and then would totally redefine the node; for example, for int data types, the binary tree node's definition would look like:

```
typedef struct _tree_int {
  int data;
  struct _tree_int *left;
  struct _tree_int *right;
} BINARY_TREE_int;
```

Now, *this* is just a minor example of the inherent sophistication and modularity provided by the C/C++ languages. Remember, the previous examples are all legal in C and require no additional C++ syntax and sophistication!

However, for as slick as this example is, you have one inherent problem. Unlike **inline** functions, which can also be used to generate macros, **#define** defined macros have no error-checking capabilities. They are strictly string search and replace operations at pass one of C/C++'s two-pass compile. Obviously, in order to generate reliable and portable code, some other means was necessary - enter the C++ **template**.

C++ Template Keyword

Templates were one of the last features added to C++ before the ANSI/ISO C++ standardization process began. As Bjarne Stroustrup (author of C++) states, "Templates were considered essential for the design of proper container classes. . . . For many people, the largest single problem with C++ is the lack of an extensive standard library. A major problem in producing such a library is that C++ does not provide a sufficiently general facility for defining 'container classes' such as lists, vectors, and associative arrays." The incorporation of templates into the C++ language led directly to the development of the STL, a standardized library of container classes and algorithms using template classes and functions.

Template Syntax

As a programmer, you undoubtedly understand the concept of functions and function calls. The function - contains a modularly designed, reusable, single problem-solving algorithm. The function call - passes the actual values needed by the function at a particular instance in the execution of the calling routine's algorithm.

C++ templates use parameters in an entirely new way: to create new functions and classes. And, unlike parameter passing to functions, templates create these new functions and classes at *compile-time*, rather than run-time.

The straightforward syntax for templates looks like:

```
template <argument_list> declaration
```

After the **template** keyword and *argument_list*, the programmer supplies the template declaration, where s/he defines the parameterized version of a class or function. The C++ compiler decides to generate different versions of the class or function based on the arguments passed to the template when it is used.

Function Templates

To understand how templates function in the STL, you need to understand that you have two types of templates: class templates and function templates. Function templates generate functions, and class templates generate classes.

The following example defines a function template that squares any data type:

```
template <class Type>
Type squareIt( Type x ) { return x * x; } //function template
```

The function template squareIt() can be passed any appropriate data *Type*. For example:

```
void main( void )
{

  cout << "The square of the integer 9 is: " << squareIt( 9 );
  cout << "The square of the unsigned int 255 is: " << squareIt( 255U );
  cout << "The square of the float 10.0: " << squareIt( 10.0 );
  //...
}
```

These three statements cause the compiler to generate, at compile-time, three unique function bodies—one instance for integer data, another for unsigned integer data, and a third for floating-point values:

```
int square(int x) { return x * x; }
unsigned int square(unsigned int x) { return x * x; }
double square(double x) { return x * x; }
```

Class Templates

The second category of templates is a class template. The following example defines a simple array container class template:

```
template < class Type, int MAX_ELEMENTS >
class Array {
  protected:
    Type *pTypeArray;
  public:
    Array()  { pTypeArray  = new Type[ MAX_ELEMENTS ]; }//constructor
    ~Array() { delete[] pTypeArray; }//destructor
  // ...
};
```

The template class definition creates an array container class of any *Type*! The first argument to the template defines what type of elements the array will hold, and the second argument defines how many rows, or number of elements, the array will hold. The array's *Type* can be anything from a simple standard C++ data type such as int, or as complex as an application-specific structure or complex object.

A program instantiates an actual tangible instance of the template class definition with almost a function-like syntax:

```
void main( void )
{
  Array < float, 10 >  fArray;

  Array < int, 25 > iArray;

  Array < MY_STRUCTURE_DEFINITION, MAX_RECORDS > strucArray;

  Array < MY_CLASS_DEFINITION, iRunTimeUsersChoice > classArray;
  //...
}
```

For each instantiation, the compiler generates a brand-new version of the *Array* class for every different combination of types passed to it. It does so at compile-time by performing a substitution of the arguments wherever they appear in the formal template definition.

The Need for Standardization

In theory, C++ templates fill the need for easy-to-use container classes. But in real life, the solution wasn't always that simple, because several obstacles got in the way. First, depending on the implementation of template container classes either from compiler to third-party vendors, template-based containers could be noticeably slower than their C counterparts. For instance, many template-based container classes relied on inheritance to do their jobs, and certain kinds of inheritance can measurably slow down a program.

Another problem with templates was compatibility. If you happened to use templates from two different vendors, compatibility conflicts could occur between them since no standard existed. But this was a lesser problem than customization. To some extent, customizing code is a normal part of working with templates. Take a class called *VehicleSalesRecord*, for instance. For this class to work with a linked list template, you would have to define operations like less-than (<), the equivalence operator (==), and possibly a greater-than operator (>). Providing these operations or requirements for every class was part of the overhead of working with any template.

Traditionally, to work with container templates, a programmer needed to customize the objects in the container, not the container template itself. The problem comes in when you need to modify the way a template works. For example, imagine your wanting to customize the way the items are sorted. With most template-based classes, you need to decipher someone else's code, modify the template source code, and re-compile your program. That requirement assumes that you have access to the original template definition. And template code modification doesn't lend itself to preserving the original intent behind templates.

With the inherent slowness in template-based container classes, along with their historically being nonstandard and not easy to customize, we needed a better way. Welcome to STL!

Summary

By design, this chapter has taken you from an introductory understanding of C/C++ and strategically highlighted those components of C++ that are fundamental STL building blocks. Chapter 3 takes these concepts and combines them with a high-level overview of STL features and syntax. This next chapter will highlight the structure of a Standard Template Library, showing you how to interpret the various libraries' contents, telling you any mandatory steps needed to use STL, and including a few coded examples.

Once you have digested the information presented in this chapter and the next, you will be fully empowered to maximize the use of any STL definition you choose!

THREE

Standard C++ Library and STL Fundamentals

Assuming that you have never used STL before, Chapter 3 stands as a bridge between the history and non-STL C++ language syntax and Chapter 4, which begins defining and using specific STL templates.

When reading this chapter, pay close attention to the two different libraries, the Standard C++ Library, which is different from, though used in conjunction with, the Standard Template Library.

The chapter begins with a discussion of the latest ANSI/ISO Language concept updates. Many of these new innovations are used within the Standard C++ Library and the Standard Template Library.

The chapter finishes with an overview of the Standard C++ Library as implemented in Microsoft Visual C++, and the Standard Template Library. By the end of the chapter, you will be able to:

1. Understand namespaces.
2. Understand and use the "new-style" casts.
3. Understand and use run-time Type Information (RTTI)
4. Name the different components of the Standard C++ Library.
5. Write simple programs using Visual C++ that use the Standard Template Library components.
6. In addition, skillfully use the Standard C++ Library exception handling and language support.

The chapter assumes that you understand basic C++ programming and have a good understanding of C++ templates (discussed in Chapter 2).

Latest C++ ANSI/ISO Language Updates

While the ANSI/ISO committee was busy incorporating STL, they took the opportunity to introduce modifications to the C++ language definition. These modifications, in most cases, implement features that the committee members admired in other languages, features that they viewed as deficiencies in traditional C++. These new changes, which consist of language additions, should not affect any previously written code.

Using namespace

We'll look at the definition for *namespace* from a bottom-up point of view. Namespaces control scope, in other words, identifier (constants, variables, functions, classes, etc.) visibility. The tightest scope is local—those identifiers declared within a function and associated at this level would be member function or method declarations. Higher up on the scale would be class scope.

Visibility issues are associated with file scope, for example, when 1.cpp, 2.cpp, and 3.cpp are combined to generate 123.exe. Identifiers declared in 1.cpp, for example, are not visible (by default) in 2.cpp and 3.cpp.

At the highest level is program or workspace scope. Historically, this worked fine until the advent of today's complex programming environment, where source files are coming at you from all directions. Today's programs are a combination of source files you write, those supplied by the compiler(s), some from the operating system itself, and third-party vendors. Under these circumstances, program scope is not sufficient to prevent identifier collisions between categories. Namespaces allow you to lock down all program identifiers, successfully preventing these types of collisions.

Collisions usually fall under the category of external, global identifiers used throughout a program. They are visible to all object modules in the application program, in third-party class and function libraries, and in the compiler's system libraries. When two variables in global scope have the same identifier, the linker generates an error.

Many compiler manufacturers initially solved this problem by assigning unique identifiers to each variable. For example, under Standard C, the compiler system prefixes its internal global identifiers with underscore characters, and programmers are told to avoid that usage to avoid conflicts.

Third-party vendors prepended unique mnemonic prefixes to global identifiers in an attempt to prevent collisions. However, even this effort failed whenever two developers chose the same prefix. The problem is that the language had no built-in mechanism with which a library publisher could stake out a so-called namespace of its own—one that would insulate its global identifiers from those of other libraries being linked into the same application.

Traditionally, a programmer had three choices to eliminating the collisions: they could get the source code, modify it, and rebuild-all, have the authors of the offending code change *their* declarations, or select an alternate code source containing the same functionality. Not a very pleasant set of alternatives!

The C++ **namespace** keyword limits an identifier's scope to the namespace identifier. All references from outside the block to the global identifiers declared in the block must, in one way or another, qualify the global identifier's reference with the namespace identifier. In actuality, this is logically similar to prepending prefixes; however, namespace identifers tend to be longer than the typical two- or three-character prefixes and stand a better chance of working.

namespace Syntax

To define a **namespace**, you encapsulate your declarations within a namespace block, as in:

```
namespace your_namespace_name {
  int ivalue;
  class my_class {/*....*/};
  // more declarations;
}
```

In the above example, any code statements within the *your_namespace_name* have direct access to the namespace's declarations. However, any code statements outside the *your_namespace_name* must use a qualifying syntax. For example, from the main() function, accessing *ivalue* would look like:

```
void main ( void )
{
  your_namespace_name::ivalue++;
}
```

The using namespace Statement

If you do not like the idea of always having to qualify an identifier with its namespace everytime you access it, you can use the **using** statement, as in:

```
using namespace your_namespace_name;
void main ( void )
{
  ivalue++;
}
```

This approach can, however, be like giving a hotel guest the key to the entire hotel instead of a single room—inviting trouble! The **using namespace** syntax provides access to all the namespace's declarations. Each application will benefit from the best selection of these two approaches.

The Selective using Statement

Somewhere between a fully qualified namespace identifier (*your_namespace_name::ivaluel++;*) and the **using namespace** ***your_namespace_name*** syntax is the simpler **using** statement. The **using** directive tells the compiler that you intend to use specific identifiers within a namespace. Using the previous examples, this would look like:

```
using your_namespace_name::ivalue;
void main ( void )
{
  ivalue++;
}
```

Just as a programmer would not choose to always use **for** loops when **while** and **do-while** alternatives are available, so too a programmer should carefully select the best, application-specific approach to namespace identifier access.

Renaming namespaces

Sometimes third-party namespace names can get in your way because of their length; for example, *your_namespace_name* is quite long. For this reason, the namespace feature allows a programmer to associate a new name with the namespace identifier, as in:

```
namespace YNN = your_namespace_name;
void main ( void )
{
  YNN::ivalue++;
}
```

static File Scope vs. Unnamed namespaces

One way to enforce file scope is with the keyword **static**. For example, if 1.cpp, 2.cpp, and 3.cpp all have the external variable declaration int ivalue; and you do not want internal linkage (meaning that all three identifiers *share* the same storage location), you precede all three declarations with the keyword **static**:

```
// 1.cpp               // 2.cpp                     // 3.cpp
static int ivalue;     static int ivalue;           static int ivalue;
void main ( void )     void some_funcs( void );     void more_funcs( void );
```

Unnamed namespaces provide the same capability, just a slightly different syntax:

```
// 1.cpp
namespace {
  int ivalue;
}
void main ( void )
{
  ivalue++;
}
```

To create an unnamed namespace, you simply omit a namespace identifier. The compiler then generates an internal identifier that is unique throughout the program. All identifiers declared within an unnamed namespace are available only within the defining file. Functions in other files, within the program's workspace, cannot reference the declarations.

New Casting Operations

With traditional style casting proving to be unsafe, error-prone, difficult to spot when reading programs and even more challenging when searched for in large bodies of source code, the newer style cast is a huge improvement. Four new types of casts exist. The general syntax looks like:

```
cast_operator <castType> (objectToCast)
```

Dynamic Casting

You use a *dynamic_cast* whenever you need to convert a base class pointer or reference to a derived class pointer or reference. The one restriction is that the base, parent, or root class must have at least one virtual function. The syntax for a *dynamic_cast* looks like:

```
dynamic_cast < castType > ( objectToCast );
```

This type of cast allows the program, at run-time, to determine whether a base class pointer or reference points to an object of a specific derived class or to an object of a class derived from the specified class.

You also use a *dynamic_cast* to upcast a pointer or reference to a derived class to a pointer or reference to one of the base, parent, or root classes in the same hierarchy. Upcasting allows a program to determine, at run-time, whether a pointer to a derived class really contains the address of an object of that class and, at the same time, whether you want to force the address into a pointer of one of the object's ancestor classes.

Static Casting

A *static_cast* implicitly converts between types that are not in the same class hierarchy. The type-checking is static, where the compiler checks to ensure that the conversion is valid, as opposed to the dynamic run-time type-checking that is used with *dynamic_cast*s. The syntax for a *static_cast* looks like:

```
static_cast < castType > ( objectToCast );
```

The *static_cast* operator can be used for operations such as converting a pointer to a base class to a pointer to a derived class. Such conversions are not always safe. For example:

```
class typeA { ... };

class typeB : public typeA { ... };

void someFunction(typeA* ptypeA, typeB* ptypeB)
{
    typeB* ptypeB2 = static_cast<typeB*>(ptypeA);  // not safe, ptypeB may
                                                   // point to just typeB

    typeA* ptypeA2 = static_cast<typeA*>(ptypeB);  // BETTER - this is a safe
                                                      conversion
    ...
}
```

In this code segment, the object pointed to by `ptypeA` may not be an object of type `typeB`, in which case the use of `*ptypeB2` could be disastrous. For instance, calling a function that is a member of the `typeB` class, but not the `typeA` class, could result in an access violation.

Newer C-Type Cast

The *reinterpret_cast* operator replaces many of the older C-type casts except those removing an identifier **const** restriction. The *reinterpret_cast* is capable of converting one pointer type into another, numbers into pointers, and vice-versa. The syntax looks like:

```
reinterpret_cast < castType > ( objectToCast );
```

The reinterpret_cast operator can be used for conversions such as **`char*`** to **`int*`**, or `Base_class*` to `anyOtherNONrelated_class*`, which are inherently unsafe.

The result of a *reinterpret_cast* cannot safely be used for anything other than being cast back to its original type. Other uses are, at best, nonportable. The following code segment demonstrates a pointer type cast in C, C++, and C++ using the *reinterpret_cast* syntax:

```
void main ( void )
{
  int * pointer_to_int;
  /* in C */
  pointer_to_int = malloc(100); /* implicit void * cast to int *,
                                   with warning */
```

```
  pointer_to_int = (int *) new int[100]; // C++ required cast of void  *
                                            to int *
  pointer_to_int = reinterpret_cast<int *>( new int[100]); // new style cast
}
```

Constant Cast

The *const_cast* operator can be used to remove the **const**, **volatile**, and **__unaligned** attribute(s) from a class. The general syntax looks like:

```
const_cast < castType > ( objectToCast )
```

With a *const_cast*, your program can cast a pointer to any object type or a pointer to a data member can, to a type that is identical except for the **const**, **volatile**, and **__unaligned** qualifiers. For pointers and references, the result will refer to the original object. For pointers to data members, the result will refer to the same member as the original (uncast) pointer to data member.

Run-Time Type Information

The *typeid* operator, found in <typeinfo>, supports the new C++ run-time type information feature. The operator returns a reference to a system-maintained object of the type *type_info*, which identifies the type of the argument. RTTI was added to the C++ language because many vendors of class libraries were implementing this functionality themselves. This addition caused incompatibilities between libraries. Thus, obviously, that support for run-time type information was needed at the language level.

The following code segment demonstrates their straightforward syntax and logical use:

```
#include <typeinfo>
#include <iostream>
using namespace std;
// ...
class someClassType { };
// ...
  someClassType sCTinstance;
  int ivalue;
  cout << "object type = " << typeid(sCTinstance).name(); // type's name
  if ( typeid ( ivalue ) == typeid ( sCTinstance ) ) // type comparisons
    cout << "I DON'T BELIEVE IT!";
```

Had this code section defined and then dynamically created a plethora of object types and instances, knowing which dynamically allocated type is in use at any point within an algorithm can be an extremely useful piece of run-time logic control.

Introduction to the Standard C++ Library

No matter how sophisticated your procedural or object-oriented, standalone or Windows application is—using every available feature of C++—as a programmer, you must invariably resort to tried 'n' true Data Structures algorithms for creating linked-lists, stacks, queues, binary trees, etc. By necessity, you have again re-invented the wheel for each application's unique user-defined data types. Along with this application-specific proprietary code comes the developer's nighmare—design changes that are not easily added in such cases and code maintenance.

Unlike many other object-oriented languages, such as SmallTalk, had these common programming components been part of the C++ language, you could avoid re-inventing data-specific algorithms. In a nutshell, that avoidance is what STL is all about. Finally, the C++ language provides you with general-purpose components for common programming tasks through the Standard C++ Library.

Some of the more interesting reusable components of the Standard C++ Library include powerful and flexible containers, and programmable algorithms. The facilities provided by the Standard C++ Library are as follows:

- **C++ Language Support** includes common type definitions used throughout the library such as predefined types, C++ program start and termination function support, support for dynamic memory allocation, support for dynamic type identification, and support for exception processing.
- **Diagnostic Tools** providing components for reporting several kinds of exceptional conditions, components for documenting program assertions, and a global variable for error number codes.
- **General C/C++ utilities** providing components used by other elements of the Standard C++ Library. This category also includes components used by the Standard Template Library (STL) and function objects, dynamic memory management utilities, and date/time utilities. These components may also be used by any C++ program. The general C/C++ utilities also include memory management components derived from the C library.
- **Strings**, including components for manipulating sequences of characters, where characters may be of type *char* or *w_char* (used in UNICODE applications), or of a type defined in a C++ program. UNICODE uses a two-byte value to represent every known written language's symbol set versus the limiting one-byte ASCII code.
- **Cultural Formatting Support** provides numeric, monetary, and date/time formatting and parsing and support for character classification and string collation.
- **STL (Standard Template Library)**, including the most widely used algorithms and data structures in data-independent format. STL headers can be grouped into three major organizing concepts: containers, iterators, and

algorithms. *Containers* are template classes that provide powerful and flexible ways to organize data: for example, vectors, lists, sets, and maps. *Iterators* are the glue that pastes together algorithms and containers.

- **Advanced Numerical Computation**, including seminumerical operations and components for complex number types, numeric arrays, generalized numeric algorithms.
- **Input/output**, including components for forward declarations of iostreams, predefined iostream objects, base iostream classes, stream buffering, stream formatting and manipulators, string streams, and file streams.
- The Standard C++ Library also incorporates the **Standard C Library**.

The Standard C++ Libraries

An application accesses Microsoft's Standard C++ Library facilities by using appropriate include files and associated static and dynamic libraries. Tables 3.1 and 3.2 list all the Standard C++ Library headers and the associated static and dynamic libraries provided by Visual C++.

Table 3.1 The Standard C++ Library Headers

algorithm	bitset	cassert	cctype
cerrno	cfloat	ciso646	climits
clocale	cmath	complex	csetjmp
csignal	cstdarg	cstddef	cstdio
cstdlib	cstring	ctime	cwchat
cwctype	deque	exception	fstream
functional	iomanip	ios	iosfwd
iostream	istream	iterator	limits
list	locale	map	memory
new	numeric	ostream	queue
set	sstream	stack	stdexcept
streambuff	string	strstream	utility
valarray	vector		

Remember, the Standard C++ Library headers have no .h file extension, in accordance with the latest ANSI/ISO C++ standard.

Microsoft also provides the static and dynamic libraries listed in Table 3.2.

Table 3.2 Static and Dynamic Libraries Included with Microsoft Visual C++

Library types	C run-time library	Standard C++ library	Old iostream library
Single Threaded	LIBC.LIB	LIBCP.LIB	LIBCI.LIB
Multithreaded	LIBCMT.LIB	LIBCPMT.LIB	LIBCIMT.LIB
Multithreaded DLL version	MSVCRT.LIB (uses MSVCRT.DLL)	MSVCPRT.LIB (uses MSVCRT.DLL)	MSVCIRT.LIB (uses MSVCIRT.DLL)
Debug Single Threaded	LIBCD.LIB	LIBCPD.LIB	LIBCID.LIB
Debug Multithreaded	LIBCMTD.LIB	LIBCPMTD.LIB	LIBCIMTD.LIB
Debug Multithreaded	MSVCRTD.LIB (uses MSVCRTD.DLL)	MSVCPRTD.LIB (uses MSVCRTD.DLL)	MSVCIRTD.LIB (uses MSVCIRTD.DLL)

Your First Standard C++ Library Application

To make you feel right at home, the following C++ program uses the Standard C++ Library iostream to print "Hello World!"

```
#include <iostream>
void main( void )
{
    cout << "Hello World!";
}
```

The code segment used the Standard C++ Library input/output component to print "Hello World!" by simply including the Standard C++ Library header <iostream>. Be sure to remember that starting with Visual C++ 4.0, a C++ program, depending on the run-time library compiler option specified (/ML[d], /MT[d], or /MD[d]), will always link with one Basic C run-time library and, depending on headers included, will link with either a Standard C++ Library (as in the example program above) or the old iostream library (as in the following coded example):

```
#include <iostream.h>
void main( void )
{
  cout << "Hellow World!";
}
```

Implementing Your Own Template

Frequently, a C++ program uses common data structures such as stacks, queues, and linked-lists. Imagine a program that requires a queue of customers and a queue of messages. You could easily implement a queue of customers, and then take the existing code and implement a queue of messages.

If the program grows and you have a need for a queue of orders, you could take the queue of messages and convert it to a queue of orders. But what if you need to make some changes to the queue implementation? This task would not be very easy because the code has been duplicated in many places. Re-inventing source code is not an intelligent approach in an object-oriented environment that encourages re-usability. Implementing a queue that can contain any arbitrary type rather than duplicating code seems to make more sense. How does one do that? The answer is to use *Type Parameterization*, more commonly referred to as *Templates*.

Templates are very useful when implementing generic constructs such as vectors, stacks, lists, and queues that can be used with any arbitrary type. C++ templates provide a way to re-use source code, as opposed to inheritance and composition, which provide a way to re-use object code.

C++ provides two types of templates: *class templates* and *function templates*. Use function templates to write generic functions: for example, searching and sorting routines that can be used with arbitrary types. The Standard Template Library generic algorithms have been implemented as function templates, and the containers have been implemented as class templates.

Your First class Template

The good news is that a class template definition looks very similar to a regular class definition, except for the prefix keyword **template**. The following example defines a stack class template—independent from any stack element type definitions:

```
template <class T>

class genericStack

{
public:
        genericStack( sizeOfStack = 25);
        ~genericStack() { delete[] stackPtr; }
        int pushElement(const T&);
        int popElement(T&) ;
        int isStackEmpty()const { return stackTop == -1 ; }
        int isStackFull() const { return stackTop == sizeOfStack - 1 ; }
private:
        int sizeOfStack ;  // number of stack elements
        int stackTop ;
        T* stackPtr ;
} ;
```

T represents any data type. Be sure to note that *T* does not have to be a class type as implied by the keyword class. *T* can be anything from a simple data type like int to a complex data structure pToArrayOfStructures *.

Function Templates Requirements

Implementing template member functions is somewhat different from implementing the regular class member functions. The declarations and definitions of the class-template member functions should all be in the same header file. Why do the declarations and definitions need to be in the same header file? Consider the following:

<table>
<tr>
<td><pre>//sample.h
template <class t>
class sample
{
public:
    sample() ;
    ~sample() ;
} ;</pre></td>
<td><pre>//sample.cpp
#include "sample.h"
template <class t>
sample<t>::sample()
{
}
template <class t>
sample<t>::~sample()
{
}</pre></td>
<td><pre>//main.cpp
#include "sample.h"
void main(void)
{
     sample<int> si ;
     sample<float> sf ;
}</pre></td>
</tr>
</table>

When compiling sample.cpp, the compiler has both the declarations and the definitions available. At this point, the compiler does not need to generate any definitions for template classes, since no instantiations exist. When the compiler compiles main.cpp, you have two instantiations: template classes sample<int> and sample<float>. At this point, the compiler has the declarations but no definitions!

Using a class Template

Using a class template is very easy. Create the required classes by plugging in the actual type for the type parameters. This process is commonly known as *instantiating* a class. Here is a sample class that uses the genericStack class template:

```
#include <iostream>
#include "stack.h"
using namespace std;
void main( void )
{
  typedef genericStack<float> floatStack;
  typedef genericStack<int> intStack;
  FloatStack actualFloatStackInstance( 10 );
```

In the above example, we defined a class template genericStack. In the program, we instantiated a genericStack of float (floatStack) and a generic-

Stack of int (intStack). Once the template classes are instantiated, you can instantiate objects of that type (for example, *actualFloatStackInstance.*)

Good programming practice is to use **typedef** while instantiating template classes. Then throughout the program, one can use the **typedef** name, with two advantages. First, **typedef**s are helpful when nesting template definitions. For example, when instantiating an int STL vector, you could use:

```
typedef vector<int, allocator<int> > intVECTOR ;
```

Secondly, should the template definition change, simply change the **typedef** definition. This practice is especially helpful when using STL components.

Class Template Parameters

The *genericStack* class template, described in the previous section, used only type parameters in the template header. You can also use nontype parameters. For example, the template header could be modified to take an *int number_of_elements* parameter as follows:

```
#define MAX_ELEMENTS 32
template <class T, int number_of_elements>
class genericStack ;
```

Then a declaration such as:

```
genericStack<float, MAX_ELEMENTS> currentStackSize;
```

could instantiate (at compile time) a *MAX_ELEMENTS* genericStack template class named *currentStackSize* (of float values); this template class would be of type *genericStack<float, 32>*.

Default Template Parameters

Let us look at the genericStack class template again:

```
template <class T, int number_of_elements> genericStack { ....};
```

C++ allows you to specify a *default template parameter*, so the definition could now look like:

```
template <class T = float, int number_of_elements = 10> genericStack { ....};
```

Then a declaration such as:

```
genericStack<> defaultStackSize;
```

would instantiate (at compile time) a 10-element *genericStack* template class named *defaultStackSize* (of float values); this template class would be of type *genericStack<float, 10>*.

If you specify a default template parameter for any formal parameter, the rules are the same as for functions and default parameters. Once you begin supplying a default parameter, all subsequent parameters must have defaults.

The Standard Template Library

The Standard Template Library is a part of the Standard C++ Library. Every C++ programmer at one time or another has implemented common data structures such as a vector, list, or queue, and common algorithms such as binary search, sort, and so on. Through STL, C++ gives programmers a set of carefully designed generic data structures and algorithms.

These generic data structures and algorithms are parameterized types (templates) that require only plugging in of actual types to be ready for use. Finally, STL brings to C++ the long promised goal of re-usable software components. More importantly, the STL substructure generates extremely efficient code size and performance.

STL Components

- **Containers** are objects that store other objects.
  sequential containers include:
    vector
    list
    deque
  associative containers include:
    map
    multimap
    set
    multiset

- **Algorithms** include generic functions that handle common tasks such as searching, sorting, comparing, and editing.

- **Iterators** are generic pointers used to interface containers and algorithms. STL algorithms are written in terms of iterator parameters, and STL containers provide iterators that can be plugged into the algorithms. Iterators include:
    input
    output
    forward
    bidirectional
    random access
    istream_iterator
    ostream_iterator

- **Function** templates are objects of any class or struct that overload the function call **operator()**. Most STL algorithms accept a function object as a parameter that can change the default behavior of the algorithm. Function template argument types include:
    plus
    minus

times
divides

The unary, logical, bitwise, and comparison operator object types include:

modulus
negate
equal_to
not_equal_to
greater
less
greater_equal
less_equal
logical_and
logical_or
logical_not

- **Adapters** modify the interface of other components. There are three kinds of STL adaptors:

  Container Adapter: stack, queue, priority_queue
  Iterator Adapter: reverse_bidirectional_iterator, back_insert_iterator, front_insert_iterator, and insert_iterator
  Function Adapters: not1, not2, bind1st, and bind2nd

The individual STL libraries and glue components are designed to work together in useful ways to produce the kind of larger and more specialized algorithms needed in today's applications.

Rules for Using STL

The following section highlights fundamental principles employed by the C++ compiler when using STL components. For example, when an object is used with an STL container, it is first copied with a call to the copy constructor, and the copy is what is actually inserted into the container. This fundamental principle means that an object held by an STL container must have a copy constructor. If an application removes an STL container object, the object is destroyed with a call to the destructor. If the STL container is destroyed, it destroys all objects it currently holds.

Frequently, STL components use compare container objects with a complete set of logical tests such as <, <=, >, >=, ==, !=. Therefore, the comparison operators must be defined for objects used with an STL component. Of course, some STL components modify the value of an object. This modification is accomplished using the assignment operator. So the assignment operator = must be defined for objects used with an STL component. Your application can use the <utility> definitions of the <=, >, >=, and != operators, which are all defined in terms of the < and ==.

The simplest way for you to guarantee that your objects will successfully interact with the STL containers is to make certain that your objects contain:

1. A copy constructor.
2. An assignment operator, =.
3. An equality comparison operator, ==.
4. A less than comparison operator, < .

Function Objects

Function objects are relatively new to the C++ programming language. Their usage may seem odd at first glance, and the syntax may appear to be confusing. A function object is an object of a class or struct type that includes an operator() member function. An operator() member function allows the creation of an object that behaves like a function. For example, a two-dimensional Array2D class could overload operator() to access an element whose row and column index are specified as arguments to operator().

```
class Array2D
{
  public:
    Array2D(int, int);
    int operator(int, int) const;
  private:
    Array<int> Array2Def;
    int rowOffset;
    int colOffset;
} ;
int Array2D::operator(int currentRow, int currentCol) const
{
  if ( currentRow > 0 && currentRow <= rowOffset && currentCol > 0 &&
currentCol <= colOffset)
    return Array2Def[currentRow, currentCol];
  else
    return (0);
}
Array2D intArray2D(10, 10);
int  intArray2D_element = intArray(5, 5);
```

Be sure to note that function objects are objects that behave like functions; as such, they can be created and must always return a value.

STL Function Objects

The Standard Template Library provides function objects for standard math operations such as addition, subtraction, multiplication, and division. STL also provides function objects for unary operations, logical operations, bitwise operations, and comparison operations. Chapter 4 lists all the function objects defined in the STL the header file **<functional>**.

The following example program demonstrates how these function objects can be used with STL algorithms to change their default behavior. The STL sort algorithm, by default, sorts in ascending order. However, by using the greater(T) function object, you can "trick" the sort algorithm to work in descending order:

```
#include <iostream>
#include <vector>
#include <functional>
#include <algorithm>
using namespace std;

void main( void )
{
  typedef vector<int, allocator<int> > iVECTOR;
  int iArray[5] = {10, 15, 22, 31, 18, 5};
  iVECTOR iVectorInstance(iArray, iArray + 5) ;

// default ascending sort
  copy(iVectorInstance.begin(), iVectorInstance.end(), out) ;
  sort(iVectorInstance.begin(), iVectorInstance.end()) ;
// use of function object to reverse sort to descinding

  copy(iVectorInstance.begin(), iVectorInstance.end(), out) ;
  sort(iVectorInstance.begin(), iVectorInstance.end(),
greater<int>()) ;
 }
```

Basically, the greater<int>(), function object passed to sort() inverts the comparison logic used by sort(), thereby tricking it into a descending algorithm. You can also use STL function objects directly in a C++ program. The following two statements:

```
float floatCalculation = (times<float>())(1.1, 2.2); // assigns 2.42
int intCalculation = (minus<int>())(15, 5); // assigns 10
```

STL Function Adapters

Function adapters help us construct a wider variety of function objects using existing function objects. Using function adapters is often easier than directly constructing a new function object type with a struct or class definition. STL provides three categories of function adapters: *negators*, *binders*, and *adapters for pointer to functions.*

Binders are function adapters that convert binary function objects into unary function objects by binding an argument to some particular value. STL provides two types of binder function objects: **binder1st<Operation>** and **binder2nd<Operation>**. A binder function object takes only a single argument. STL provides two template functions, **bind1st** and **bind2nd**, to create binder function objects.

The functions **bind1st** and **bind2nd** each take as arguments a binary function object *f* and a value *x*. **bind1st** returns a function object of type **binder1st<Operation>**, and **bind2nd** returns a function object of type **binder2nd<Operation>**. Here are the function prototypes for the **bind1st** and **bind2nd** functions:

```
template <class Operation, class T>
binder1st<Operation> bind1st(const Operation& f, const T& x) ;
template <class Operation, class T>
binder2nd<Operation> bind2nd(const Operation& f, const T& x) ;
```

Look at this first example:

```
int iGreater = (bind2nd(greater<int>(), 15))(actual_int_value)
```

Assume that *actual_int_value* is defined as type **int**, and the above statement could have been rewritten as:

```
int iGreater = (greater<int>())(actual_int_value, 15)
```

Negators are the second type of function adaptors. Negators are used to return the complement of a result obtained by applying a provided unary or binary operation. STL provides two types of negator function objects: **unary_negate<Operation>** and **binary_negate<Operation>**. A negator function object takes only a single argument.

The two template functions, **not1** and **not2**, create negator function objects. The function **not1** takes a unary function object *f* as its argument and returns a function object of type **unary_negate<Operation>**. The function **not2** takes a binary function object *f* as its argument and returns a function object of type **binary_negate<Operation>**. Here are the function prototypes for the **not1** and **not2** functions:

```
template <class Operation>
unary_negate<Operation> not1(const Operation& f) ;
template <class Operation>
binary_negate<Operation> not2(const Operation& f) ;
```

The following code segment demonstrates find_if() used with the **not1** function used to locate the first element in the array that is not greater than 15:

```
int iArray[25] = {/* your initialization code here */};
int* offset = find_if(iArray, iArray+25, not1(bind2nd(greater<int>(), 15)));
```

The function **bind2nd** creates a unary function object that returns the result of the comparison int > 15. The function **not1** takes the unary function object as an argument and creates another function object. This function object merely negates the results of the comparison int > 15. This next statement uses the **not2** function in a game playing match by causing the **greater** function object to trigger an ascending **sort** order:

```
sort(iVectorInstance.begin(), iVectorInstance.end(), not2(greater<int>())) ;
```

Pointer-to-Function Adapters

STL provides two types of pointer-to-function objects: pointer_to_unary_function<Arg, Result> and pointer_to_binary_function<Arg1, Arg2, Result>. An application can use adapters for pointers to functions to convert existing binary or unary functions to function objects. Adapters for pointers to functions allow the programmer to utilize the existing code to uniquely extend the library.

The pointer_to_unary_function function object takes one argument of type Arg, and the pointer_to_binary_function takes two arguments of type Arg1 and Arg2. STL provides two versions of the template function ptr_fun to create pointer-to-function function objects.

The first version of ptr_fun takes a unary function f as its argument and returns a function object of type pointer_to_unary_function<Arg, Result>. The second version of ptr_fun takes a binary function f as its argument and returns a function object of type pointer_to_binary_function<Arg1, Arg2, Result>. Here are the function prototypes for the ptr_fun functions:

```
template<class Arg, class Result>
    class pointer_to_unary_function
        : public unary_function<Arg, Result> {
public:
    explicit pointer_to_unary_function(Result (*pf)(Arg));
    Result operator()(const Arg x) const;
};
```

The template class stores a copy of `pf`. It defines its member function `operator()` as returning `(*pf)(x)`.

Standard Template Library Algorithms

This section serves to introduce the STL algorithm fundamentals and present some examples. Remembering some basic rules will help you to understand the algorithms and how to use them. STL provides generic parameterized, iterator-based functions (a fancy description for template functions). These functions implement some common array-based utilities, including searching, sorting, comparing, and editing. The STL algorithms are user programmable. What this means is that you can modify the default behavior of an algorithm to suit your needs. For example, the sort algorithm:

```
sort(first, last) ; //sorts elements of a sequence
                    //in ascending order by default.
```

In this case, the STL algorithm assumes that an operator == or operator < exists, and uses it to compare elements. The default behavior of the STL algorithms can be changed by specifying a predicate. The predicate function could be a C++ function. For example, sort_descending is a C++ function that compares two elements. In this case, the sort algorithm takes a function pointer, as follows:

```
sort(first, last, sort_descending);
```

Or the predicate function could be a function object. Either define a function object, or use the function objects provided by STL. For example (as seen earlier):

```
sort(first, last, greater<int>());
```

Every algorithm operates on a range of sequence. A sequence is a range of elements in an array or container, or user-defined data structures delimited by a pair of iterators. The identifier first points to the first element in the sequence. The identifier last points one element beyond the end of the region you want the algorithm to process. A common notation used to represent the sequence is [first, last). This is a notation for an open interval. The notation [first, last) implies that the sequence ranges from first to last, including first but not including last. The algorithm will increment an internal iterator with the ++ operator until it equals last. The element pointed to by last will not be processed by the algorithm.

STL algorithms do not perform range or validity checking on the iterator or pointer values. Many algorithms work with two sequences. For example, the copy algorithm takes three parameters, as follows:

```
copy(firstValue1, lastValue1, firstValue2);
```

If the second sequence is shorter than the first, copy will blindly continue writing into unconnected areas of memory. Some STL algorithms also create an in-place version and a copying version. For example:

```
reverse(first, last); // places results in original container
reverse_copy(firstValue1, lastValue1, firstValue1); // results in
duplicate location
```

The STL generic algorithms can be divided into four main categories. Nonmutating-Sequence Algorithms operate on containers without, in general, modifying the contents of the container. Mutating-Sequence Algorithms typically modify the containers on which they operate. The Sorting-Related Algorithms include sorting and merging algorithms, binary searching algorithms, and set operations on sorted sequences. Finally, a small collection of Generalized Numeric Algorithms is defined in the files: <algorithm>, <functional>, and <numeric>.

Standard C++ Library Language Support

The language support section of the Standard C++ Library provides common type definitions used throughout the library, characteristics of pre-defined types, functions supporting start and termination of C++ programs, support for dynamic memory allocation, support for dynamic type identification, support for exception processing, and other run-time support.

cstddef

This header file basically includes stddef.h. Two macros, NULL and offsetof, and two types, ptrdiff_t and size_t, are specifically listed in this section of the standard. To determine the distance (or the number of elements) between two elements, you can use the distance() function. If you pass it an iterator pointing to the first element and one pointing to the third element, it will return a 2. The distance function is in the utility header file and it takes two iterators as parameters and returns a number of type difference_type. Difference_type maps are an int.

Implementation Properties: limits, climits, cfloat

The numeric_limits component provides information about properties of fundamental types. Specializations are provided for each fundamental type such as int, floating point, and bool. The member is_specialized returns true for the specializations of numeric_limits for the fundamental types. The numeric_limits class is defined in the limits header file:

```
template<class T>  class numeric_limits {
public:
static const bool has_denorm;
static const bool has_denorm_loss;
static const bool has_infinity;
static const bool has_quiet_NaN;
static const bool has_signaling_NaN;
static const bool is_bounded;
static const bool is_exact;
static const bool is_iec559;
static const bool is_integer;
static const bool is_modulo;
static const bool is_signed;
static const bool is_specialized;
static const bool tinyness_before;
static const bool traps;
static const float_round_style round_style;
static const int digits;
static const int digits10;
static const int max_exponent;
static const int max_exponent10;
static const int min_exponent;
static const int min_exponent10;
static const int radix;
static T denorm_min() throw();
static T epsilon() throw();
static T infinity() throw();
static T max() throw();
static T min() throw();
static T quiet_NaN() throw();
static T round_error() throw();
static T signaling_NaN() throw();
};
```

Exception Handling

The C++ Standard Library exception class defines the base class for the types of objects thrown as exceptions. The exception header file defines the exception class that is the base class for all exceptions thrown by the C++ Standard Library. The following code would catch any exception thrown by classes and functions in the Standard C++ Library:

```
try {
   // your code here
}
catch ( const exception &ex)
{
   cout << "exception: " << ex.what();
}
```

The exception class is defined in the header file exception, as follows:

```
class exception {
public:
    exception() throw();
    exception(const exception& rhs) throw();
    exception& operator=(const exception& rhs) throw();
    virtual ~exception() throw();
    virtual const char *what() const throw();
private:
// ...
};
```

Additional Support

Each of these headers files—cstdarg, csetjmp, ctime, csignal, cstdlib—includes the corresponding C header file, stdarg.h, setjmp.h, time.h, signal.h, and stdlib.h. Macros, types, and functions listed for each of these in the Standard C++ Library are as follows:

File	Macros	Types	Functions
cstdarg	va_arg, va_end,va_start	va_list	
csetjmp	Macro: setjmp	jmp_buf	longjmp
ctime	CLOCKS_PER_SEC	clock_t	clock
csignal	SIGABRT, SIGILL, SIGSEGV, SIG_DFL, SIG_IGN, SIGFPE, SIGINT, SIGTERM, SIG_ERR	sig_atomic_t	raise, signal
cstdlib	getenv, system		

Summary

These last two chapters may have clouded the goal of STL—that being *simplicity*. Unfortunately, this kind of generic, bulletproof, robust code capability does not come easily. From the confusing library names, the Standard C++ Library and Standard Template Library, to the interactions between templates, algorithms, iterators, binders, and beyond, STL intimidates.

Chapters 2 and 3 served to reverse engineer STL components down to their simpler C++ and even C underpinnings. With a little persistance and initially some patience, you should be able to now start using the simpler STL routines. You can find these starting in Chapter 5. Chapter 4 uses the syntax and logic explained in Chapters 2 and 3 to enumerate and use, by example, the STL <utility> and <functional> support libraries.

FOUR

STL Support Templates

Just as every solid building starts with proper footers and a strong foundation, so too do C++ applications need the correct building blocks in order for the entire structure to stand. Before discussing the structural requirements for any application using the STL, you need to recognize the syntax evolution behind the new Standard C++ libraries. These are separate library routines used by most C/C++ applications and have nothing directly to do with STL.

The Standard C++ library is a separate entity from the Standard Template Library.

The Standard C++ library encompasses all the latest ANSI C++, including the Standard Template library and a new iostream library. The Standard C++ library provides new functionality, such as numerous algorithms that manipulate C++ objects, and a migration path for developers who want to move to the standard iostream.

The Standard C++ library is a set of 51 header files. The new header files do not have the `.h` extension. The Standard C++ library also has 18 standard C headers with the `.h` extension, for example, `errno.h` and `stdio.h`.

The main difference between the Standard C++ library and previous run-ti libraries is in the iostream library. Details of the iostream implementation have changed, and you cannot mix calls to the old iostream library and to the new Standard C++ library.

From iostream.h to <iostream>

Traditional C++ applications have always accessed library routines with the straightforward **#include <*filename*.h>** syntax, as in:

```
#include <fstream.h>
#include <iomanip.h>
#include <ios.h>
#include <iostream.h>
#include <istream.h>
#include <ostream.h>
#include <strstrea.h>
```

Under the new ANSI C/C++/ISO standard, to use the new Standard C++ library, you include one or more of the Standard C++ library header files in your code, with a different syntax, as in:

```
#include <iostream>
```

The new header files do not have the `.h` extension. You should *not* use the old iostream header files (`fstream.h`, `iomanip.h`, `ios.h`, `iostream.h`, `istream.h`, `ostream.h`, `streamb.h`, and `strstrea.h`). You cannot mix calls to the old iostream library and the new Standard C++ library.

The good news is that many of the new Standard C++ iostream header files—`fstream`, `iomanip`, `ios`, `iosfwd`, `iostream`, `istream`, `ostream`, `sstream`, `streambuf`, and `strstream`—have names that are the same as or similar to the old iostream header files but without the `.h` extension. If you include the new Standard C++ header files, the run-time library files that contain the Standard C++ library will be the default libraries.

From iosream.h to <iostream>

The most fundamental difference between the Standard C++ library and previous run-time libraries is in the iostream library. Many of the underlying details of the iostream implementation have changed.

For some applications, you may have to rewrite parts of your code that use iostream if you want to link with the Standard C++ library by removing any old iostream headers, such as `fstream.h`, `iomanip.h`, `ios.h`, `iostream.h`, `istream.h`, `ostream.h`, `streamb.h`, and `strstrea.h`, included in your code. They are replaced with one or more of the new Standard C++ iostream headers `fstream`, `iomanip`, `ios`, `iosfwd`, `iostream`, `istream`, `ostream`, `sstream`, `streambuf`, and `strstream`, all without the `.h` extension.

One option for older applications making heavy use of iostream is to simply link with the new Standard C++ library. In this case, leave the old iostream headers in your code, and the old iostream library will automatically be linked. However, you cannot include any of the new Standard C++ library headers. You cannot mix calls to the old iostream library and the new Standard C++ library.

The following section explains the differences in the new Standard C++ iostream library and the old iostream library. In the new Standard C++ iostream library:

- open functions no longer have a third protection parameter.
- you can no longer create streams from file handles.
- no open ofstream objects exists with the ios::out flag by itself; instead, you combine the flag with another ios enumerator in a logical AND, for example, with ios::in or ios::nocreate.
- ios::unsetf returns void instead of the previous value.
- istream::get(char& rchar) does not assign to rchar if an error occurs.
- istream::get(char* pchar, int nCount, char cdelim) is different in three ways:
    - when nothing is read, failbit is set.
    - istream::seekg with an invalid parameter does not set failbit.
    - the return type streampos is a class with overloaded operators. In functions that return a streampos value (such as istream::tellg, ostream::tellp, strstreambuf::seekoff, and strstreambuf::seekpos), you should cast the return value to the type required: streamoff, fpos_t, or mbstate_t.
- the first function parameter falloc in strstreambuf::strstreambuf takes a size_t argument, not the older type long.
- the following list enumerates elements of the old iostream library that are not elements of the new iostream library:
    - attach the member function of filebuf, fstream, ifstream, and ofstream
    - filebuf::openprot and filebuf::setmode
    - ios::bitalloc, ios::nocreate, ios::noreplace, and ios::sync_with_stdio
    - streambuf::out_waiting, and streambuf::setbuf

Exception Handling Under the New ANSI C/C++/ISO Standard

A special warning to programmers: when using Microsoft's Visual C++ Standard C++ library, all applications must be compiled with C++ exception handling enabled. Microsoft's Visual C++ exception handling is enabled by default; however, you can manually enable exception handling by selecting the **Enable exception handling** option in the **C++ Language** category of the **C/C++** tab in the **Project Settings** dialog box, or by using the /GX compiler switch.

The <utility> and <functional> Templates

The <utility> and <functional> templates are very rarely used by themselves. Instead, they can be viewed as adding additional functionality to the other Standard Template Libraries. Since they are such a frequent component of mainstream STL applications, the time to view their definitions and capabilities is worthwhile. These two libraries are also a gentle way to wade into the sea of STL syntax.

<utility> Template Syntax

The header file <utility> defines global versions of the **<=**, **>**, **>=**, and **!=** operators, which are all defined in terms of the **<** and **==**. In principle, STL assumes that all object containers have at least the following:

- An assignment operator (**=**)
- An equality comparison operator (**==**)
- A less than comparison operator (**<**)
- A copy constructor

This section examines the syntax used to support the <utility> template. The following listing shows the template prototypes and the related template methods:

```
template<class T, class U>
    struct pair;
template<class T, class U>
    pair<T, U> make_pair(const T& x, const U& y);
template<class T, class U>
    bool operator==(const pair<T, U>& x, const pair<T, U>& y);
template<class T, class U>
    bool operator!=(const pair<T, U>& x, const pair<T, U>& y);
template<class T, class U>
    bool operator<(const pair<T, U>& x, const pair<T, U>& y);
template<class T, class U>
    bool "operator>(const pair<T, U>& x, const pair<T, U>& y);
template<class T, class U>
    bool operator<=(const pair<T, U>& x, const pair<T, U>& y);
template<class T, class U>
    bool ="operator>=(const pair<T, U>& x, const pair<T, U>& y);
namespace rel_ops {
    template<class T>
        bool operator!=(const T& x, const T& y);
    template<class T>
        bool operator<=(const T& x, const T& y);
    template<class T>
        bool "operator>(const T& x, const T& y);
```

```
template<class T>
    bool ="operator>=(const T& x, const T& y);
    };
};
```

Include the STL standard header `<utility>` to define several templates of general use throughout the Standard Template Library. Four template operators—`operator!=`, `operator<=`, `operator>`, and `operator>=`—define a total ordering on pairs of operands of the same type, given definitions of `operator==` and `operator<`. If an implementation supports namespaces, these template operators are defined in the *rel_ops* namespace, nested within the `std` namespace.

To use the <utility> template operators, you use the following syntax:

```
using namespace std::rel_ops;
```

which promotes the template operators into the current namespace.

Those familiar to C/C++ programming know that frequently, in order to understand a particular definition, declaration, or statement, you have to nest backwards through many levels of predefined identifiers (constants, variables, functions, and classes). The same holds true for the STL library. The following section saves you the time of doing this nesting for all related support definitions.

struct pair

```
template<class T, class U>
    struct pair {
    typedef T first_type;
    typedef U second_type
    T first;
    U second;
    pair();
    pair(const T& x, const U& y);
    template<class V, class W>
    pair(const pair<V, W>& pr);
  };
```

You use the pair template class to store pairs of objects. *first* is assigned the type *T*, and *second* the type *U*. The type definition *first_type* is the same as the template parameter *T*, and *second_type* is the same as the template parameter *U*. The first (default) constructor initializes *first* to *T()* and `second` to *U()*. The second constructor initializes `first` to `x` and `second` to `y`. The third (template) constructor initializes `first` to `pr.first` and `second` to `pr.second`. `T` and `U` each need supply only a single-argument constructor and a destructor.

make_pair

```
template<class T, class U>
    pair<T, U> make_pair(const T& x, const U& y);
```

The template function returns `pair<T, U>(x, y)`.

<utility> Template Overloaded Operators

The <utility> template overloads the operators shown in Table 4.1

Table 4.1 Overloaded <utility> template operators.

Overload Operators	Returns
`bool operator==(const pair<T, U>& x, const pair<T, U>& y);`	`x.first == y.first && x.second == y.second`
`bool operator!=(const T& x, const T& y);` `bool operator!=(const pair<T, U>& x, const pair<T, U>& y);`	`!(x == y)`
`bool operator<(const pair<T, U>& x, const pair<T, U>& y);` `bool operator<(const pair<T, U>& x, const pair<T, U>& y);`	`x.first < y.first || !(y.first < x.first && x.second < y.second`
`bool operator>(const T& x, const T& y);` `bool operator>(const pair<T, U>& x, const pair<T, U>& y);`	`y < x`
`bool operator<=(const T& x, const T& y);` `bool operator<=(const pair<T, U>& x, const pair<T, U>& y);`	`!(y < x)`
`bool operator>=(const T& x, const T& y);` `bool operator>=(const pair<T, U>& x, const pair<T, U>& y);`	`!(x < y)`

The mak_par.cpp Application

The first example application, mak_par.cpp, shows how the <utility> make_pair() method is used to create, and use a pair of data types:

```
// mak_par.cpp
// Testing <utility>
// make_pair()
// Chris H. Pappas and William H. Murray, 1999


#include <utility>
```

```
#include <iostream>

using namespace std;

// STL id_PAIR, struct pair typedef using int and char
member types

typedef struct pair<int,char> ic_PAIR;

void main(void){

 // create storage for and initialize
 // an_int_char_pair using make_pair()

 ic_PAIR an_int_char_pair = make_pair(15,'c');


 // output the individual members
 cout << an_int_char_pair.first
      << " "
      << an_int_char_pair.second
      << endl;


 // assign new member values
 an_int_char_pair.first = 20;
 an_int_char_pair.second = 'a';


 // output the new values
 cout << an_int_char_pair.first
      << " "
      << an_int_char_pair.second
      << endl;
}
```

The straightforward output from the program looks like:

```
15 c
20 a
```

The util_oprs.cpp Application

This next example uses an **int**, **double** *pair* to test the overloaded <utility> operators:

```
// util_oprs.cpp
// Testing <utility>
// ==, !=, <, <=, >, >=
// Chris H. Pappas and William H. Murray, 1999
```

```
#include <iostream>
#include <utility>

using namespace std ;

// STL id_PAIR, struct pair typedef usingint and double member types

typedef struct pair<int, double> id_PAIR;

void main(void)
{
 id_PAIR pair33_56a(33,5.6);
 id_PAIR pair22_56 (22,5.6);
 id_PAIR pair33_95 (33,9.5);
 id_PAIR pair33_56b(33,5.6);

// output original values

 cout << "pair33_56a = ( " << pair33_56a.first << " , " << pair33_56a.second <<
" )" << endl;
 cout << "pair22_56 = ( " << pair22_56.first << " , " << pair22_56.second << "
)" << endl;
 cout << "pair33_95 = ( " << pair33_95.first << " , " << pair33_95.second << "
)" << endl;
 cout << "pair33_56b = ( " << pair33_56b.first << " , " << pair33_56b.second <<
" )" << endl;

 cout << "\n\n\n";

// test for equality ==

 cout << ((pair33_56a == pair33_56b) ?
    "pair33_56a and pair33_56b are equal \n" :
    "pair33_56a and pair33_56b are not equal \n");

// test for non-equality !=

 cout << ((pair22_56 != pair33_95) ?
    "pair22_56 and pair33_95 are not equal \n" :
    "pair22_56 and pair33_95 are equal \n");

 cout << "\n\n";

// test for greater than >

 cout << ((pair33_56a > pair33_95) ?
    "pair33_56a is greater than pair33_95 \n" :
    "pair33_56a is not greater than pair33_95 \n");

// test for greater than or equal >=

 cout << ((pair33_56a >= pair33_95) ?
    "pair33_56a is greater than or equal to pair33_95 \n" :
    "pair33_56a is not greater than or equal to pair33_95 \n");

 cout << "\n\n";

// test for less than <
```

```
 cout << ((pair33_95 < pair33_56a) ?
    "pair33_95 is less than pair33_56a \n" :
    "pair33_95 is not less than pair33_56a \n");

// test for less than or equal <=

 cout << ((pair33_95 < pair33_56a) ?
    "pair33_95 is less than or equal to pair33_56a \n" :
    "pair33_95 is not less than or equal to pair33_56a \n");
}
```

The output from the program looks like:

```
pair33_56a = ( 33 , 5.6 )
pair22_56 = ( 22 , 5.6 )
pair33_95 = ( 33 , 9.5 )
pair33_56b = ( 33 , 5.6 )

pair33_56a and pair33_56b are equal
pair22_56 and pair33_95 are not equal

pair33_56a is not greater than pair33_95
pair33_56a is not greater than or equal to pair33_95

pair33_95 is not less than pair33_56a
pair33_95 is not less than or equal to pair33_56
```

<functional> Template Syntax

As mentioned earlier, both the <utility> and <functional> templates are viewed as support libraries. You use the <functional> STL for defining several templates that help construct predicates for the templates defined in `<algorithm>` and <numeric>. The syntax for the <functional> library looks like:

```
namespace std {
// TEMPLATE CLASSES
template<class Arg, class Result>
    struct unary_function;
template<class Arg1, class Arg2, class Result>
    struct binary_function;
template<class T>
    struct plus;
template<class T>
    struct minus;
template<class T>
    struct multiplies;
template<class T>
    struct divides;
template<class T>
    struct modulus;
template<class T>
```

```
    struct negate;
template<class T>
    struct equal_to;
template<class T>
    struct not_equal_to;
template<class T>
    struct greater;
template<class T>
    struct less;
template<class T>
    struct greater_equal;
template<class T>
    struct less_equal;
template<class T>
    struct logical_and;
template<class T>
    struct logical_or;
template<class T>
    struct logical_not;
template<class Pred>
    struct unary_negate;
template<class Pred>
    struct binary_negate;
template<class Pred>
    class binder1st;
template<class Pred>
    class binder2nd;
template<class Arg, class Result>
    class pointer_to_unary_function;
template<class Arg1, class Arg2, class Result>
    class pointer_to_binary_function;
template<class R, class T>
    struct mem_fun_t;
template<class R, class T, class A>
    struct mem_fun1_t;
template<class R, class T>
    struct mem_fun_ref_t;
template<class R, class T, class A>
    struct mem_fun1_ref_t;

// TEMPLATE FUNCTIONS
template<class Pred>
    unary_negate<Pred> not1(const Pred& pr);
template<class Pred>
    binary_negate<Pred> not2(const Pred& pr);
template<class Pred, class T>
    binder1st<Pred> bind1st(const Pred& pr, const T& x);
template<class Pred, class T>
    binder2nd<Pred> bind2nd(const Pred& pr, const T& x);
template<class Arg, class Result>
```

```
    pointer_to_unary_function<Arg, Result>
        ptr_fun(Result (*)(Arg));
template<class Arg1, class Arg2, class Result>
    pointer_to_binary_function<Arg1, Arg2, Result>
        ptr_fun(Result (*)(Arg1, Arg2));
template<class R, class T>
    mem_fun_t<R, T> mem_fun(R (T::*pm)());
template<class R, class T, class A>
    mem_fun1_t<R, T, A> mem_fun1(R (T::*pm)(A arg));
template<class R, class T>
    mem_fun_ref_t<R, T> mem_fun_ref(R (T::*pm)());
template<class R, class T, class A>
    mem_fun1_ref_t<R, T, A> mem_fun1_ref(R (T::*pm)(A arg));
    };
```

When you include the STL standard header `<functional>`, you gain access to several templates that help construct function objects. These are objects of a class that defines `operator()`. Later chapters will demonstrate how function objects behave much like function pointers, except that the object can store additional information that can be used during a function call.

The following section saves you the time to cross-reference nested definitions used by the <functional> template.

unary_function

```
template<class Arg, class Result>
    struct unary_function {
    typedef Arg argument_type;
    typedef Result result_type;
    };
```

The template class serves as a base for classes that define a member function of the form:

```
result_type operator()(argument_type)
```

Hence, all such unary functions can refer to their sole argument type as `argument_type` and their return type as `result_type`.

binary_function

```
template<class Arg1, class Arg2, class Result>
    struct binary_function {
    typedef Arg1 first_argument_type;
    typedef Arg2 second_argument_type;
    typedef Result result_type;
    };
```

The template class serves as a base for classes that define a member function of the form:

`result_type operator()(first_argument_type, second_argument_type)`

This definition allows all such binary functions to refer to their first argument type as `first_argument_type`, their second argument type as `second_argument_type`, and their return type as `result_type`.

plus

```
template<class T>
    struct plus : public binary_function<T, T, T> {
    T operator()(const T& x, const T& y) const;
    };
```

The template class defines a member function returning `x + y`.

minus

```
template<class T>
    struct minus : public binary_function<T, T, T> {
    T operator()(const T& x, const T& y) const;
    };
```

The template class defines a member function returning `x - y`.

multiplies

```
template<class T>
    struct multiplies : public binary_function<T, T, T> {
    T operator()(const T& x, const T& y) const;
    };
```

The template class defines a member function returning `x * y`.

divides

```
template<class T>
    struct divides : public binary_function<T, T, T> {
    T operator()(const T& x, const T& y) const;
    };
```

The template class defines a member function returning `x / y`.

modulus

```
template<class T>
    struct modulus : public binary_function<T, T, T> {
    T operator()(const T& x, const T& y) const;
    };
```

The template class defines a member function returning `x % y`.

negate

```
template<class T>
    struct negate : public unary_function<T, T> {
    T operator()(const T& x) const;
    };
```

The template class defines a member function returning `-x`.

equal_to

```
template<class T>
    struct equal_to : public binary_function<T, T, bool> {
    bool operator()(const T& x, const T& y) const;
    };
```

The template class defines a member function returning `x == y`.

not_equal_to

```
template<class T>
    struct not_equal_to : public binary_function<T, T, bool> {
    bool operator()(const T& x, const T& y) const;
    };
```

The template class defines a member function returning `x != y`.

greater

```
template<class T>
    struct greater : public binary_function<T, T, bool> {
    bool operator()(const T& x, const T& y) const;
    };
```

The template class defines a member function returning `x > y`. The member function defines a *total ordering*, even if `T` is an object pointer type.

less

```
template<class T>
    struct less : public binary_function<T, T, bool> {
    bool operator()(const T& x, const T& y) const;
    };
```

The template class defines a member function returning `x < y`. The member function defines a *total ordering*, even if `T` is an object pointer type.

greater_equal

```
template<class T>
    struct greater_equal : public binary_function<T, T, bool> {
    bool operator()(const T& x, const T& y) const;
    };
```

The template class defines a member function returning `x >= y`.

less_equal

```
template<class T>
    struct less_equal : public binary_function<T, T, bool> {
    bool operator()(const T& x, const T& y) const;
    };
```

The template class defines a member function returning `x <= y`.

logical_and

```
template<class T>
    struct logical_and : public binary_function<T, T, bool> {
    bool operator()(const T& x, const T& y) const;
    };
```

The template class defines a member function returning `x && y`.

logical_or

```
template<class T>
    struct logical_or : public binary_function<T, T, bool> {
    bool operator()(const T& x, const T& y) const;
    };
```

The template class defines a member function returning `x || y`.

logical_not

```
template<class T>
    struct logical_not : public unary_function<T, bool> {
    bool operator()(const T& x) const;
    };
```

The template class defines a member function returning `!x`.

unary_negate

```
template<class Pred>
    class unary_negate
        : public unary_function<Pred::argument_type, bool>
{
public:
    explicit unary_negate(const Pred& pr);
    bool operator()(const argument_type& x) const;
    };
```

The template class stores a copy of `pr`, which must be a unary function object. It defines a member function `operator()` returning `!pr(x)`.

binary_negate

```
template<class Pred>
    class binary_negate
        : public binary_function<Pred::first_argument_type,
            Pred::second_argument_type, bool> {
public:
    explicit binary_negate(const Pred& pr);
    bool operator()(const first_argument_type& x,
        const second_argument_type& y) const;
    };
```

The template class stores a copy of `pr`, which must be a binary function object. It defines a member function `operator()` returning `!pr(x, y)`.

binder1st

```
template<class Pred>
    class binder1st
        : public unary_function<Pred::second_argument_type,
            Pred::result_type> {
public:
    binder1st(const Pred& pr, const Pred::first_argument_type x);
    result_type operator()(const argument_type& y) const;
protected:
    Pred op;
    Pred::first_argument_type value;
    };
```

The template class stores a copy of `pr`, which must be a binary function object, in `op`, and a copy of `x` in `value`. It defines a member function `operator()` returning `op(value, y)`.

binder2nd

```
template<class Pred>
    class binder2nd
        : public unary_function<Pred::first_argument_type,
            Pred::result_type> {
public:
    binder2nd(const Pred& pr, const Pred::second_argument_type y);
    result_type operator()(const argument_type& x) const;
protected:
    Pred op;
    Pred::second_argument_type value;
    };
```

The template class stores a copy of pr, which must be a binary function object, in op, and a copy of y in value. It defines a member function operator() returning op(x, value).

pointer_to_unary_function

```
template<class Arg, class Result>
    class pointer_to_unary_function
        : public unary_function<Arg, Result> {
public:
    explicit pointer_to_unary_function(Result (*pf)(Arg));
    Result operator()(const Arg x) const;
    };
```

The template class stores a copy of pf. It defines a member function operator() returning (*pf)(x).

pointer_to_binary_function

```
template<class Arg1, class Arg2, class Result>
    class pointer_to_binary_function
        : public binary_function<Arg1, Arg2, Result> {
public:
    explicit pointer_to_binary_function(Result (*pf)(Arg1, Arg2));
    Result operator()(const Arg1 x, const Arg2 y) const;
    };
```

The template class stores a copy of pf. It defines a member function operator() returning (*pf)(x, y).

mem_fun_t

```
template<class R, class T>
    struct mem_fun_t : public unary_function<T *, R> {
    explicit mem_fun_t(R (T::*pm)());
    R operator()(T *p);
    };
```

The template class stores a copy of pm, which must be a pointer to a member function of class T, in a private member object. It defines a member function operator() returning (p->*pm)().

mem_fun1_t

```
template<class R, class T, class A>
    struct mem_fun1_t : public binary_function<T *, A, R> {
    explicit mem_fun1_t(R (T::*pm)(A));
    R operator()(T *p, A arg);
    };
```

The template class stores a copy of pm, which must be a pointer to a member function of class T, in a private member object. It defines a member function operator() returning (p->*pm)(arg).

mem_fun_ref_t

```
template<class R, class T>
    struct mem_fun_ref_t : public unary_function<T *, R> {
    explicit mem_fun_t(R (T::*pm)());
    R operator()(T& x);
    };
```

The template class stores a copy of pm, which must be a pointer to a member function of class T, in a private member object. It defines a member function operator() returning (x.*Pm)().

mem_fun1_ref_t

```
template<class R, class T, class A>
    struct mem_fun1_ref_t : public binary_function<T *, A, R> {
    explicit mem_fun1_ref_t(R (T::*pm)(A));
    R operator()(T& x, A arg);
    };
```

The template class stores a copy of pm, which must be a pointer to a member function of class T, in a private member object. It defines a member function operator() returning (x.*pm)(arg).

<functional> Template Functions

The <functional> template functions are shown in Table 4.2, along with a brief description of their purpose and return values:

Table 4.2 <functional> template functions.

Template Method	Description
`not1(const Pred& pr)`	The template function returns `unary_negate<Pred>(pr)`.
`not2(const Pred& pr)`	The template function returns `binary_negate<Pred>(pr)`.
`bind1st(const Pred& pr, const T& x);`	The function returns `binder1st<Pred>(pr, Pred::first_argument_type(x))`.
`bind2nd(const Pred& pr, const T& y);`	The function returns `binder2nd<Pred>(pr, Pred::second_argument_type(y))`.
`ptr_fun(Result (*pf)(Arg))` `ptr_fun(Result (*pf)(Arg1, Arg2))`	The first template function returns `pointer_to_unary_function<Arg, Result>(pf)`. The second template function returns `pointer_to_binary_function<Arg1, Arg2, Result>(pf)`.
`mem_fun(R (T::*pm)())`	The template function returns `mem_fun_t<R, T>(pm)`.
`mem_fun1(R (T::*pm)(A))`	The template function returns `mem_fun1_t<R, T, A>(pm)`.
`mem_fun_ref(R (T::*pm)())`	The template function returns `mem_fun_ref_t<R, T>(pm)`.
`mem_fun1_ref(R (T::*pm)(A))`	The template function returns `mem_fun1_ref_t<R, T, A>(pm)`.

The following sections demonstrates the use of the STL <functional> template.

The functnl.cpp Application

The following program instantiates the plus, minus, multiplies, and divides templates for the standard C/C++ integer data type:

```
// functnl.cpp
// Testing <functional>
// plus<>, minus<>, multiplies<>, divides<>
// Chris H. Pappas and William H. Murray, 1999
```

```
#include <iostream>
#include <functional>

using namespace std ;

class functional_tmplts : public plus<int>, public minus<int>,
 public multiplies<int>, public divides<int>
{
public:

 int iValue1;

 // Overloaded constructors
 functional_tmplts() {iValue1 = 0 ;}
 functional_tmplts(int aValue1 ){iValue1 = aValue1;}

 // Overloaded operators
 result_type operator+(second_argument_type iValue2_to_add)
                                  {return iValue1 + iValue2_to_add;}
 result_type operator-(second_argument_type iValue2_to_sub)
                                  {return iValue1 - iValue2_to_sub;}
 result_type operator*(second_argument_type iValue2_to_mul)
                                  {return iValue1 * iValue2_to_mul;}
 result_type operator/(second_argument_type iValue2_to_divby)
                                  {return iValue1 / iValue2_to_divby;}

};

ostream& operator<<(ostream& os, const functional_tmplts& obj )
{
 os << obj.iValue1 ;
 return os ;
}

void main(void)
{
 functional_tmplts iFirstResult,iSecondResult,
                  iThirdResult,iFourthResult,iFifthResult;

 cout << "Testing <functional> STL library \n\n";

 iFirstResult = 10;
 cout << "iFirstResult = "
                  << iFirstResult << endl ;

 iSecondResult = iFirstResult + 10;
 cout << "iSecondResult = iFirstResult + 10 = "
                  << iSecondResult << endl ;

 iThirdResult = iSecondResult - 5;
```

```
    cout << "iThirdResult = iSecondResult - 5 = "
                    << iThirdResult << endl ;

    iFourthResult = iThirdResult * 2;
    cout << "iFourthResult = iThirdResult * 2 = "
                    << iFourthResult << endl ;

    iFifthResult = iFourthResult / 15;
    cout << "iFifthResult = iFourthResult / 15 = "
                    << iFifthResult << endl ;
}
```

Summary

In this chapter, you learned to separate the Standard C++ Library from the C++ Standard Template Library. You saw how to facilitate STL; certain components of historic C++ needed updating, in particular, iostream.h. You also looked at the two "support" templates, <utility> and <functional>, which are frequently combined with additional templates increasing their usability. These will be used in many of the example programs in following chapters.

FIVE

The STL <algorithm> Template

The <algorithm> template functions and classes work on containers. Although each individual container provides support for its own basic operations, the standard algorithms provide more extended or complex actions. They also allow you to work with two different types of containers at the same time.

The <algorithm> template functions allow you to sort, compare, merge, insert, delete, swap, copy, fill, and do many other container element manipulations. This chapter is used to introduce STL <algorithm> fundamentals and present several examples you can use to model additional applications. With over sixty <algorithm> template functions available, remembering some basic rules will help you to understand the algorithms themselves and how to use them.

The C++ STL provides generic parameterized, iterator-based functions (Chapter 6 discusses the STL iterators in detail) that implement some common array-based utilities, including searching, sorting, comparing, and editing. The default behavior of the STL algorithms can be changed by specifying a predicate or modifying a function template. For example, the sort algorithm has a formal third argument specifying the sort type, as in ***sort_descending****, or an STL template function like greater< ... >().*

Every <algorithm> template function operates on a sequence. A sequence is a range of elements in an array or container, or user-defined data structures delimited by a pair of iterators. The identifier

first *points to the first element in the sequence. The identifier* ***last*** *points one element beyond the end of the region you want the algorithm to process.*

Many <algorithm> function templates use the (...first,last) sequence. This syntax implies that the sequence ranges from first to last, including first but not including last. <algorithm> template funtions use the increment operator until it equals ***last****. The element pointed to by* ***last*** *will not be processed by the algorithm.*

Certain STL algorithms will create an instance copy of a container. For example, the reverse(first, last) template function call adjusts container contents in the original container, and reverse_copy(first, last), generates a copy of the container with the adjusted element contents.

<algorithm> Template Syntax

The following listing gives the syntax for the <algorithm> template.

```
namespace std {
template<class InIt, class Fun>
    Fun for_each(InIt first, InIt last, Fun f);
template<class InIt, class T>
    InIt find(InIt first, InIt last, const T& val);
template<class InIt, class Pred>
    InIt find_if(InIt first, InIt last, Pred pr);
template<class FwdIt1, class FwdIt2>
    FwdIt1 find_end(FwdIt1 first1, FwdIt1 last1,
        FwdIt2 first2, FwdIt2 last2);
template<class FwdIt1, class FwdIt2, class Pred>
    FwdIt1 find_end(FwdIt1 first1, FwdIt1 last1,
        FwdIt2 first2, FwdIt2 last2, Pred pr);
template<class FwdIt1, class FwdIt2>
    FwdIt1 find_first_of(FwdIt1 first1, FwdIt1 last1,
        FwdIt2 first2, FwdIt2 last2);
template<class FwdIt1, class FwdIt2, class Pred>
    FwdIt1 find_first_of(FwdIt1 first1, FwdIt1 last1,
        FwdIt2 first2, FwdIt2 last2, Pred pr);
template<class FwdIt>
    FwdIt adjacent_find(FwdIt first, FwdIt last);
template<class FwdIt, class Pred>
    FwdIt adjacent_find(FwdIt first, FwdIt last, Pred pr);
    size_t count(InIt first, InIt last,
        const T& val, Dist& n);
template<class InIt, class Pred, class Dist>
    size_t count_if(InIt first, InIt last,
        Pred pr);
template<class InIt1, class InIt2>
```

```
    pair<InIt1, InIt2> mismatch(InIt1 first, InIt1 last, InIt2 x);
template<class InIt1, class InIt2, class Pred>
    pair<InIt1, InIt2> mismatch(InIt1 first, InIt1 last,
        InIt2 x, Pred pr);
template<class InIt1, class InIt2>
    bool equal(InIt1 first, InIt1 last, InIt2 x);
template<class InIt1, class InIt2, class Pred>
    bool equal(InIt1 first, InIt1 last, InIt2 x, Pred pr);
template<class FwdIt1, class FwdIt2>
    FwdIt1 search(FwdIt1 first1, FwdIt1 last1,
        FwdIt2 first2, FwdIt2 last2);
template<class FwdIt1, class FwdIt2, class Pred>
    FwdIt1 search(FwdIt1 first1, FwdIt1 last1,
        FwdIt2 first2, FwdIt2 last2, Pred pr);
template<class FwdIt, class Dist, class T>
    FwdIt search_n(FwdIt first, FwdIt last,
        Dist n, const T& val);
template<class FwdIt, class Dist, class T, class Pred>
    FwdIt search_n(FwdIt first, FwdIt last,
        Dist n, const T& val, Pred pr);
template<class InIt, class OutIt>
    OutIt copy(InIt first, InIt last, OutIt x);
template<class BidIt1, class BidIt2>
    BidIt2 copy_backward(BidIt1 first, BidIt1 last, BidIt2 x);
template<class T>
    void swap(T& x, T& y);
template<class FwdIt1, class FwdIt2>
    FwdIt2 swap_ranges(FwdIt1 first, FwdIt1 last, FwdIt2 x);
template<class FwdIt1, class FwdIt2>
    void iter_swap(FwdIt1 x, FwdIt2 y);
template<class InIt, class OutIt, class Unop>
    OutIt transform(InIt first, InIt last, OutIt x, Unop uop);
template<class InIt1, class InIt2, class OutIt, class Binop>
    OutIt transform(InIt1 first1, InIt1 last1, InIt2 first2,
        OutIt x, Binop bop);
template<class FwdIt, class T>
    void replace(FwdIt first, FwdIt last,
        const T& vold, const T& vnew);
template<class FwdIt, class Pred, class T>
    void replace_if(FwdIt first, FwdIt last,
        Pred pr, const T& val);
template<class InIt, class OutIt, class T>
    OutIt replace_copy(InIt first, InIt last, OutIt x,
        const T& vold, const T& vnew);
template<class InIt, class OutIt, class Pred, class T>
    OutIt replace_copy_if(InIt first, InIt last, OutIt x,
        Pred pr, const T& val);
template<class FwdIt, class T>
    void fill(FwdIt first, FwdIt last, const T& x);
template<class OutIt, class Size, class T>
```

```
    void fill_n(OutIt first, Size n, const T& x);
template<class FwdIt, class Gen>
    void generate(FwdIt first, FwdIt last, Gen g);
template<class OutIt, class Pred, class Gen>
    void generate_n(OutIt first, Dist n, Gen g);
template<class FwdIt, class T>
    FwdIt remove(FwdIt first, FwdIt last, const T& val);
template<class FwdIt, class Pred>
    FwdIt remove_if(FwdIt first, FwdIt last, Pred pr);
template<class InIt, class OutIt, class T>
    OutIt remove_copy(InIt first, InIt last, OutIt x, const T& val);
template<class InIt, class OutIt, class Pred>
    OutIt remove_copy_if(InIt first, InIt last, OutIt x, Pred pr);
template<class FwdIt>
    FwdIt unique(FwdIt first, FwdIt last);
template<class FwdIt, class Pred>
    FwdIt unique(FwdIt first, FwdIt last, Pred pr);
template<class InIt, class OutIt>
    OutIt unique_copy(InIt first, InIt last, OutIt x);
template<class InIt, class OutIt, class Pred>
    OutIt unique_copy(InIt first, InIt last, OutIt x, Pred pr);
template<class BidIt>
    void reverse(BidIt first, BidIt last);
template<class BidIt, class OutIt>
    OutIt reverse_copy(BidIt first, BidIt last, OutIt x);
template<class FwdIt>
    void rotate(FwdIt first, FwdIt middle, FwdIt last);
template<class FwdIt, class OutIt>
    OutIt rotate_copy(FwdIt first, FwdIt middle, FwdIt last, OutIt x);
template<class RanIt>
    void random_shuffle(RanIt first, RanIt last);
template<class RanIt, class Fun>
    void random_shuffle(RanIt first, RanIt last, Fun& f);
template<class BidIt, class Pred>
    BidIt partition(BidIt first, BidIt last, Pred pr);
template<class FwdIt, class Pred>
    FwdIt stable_partition(FwdIt first, FwdIt last, Pred pr);
template<class RanIt>
    void sort(RanIt first, RanIt last);
template<class RanIt, class Pred>
    void sort(RanIt first, RanIt last, Pred pr);
template<class BidIt>
    void stable_sort(BidIt first, BidIt last);
template<class BidIt, class Pred>
    void stable_sort(BidIt first, BidIt last, Pred pr);
template<class RanIt>
    void partial_sort(RanIt first, RanIt middle, RanIt last);
template<class RanIt, class Pred>
    void partial_sort(RanIt first, RanIt middle, RanIt last, Pred pr);
template<class InIt, class RanIt>
```

```
    RanIt partial_sort_copy(InIt first1, InIt last1,
        RanIt first2, RanIt last2);
template<class InIt, class RanIt, class Pred>
    RanIt partial_sort_copy(InIt first1, InIt last1,
        RanIt first2, RanIt last2, Pred pr);
template<class RanIt>
    void nth_element(RanIt first, RanIt nth, RanIt last);
template<class RanIt, class Pred>
    void nth_element(RanIt first, RanIt nth, RanIt last, Pred pr);
template<class FwdIt, class T>
    FwdIt lower_bound(FwdIt first, FwdIt last, const T& val);
template<class FwdIt, class T, class Pred>
    FwdIt lower_bound(FwdIt first, FwdIt last, const T& val, Pred pr);
template<class FwdIt, class T>
    FwdIt upper_bound(FwdIt first, FwdIt last, const T& val);
template<class FwdIt, class T, class Pred>
    FwdIt upper_bound(FwdIt first, FwdIt last, const T& val, Pred pr);
template<class FwdIt, class T>
    pair<FwdIt, FwdIt> equal_range(FwdIt first, FwdIt last,
        const T& val);
template<class FwdIt, class T, class Pred>
    pair<FwdIt, FwdIt> equal_range(FwdIt first, FwdIt last,
        const T& val, Pred pr);
template<class FwdIt, class T>
    bool binary_search(FwdIt first, FwdIt last, const T& val);
template<class FwdIt, class T, class Pred>
    bool binary_search(FwdIt first, FwdIt last, const T& val,
        Pred pr);
template<class InIt1, class InIt2, class OutIt>
    OutIt merge(InIt1 first1, InIt1 last1,
        InIt2 first2, InIt2 last2, OutIt x);
template<class InIt1, class InIt2, class OutIt, class Pred>
    OutIt merge(InIt1 first1, InIt1 last1,
        InIt2 first2, InIt2 last2, OutIt x, Pred pr);
template<class BidIt>
    void inplace_merge(BidIt first, BidIt middle, BidIt last);
template<class BidIt, class Pred>
    void inplace_merge(BidIt first, BidIt middle, BidIt last, Pred pr);
template<class InIt1, class InIt2>
    bool includes(InIt1 first1, InIt1 last1,
        InIt2 first2, InIt2 last2);
template<class InIt1, class InIt2, class Pred>
    bool includes(InIt1 first1, InIt1 last1,
        InIt2 first2, InIt2 last2, Pred pr);
template<class InIt1, class InIt2, class OutIt>
    OutIt set_union(InIt1 first1, InIt1 last1,
        InIt2 first2, InIt2 last2, OutIt x);
template<class InIt1, class InIt2, class OutIt, class Pred>
    OutIt set_union(InIt1 first1, InIt1 last1,
        InIt2 first2, InIt2 last2, OutIt x, Pred pr);
```

```
template<class InIt1, class InIt2, class OutIt>
    OutIt set_intersection(InIt1 first1, InIt1 last1,
        InIt2 first2, InIt2 last2, OutIt x);
template<class InIt1, class InIt2, class OutIt, class Pred>
    OutIt set_intersection(InIt1 first1, InIt1 last1,
        InIt2 first2, InIt2 last2, OutIt x, Pred pr);
template<class InIt1, class InIt2, class OutIt>
    OutIt set_difference(InIt1 first1, InIt1 last1,
        InIt2 first2, InIt2 last2, OutIt x);
template<class InIt1, class InIt2, class OutIt, class Pred>
    OutIt set_difference(InIt1 first1, InIt1 last1,
        InIt2 first2, InIt2 last2, OutIt x, Pred pr);
template<class InIt1, class InIt2, class OutIt>
    OutIt set_symmetric_difference(InIt1 first1, InIt1 last1,
        InIt2 first2, InIt2 last2, OutIt x);
template<class InIt1, class InIt2, class OutIt, class Pred>
    OutIt set_symmetric_difference(InIt1 first1, InIt1 last1,
        InIt2 first2, InIt2 last2, OutIt x, Pred pr);
template<class RanIt>
    void push_heap(RanIt first, RanIt last);
template<class RanIt, class Pred>
    void push_heap(RanIt first, RanIt last, Pred pr);
template<class RanIt>
    void pop_heap(RanIt first, RanIt last);
template<class RanIt, class Pred>
    void pop_heap(RanIt first, RanIt last, Pred pr);
template<class RanIt>
    void make_heap(RanIt first, RanIt last);
template<class RanIt, class Pred>
    void make_heap(RanIt first, RanIt last, Pred pr);
template<class RanIt>
    void sort_heap(RanIt first, RanIt last);
template<class RanIt, class Pred>
    void sort_heap(RanIt first, RanIt last, Pred pr);
template<class T>
    const T& max(const T& x, const T& y);
template<class T, class Pred>
    const T& max(const T&  x, const T& y, Pred pr);
template<class T>
    const T& min(const T& x, const T& y);
template<class T, class Pred>
    const T& min(const T& x, const T& y, Pred pr);
template<class FwdIt>
    FwdIt max_element(FwdIt first, FwdIt last);
template<class FwdIt, class Pred>
    FwdIt max_element(FwdIt first, FwdIt last, Pred pr);
template<class FwdIt>
    FwdIt min_element(FwdIt first, FwdIt last);
template<class FwdIt, class Pred>
    FwdIt min_element(FwdIt first, FwdIt last, Pred pr);
```

```
template<class InIt1, class InIt2>
    bool lexicographical_compare(InIt1 first1, InIt1 last1,
        InIt2 first2, InIt2 last2);
template<class InIt1, class InIt2, class Pred>
    bool lexicographical_compare(InIt1 first1, InIt1 last1,
        InIt2 first2, InIt2 last2, Pred pr);
template<class BidIt>
    bool next_permutation(BidIt first, BidIt last);
template<class BidIt, class Pred>
    bool next_permutation(BidIt first, BidIt last, Pred pr);
template<class BidIt>
    bool prev_permutation(BidIt first, BidIt last);
template<class BidIt, class Pred>
    bool prev_permutation(BidIt first, BidIt last, Pred pr);
    };
```

<algorithm> Template Methods

The <algorithm> template provides the template functions shown in Table 5.1

Table 5.1 The <algorithm> template functions

Method	Description
FwdIt adjacent_find(FwdIt first, FwdIt last); FwdIt adjacent_find(FwdIt first, FwdIt last, Pred pr);	This template function returns the lowest N in the range [0, last - first) where N + 1 != last - first and the predicate *(first + N) == *(first + N + 1) is true. It then returns first + N. If no such value exists, the function returns last. The second template function use of the predicate is pr(*(first + N), *(first + N + 1)).
bool binary_search(FwdIt first, FwdIt last, const T& val); bool binary_search(FwdIt first, FwdIt last, const T& val, Pred pr);	This first template function determines whether a value of N exists in the range [0, last - first) for which *(first + N) has equivalent ordering to val, where the elements designated by iterators in the range [first, last) form a sequence ordered by operator<. If so, the function returns true. If no such value exists, it returns false.
OutIt copy(InIt first, InIt last, OutIt x);	This template function evaluates *(x + N) = *(first + N)) once for each N in the range [0, last - first). This template function returns x + N. If x and first designate regions of storage, x must not be in the range [first, last).

Table 5.1 The <algorithm> template functions *(continued)*

Method	Description
BidIt2 copy_backward(BidIt1 first, BidIt1 last, BidIt2 x);	This template function evaluates *(x - N - 1) = *(last - N - 1)) once for each N in the range [0, last - first), for decreasing values of N beginning with the highest value. It then returns x - (last - first). If x and first designate regions of storage, x must not be in the range [first, last).
size_t count(InIt first, InIt last, const T& val);	This template function sets a count n to zero. It then executes ++n for each N in the range [0, last - first) for which the predicate *(first + N) == val is true, returning n. It evaluates the predicate exactly last - first times.
size_t count_if(InIt first, InIt last, Pred pr);	This template function sets a count n to zero. It then executes ++n for each N in the range [0, last - first) for which the predicate pr(*(first + N)) is true, evaluating the predicate exactly last - first times.
bool equal(InIt1 first, InIt1 last, InIt2 x); bool equal(InIt1 first, InIt1 last, InIt2 x, Pred pr);	This template function returns true only if, for each N in the range [0, last1 - first1), the predicate *(first1 + N) == *(first2 + N) is true evaluating the predicate once, at most, for each N.

pair<FwdIt, FwdIt> equal_range(FwdIt first, FwdIt last, const T& val);
template<class FwdIt, class T, class Pred>
pair<FwdIt, FwdIt> equal_range(FwdIt first, FwdIt last, const T& val, Pred pr);
	This template function effectively returns pair(lower_bound(first, last, val), upper_bound(first, last, val)). The elements designated by iterators in the range [first, last) form a sequence ordered by operator<.

void fill(FwdIt first, FwdIt last, const T& x);	This template function evaluates *(first + N) = x once for each N in the range [0, last - first).
void fill_n(OutIt first, Size n, const T& x);	This template function evaluates *(first + N) = x once for each N in the range [0, n).
void generate(FwdIt first, FwdIt last, Gen g);	This template function evaluates *(first + N) = g() once for each N in the range [0, last - first).
InIt find(InIt first, InIt last, const T& val);	This template function determines the lowest value of N in the range [0, last - first) where the predicate *(first + N) == val is true, returning first + N. If no such value exists, the function returns last.

Table 5.1 The <algorithm> template functions *(continued)*

Method	Description
FwdIt1 find_end(FwdIt1 first1, FwdIt1 last1, FwdIt2 first2, FwdIt2 last2); template<class FwdIt1, class FwdIt2, class Pred> FwdIt1 find_end(FwdIt1 first1, FwdIt1 last1, FwdIt2 first2, FwdIt2 last2, Pred pr);	This template function determines the highest value of N in the range [0, last1 - first1 - (last2 - first2)) for each M in the range [0, last2 - first2), the predicate *(first1 + N + M) == *(first2 + N + M) is true, returning first1 + N. If no such value exists, the function returns last1. It evaluates the predicate (last2 - first2) * (last1 - first1 - (last2 - first2) + 1) times, at most. The second template function is the same, except that the predicate is pr(*(first1 + N + M), *(first2 + N + M)).
FwdIt1 find_first_of(FwdIt1 first1, FwdIt1 last1, FwdIt2 first2, FwdIt2 last2); FwdIt1 find_first_of(FwdIt1 first1, FwdIt1 last1, FwdIt2 first2, FwdIt2 last2, Pred pr);	This template function determines the lowest value of N in the range [0, last1 - first1) such that for some M in the range [0, last2 - first2), the predicate *(first1 + N) == *(first2 + M) is true, returning first1 + N.
InIt find_if(InIt first, InIt last, Pred pr);	This template function determines the lowest value of N in the range [0, last - first) where the predicate pred(*(first + N)) is true, returning first + N. Otherwise, the function returns last.
Fun for_each(InIt first, InIt last, Fun f);	This template function evaluates f(*(first + N)) once for each N in the range [0, last - first). It then returns f. The call f(*(first + N)) must not alter *(first + N).
void generate(FwdIt first, FwdIt last, Gen g);	This template function evaluates *(first + N) = g() once for each N in the range [0, last - first).
void generate_n(OutIt first, Dist n, Gen g);	This template function evaluates *(first + N) = g() once for each N in the range [0, n).
bool includes(InIt1 first1, InIt1 last1, InIt2 first2, InIt2 last2); template<class InIt1, class InIt2, class Pred> bool includes(InIt1 first1, InIt1 last1, InIt2 first2, InIt2 last2, Pred pr);	The first template function determines whether a value of N exists in the range [0, last2 - first2) such that, for each M in the range [0, last1 - first1), *(first + M) and *(first + N) do not have equivalent ordering, where the elements designated by iterators in the ranges [first1, last1) and [first2, last2) each form a sequence ordered by operator<. If so, the function returns false. If no such value exists, it returns true.

The <algorithm> template functions *(continued)*

Method	Description

void inplace_merge(BidIt first, BidIt middle, BidIt last);
template<class BidIt, class Pred>
void inplace_merge(BidIt first, BidIt middle, BidIt last, Pred pr);
	The first template function reorders the sequences designated by iterators in the ranges [first, middle) and [middle, last), each ordered by operator<, to form a merged sequence of length last - first beginning at first, also ordered by operator<. The merge occurs without altering the relative order of elements within either original sequence.

void iter_swap(FwdIt1 x, FwdIt2 y);	This template function leaves the value originally stored in *y subsequently stored in *x, and the value originally stored in *x subsequently stored in *y.

bool lexicographical_compare(InIt1 first1, InIt1 last1, InIt2 first2, InIt2 last2);
template<class InIt1, class InIt2, class Pred>
bool lexicographical_compare(InIt1 first1, InIt1 last1, InIt2 first2, InIt2 last2, Pred pr);
	The first template function determines K, the number of elements to compare as the smaller of last1 - first1 and last2 - first2. The second template function operates the same, except that it replaces operator<(X, Y) with pr(X, Y).

FwdIt lower_bound(FwdIt first, FwdIt last, const T& val); template<class FwdIt, class T, class Pred> FwdIt lower_bound(FwdIt first, FwdIt last, const T& val, Pred pr);	The first template function determines the lowest value of N in the range [0, last - first) such that, for each M in the range [0, N), the predicate *(first + M) < val is true, where the elements designated by iterators in the range [first, last) form a sequence ordered by operator<. It then returns first + N. The second template function operates the same, except that it replaces operator<(X, Y) with pr(X, Y).
void make_heap(RanIt first, RanIt last); template<class RanIt, class Pred> void make_heap(RanIt first, RanIt last, Pred pr);	The first template function reorders the sequence designated by iterators in the range [first, last) to form a heap ordered by operator<. The function evaluates the ordering predicate X < Y at most 3 * (last - first) times. The second template function operates the same, except that it replaces operator<(X, Y) with pr(X, Y).

const T& max(const T& x, const T& y);
template<class T, class Pred>
const T& max(const T& x, const T& y, Pred pr);
	The first template function returns y if x < y. Otherwise, it returns x. T need supply only a single-argument constructor and a destructor. The second template function operates the same, except that it replaces operator<(X, Y) with pr(X, Y). Microsoft-specific: To avoid conflicts with min and max in WINDEF.H, use _MIN and _MAX instead. These macros evaluate to _cpp_min and _cpp_max, respectively.

Table 5.1 The <algorithm> template functions *(continued)*

Method	Description
FwdIt max_element(FwdIt first, FwdIt last); template<class FwdIt, class Pred> FwdIt max_element(FwdIt first, FwdIt last, Pred pr);	The first template function determines the lowest value of N in the range [0, last - first), such that for each M in the range [0, last - first), the predicate *(first + N) < *(first + M) is false. It then returns first + N.
OutIt merge(InIt1 first1, InIt1 last1, InIt2 first2, InIt2 last2, OutIt x); template<class InIt1, class InIt2, class OutIt, class Pred> OutIt merge(InIt1 first1, InIt1 last1, InIt2 first2, InIt2 last2, OutIt x, Pred pr);	The first template function determines K, the number of elements to copy as (last1 - first1) + (last2 - first2). It then alternately copies two sequences, designated by iterators in the ranges [first1, last1) and [first2, last2) and each ordered by operator<, to form a merged sequence of length K beginning at x, also ordered by operator<. The function then returns x + K.
const T& min(const T& x, const T& y); template<class T, class Pred> const T& min(const T& x, const T& y, Pred pr);	The first template function returns y if y < x. Otherwise, it returns x. T need supply only a single-argument constructor and a destructor. The second template function operates the same, except that it replaces operator<(X, Y) with pr(X, Y). Microsoft-specific: To avoid conflicts with min and max in WINDEF.H, use _MIN and _MAX instead. These macros evaluate to _cpp_min and _cpp_max, respectively.
FwdIt min_element(FwdIt first, FwdIt last); template<class FwdIt, class Pred> FwdIt min_element(FwdIt first, FwdIt last, Pred pr);	The first template function determines the lowest value of N in the range [0, last - first), such that for each M in the range [0, last - first), the predicate *(first + M) < *(first + N) is false. It then returns first + N. Therefore, the function determines the lowest position that contains the smallest value in the sequence. The function evaluates the ordering predicate X < Y exactly max((last - first) - 1, 0) times. The second template function operates the same, except that it replaces operator<(X, Y) with pr(X, Y).
pair<InIt1, InIt2> mismatch(InIt1 first, InIt1 last, InIt2 x); template<class InIt1, class InIt2, class Pred> pair<InIt1, InIt2> mismatch(InIt1 first, InIt1 last, InIt2 x, Pred pr);	The first template function determines the lowest value of N in the range [0, last1 - first1) for which the predicate !(*(first1 + N) == *(first2 + N)) is true. It then returns pair(first1 + N, first2 + N). If no such value exists, N has the value last1 - first1. The function evaluates the predicate once, at most, for each N.The second template function operates the same, except that the predicate is pr(*(first1 + N), *(first2 + N)).

Table 5.1 The <algorithm> template functions *(continued)*

Method	Description

bool next_permutation(BidIt first, BidIt last);
template<class BidIt, class Pred>
bool next_permutation(BidIt first, BidIt last, Pred pr);
	The first template function determines a repeating sequence of permutations, whose initial permutation occurs when the sequence designated by iterators in the range [first, last) is ordered by operator<. (The elements are sorted in ascending order.) It then reorders the elements in the sequence, by evaluating swap(X, Y) for the elements X and Y zero or more times, to form the next permutation. The second template function operates the same, except that it replaces operator<(X, Y) with pr(X, Y).

void nth_element(RanIt first, RanIt nth, RanIt last);
template<class RanIt, class Pred>
void nth_element(RanIt first, RanIt nth, RanIt last, Pred pr);
	The first template function reorders the sequence designated by iterators in the range [first, last) such that for each N in the range [0, nth - first) and for each M in the range [nth - first, last - first), the predicate !(*(first + M) < *(first + N)) is true. The second template function operates the same, except that it replaces operator<(X, Y) with pr(X, Y).

void partial_sort(RanIt first, RanIt middle, RanIt last);
template<class RanIt, class Pred>
void partial_sort(RanIt first, RanIt middle, RanIt last, Pred pr);
	The first template function reorders the sequence designated by iterators in the range [first, last) such that for each N in the range [0, middle - first) and for each M in the range (N, last - first), the predicate !(*(first + M) < *(first + N)) is true. The second template function operates the same, except that it replaces operator<(X, Y) with pr(X, Y).

RanIt partial_sort_copy(InIt first1, InIt last1, RanIt first2, RanIt last2); template<class InIt, class RanIt, class Pred> RanIt partial_sort_copy(InIt first1, InIt last1, RanIt first2, RanIt last2, Pred pr);	The first template function determines K, the number of elements to copy, as the smaller of last1 - first1 and last2 - first2. It then copies and reorders K of the sequence designated by iterators in the range [first1, last1) such that the K elements copied to first2 are ordered by operator<. The second template function operates the same, except that it replaces operator<(X, Y) with pr(X, Y).

Table 5.1 The <algorithm> template functions *(continued)*

Method	Description
BidIt partition(BidIt first, BidIt last, Pred pr);	This template function reorders the sequence designated by iterators in the range [first, last) and determines the value K such that for each N in the range [0, K), the predicate pr(*(first + N)) is true, and for each N in the range [K, last - first), the predicate pr(*(first + N)) is false. The function then returns first + K. The predicate must not alter its operand. The function evaluates pr(*(first + N)) exactly last - first times and swaps (last - first) / 2 pairs of elements, at most.

void pop_heap(RanIt first, RanIt last);
template<class RanIt, class Pred>
void pop_heap(RanIt first, RanIt last, Pred pr);
	The first template function reorders the sequence designated by iterators in the range [first, last) to form a new heap, ordered by operator< and designated by iterators in the range [first, last - 1), leaving the original element at *first subsequently at *(last - 1). The original sequence must designate an existing heap, also ordered by operator<. Therefore, first != last must be true and *(last - 1) is the element to remove from (pop off) the heap.
	The function evaluates the ordering predicate X < Y ceil(2 * log(last - first)) times, at most.The second template function operates the same, except that it replaces operator<(X, Y) with pr(X, Y).

bool prev_permutation(BidIt first, BidIt last);
template<class BidIt, class Pred>
bool prev_permutation(BidIt first, BidIt last, Pred pr);
	The first template function determines a repeating sequence of permutations, whose initial permutation occurs when the sequence designated by iterators in the range [first, last) is the reverse of one ordered by operator<. (The elements are sorted in descending order.) It then reorders the elements in the sequence, by evaluating swap(X, Y) for the elements X and Y zero or more times, to form the next permutation. The second template function operates the same, except that it replaces operator<(X, Y) with pr(X, Y).

Table 5.1 The <algorithm> template functions *(continued)*

Method	Description

void push_heap(RanIt first, RanIt last);
template<class RanIt, class Pred>
void push_heap(RanIt first, RanIt last, Pred pr);
	The first template function reorders the sequence designated by iterators in the range [first, last) to form a new heap ordered by operator<. Iterators in the range [first, last - 1) must designate an existing heap, also ordered by operator<. The second template function operates the same, except that it replaces operator<(X, Y) with pr(X, Y).

void random_shuffle(RanIt first, RanIt last);
template<class RanIt, class Fun>
void random_shuffle(RanIt first, RanIt last, Fun& f);
	The first template function evaluates swap(*(first + N), *(first + M)) once for each N in the range [1, last - first), where M is a value from some uniform random distribution over the range [0, N). Therefore, the function randomly shuffles the order of elements in the sequence. The second template function operates the same, except that M is (Dist)f((Dist)N), where Dist is the type iterator_traits::distance_type.

FwdIt remove(FwdIt first, FwdIt last, const T& val);	This template function effectively assigns first to X, and then executes the statement: if (!(*(first + N) == val)) *X++ = *(first + N); once for each N in the range [0, last - first). It then returns X.

OutIt remove_copy(InIt first, InIt last, OutIt x, const T& val);	This template function effectively executes the statement:
	if (!(*(first + N) == val))
	*x++ = *(first + N);
	once for each N in the range [0, last - first). It then returns x.

OutIt remove_copy_if(InIt first, InIt last, OutIt x, Pred pr);	This template function effectively executes the statement:
	if (!pr(*(first + N)))
	*x++ = *(first + N);
	once for each N in the range [0, last - first). It then returns x.

FwdIt remove_if(FwdIt first, FwdIt last, Pred pr);	This template function effectively assigns first to X, and then executes the statement: if (!pr(*(first + N))) *X++ = *(first + N); once for each N in the range [0, last - first). It then returns X.

Table 5.1 The <algorithm> template functions *(continued)*

Method	Description
void replace(FwdIt first, FwdIt last, const T& vold, const T& vnew);	This template function executes the statement: if (*(first + N) == vold) *(first + N) = vnew; once for each N in the range [0, last - first).
OutIt replace_copy(InIt first, InIt last, OutIt x, const T& vold, const T& vnew);	This template function executes the statement: if (*(first + N) == vold) *(x + N) = vnew; else *(x + N) = *(first + N) once for each N in the range [0, last - first).If x and first designate regions of storage, the range [x, x + (last - first)) must not overlap the range [first, last).
OutIt replace_copy_if(InIt first, InIt last, OutIt x, Pred pr, const T& val);	This template function executes the statement: if (pr(*(first + N))) *(x + N) = val; else *(x + N) = *(first + N) once for each N in the range [0, last - first). If x and first designate regions of storage, the range [x, x + (last - first)) must not overlap the range [first, last).
void replace_if(FwdIt first, FwdIt last, Pred pr, const T& val);	This template function executes the statement: if (pr(*(first + N))) *(first + N) = val; once for each N in the range [0, last - first).
void reverse(BidIt first, BidIt last);	This template function evaluates swap(*(first + N), *(last - 1 - N) once for each N in the range [0, (last - first) / 2). Therefore, the function reverses the order of elements in the sequence.
OutIt reverse_copy(BidIt first, BidIt last, OutIt x);	This template function evaluates *(x + N) = *(last - 1 - N) once for each N in the range [0, last - first). It then returns x + (last - first).
void rotate(FwdIt first, FwdIt middle, FwdIt last);	This template function leaves the value originally stored in *(first + (N + (middle - last)) % (last - first)) subsequently stored in *(first + N) for each N in the range [0, last - first).

Table 5.1 The <algorithm> template functions *(continued)*

Method	Description
OutIt rotate_copy(FwdIt first, FwdIt middle, FwdIt last, OutIt x);	This template function evaluates *(x + N) = *(first + (N + (middle - first)) % (last - first)) once for each N in the range [0, last - first).
FwdIt1 search(FwdIt1 first1, FwdIt1 last1, FwdIt2 first2, FwdIt2 last2); template<class FwdIt1, class FwdIt2, class Pred> FwdIt1 search(FwdIt1 first1, FwdIt1 last1, FwdIt2 first2, FwdIt2 last2, Pred pr);	The first template function determines the lowest value of N in the range [0, (last1 - first1) - (last2 - first2)) such that for each M in the range [0, last2 - first2), the predicate *(first1 + N + M) == *(first2 + M) is true. It then returns first1 + N. The second template function operates the same, except that the predicate is pr(*(first1 + N + M), *(first2 + M)).
FwdIt search_n(FwdIt first, FwdIt last, Dist n, const T& val); template<class FwdIt, class Dist, class T, class Pred> FwdIt search_n(FwdIt first, FwdIt last, Dist n, const T& val, Pred pr);	The first template function determines the lowest value of N in the range [0, (last - first) - n) such that for each M in the range [0, n), the predicate *(first + N + M) == val is true. It then returns first + N. The second template function operates the same, except that the predicate is pr(*(first + N + M), val).
OutIt set_difference(InIt1 first1, InIt1 last1, InIt2 first2, InIt2 last2, OutIt x); template<class InIt1, class InIt2, class OutIt, class Pred> OutIt set_difference(InIt1 first1, InIt1 last1, InIt2 first2, InIt2 last2, OutIt x, Pred pr);	The first template function alternately copies values from two sequences designated by iterators in the ranges [first1, last1) and [first2, last2), both ordered by operator<, to form a merged sequence of length K beginning at x, also ordered by operator<. The function then returns x + K. The merge occurs without altering the relative order of elements within either sequence. The second template function operates the same, except that it replaces operator<(X, Y) with pr(X, Y).
OutIt set_intersection(InIt1 first1, InIt1 last1, InIt2 first2, InIt2 last2, OutIt x); template<class InIt1, class InIt2, class OutIt, class Pred> OutIt set_intersection(InIt1 first1, InIt1 last1, InIt2 first2, InIt2 last2, OutIt x, Pred pr);	The first template function alternately copies values from two sequences designated by iterators in the ranges [first1, last1) and [first2, last2), both ordered by operator<, to form a merged sequence of length K beginning at x, also ordered by operator<. The function then returns x + K.
OutIt set_symmetric_difference(InIt1 first1, InIt1 last1, InIt2 first2, InIt2 last2, OutIt x); template<class InIt1, class InIt2, class OutIt, class Pred> OutIt set_symmetric_difference(InIt1 first1, InIt1 last1, InIt2 first2, InIt2 last2, OutIt x, Pred pr);	The first template function alternately copies values from two sequences designated by iterators in the ranges [first1, last1) and [first2, last2), both ordered by operator<, to form a merged sequence of length K beginning at x, also ordered by operator<. The function then returns x + K.

Table 5.1 The <algorithm> template functions *(continued)*

Method	Description
OutIt set_union(InIt1 first1, InIt1 last1, InIt2 first2, InIt2 last2, OutIt x); template<class InIt1, class InIt2, class OutIt, class Pred> OutIt set_union(InIt1 first1, InIt1 last1, InIt2 first2, InIt2 last2, OutIt x, Pred pr);	The first template function alternately copies values from two sequences designated by iterators in the ranges [first1, last1) and [first2, last2), both ordered by operator<, to form a merged sequence of length K beginning at x, also ordered by operator<. The function then returns x + K.
void sort(RanIt first, RanIt last); template<class RanIt, class Pred> void sort(RanIt first, RanIt last, Pred pr);	The first template function reorders the sequence designated by iterators in the range [first, last) to form a sequence ordered by operator. The second template function operates the same, except that it replaces operator<(X, Y) with pr(X, Y).
void sort_heap(RanIt first, RanIt last); template<class RanIt, class Pred> void sort_heap(RanIt first, RanIt last, Pred pr);	The first template function reorders the sequence designated by iterators in the range [first, last) to form a sequence that is ordered by operator <. The original sequence must designate a heap, also ordered by operator <.
FwdIt stable_partition(FwdIt first, FwdIt last, Pred pr);	This template function reorders the sequence designated by iterators in the range [first, last) and determines the value K such that for each N in the range [0, K) the predicate pr(*(first + N)) is true, and for each N in the range [K, last - first) the predicate pr(*(first + N)) is false.
void stable_sort(RanIt first, RanIt last); template<class RanIt, class Pred> void stable_sort(RanIt first, RanIt last, Pred pr);	The first template function reorders the sequence designated by iterators in the range [first, last) to form a sequence ordered by operator <.
void swap(T& x, T& y);	This template function leaves the value originally stored in y subsequently stored in x, and the value originally stored in x subsequently stored in y.
FwdIt2 swap_ranges(FwdIt1 first, FwdIt1 last, FwdIt2 x);	This template function evaluates swap(*(first + N), *(x + N)) once for each N in the range [0, last - first). It then returns x + (last - first). If x and first designate regions of storage, the range [x, x + (last - first)) must not overlap the range [first, last).

Table 5.1 The <algorithm> template functions *(continued)*

Method	Description
OutIt transform(InIt first, InIt last, OutIt x, Unop uop); template<class InIt1, class InIt2, class OutIt, class Binop> OutIt transform(InIt1 first1, InIt1 last1, InIt2 first2, OutIt x, Binop bop);	The first template function evaluates *(x + N) = uop(*(first + N)) once for each N in the range [0, last - first). It then returns x + (last - first). The call uop(*(first + N)) must not alter *(first + N). The second template function evaluates *(x + N) = bop(*(first1 + N), *(first2 + N)) once for each N in the range [0, last1 - first1). It then returns x + (last1 - first1). The call bop(*(first1 + N), *(first2 + N)) must not alter either *(first1 + N) or *(first2 + N).
FwdIt unique(FwdIt first, FwdIt last); template<class FwdIt, class Pred> FwdIt unique(FwdIt first, FwdIt last, Pred pr);	The first template function effectively assigns first to X, then executes the statement: if (N == 0 || !(*(first + N) == V)) V = *(first + N), *X++ = V; once for each N in the range [0, last - first). It then returns X.
OutIt unique_copy(InIt first, InIt last, OutIt x); template<class InIt, class OutIt, class Pred> OutIt unique_copy(InIt first, InIt last, OutIt x, Pred pr);	The first template function effectively executes the statement: if (N == 0 || !(*(first + N) == V)) V = *(first + N), *x++ = V; once for each N in the range [0, last - first). It then returns x.
FwdIt upper_bound(FwdIt first, FwdIt last, const T& val); template<class FwdIt, class T, class Pred> FwdIt upper_bound(FwdIt first, FwdIt last, const T& val, Pred pr);	The first template function determines the highest value of N in the range [0, last - first) such that, for each M in the range [0, N) the predicate *(first + M) < val is true, where the elements designated by iterators in the range [first, last) form a sequence ordered by operator<. It then returns first + N. The second template function operates the same, except that it replaces operator<(X, Y) with pr(X, Y).

Sample Code

The following four programs—find.cpp, mdshfl.cpp, removif.cpp, and setunon.cpp—demonstrate several of the <algorithm> template functions. These examples lay down the fundamental syntax requirements for using the <algorithm> template functions and STL iterators (discussed in Chapter 6).

The find.cpp Application

The first example application, find.cpp, shows how the find() function template can be used to locate the first occurrence of a matching element within a sequence. The syntax for find() looks like:

```
template<class InIt, class T>
    InIt find(InIt first, InIt last, const T& val);
```

Find() expects two input iterators (see Chapter 6), the address of the comparison value, and returns an input iterator. The program looks like:

```
// find.cpp
// Testing <algorithm>
// find()
// Chris H. Pappas and William H. Murray, 1999

#include <iostream>
#include <algorithm>

using namespace std;

#define MAX_ELEMENTS 5

void main( void )
{
  // simple character array declaration and initialization
  char cArray[MAX_ELEMENTS] = { 'A', 'E', 'I', 'O', 'U' } ;

  char *pToMatchingChar, charToFind = 'I';

  // find() passed the array to search, length +1, and charToFind ptr
  pToMatchingChar = find(cArray, cArray + MAX_ELEMENTS, charToFind);

  if( pToMatchingChar!= cArray + MAX_ELEMENTS )
    cout << "The first occurrence of " << charToFind
         << " was at offset " << pToMatchingChar - cArray;
  else
    cout << "Match NOT found!";
};
```

Remember, all you need to do to use any STL template function is the proper include statement:

```
#include <algorithm> // for this chapter
```

and the using statement:

```
using namespace std;
```

The program first defines the character array *cArray* and initializes it to uppercase vowels. The program then searches the array, using the find() function template, for the letter 'I' and reports its offset into the *cArray* if found. The output from the program looks like:

```
The first occurrence of I was at offset 2
```

The rndshfl.cpp Application

Randomization of data is an extremely important component to many applications, whether it's the random shuffle of a deck of electronic poker cards, to truly random test data. The following application uses the random_shuffle() template function to randomize the contents of an array of characters. This simple example can be easily modified to work on any container element type.

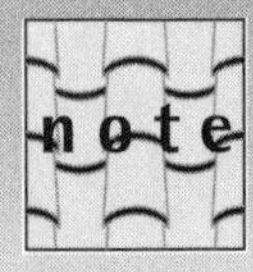

Several of the applications use additional STL templates. Each chapter will emphasize, in the discussion, only those code segments relating to that chapter's STL template. Without this approach, each chapter would endlessly digress. With patience and practice, you will soon understanding how the support STL templates work together, in much the same way someone learning to speak a new language may know *how* to use a verb without really knowing the details of sentence construction.

The syntax for random_shuffle() looks like:

```
template<class RanIt>
    void random_shuffle(RanIt first, RanIt last);
```

random_shuffle requires two random access iterator formal arguments (discussed in Chapter 6). The program looks like:

```
// rndshuf.cpp
// Testing <algorithm>
// random_shuffle()
// Chris H. Pappas and William H. Murray, 1999

#include <iostream>
#include <algorithm>
#include <vector>

using namespace std;

#define MAX_ELEMENTS 5

void main( void )
{
  // typedef for char vector class and iterator
  typedef vector<char> cVectorClass;
  typedef cVectorClass::iterator cVectorClassIt;

                //instantiation of character vector
```

```
            cVectorClass cVowels(MAX_ELEMENTS);

  // additional iterators
  cVectorClassIt start, end, pToCurrentcVowels;

  cVowels[0] = 'A';
  cVowels[1] = 'E';
  cVowels[2] = 'I';
  cVowels[3] = 'O';
  cVowels[4] = 'U';

  start = cVowels.begin();    // location of first cVowels
  end = cVowels.end();        // one past the last cVowels

  cout << "Original order looks like: ";
  cout << "{ ";
  for(pToCurrentcVowels = start; pToCurrentcVowels != end;
      pToCurrentcVowels++)
        cout << *pToCurrentcVowels << " ";
    cout << "}\n" << endl;

    random_shuffle(start, end); // <algorithm> template function

    cout << "Shuffled order looks like: ";
    cout << "{ " ;
    for(pToCurrentcVowels = start; pToCurrentcVowels != end;
                    pToCurrentcVowels++)
      cout << *pToCurrentcVowels << " ";
    cout << "}" << endl;
}
```

Notice that the application incorporates two STL templates: <vector> and <algorithm>. The STL <vector> template provides the definitions necessary to create the character vector container, while <algorithm> defines the random_shuffle() template function. The application uses the <vector> templates begin() and end() to locate the front and back offset addresses into the *cVowels* container. These two parameters are then passed to the random_shuffle() template function so that the algorithm knows where the container starts and ends in memory. The output from the program looks like:

```
Original order looks like: { A E I O U }

Shuffled order looks like: { U O A I E }
```

The removif.cpp Application

This next application uses the remove_if() template function along with the <functional> less_equal() template to remove any container elements matching the test value. The syntax for remove_if() looks like:

```
FwdIt remove_if(FwdIt first, FwdIt last, Pred pr);
template<class InIt, class OutIt, class T>
```

remove_if() is passed two forward iterators (discussed in Chapter 6) and a predicate telling remove_if() what comparison test to perform. The program looks like:

```
// removif.cpp
// Testing <algorithm>
// remove_if()
// Chris H. Pappas and William H. Murray, 1999

#include <iostream>
#include <algorithm>
#include <vector>
#include <functional>

using namespace std;

#define MAX_ELEMENTS 10

void main( void )
{
  typedef vector<int> cVectorClass ;
  typedef cVectorClass::iterator cVectorClassIt;

  cVectorClass iVector(MAX_ELEMENTS);

  cVectorClassIt start, end, pToCurrentint, last;

  start = iVector.begin();   // location of first iVector
  end = iVector.end();       // location of one past last iVector

  iVector[0] =  7;
  iVector[1] = 16;
  iVector[2] = 11;
  iVector[3] = 10;
  iVector[4] = 17;
  iVector[5] = 12;
  iVector[6] = 11;
  iVector[7] =  6;
  iVector[8] = 13;
  iVector[9] = 11;

  cout << "Original order: {";

  for(pToCurrentint = start; pToCurrentint != end;
      pToCurrentint++)
    cout << *pToCurrentint << " " ;
  cout << " }\n" << endl ;
```

```
  // call to remove all values less than or equal to the value 11
  last = remove_if(start, end, bind2nd(less_equal<int>(), 11) ) ;

  cout << end-last << " elements were removed.\n" << endl;

  cout << "The " << MAX_ELEMENTS-(end-last)
       << " valid remaining elements are: { " ;
  for(pToCurrentint = start; pToCurrentint != last;
      pToCurrentint++)
    cout << *pToCurrentint << " " ;
    cout << " }\n" << endl ;

}
```

Although many components of this application are similar to the two previous examples, this program uses the <functional> template function bind2nd() along with the less_equal template class, as the second argument to remove_if(), to find all occurrences with values less than or equal to the integer value 11. The output from the program looks like:

```
Original order: { 7 16 11 10 17 12 11 6 13 11 }
6 elements were removed.
The 4 valid remaining elements are: { 16 17 12 13 }
```

Notice that the values 7, 11, 10, 11, 6, and 11 were removed, respectively.

The setunon.cpp Application

This last application uses the <algorithm> sort() and set_union() template functions. First the program instantiates two integer vectors, *iVector1* and *iVector2*, and a third, *iUnionedVector*, twice the length of the first two. Sorting is necessary for the set_union() template function to correctly locate and eliminate all duplicate values. The syntax for set_union() looks like:

```
template<class InIt1, class InIt2, class OutIt>
    OutIt set_union(InIt1 first1, InIt1 last1,
        InIt2 first2, InIt2 last2, OutIt x);
```

set_union() uses four input iterators (discussed in Chapter 6) and one output iterator to point to the comparison containers and output the results, respectively. The program looks like:

```
// setunon.cpp
// Testing <algorithm>
// set_union()
// Chris H. Pappas and William H. Murray, 1999

#include <iostream>
#include <algorithm>
#include <vector>
```

```
#include <functional>

using namespace std;

#define MAX_ELEMENTS 10

void main( void )
{
  typedef vector<int> cVectorClass ;
  typedef cVectorClass::iterator cVectorClassIt;


  cVectorClass iVector1(MAX_ELEMENTS), iVector2(MAX_ELEMENTS),
              iUnionedVector(2 * MAX_ELEMENTS) ;

  cVectorClassIt start1, end1,
                start2, end2,
                      pToCurrentint, unionStart;

  start1 = iVector1.begin();   // location of first iVector1
  end1 = iVector1.end();       // location of one past last iVector1

  start2 = iVector2.begin();   // location of first iVector2
  end2 = iVector2.end();       // location of one past last iVector2

  // locating the first element address of result union container

  unionStart = iUnionedVector.begin();

  iVector1[0] =  7; iVector2[0] = 14;
  iVector1[1] = 16; iVector2[1] = 11;
  iVector1[2] = 11; iVector2[2] =  2;
  iVector1[3] = 10; iVector2[3] = 19;
  iVector1[4] = 17; iVector2[4] = 20;
  iVector1[5] = 12; iVector2[5] =  7;
  iVector1[6] = 11; iVector2[6] =  1;
  iVector1[7] =  6; iVector2[7] =  0;
  iVector1[8] = 13; iVector2[8] = 22;
  iVector1[9] = 11; iVector2[9] = 18;

  cout << "iVector1 as is : { ";

  for(pToCurrentint = start1; pToCurrentint != end1;
      pToCurrentint++)
    cout << *pToCurrentint << " " ;
  cout << "}\n" << endl ;

  cout << "iVector2 as is : { ";

  for(pToCurrentint = start2; pToCurrentint != end2;
      pToCurrentint++)
```

```
    cout << *pToCurrentint << " " ;
  cout << "}\n" << endl ;

  // sort of both containers necessary for correct union
  sort(start1,end1);
  sort(start2,end2);

  cout << "\niVector1 sorted: { ";

  for(pToCurrentint = start1; pToCurrentint != end1;
      pToCurrentint++)
    cout << *pToCurrentint << " " ;
    cout << "}\n" << endl ;

  cout << "\niVector2 sorted: { ";

  for(pToCurrentint = start2; pToCurrentint != end2;
      pToCurrentint++)
    cout << *pToCurrentint << " " ;
    cout << "}\n" << endl;

  // call to set_union() with all necessary pointers
  set_union(start1,end1,start2,end2,unionStart);

  cout << "After calling set_union()\n" << endl ;

  cout << "iUnionedVector { " ;
  for(pToCurrentint = iUnionedVector.begin();
      pToCurrentint != iUnionedVector.end(); pToCurrentint++)
    cout << *pToCurrentint << " " ;
  cout << "}\n" << endl ;
}
```

The output from the program looks like:

```
iVector1 as is : { 7 16 11 10 17 12 11 6 13 11 }
iVector2 as is: { 14 11 2 19 20 7 1 0 22 18 }
iVector1 sorted: { 6 7 10 11 11 11 12 13 16 17 }
ivector2 sorted: { 0 1 2 7 11 14 18 19 20 22 }
After calling set_union():
iUnionedVector { 0 1 2 6 7 10 11 11 11 12 13 14 16 17 18 19 20 22 0 0 }
```

Notice that the union of *ivector1*'s and *iVector2*'s value of 11 removes their duplicate occurrences, explaining the last two 0s in *iUnionedVector*, indicating null elements.

Summary

In this chapter, you explored several of the STL <algorithm> template functions as used on integer <vector> classes. The applications demonstrated how to find a container element, randomly shuffle container contents, scan a container for certain comparison conditions (less-than-or-equal-to) and perform a union. Chapter 6 defines and uses the STL <iterator> header that defines several templates used to define and manipulate iterators. You may wish to return to this chapter, after reading Chapter 6, for additional understanding of how the four algorithms discussed here use iterators.

SIX

The STL <iterator> Template

The STL <iterator> template is an extremely important component of STL. Whereas many of the other STL templates, such as container types, are easier to digest and use, in actuality STL is composed of many interrelated components. Iterators are every bit as important as containers, algorithms, and allocators.

The ANSI/ISO committee defines an iterator as a generalized pointer that allows a programmer to work with different data structures (or containers) in a uniform manner. Structurally, an iterator is a pointer data type, although with a few surprising subtleties of its own. Like all pointers, for example:

```
int * pi, or float * pf, or MYCLASS* pmyclass
```

iterators are defined in terms of where they point. Their syntax:

```
container<Type>::iterator iterator_instance;
```

begins with the type of container with which the iterator is associated. The syntax looks slightly different from your standard pointer syntax, by being associated with a template type instead of a simple data type. In the example above, *iterator_instance* is going to be a pointer to elements in a container that holds objects of type *Type*. Dereferencing *iterator_instance* yields a reference to an object of type *Type*.

Since iterators allow algorithms to access the elements of any container type, in a uniform way, you can generate code solutions that are easily ported to different application needs. For example, the following example uses the iterators *InIt* and *OutIt* to copy the elements of one container to another:

```
template <class InIt, class OutIt>
OutIt copy(InIt first, InIt last, OutIt copiedContainer)
  {
    while( first != last ) *copiedContainer++ = *first++;
    return copiedContainer;
  }
```

Here the copy() template function works by using the iterator interface. It expects the input and output iterators to provide the basic set of three operations: operator*(), which returns a reference to the container's content_type, operator!=(), a template function that determines when it's time to exit the main loop, and operarator++(), used to move to the next container element in both the source and destination containers.

Since all the different iterator types used in STL support these basic operations, the <algorithm> copy() template function can work on *any* container type. With iterators not caring about a container's type or element type, you do not have to write custom versions of your algorithm for each container class.

Iterator Hierarchy

The following list of iterators begins with the simplest and most straightforward, on up to those iterators with the most capabilities. At the bottom of the tree are Input and Output iterators, followed by Forward, Bidirectional, and finally at the top of the tree, Random Access iterators.

Input and Output Iterators

Both the input and output iterators are pointers to container elements. The only operations allowed on these iterators are pointer dereferencing and incrementing. Each specific location can be dereferenced only *once* in order to reference or store an individual container element.

Forward Iterators

Unlike input and output iterators, forward iterators return a true reference when the pointer is dereferenced so that it can be read and written to multiple times.

Bidirectional Iterators

Bidirectional iterators do forward iterators one better by allowing the pointer to be decremented, not just incremented. Any container that uses this iterator is no longer limited to single-pass algorithms.

Random Iterators

As their name implies, random iterators behave most closely to true pointer variables in that they can be both incremented and decremented, or have a constant value added to or subtracted from it.

Legal Iterator Range

If you have had a Data Structures course somewhere in your software engineering career, you are intimately aware of the debugging nightmare that pointer variables introduce into your program. Iterators are no exception. The biggest problem associated with pointer variables is pointing with a garbage address. To avoid this disaster when you start working with iterators, you need to adopt the STL philosophy of using an interator's range. Most STL template functions that work on containers do so over the range of the container. A container's range is defined by the begin() and end() template functions; for example:

```
for( vector<float>::iterator pElement = ctr.begin(); pElementlll !=
  ctr.end(); pElement++ )
```

constructs a well formed **for** loop with the iterator (*pElement*) always within a valid range.

One important concept to grasp when dealing with iterators, which, remember, are most closely related to pointer variable types, is that you do *not* compare their values with the standard pointer value NULL, or ask whether one iterator is greater than or less than another. Instead, you use iterators in pairs to define the range over which the algorithm operates.

Important Naming Conventions

Not all algorithms support all iterator types. This fact could present a problem to you, the user of STL, were it not for certain naming conventions. For example, the sort() template function needs a random access iterator, not just one starting at crt.begin() and ending at crt.end(). In an attempt to avoid this type of confusion, the STL uses a standardized naming of the class arguments used to parameterize template functions.

Microsoft uses a very consistent naming convention that you will soon pick up on as you continue through the examples in this chapter and the remainder of the book. For example, look at the following STL definition for the <algorithm> sort():

```
template<class RanIt> void sort(RanIt first, RanIt last);
```

In this definition, *first* and *last* are defined by a random iterator *RanIt*. The following list describes these important default names: The name of an iterator type indicates the category of iterators required for that type. In order of increasing power, the categories are summarized here as:

1. `OutIt`—An output iterator `X` can have only a value `V` stored indirectly on it, after which it must be incremented before the next.
2. `InIt`—An input iterator `X` can represent a singular value that indicates end-of-sequence. If such an iterator does not compare equal to its end-of-sequence value, it can have a value `V` accessed indirectly on it any number of times. To progress to the next value, or end-of-sequence, you increment it, as in `++X`, `X++`. Once you increment any copy of an input iterator, none of the other copies can safely be compared, dereferenced, or incremented.
3. `FwdIt`—A forward iterator `X` can take the place of an output iterator or an input iterator. You can read what you just wrote through a forward iterator. And you can make multiple copies of a forward iterator, each of which can be dereferenced and incremented independently.
4. `BidIt`—A bidirectional iterator `X` can take the place of a forward iterator. You can, however, also decrement a bidirectional iterator, as in `--X`, `X--`.
5. `RanIt`—A random-access iterator `X` can take the place of a bidirectional iterator. You can also perform much the same integer arithmetic on a random-access iterator that you can on an object pointer.

Table 6.1 lists the iterators you can use to perform, read, write, or read/write container element access:

Table 6.1 Read, Write, Read/Write Iterators

Mode	Legal Iterator Type(s)
Write-Only Iterators	`output iterator` (**`FwdIt`**) `forward iterator` (**`BidIt`**) `bidirectional iterator` (**`RanIt`**) `random-access iterator`
Read-Only Iterators	`input iterator` (**`FwdIt`**) `forward iterator` (**`BidIt`**) `bidirectional iterator` (**`RanIt`**) `random-access iterator`
Read/Write Iterators	`forward iterator` (**`BidIt`**) `bidirectional iterator` (**`RanIt`**) `random-access iterator`

<iterator> Template Syntax

The following listing gives the syntax for the <iterator> template.

```
namespace std {
struct input_iterator_tag;
struct output_iterator_tag;
struct forward_iterator_tag;
struct bidirectional_iterator_tag;
struct random_access_iterator_tag;
template<class C, class T, class Dist>
    struct iterator;
template<class It>
    struct iterator_traits;
template<class T>
    struct iterator_traits<T *>
template<class BidIt, class T, class Ref,
    class Ptr, class Dist>
    class reverse_bidirectional_iterator;
template<class RanIt, class T, class Ref,
    class Ptr, class Dist>
    class reverse_iterator;
template<class Cont>
    class back_insert_iterator;
template<class Cont>
    class front_insert_iterator;
template<class Cont>
    class insert_iterator;
template<class T, class Dist>
    class istream_iterator;
template<class T>
    class ostream_iterator;
template<class E, class T>
    class istreambuf_iterator;
template<class E, class T>
    class ostreambuf_iterator;
```

```
//      TEMPLATE FUNCTIONS
template<class BidIt, class T, class Ref, class Ptr, class Dist>
    bool operator==(
        const reverse_bidirectional_iterator<BidIt, T, Ref,
            Ptr, Dist>& lhs,
        const reverse_bidirectional_iterator<BidIt, T, Ref,
            Ptr, Dist>& rhs);
template<class RanIt, class T, class Ref, class Ptr, class Dist>
    bool operator==(
        const reverse_iterator<RanIt, T, Ref, Ptr, Dist>& lhs,
        const reverse_iterator<RanIt, T, Ref, Ptr, Dist>& rhs);
template<class T, class Dist>
    bool operator==(
        const istream_iterator<T, Dist>& lhs,
        const istream_iterator<T, Dist>& rhs);
template<class E, class T>
    bool operator==(
        const istreambuf_iterator<E, T>& lhs,
        const istreambuf_iterator<E, T>& rhs);
template<class BidIt, class T, class Ref, class Ptr, class Dist>
    bool operator!=(
        const reverse_bidirectional_iterator<BidIt, T, Ref,
            Ptr, Dist>& lhs,
        const reverse_bidirectional_iterator<BidIt, T, Ref,
            Ptr, Dist>& rhs);
template<class RanIt, class T, class Ref, class Ptr, class Dist>
    bool operator!=(
        const reverse_iterator<RanIt, T, Ref, Ptr, Dist>& lhs,
        const reverse_iterator<RanIt, T, Ref, Ptr, Dist>& rhs);
template<class T, class Dist>
    bool operator!=(
        const istream_iterator<T, Dist>& lhs,
        const istream_iterator<T, Dist>& rhs);
```

```
template<class E, class T>
    bool operator!=(
        const istreambuf_iterator<E, T>& lhs,
        const istreambuf_iterator<E, T>& rhs);
template<class RanIt, class T, class Ref, class Ptr, class Dist>
    bool operator<(
        const reverse_iterator<RanIt, T, Ref, Ptr, Dist>&mmp lhs,
        const reverse_iterator<RanIt, T, Ref, Ptr, Dist>& rhs);
template<class RanIt, class T, class Ref, class Ptr, class Dist>
    bool "operator>(
        const reverse_iterator<RanIt, T, Ref, Ptr, Dist>&mmp lhs,
        const reverse_iterator<RanIt, T, Ref, Ptr, Dist>& rhs);
template<class RanIt, class T, class Ref, class Ptr, class Dist>
    bool operator<=(
        const reverse_iterator<RanIt, T, Ref, Ptr, Dist>&mmp lhs,
        const reverse_iterator<RanIt, T, Ref, Ptr, Dist>& rhs);
template<class RanIt, class T, class Ref, class Ptr, class Dist>
    bool ="operator>=(
        const reverse_iterator<RanIt, T, Ref, Ptr, Dist>&mmp lhs,
        const reverse_iterator<RanIt, T, Ref, Ptr, Dist>& rhs);
template<class RanIt, class T, class Ref, class Ptr, class Dist>
    Dist operator-(
        const reverse_iterator<RanIt, T, Ref, Ptr, Dist>& lhs,
        const reverse_iterator<RanIt, T, Ref, Ptr, Dist>& rhs);
template<class RanIt, class T, class Ref, class Ptr, class Dist>
    reverse_iterator<RanIt, T, Ref, Ptr, Dist> operator+(
        Dist n,
        const reverse_iterator<RanIt, T, Ref, Ptr, Dist>& rhs);
template<class Cont>
    back_insert_iterator<Cont> back_inserter(Cont& x);
template<class Cont>
    front_insert_iterator<Cont> front_inserter(Cont& x);
template<class Cont, class Iter>
    insert_iterator<Cont> inserter(Cont& x, Iter it);
```

```
template<class InIt, class Dist>
    void advance(InIt& it, Dist n);
template<class Init, class Dist>
    ptrdiff_t distance(InIt first, InIt last);
    };
```

<iterator> Class Definitions

The following section lists the class definitions used by the STL <iterator> templates.

ITERATOR

```
template<class C, class T, class Dist = ptrdiff_t>
    struct iterator {
    typedef C iterator_category;
    typedef T value_type;
    typedef Dist distance_type;
    };
```

The template class is used as a base type for all iterators. It defines the member types `iterator_category`, `value_type`, and `distance_type`.

ITERATOR_TRAITS

```
template<class It>
    struct iterator_traits {
    typedef It::iterator_category iterator_category;
    typedef It::value_type value_type;
    typedef It::distance_type distance_type;
    };
```

This template class determines several critical types associated with the iterator type `It`. It defines the member types `iterator_category`, `value_type`, and `distance_type`.

REVERSE_BIDIRECTIONAL_ITERATOR

```
template<class BidIt,
    class T = iterator_traits<BidIt>::value_type,
    class Ref = T&,
    class Ptr = T *, class Dist = ptrdiff_t>
```

```
    class reverse_bidirectional_iterator
        : public iterator<bidirectional_iterator_tag, T, Dist> {
public:
    typedef BidIt iter_type;
    typedef Ref reference_type;
    typedef Ptr pointer_type;
    reverse_bidirectional_iterator();
    explicit reverse_bidirectional_iterator(BidIt x);
    BidIt base() const;
    Ref operator*() const;
    Ptr "operator->() const;
    reverse_bidirectional_iterator& operator++();
    reverse_bidirectional_iterator operator++(int);
    reverse_bidirectional_iterator& operator--();
    reverse_bidirectional_iterator operator--();
protected:
    BidIt current;
    };
```

This template class describes an object that behaves like a bidirectional iterator of class iterator<bidirectional_iterator_tag, T, Dist>. It stores a bidirectional iterator of type BidIt in the protected object current. Incrementing the object x of type reverse_bidirectional_iterator decrements x.current, and decrementing x increments x.current.

REVERSE_ITERATOR

```
template<class RanIt,
    class T = iterator_traits<RanIt>::value_type,
    class Ref = T&,
    class Ptr = T *, class Dist = ptrdiff_t>
    class reverse_iterator
        : public iterator<random_access_iterator_tag, T, Dist> {
public:
    typedef RanIt iter_type;
    typedef Ref reference_type;
    typedef Ptr pointer_type;
```

```
    reverse_iterator();
    explicit reverse_iterator(RanIt x);
    RanIt base() const;
    Ref operator*() const;
    Ptr "operator->() const;
    reverse_iterator& operator++();
    reverse_iterator operator++(int);
    reverse_iterator& operator--();
    reverse_iterator operator--();
    reverse_iterator& operator+=(Dist n);
    reverse_iterator operator+(Dist n) const;
    reverse_iterator& operator-=(Dist n);
    reverse_iterator operator-(Dist n) const;
    Ref operator[](Dist n) const;
protected:
    RanIt current;
    };
```

This template class describes an object that behaves like a random-access iterator of class iterator<random_access_iterator_tag, T, Dist>. It stores a random-access iterator of type RanIt in the protected object current. Incrementing the object x of type reverse_iterator decrements x.current, and decrementing x increments x.current

BACK_INSERT_ITERATOR

```
template<class Cont>
    class back_insert_iterator
        : public iterator<output_iterator_tag, void, void> {
public:
    typedef Cont container_type;
    typedef Cont::value_type value_type;
    explicit back_insert_iterator(Cont& x);
    back_insert_iterator& operator=(const Cont::value_type& val);
    back_insert_iterator& operator*();
    back_insert_iterator& operator++();
    back_insert_iterator operator++(int);
```

```
protected:
    Cont& container;
    };
```

This template class describes an output iterator that inserts elements into a container of type Cont, which it accesses via the protected reference object it stores called container.

FRONT_INSERT_ITERATOR

```
template<class Cont>
    class front_insert_iterator
        : public iterator<output_iterator_tag, void, void> {
public:
    typedef Cont container_type;
    typedef Cont::value_type value_type;
    explicit front_insert_iterator(Cont& x);
    front_insert_iterator& operator=(const Cont::value_type& val);
    front_insert_iterator& operator*();
    front_insert_iterator& operator++();
    front_insert_iterator operator++(int);
protected:
    Cont& container;
    };
```

This template class describes an output iterator object. It inserts elements into a container of type Cont, which it accesses via the protected reference object it stores called container.

INSERT_ITERATOR

```
template<class Cont>
    class insert_iterator
        : public iterator<output_iterator_tag, void, void> {
public:
    typedef Cont container_type;
    typedef Cont::value_type value_type;
    explicit insert_iterator(Cont& x, Cont::iterator it);
    insert_iterator& operator=(const Cont::value_type& val);
    insert_iterator& operator*();
```

```
    insert_iterator& operator++();
    insert_iterator& operator++(int);
protected:
    Cont& container;
    Cont::iterator iter;
    };
```

This template class describes an output iterator object. It inserts elements into a container of type Cont, which it accesses via the protected reference object it stores called container. It also stores the protected iterator object of class Cont::iterator called iter.

ISTREAM_ITERATOR

```
template<class U, class E = char, class T = char_traits<E> >
    class istream_iterator
        : public iterator<input_iterator_tag, U, ptrdiff_t> {
public:
    typedef E char_type;
    typedef T traits_type;
    typedef basic_istream<E, T> istream_type;
    istream_iterator();
    istream_iterator(istream_type& is);
    const U& operator*() const;
    const U *"operator->() const;
    istream_iterator<U, E, T>& operator++();
    istream_iterator<U, E, T> operator++(int);
    };
```

This template class describes an input iterator that extracts objects of class U from an input stream, which it accesses via an object it stores, of type pointer to basic_istream<E, T>. If the extraction fails, the object effectively replaces the stored pointer with a null pointer.

OSTREAM_ITERATOR

```
template<class U, class E=char, class Tr=char_traits<E> >
    class ostream_iterator
        : public iterator<output_iterator_tag, void, void> {
public:
```

```
    typedef U value_type;
    typedef E char_type;
    typedef T traits_type;
    typedef basic_ostream<E, T> ostream_type;
    ostream_iterator(ostream_type& os);
    ostream_iterator(ostream_type& os, const E *delim);
    ostream_iterator<U, E, T>& operator=(const U& val);
    ostream_iterator<U, E, T>& operator*();
    ostream_iterator<U, E, T>& operator++();
    ostream_iterator<U, E, T> operator++(int);
    };
```

This template class describes an output iterator that inserts objects of class U into an output stream, which it accesses via an object it stores, of type pointer to basic_ostream<E, T>.

OSTREAMBUF_ITERATOR

```
template<class E, class T = char_traits<E> >
    class ostreambuf_iterator
        : public iterator<output_iterator_tag, void, void> {
public:
    typedef E char_type;
    typedef T traits_type;
    typedef basic_streambuf<E, T> streambuf_type;
    typedef basic_ostream<E, T> ostream_type;
    ostreambuf_iterator(streambuf_type *sb) throw();
    ostreambuf_iterator(ostream_type& os) throw();
    ostreambuf_iterator& operator=(E x);
    ostreambuf_iterator& operator*();
    ostreambuf_iterator& operator++();
    T1 operator++(int);
    bool failed() const throw();
    };
```

This template class describes an output iterator that inserts elements of class E into an output stream buffer.

<iterator> Template Overloaded Operators

The <iterator> template overloads the operators shown in Table 6.2

Table 6.2 Overloaded operators for <iterator>

Overloaded Operators
template<class BidIt, class T, class Ref, class Ptr, class Dist> bool operator==(const reverse_bidirectional_iterator<BidIt, T, Ref, Ptr, Dist>& lhs, const reverse_bidirectional_iterator<BidIt, T, Ref, Ptr, Dist>& rhs);
template<class RanIt, class T, class Ref, class Ptr, class Dist> bool operator==(const reverse_iterator<RanIt, T, Ref, Ptr, Dist>& lhs, const reverse_iterator<RanIt, T, Ref, Ptr, Dist>& rhs);
template<class T, class Dist> bool operator==(const istream_iterator<T, Dist>& lhs, const istream_iterator<T, Dist>& rhs);
template<class E, class T> bool operator==(const istreambuf_iterator<E, T>& lhs, const istreambuf_iterator<E, T>& rhs);
template<class BidIt, class T, class Ref, class Ptr, class Dist> bool operator!=(const reverse_bidirectional_iterator<BidIt, T, Ref, Ptr, Dist>& lhs, const reverse_bidirectional_iterator<BidIt, T, Ref, Ptr, Dist>& rhs);
template<class RanIt, class T, class Ref, class Ptr, class Dist> bool operator!=(const reverse_iterator<RanIt, T, Ref, Ptr, Dist>& lhs, const reverse_iterator<RanIt, T, Ref, Ptr, Dist>& rhs);
template<class T, class Dist> bool operator!=(const istream_iterator<T, Dist>& lhs, const istream_iterator<T, Dist>& rhs);
template<class E, class T> bool operator!=(const istreambuf_iterator<E, T>& lhs, const istreambuf_iterator<E, T>& rhs);
template<class RanIt, class T, class Ref, class Ptr, class Dist> bool operator<(const reverse_iterator<RanIt, T, Ref, Ptr, Dist>&mmp lhs, const reverse_iterator<RanIt, T, Ref, Ptr, Dist>& rhs);
template<class RanIt, class T, class Ref, class Ptr, class Dist> bool "operator>(const reverse_iterator<RanIt, T, Ref, Ptr, Dist>&mmp lhs, const reverse_iterator<RanIt, T, Ref, Ptr, Dist>& rhs);
template<class RanIt, class T, class Ref, class Ptr, class Dist> bool operator<=(const reverse_iterator<RanIt, T, Ref, Ptr, Dist>&mmp lhs, const reverse_iterator<RanIt, T, Ref, Ptr, Dist>& rhs);
template<class RanIt, class T, class Ref, class Ptr, class Dist> bool ="operator>=(const reverse_iterator<RanIt, T, Ref, Ptr, Dist>&mmp lhs, const reverse_iterator<RanIt, T, Ref, Ptr, Dist>& rhs);
template<class RanIt, class T, class Ref, class Ptr, class Dist> Dist operator-(const reverse_iterator<RanIt, T, Ref, Ptr, Dist>& lhs, const reverse_iterator<RanIt, T, Ref, Ptr, Dist>& rhs);
template<class RanIt, class T, class Ref, class Ptr, class Dist> reverse_iterator<RanIt, T, Ref, Ptr, Dist> operator+(Dist n, const reverse_iterator<RanIt, T, Ref, Ptr, Dist>& rhs);

<iterator> Template Iterators

The <iterator> template provides the iterators shown in Table 6.3.

Table 6.3 Iterators

Iterators
template<class Cont> back_insert_iterator<Cont> back_inserter(Cont& x);
template<class Cont> front_insert_iterator<Cont> front_inserter(Cont& x);
template<class Cont, class Iter> insert_iterator<Cont> inserter(Cont& x, Iter it);
template<class InIt, class Dist> void advance(InIt& it, Dist n); template<class Init, class Dist> ptrdiff_t distance(InIt first, InIt last); };

The iteratr1.cpp Application

The following application uses three iterators: **vector::begin**, which returns an iterator to start the traversal of the vector; **vector::end**, which returns an iterator for the last element of the vector; and **vector::traverse**, which traverses the vector. The program first creates a vector instance named *iVectorInstance*, and then initializes the vector's contents with the offset address into the vector:

```
// iteratr1.cpp
// Testing <iterator>
// ::iterator
// Chris H. Pappas and Willliam H. Murray, 1999

#include <iostream>
#include <vector>


using namespace std ;

#define MAX_ELEMENTS 10

typedef vector<int> iVector;
```

```
void ShowVector(iVector &iVectorInstance);

void main( void )
{
  iVector iVectorInstance;

  // Initialize vector elements with
  // the offset's value
  for (int offsetAndValue = 0; offsetAndValue < MAX_ELEMENTS;
       offsetAndValue++)
         iVectorInstance.push_back(offsetAndValue);

  // Iterator used to traverse vector elements
  iVector::iterator actualIterator;

  // Output original contents of iVectorInstance.
  cout << "iVectorInstance with the last element: ";
  for (actualIterator  = iVectorInstance.begin();
       actualIterator != iVectorInstance.end();
       actualIterator++)
         cout << *actualIterator << " ";

  cout << "\n\n";

  // Use <vector> erase() to delete last value
  iVectorInstance.erase(iVectorInstance.end() -1);

  // Output contents of iVectorInstance.minus last element
  cout << "iVectorInstance minus the last element: ";
  for (actualIterator = iVectorInstance.begin();
       actualIterator != iVectorInstance.end();
       actualIterator++)
         cout << *actualIterator << " ";
}
```

The program finishes by first printing the original vector's contents, then deleting the last element, and finally printing the modified container. The output from the program looks like:

```
iVectoInstance with the last element: 0 1 2 3 4 5 6 7 8 9
iVectorInstance minus the last element 0 1 2 3 4 5 6 7 8
```

The iteratr2.cpp Application

For a change, the following application uses a <list> instead of a <vector> container to hold a series of words. The program uses a list::iterator, a list::difference_type (holding the type of element pointers it will be subtracting), and the advance() template function, which moves the input iterator *n* elements.

```
// iteratr2.cpp
// Testing <iterator>
// ::iterator
// Chris H. Pappas and William H. Murray, 1999

#include <list>
#include <string>
#include <iostream>

using namespace std ;

typedef list<string> strClassList;

void main( void ) {

  strClassList List;

  // iterator used to traverse list of strings
  strClassList::iterator iteratorForListElements;

  // list::difference_type describes an object that represents
  // the difference between the addresses of any two elements.
```

```
  strClassList::difference_type distance_between;

  List.push_back("Sun,");
  List.push_back("Sand,");
  List.push_back("Ocean,");
  List.push_back("Beach,");
  List.push_back("Lotion,");
  List.push_back("equals ");
  List.push_back("Ahhhhhh!");

  // output the list
  iteratorForListElements = List.begin();
  cout << "The vacation begins: ";
  for( int i = 0; i < 7 ; i++, iteratorForListElements++ )
    cout << *iteratorForListElements  << "  ";

  // Find the first element
  iteratorForListElements=List.begin();

  cout << "\n\nUsing advance() to locate the KEY word :) \n";

  advance(iteratorForListElements,2); // move iterator two elements

  cout << "\nThe magic word is " << *iteratorForListElements << endl;

  // calculating the distance between first and third elements
  distance_between = distance( List.begin(), iteratorForListElements);

  // Output difference
  cout << "\nThe distance between the elements is : " <<
distance_between;
}
```

Notice that both programs declare container iterators using the identical syntax, just different container types:

```
iVector::iterator actualIterator;
strClassList::iterator iteratorForListElements;
```

The following statement defines which container element type *distance_between* will need to subtract:

```
strClassList::difference_type distance_between;
```

Next the program uses the list::push_back() method to insert an element with the current string constant at the end of the list container. At this point, the list iterator needs the address to the first container element:

```
iteratorForListElements = List.begin();
```

before it can begin traversing the list and outputting its contents. Once the **for** loop executes, the iterator needs resetting back to the beginning of the list container so that it may be advanced *n* elements from the beginning.

The advance() template function moves the list pointer two elements forward:

```
advance(iteratorForListElements,2); // move iterator two elements
```

The distance() template function uses the advanced iterator's address and compares it with the beginning of the list:

```
distance_between = distance( List.begin(), iteratorForListElements);
```

The output from the vacation plans looks like:

```
The vacation begins: Sun, Sand, Ocean, Beach, Lotion, equals Ahhhhhh!
Using advance() to locate the KEY word :)
The magic word is Ocean,
The distance between the elements is: 2
```

Summary

In this chapter, you looked at the similarities and differences between standard C/C++ pointers and STL iterators. The advantage of iterators involves their generic syntax that allows them to work on any container-type/element-type. You also discovered that when using template functions with iterator arguments, you must pay close attention to the required iterator type (input, output, random, etc.) and Microsoft's naming conventions for each category. At this point, you may wish to go back through previous chapters' example programs, since just about every application you could write using STL uses iterators.

The good news is that with <utility>, <functional>, <algorithm>, and <iterator> STL routines behind you, you are ready to knowledgeably understand how the remaining STL definitions (<vector>, <stack>, <queue>, <list>, etc.) interface, providing extremely powerful, portable, and generic code solutions for today's applications.

S E V E N

The <vector> Template

Question: If <vector> containers are arrays, then are arrays <vector> containers? Answer: No! Okay, here's the good news: using <vector> containers is logically and syntactically very similar to using simple C/C++ arrays. The great news is that unlike statically allocated arrays, <vector> containers are dynamic. Dynamic in the sense of linked-list technology, meaning that the <vector> container can grow and shrink its size to maximize the use of RAM.

The term *vector* is commonly used to mean an indexed collection of similarly typed values. In C++, we can represent this abstract concept as a one-dimensional array. Recall that an array is a fixed-size collection of values of homogeneous data types, indexed by integer keys. The number of elements held by the array is provided as part of the declaration. The following, for example, creates an array of ten float values:

```
float fArray[10];
```

Legal index values range from zero to one less than the size of the collection. Values are accessed using the subscript operator. A programmer can think of the elements of an array as being placed end-to-end in memory. The underlying C++ language provides only a primitive mechanism for the support of one-dimensional arrays, and this mechanism provides few safeguards. Most importantly, index values are *not* checked against declared bounds at run time.

The problem is compounded by the fact that you have no way to determine from the value of a simple C++ array the extent, or number of elements, it should contain. Furthermore, even fewer high-level operations are defined for the array type than for character strings. By adding a new abstraction layer on top of the basic language framework, we can correct many of these deficiencies.

Templatized Vectors

A vector viewed as a data abstraction is different in one very important respect from the data types we have previously investigated. As an abstract concept, the idea of a vector describes an incomplete data type. The solution of any particular problem might require a vector of integers, a vector of floating-point values, or even a vector of strings. In order to abstract the concept of a vector, out of these more concrete realizations, we need a facility to parameterize a type description with another type. That is, we need some way to describe the idea of a vector of type T, where T represents an unknown type.

Within a vector class description, the unknown parameter type T can be used in any situation requiring the use of a type name. This possibility allows you to declare an instance variable as a pointer to T, and we can declare an operator as returning a T reference. In the copy constructor, we need to refer to an object of the same type as the receiver. Although only the keyword vector is used, it is implicitly assumed to mean vector of T.

Instantiating Vectors

In order to use a template class as a type, you have to provide bindings for the unknown argument types. This goal is accomplished by providing the element type in a list, again surrounded by angle brackets. For example, the following declares a vector of five integer values, each entry initialized to 0,; a vector consisting of 20 un-initialized, float-precision values; and a vector of ten strings, all initialized to the string “abc.”:

```
// overloaded <vector> constructors
vector<int> iVector(5,0);
vector<float> fVector(20);
vector<string> szVector(10,"abc");
```

Understanding Vector Template Functions

The following template function max(), which appears in the STL, is used to compute the maximum of two arguments. This functionality is parameterized using the template syntax:

```
template <class T> max(T a, T b)
{
  if( a < b )
    return b;
  return a:
}
```

The template function will work as long as the arguments are of a type that can be compared. Thus, the function will work with integers, floating-point precision, and strings. Many of the template functions used by the <vector> template library use this data-independent syntax.

Accessing <vector> Elements

Accessing an individual <vector> element is no more difficult than accessing a simple array element. The syntax looks identical:

```
standardArrayElementReference[ 1 ];
myVectorInstanceElementReference[ 1 ];
```

The syntax changes slightly when traversing an entire <vector> versus an array. Look at the two equivalent statements that follow:

```
// traversing a simple array
for( int offset = 0; offset < MAX_ELEMENTS; offset++)...
// traversing a <vector> instance
vector<int>::iterator iteratorOffset;
for( iteratorOffset = myVector.front(); iteratorOffset != myVector.end();
     iteratorOffset++)...
```

Similar to the <string> template, the <vector> template contains a type definition for the name iterator. This permits an iterator to be easily declared for any particular type of vector value. The template functions begin() and end() yield random access iterators for the vector. Again, note that the iterators yielded by these operations can become invalidated after insertions or removal of elements.

Insertion and Removal of <vector> Elements

You use the <vector> template functions push_back(), insert(), pop_back(), and erase() to insert and remove <vector> elements. The template function push_back() takes a new value as argument and inserts the element at the end of the vector, increasing the size of the vector by one. The more general template function insert() takes as arguments an iterator and a value, and inserts the new element preceding the position specified by the iterator. Again, the size of the vector is increased by one.

The <vector> template function pop_back() removes the last element of the vector, reducing the size of the vector by one. The more general template function erase() is overloaded. In the easier form, a single location is specified using an iterator, and the value denoted by the iterator is removed from the vector. Again the size of the vector is then reduced by one. The more general form of erase() takes two iterator arguments, which specify a range of values within the vector. All elements within this range are removed, regardless of the number of elements being removed.

The template function swap() takes as argument another vector that holds the same type of elements. The values of the two vectors are then exchanged; after the operation, all values from the argument will be held by the receiving vector, and all elements in the current vector will be held by the argument.

Two Different Vector Size Descriptors

Unlike a standard C++ array, which has a fixed size determined by the declaring statement, <vector> vectors are dynamic in size, growing and shrinking as needed. However, vectors have two different sizes associated with them. The first is the number of elements currently in the vector; the second is the maximum size to which the vector can grow, without actually allocating that new storage. The <vector> template function size() fulfills the first category—returning the actual number of vector elements, while capacity() returns your "wish list" for the total number of elements to be stored.

We can therefore deduce that inserting and deleting vector elements always changes the vector's size but may or may not change its capacity. An insertion that causes the size to exceed the capacity generally results in a new block of memory being allocated to hold the vector elements. Values are then copied into this new memory, using the assignment operator appropriate to the element type, and the old memory is deleted. This approach can generate a significant performance hit on your algorithm should the vector be large in size.

The <vector> template function reserve() is a directive to the vector, indicating that the vector is expected to grow to at least the given size. If the argument used with reserve() is larger than the current capacity, then a reallocation occurs and the argument value becomes the new capacity. If subsequent inserts cause the vector to grow even larger than this new value, the vector can grow even larger. The reserved value is not a fixed delimiter, but an application's best guess at the maximum vector size. When the capacity is already in excess of the reserved size request, no reallocation takes place. Remember, calling reserve() does *not* change the actual size of the vector, nor the element values themselves.

Caution is the word; dealing with pointers to vectors as a reallocation invalidates *all* references, pointers, and iterators denoting elements being held by a vector. This means that to lock onto an iterator's address is dangerous if you think that the address associated with the pointer will *never* change:

```
vector<double>::iterator FrontOfVectorConstant;
FrontOfVectorConstant = myVector.begin();
// code using FrontOfVectorConstant instead of myVector.begin()...
```

Other <vector> Operations

Although the <vector> template does not directly provide any template function that can be used to determine whether a specific value is contained in the collection, the generic <algorithm> template functions find() or count() can be used for these purposes. Chapter 5 discusses the <algorithm> template. Table 7.1 shows its more <vector> related components.

Table 7.1 <algorithm> Related <vector> Template Functions

Related <algorithm> Template Functions	**Description**
fill()	Fills a vector with a given initial value.
copy()	Copies one sequence into another.
max_element()	Finds the largest value in a collection.
min_element()	Finds the smallest value in a collection.
reverse()	Reverses the container's elements.
count()	Counts the elements that match a target value, incrementing a counter.
count_if()	Counts elements that satisfy the unary template function passed to it, incrementing a counter.

Table 7.1 <algorithm> Related <vector> Template Functions *(continued)*

Related <algorithm> Template Functions	Description
transform()	Transforms elements using the unary template function passed to it, from source container to destination container.
find()	Finds a value for which the template function passed to it returns true, returning an iterator for the matching element's location.
find_if()	Finds a value in the container, returning an iterator to the matching element.
replace()	Replaces the target element with new value.
replace_if()	Replaces elements for which a unary template function passed to it returns true, with replacement value.
sort()	Places elements in ascending order.
for_each()	Executes a template function passed to it, on each container element.
iter_swap()	Swaps the values specified by two iterators.

Table 7.2 lists the <algorithm> template functions you may choose to use with sort().

Table 7.2 <algorithm> template functions used with sort()

Related <algorithm> Template Functions	Description
merge()	Merges two sorted collections into a third container.
inplace_merge()	Merges two adjacent sorted sequences into one.
binary_search()	Searches for elements within a container, and returns true or false.
lower_bound()	Finds the first element larger than or equal to the specified value, and returns an iterator pointing to the match.
upper_bound()	Finds the first element greater than the value specified, and returns an iterator pointing to the match.

<vector> Template Syntax

The following listing gives the syntax for the <vector> template.

```
namespace std {
template<class T, class A>
    class vector;
template<class A>
    class "vector<bool, A>;
//    TEMPLATE FUNCTIONS
template<class T, class A>
    bool operator==(
        const vector<T, A>& lhs,
        const vector<T, A>& rhs);
template<class T, class A>
    bool operator!=(
        const vector<T, A>& lhs,
        const vector<T, A>& rhs);
template<class T, class A>
    bool operator<(
        const vector<T, A>& lhs,
        const vector<T, A>& rhs);
template<class T, class A>
    bool "operator>(
        const vector<T, A>& lhs,
        const vector<T, A>& rhs);
template<class T, class A>
    bool operator<=(
        const vector<T, A>& lhs,
        const vector<T, A>& rhs);
template<class T, class A>
    bool ="operator>=(
        const vector<T, A>& lhs,
        const vector<T, A>& rhs);
template<class T, class A>
    void swap(
        const vector<T, A>& lhs,
        const vector<T, A>& rhs);
    };
```

Include the STL standard header <vector> to define the container template class `vector` and three supporting templates:

```
template<class T, class A = allocator<T> >
    class vector {
public:
    typedef A allocator_type;
    typedef A::size_type size_type;
    typedef A::difference_type difference_type;
    typedef A::reference reference;
    typedef A::const_reference const_reference;
```

```
    typedef A::value_type value_type;
    typedef T0 iterator;
    typedef T1 const_iterator;
    typedef reverse_iterator<iterator, value_type,
        reference, A::pointer, difference_type>
            reverse_iterator;
    typedef reverse_iterator<const_iterator, value_type,
        const_reference, A::const_pointer, difference_type>
            const_reverse_iterator;
    explicit vector(const A& al = A());
    explicit vector(size_type n, const T& v = T(), const A& al = A());
    vector(const vector& x);
    vector(const_iterator first, const_iterator last,
        const A& al = A());
    void reserve(size_type n);
    size_type capacity() const;
    iterator begin();
    const_iterator begin() const;
    iterator end();
    iterator end() const;
    reverse_iterator rbegin();
    const_reverse_iterator rbegin() const;
    reverse_iterator rend();
    const_reverse_iterator rend() const;
    void resize(size_type n, T x = T());
    size_type size() const;
    size_type max_size() const;
    bool empty() const;
    A get_allocator() const;
    reference at(size_type pos);
    const_reference at(size_type pos) const;
    reference operator[](size_type pos);
    const_reference operator[](size_type pos);
    reference front();
    const_reference front() const;
    reference back();
    const_reference back() const;
    void push_back(const T& x);
    void pop_back();
    void assign(const_iterator first, const_iterator last);
    void assign(size_type n, const T& x = T());
    iterator insert(iterator it, const T& x = T());
    void insert(iterator it, size_type n, const T& x);
    void insert(iterator it,
        const_iterator first, const_iterator last);
    iterator erase(iterator it);
    iterator erase(iterator first, iterator last);
    void clear();
    void swap(vector x);
protected:
    A allocator;
    };
```

<vector> Template typedefs

Table 7.3 defines the typedefs used by the <vector> template.

Table 7.3 typedefs used by the <vector> template

Overloaded Operator	Description
`typedef A allocator_type;`	The type is a synonym for the template parameter A.
`typedef A::size_type size_type;`	The unsigned integer type describes an object that can represent the length of any controlled sequence.
`typedef A::difference_type difference_type;`	The signed integer type describes an object that can represent the difference between the addresses of any two elements in the controlled sequence.
`typedef A::reference reference;`	The type describes an object that can serve as a reference to an element of the controlled sequence.
`typedef A::const_reference const_reference;`	The type describes an object that can serve as a constant reference to an element of the controlled sequence.
`typedef A::value_type value_type;`	The type is a synonym for the template parameter T.
`typedef T0 iterator;`	The type describes an object that can serve as a random-access iterator for the controlled sequence.
`typedef T1 const_iterator;`	The type describes an object that can serve as a constant random-access iterator for the controlled sequence.
`typedef reverse_iterator<iterator, value_type, reference, A::pointer, difference_type> reverse_iterator;`	The type describes an object that can serve as a reverse iterator for the controlled sequence.
`typedef reverse_iterator<const_iterator, value_type, const_reference, A::const_pointer, difference_type> const_reverse_iterator;`	The type describes an object that can serve as a constant reverse iterator for the controlled sequence.

<vector> Overloaded Operators

Table 7.4 lists the overloaded operators used in the <vector> template.

Table 7.4 Overloaded <vector> template operators.

Overloaded Operator Template Function	Description
`bool operator==( const vector <T, A>& lhs, const vector <T, A>& rhs);`	The template function overloads `operator==` to compare two objects of template class `vector`. The function returns `lhs.size() == rhs.size() && equal(lhs. begin(), lhs. end(), rhs.begin())`.
`bool operator!=( const vector <T, A>& lhs, const vector <T, A>& rhs);`	The template function returns `!(lhs == rhs)`.
`bool operator<( const vector <T, A>& lhs, const vector <T, A>& rhs);`	The template function overloads `operator<` to compare two objects of template class `vector`. The function returns `lexicographical_compare(lhs. begin(), lhs. end(), rhs.begin(), rhs.end())`.
`bool operator>( const vector <T, A>& lhs, const vector <T, A>& rhs);`	The template function returns `rhs < lhs`.
`bool operator<=( const vector <T, A>& lhs, const vector <T, A>& rhs);`	The template function returns `!(rhs < lhs)`.
`bool operator>=( const vector <T, A>& lhs, const vector <T, A>& rhs);`	The template function returns `!(lhs < rhs)`.
`void swap( const vector <T, A>& lhs, const vector <T, A>& rhs);`	The template function executes `lhs.swap(rhs)`.

<vector> Template Methods

The <vector> template provides the methods shown in Table 7.5. This table lists the template methods, along with a short description of each method and returned values.

The template class describes an object that controls a varying-length sequence of elements of type T. The sequence is stored as an array of T. The object allocates and frees storage for the sequence it controls through a protected object named `allocator`, of class `A`. Such an allocator object must

Table 7.5 <vector> template methods

Template Method	Description
`explicit vector(const A& al = A());` `explicit vector(size_type n, const T& v = T(), const A& al = A());` `vector(const vector& x);` `vector(const_iterator first, const_iterator last, const A& al = A());`	vector constructors store the allocator object `al` (or, for the copy constructor, `x.get_allocator()`) in `allocator` and initialize the controlled sequence. The first constructor implies an empty initial controlled sequence. The second constructor supplies a repetition of `n` elements of value `x`. The third constructor requests a copy of the sequence controlled by `x`. The last constructor specifies the sequence `[first, last)`
`void reserve(size_type n);`	Guarantees that `capacity()` returns at least `n`.
`size_type capacity() const;`	Returns the storage currently allocated to hold the controlled sequence, a value at least as large as `size()`.
`const_iterator begin() const;` `iterator begin();`	Returns a random-access iterator that points at the first element of the sequence (or just beyond the end of an empty sequence).
`const_iterator end() const;` `iterator end();`	Returns a random-access iterator that points just beyond the end of the sequence.
`const_reverse_iterator rbegin() const;` `reverse_iterator rbegin();`	Returns a reverse iterator that points just beyond the end of the controlled sequence. Pointer to the beginning of the reverse sequence.
`const_reverse_iterator rend() const;` `reverse_iterator rend();`	Returns a reverse iterator that points at the first element of the sequence (or just beyond the end of an empty sequence). Pointer to the end of the reverse sequence.
`void resize(size_type n, T x = T());`	Guarantees `size()` returns `n`. If it must lengthen the controlled sequence, it appends elements with value `x`.
`size_type size() const;`	Returns the length of the controlled sequence.
`size_type max_size() const;`	Returns the length of the longest sequence that the object can control.
`bool empty() const;`	Returns true for an empty controlled sequence.
`A get_allocator() const;`	Returns `allocator`.
`const_reference at(size_type pos) const;` `reference at(size_type pos);`	Returns a reference to the element of the controlled sequence at position `pos`. If that position is invalid, the function throws an object of class `out_of_range`.

Table 7.5 <vector> template methods *(continued)*

Template Method	Description
`const_reference operator[](size_type pos) const;` `reference operator[](size_type pos);`	Returns a reference to the element of the controlled sequence at position `pos`. If that position is invalid, the behavior is undefined.
`reference front();` `const_reference front() const;`	Returns a reference to the first element of the controlled sequence, which must be non-empty.
`reference back();` `const_reference back() const;`	Returns a reference to the last element of the controlled sequence, which must be non-empty.
`void pop_back();`	The member function removes the last element of the controlled sequence, which must be non-empty.
`void assign(const_iterator first, const_iterator last);` `void assign(size_type n, const T& x = T());`	The first member function replaces the sequence controlled by `*this` with the sequence `[first, last)`. The second member function replaces the sequence controlled by `*this` with a repetition of `n` elements of value `x`.
`iterator insert(iterator it, const T& x = T());` `void insert(iterator it, size_type n, const T& x);` `void insert(iterator it, const_iterator first, const_iterator last);`	Each member functions inserts, before the element pointed to by `it` in the controlled sequence, a sequence specified by the remaining operands. The first member function inserts a single element with value `x` and returns an iterator that points to the newly inserted element. The second member function inserts a repetition of `n` elements of value `x`. The last member function inserts the sequence `[first, last)`.
`iterator erase(iterator it);` `iterator erase(iterator first, iterator last);`	The first member function removes the element of the controlled sequence pointed to by `it`. The second member function removes the elements of the controlled sequence in the range `[first, last)`. Both return an iterator that designates the first element remaining beyond any elements removed, or `end()` if no such element exists. Erasing `N` elements causes `N` destructor calls and an assignment for each of the elements between the insertion point and the end of the sequence. No reallocation occurs, so iterators and references become invalid only from the first element erased through the end of the sequence.
`void clear() const;`	Calls `erase( begin(), end())`.

Table 7.5 <vector> template methods *(continued)*

Template Method	Description
`void swap(vector& str);`	Swaps the controlled sequences between `*this` and `str`. If `allocator == str.allocator`, it does so in constant time. Otherwise, it performs a number of element assignments and constructor calls proportional to the number of elements in the two controlled sequences.

have the same external interface as an object of template class allocator. Note that allocator is not copied when the object is assigned.

Vector reallocation occurs when a member function must grow the controlled sequence beyond its current storage capacity. Other insertions and erasures may alter various storage addresses within the sequence. In all such cases, iterators or references that point at altered portions of the controlled sequence become invalid.

Sample Code

The following sample applications demonstrate many of the more frequently used <vector> template functions, overloaded operators, and areas of caution when using this template library.

The vector1.cpp Application

This first application demonstrates the dimensioning of vector containers, from the initial instantiation of the vector, to dynamically allocated "guess" length, to actually increasing the size of the container.

```
// vector1.cpp
// Testing <vector>
// push_back(), size(), capacity(), max_size(), reserve(), resize()
// Chris H. Pappas and William H. Murray, 1999


// When symbols are longer than 255 characters, the warning is
disabled.
#pragma warning(disable:4786)

#include <vector>
#include <iomanip>
#include <iostream>

using namespace std ;
```

```
typedef vector<int> iVector;

void main( void )
{
    // Instantiation of 0 element integer vector
    iVector iVectorInstance;

    // Inserting a 5, at the end of the vector
    iVectorInstance.push_back(5);

    // Current vector statistics.
    cout << "Current statistics:" << endl;
    cout << "iVectorInstance's current size: "
                     <<  setw(10) << iVectorInstance.size() << endl;
    cout << "iVectorInstance's maximum size: "
                     <<  iVectorInstance.max_size() << endl;
    cout << "iVectorInstance's capacity    : "
                     <<  setw(10) << iVectorInstance.capacity() <<
endl;

    // See if room is available for a total of 15 elements
    iVectorInstance.reserve(15);
    cout << "\nReserving storage for 15 elements:" << endl;
    cout << "iVectorInstance's size is     : "
                     <<  setw(10) << iVectorInstance.size() << endl;
    cout << "iVectorInstance's maximum size: "
                     <<  setw(10) << iVectorInstance.max_size() <<
endl;
    cout << "iVectorInstance's capacity is : "
                     <<  setw(10) << iVectorInstance.capacity() <<
endl;

    // Demanding room for at least 25 elements
    iVectorInstance.resize(25);
    cout << "\nAfter resizing storage for 25 elements:" << endl;
    cout << "iVectorInstance's size is     : "
                     <<  setw(10) << iVectorInstance.size() << endl;
    cout << "iVectorInstance's maximum size: "
                     <<  iVectorInstance.max_size() << endl;
    cout << "iVectorInstance's capacity is : "
                     <<  setw(10) << iVectorInstance.capacity() <<
endl;
}
```

The program begins with the following typedef:

```
typedef vector<int> iVector;
```

that defines *iVector* as an integer vector type. Next the *iVectorInstance* is instantiated:

```
iVector iVectorInstance;
```

Notice that the container does *not* specify any fixed length. The first action on the vector is to insert the integer value *5* into the container using the push_back() template function:

```
iVectorInstance.push_back(5);
```

The next series of statements output the containers size(), max_size(), and capacity(), all with template functions:

```
cout << "Current statistics:" << endl;
    cout << "iVectorInstance's current size: "
         <<  setw(10) << iVectorInstance.size() << endl;
    cout << "iVectorInstance's maximum size: "
         <<  iVectorInstance.max_size() << endl;
    cout << "iVectorInstance's capacity    : "
         <<  setw(10) << iVectorInstance.capacity() << endl;
```

This series of statements repeats the same statistics based on two container size-changing statements. The first looks like:

```
iVectorInstance.reserve(15);
```

Remember that reserve() only checks to see whether the requested size could indeed fit in available RAM, and does *not* actually increase the actual size of the container. The second dimension change comes from the following statement:

```
iVectorInstance.resize(25);
```

Unlike reserve(), resize() physically increases the maximum number of elements. Look at the output from the program and notice the effect on the various container statistics:

```
Current statistics:
iVectorInstance's current size:          1
iVectorInstance's maximum size: 1073741823
iVectorInstance's capacity    :          1

Reserving storage for 15 elements:
iVectorInstance's size is     :          1
iVectorInstance's maximum size: 1073741823
iVectorInstance's capacity is :         15

After resizing storage for 25 elements:
iVectorInstance's size is     :         25
iVectorInstance's maximum size: 1073741823
iVectorInstance's capacity is :            25
```

Notice that the reserve() request did *not* change the number of elements from *1* to *15*, but *did* change the capacity to *15*. However, resize() changed both the *size* and *capacity*. Also notice the maximum_size(), which returns the length of the longest sequence that the object can control, remains constant.

The vector2.cpp Application

This next example demonstrates how to access vector elements using iterators and various insert() and erase() operations. Pay particular attention to how you syntactically and logically access vector elements:

```
// vector2.cpp
// Testing <vector>
// push_back(), insert(), delete(), begin(), end()
// Chris H. Pappas and William H. Murray, 1999


// When symbols are longer than 255 characters, the warning is
disabled.
#pragma warning(disable:4786)

#include <vector>
#include <iostream>

using namespace std ;

typedef vector<char> cVector;

void main( void )
{
    // Instantiation of 0 element integer vector
    cVector cVectorInstance;

    // Inserting five vowels
    cVectorInstance.push_back('A');
    cVectorInstance.push_back('E');
    cVectorInstance.push_back('I');
    cVectorInstance.push_back('O');
    cVectorInstance.push_back('Y');

    // Accessing vector elements using array syntax - DANGEROUS
    for(int i = 0; i < 5; i++)
      cout << cVectorInstance[i];
    cout << endl;

    // Accessing vector elements using iterators - BEST APPROACH
    vector<char>::iterator p = cVectorInstance.begin();
    while(p != cVectorInstance.end()) {
      cout << *p;
      p++;
    }
    cout << endl;

    // Inserting a NEW fifth element extending the vector's size
    p = cVectorInstance.begin();
```

```
    p += 4; // moves pointer to fifth element's address
    cVectorInstance.insert(p,'U');

    // Accessing the NEW list
    p = cVectorInstance.begin();
    while(p != cVectorInstance.end()) {
      cout << *p;
      p++;
    }
    cout << endl;

    // Deleting the sixth element 'Y'
    p = cVectorInstance.end();
    cVectorInstance.erase(--p);

    // Printing the modified container
    p = cVectorInstance.begin();
    while(p != cVectorInstance.end()) {
      cout << *p;
      p++;
    }
}
```

Most of the initial program statements should now look familiar to you, so the discussion begins with the two methods for accessing container elements:

```
// Accessing vector elements using array syntax - DANGEROUS
for(int i = 0; i < 5; i++)
  cout << cVectorInstance[i];
cout << endl;
```

Although this for loop works, it is not the most generalized approach and breaks many of the STL rules. In particular, it is hardwired to the element count. The better, standard STL approach below uses the begin() and end() template functions, along with the iterator *p* to perform the task:

```
// Accessing vector elements using iterators - BEST APPROACH
vector<char>::iterator p = cVectorInstance.begin();
while(p != cVectorInstance.end()) {
  cout << *p;
  p++;
}
```

The next three statements insert a new fifth vowel into the container, preceding the current fifth element of *Y*:

```
p = cVectorInstance.begin();
p += 4; // moves pointer to fifth element's address
cVectorInstance.insert(p,'U');
```

The re-initialization of *p* is necessary, since the previous loop moved the pointer beyond the end of the vector container. Pointer arithmetic is next employed to move *p* to the address of the fifth element, followed by a call to the insert() template function. This function accepts an iterator, *p*, and valid element type, *U*.

In order to output the updated container, iterator *p* needs resetting:

```
p = cVectorInstance.begin();
while(p != cVectorInstance.end()) {
  cout << *p;
  p++;
}
```

The final two statements:

```
p = cVectorInstance.end();
cVectorInstance.erase(--p);
```

reset *p* one more time, only this time to the end of the container. Exercise caution; the template function end() returns an interator *one beyond the end* of the container. This explains the prefix decrement of *p* in the template function call statement (*--p*). Lastly, the template function erase() removes the element at the specified location. The template function could have removed a range of values with just a slightly different syntax:

```
cVectorInstance.erase(initializedIterator, initializedIterator + n);
```

The output from the program looks like:

```
AEIOY
AEIOY
AEIOUY
AEIOU
```

Summary

In this chapter, you learned all the necessary fundamentals for using a <vector> container. You learned about various dimension descriptors and template functions; how to traverse a vector container with iterators; the DOs and DON'Ts of finding the beginning and ending address for a container via the template functions begin() and end(); how to insert and erase elements; and finally, that the end() template function does *not* return an iterator to the last element, but one beyond. In Chapter 8, you'll investigate the <stack> template container. This is a much simpler container, since all the action takes place at only one end, the top.

EIGHT

The STL <stack> Template

This chapter details the concepts of a stack as they apply to the STL <stack> template. The <stack> and <queue> (Chapter 9) data types in the STL are interesting because they are not provided as true standalone data types, but rather are constructed as adaptors placed on top of other containers. This chapter illustrates the use of these abstractions in the solution of several programming problems.

Many everyday objects provide most people with a good intuitive understanding of the stack and queue data abstractions. An excellent example of a stack is a pile of papers on a desk (not segued); an even better example is a stack of dishes in a cupboard. The pivotal characteristic for both is that the item on the top is most easily accessed, with new items being added to the collection by placing them above all the current items in the stack. Items removed from a stack are those most recently added or last-in-first-out (LIFO).

Stacks are used by compilers (internal coding) and programmers to solve an array of problems. For example, compilers use stacks to allocate space for parameters and local variables. Each function call made by a program translates into machine code that increments a memory stack to create space for the parameters and local variables associated with the function. This use of a stack to perform memory allocation has many advantages. It allows recursive procedures that possess, in each iteration, a unique data area for local variables. The release of memory simply means decrementing the stack, and invoking destructors for any values that define destructors. This construct allows the maximum use of memory, since no more memory is required for the stack than is absolutely necessary for the parameters and local variables in use at any one instance.

C++ uses a stack to implement the input stream mechanism. The stream data structure maintains two data areas. It must hold a pointer to the file from which the raw characters are obtained. It also maintains a stack of characters that have been pushed back into the input. This allows the method putback() to return a character to an input stream. A subsequent character read operation will first yield the pushed-back character, before continuing with the remainder of input from the file.

Adaptors

STL implements both stacks and queues as adaptors. So they do not directly implement the structures that hold the data values, but are instead built on top of other containers. In other words, they adapt the interface to these containers, providing names for the operations that make sense in the context of their use.

Any container that defines the internal type *T* and that implements the operations empty(), size(), back(), push_back(), and pop_back() can be used as a container for a stack. Both the <vector> and <list> templates support these operations, as well as the STL <dequeue> (discussed in Chapter 9).

Care is needed when selecting the container type. Recall from Chapter 7 that vectors grow dynamically but seldom shrink. On the other hand, space for a list both grows and shrinks as elements are added and removed from the collection. But, for a given size collection, a vector will use less overall memory space than will a list. For this reason, a vector, queue, or dequeue is a good candidate container if the size of the collection being maintained by a stack will remain relatively stable in size. You should select a list container when the collection will vary widely in size during program execution.

To appreciate these differences, consider the underlying container in response to the stack operations. The capacity (defined in Chapter 8) of a vector is given by the largest number of elements it has been asked to hold until a specific point in time, whereas the size of a vector (also defined in Chapter 8) represents the number of elements the vector currently holds. A push_back() will simply increase the size, unless the size reaches the capacity, in which case a memory reallocation is performed, creating a larger buffer. However, in a list container, only the elements currently in the collection are maintained. Each push() operation causes a new memory allocation, and each pop() returns the memory location to the pool of available memory.

<stack> Template Syntax

The following listing gives the syntax for the <stack> template.

```
template<class T,
    class Cont = deque<T> >
    class stack {
public:
    typedef Cont::allocator_type allocator_type;
    typedef Cont::value_type value_type;
    typedef Cont::size_type size_type;
    explicit stack(const allocator_type& al = allocator_type()) const;
    bool empty() const;
    size_type size() const;
    allocator_type get_allocator() const;
    value_type& top();
    const value_type& top() const;
    void push(const value_type& x);
    void pop();
protected:
    Cont c;
    };
```

The <stack> template class describes an object that controls a varying-length sequence of elements. The object allocates and frees storage for the sequence it controls through a protected object named `c`, of class `Cont`. The type `T` of elements in the controlled sequence must match `value_type`. An object of class `Cont` must supply several public members defined the same as for `deque`, `list`, and `vector` (all of which are suitable candidates for class `Cont`). The required members are:

```
typedef T value_type;
typedef T0 size_type;
Cont(const allocator_type& al);
bool empty() const;
size_type size() const;
allocator_type get_allocator() const;
value_type& back();
const value_type& back() const;
void push_back(const value_type& x);
void pop_back();
```

<stack> Template Overloaded Operators

The <stack> template overloads the operators shown in Table 8.1.

Table 8.1 Overloaded operators for <stack>

Overloaded Operators
bool operator==(const stack<T, Cont>& lhs, const stack<T, Cont>&);
bool operator!=(const stack<T, Cont>& lhs, const stack<T, Cont>&);
bool operator<(const stack<T, Cont>& lhs, const stack<T, Cont>&);
bool "operator>(const stack<T, Cont>& lhs, const stack<T, Cont>&);
bool operator<=(const stack<T, Cont>& lhs, const stack<T, Cont>&);
bool ="operator>=(const stack<T, Cont>& lhs, const stack<T, Cont>&);

<stack> Template Methods

The <stack> template provides the methods shown in Table 8.2.

Table 8.2 <stack> template methods and descriptions

Method	Description
explicit stack(const allocator_type& al = allocator_type()) const;	The constructor initializes the stored object with c(al), to specify an empty initial controlled sequence.
bool empty() const;	Returns true for an empty controlled sequence.
size_type size() const;	Returns the length of the controlled sequence.
allocator_type get_allocator() const;	Returns c.get_allocator().
value_type& top(); const value_type& top() const;	Returns a reference to the last element of the controlled sequence, which must be non-empty.
void push(const value_type& x);	Inserts an element with value x at the end of the controlled sequence.
void pop();	Removes the last element of the controlled sequence, which must be non-empty.

Sample Code

The following example uses the <stack> STL template to convert an infix expression into postfix. Infix expressions are the way most people think of numeric calculations such as 4 * (16 + 2 * 8) + 22. However, considering all the arithmetic operators available in mathematics, writing a compiler to correctly translate an infinite combination would require a very inefficient, time-consuming algorithm. Instead, compilers first take an infix expression, translate it into postfix, and then translate the postfix equation into machine code (postfix notation places the operators *after* the operands, for example A B + instead of the infix A + B). What looks like unnecessary overprocessing on the surface ends up saving execution time. Although the program that follows may initially look quite complicated, in essence it is a fraction of the code that would be necessary for a compiler to decipher an arithmetic equation using infix notation.

The stack.cpp Application

The following <stack> template application is based on a user-defined, stack element type of *OPERATORS*. This enumerated type arranges the arithmetic operators from lowest precedence (ordinal value of 0) to highest (in this case, *divideop* or 4):

```
// stack.cpp
// Testing <stack>
// push(), pop() top(), empty()
// Chris H. Pappas and William H. Murray, 1999

#pragma warning(disable:4786)
#include <stack>
#include <list>
#include <string>
#include <iostream>
#include <cctype>     // isdigit()

using namespace std ;

typedef enum tagOPERATORS { leftparenthesis, plusop,
                            minusop, multiplyop,
                            divideop } OPERATORS;

typedef stack<OPERATORS> CONVERSIONSTACK;


string ConvertOpToString(OPERATORS CurrentOperator);
void processOperator(OPERATORS currentOperator,
                     stack<OPERATORS>& ConversionStack,
                     string& result);
```

```
void main( void )
{
  CONVERSIONSTACK ConversionStack;

  string infix("4 * (16 + 2 * 8) + 22");
  string result("");
  int offset = 0;

  while(infix[offset] != '\0') {
    if(isdigit(infix[offset])) { // process values
     while(isdigit(infix[offset]))
       result += infix[offset++];
     result += " ";
   }
   else
     switch(infix[offset++]) { // process non-values
       case '(': ConversionStack.push(leftparenthesis);
                 break;
         case ')': while(ConversionStack.top() != leftparenthesis)
                 {
                       result += ConvertOpToString(ConversionStack.top());
                       ConversionStack.pop();
                }
                       ConversionStack.pop();
                       break;
         case '+': processOperator(plusop, ConversionStack, result);
                 break;
         case '-': processOperator(minusop, ConversionStack, result);
                 break;
         case '*': processOperator(multiplyop, ConversionStack, result);
                 break;
         case '/': processOperator(divideop, ConversionStack, result);
                  break;
         }
   }

   while(!ConversionStack.empty()) { // empty the stack
     result += ConvertOpToString(ConversionStack.top());
     ConversionStack.pop();
  }
  cout << result;
}

string ConvertOpToString(OPERATORS CurrentOperator)
{
  switch(CurrentOperator) {
    case plusop     : return " + ";
    case minusop    : return " - ";
    case multiplyop : return " * ";
```

```
    case divideop    : return " / ";
  }
}

void processOperator(OPERATORS currentOperator, stack<OPERATORS>& ConversionStack,
                string& result)
{
  while( (!ConversionStack.empty()) && (currentOperator <
ConversionStack.top()) ) {
    result += ConvertOpToString(ConversionStack.top());
                ConversionStack.pop();
  }
  ConversionStack.push(currentOperator);
}
```

The program begins by defining the stack element type OPERATORS:

```
typedef enum tagOPERATORS { leftparenthesis, plusop,
                            minusop, multiplyop,
                              divideop } OPERATORS;
```

Next, using Microsoft styling conventions, a typedef creates the *CONVERSIONSTACK* type. Notice that the stack element type is *OPERATORS*:

```
typedef stack<OPERATORS> CONVERSIONSTACK;
```

The instantiation of *ConversionStack* takes the form (seen inside main()):

```
CONVERSIONSTACK ConversionStack;
```

For the sake of clarity, a sample infix expression is wired into the program, avoiding superfluous I/O statements to interactively accept and verify any infix expression:

```
string infix("4 * (16 + 2 * 8) + 22");
```

The algorithm parses the *infix* string immediately, appending numeric constants to the *result* string:

```
while(infix[offset] != '\0') {
    if(isdigit(infix[offset])) { // process values
      while(isdigit(infix[offset]))
        result += infix[offset++];
      result += " ";
    }
```

Operators, such as + and *, cannot be output until both their arguments have been processed. Therefore, they must be saved on the *ConversionStack*. If an operator being pushed onto the stack has a lower precedence level than the current top of stack, then the top of stack is popped and appended to *result*.

```
while( (!ConversionStack.empty()) && (currentOperator < ConversionStack.top()) ) {
    result += ConvertOpToString(ConversionStack.top());
    ConversionStack.pop();
  }
  ConversionStack.push(currentOperator);
```

A left parenthesis is immediately pushed on the *ConversionStack*, regardless of the precedence of the current top of stack.

```
case '(': ConversionStack.push(leftparenthesis);
```

A left parenthesis will be considered to have a precedence lower than any other symbol, and thus will never be popped off the stack. Instead, a right parenthesis will cause the stack to be popped and output until the corresponding left parenthesis is found. Notice the use of the template function top(), used to access the current stack top *OPERATOR*:

```
case ')': while(ConversionStack.top() != leftparenthesis)
          {
            result += ConvertOpToString(ConversionStack.top());
            ConversionStack.pop();
          }
           ConversionStack.pop();
```

The left parenthesis is popped, but not appended to *result*. Finally, when the end of the *infix* expression is reached, the *ConversionStack* is popped until empty, appending symbols to the *result* string. The code segment uses the template function empty() to know when all *OPERATOR*s have been processed:

```
while(!ConversionStack.empty()) { // empty the stack
     result += ConvertOpToString(ConversionStack.top());
     ConversionStack.pop();
  }
```

You need to convert the enumerated representation of operators to strings that can be appended to *result* and explain the presence of *ConvertOpToString()*:

```
string ConvertOpToString(OPERATORS CurrentOperator)
{
  switch(CurrentOperator) {
    case plusop     : return " + ";
    case minusop    : return " - ";
    case multiplyop : return " * ";
    case divideop   : return " / ";
  }
}
```

The output from the program looks like:

```
4 16 2 8  *  +  * 22  +
```

Summary

In this chapter, you learned about the logical operations of a stack last-in-first-out or LIFO. You also discovered that the <stack> template does not directly implement its own data structures, but instead is considered one example of an adaptor class. Adaptors modify existing container functionality. The sample program demonstrated the most frequently used <stack> template functions empty(), push(), pop(), and top(), to convert an arithmetic expression from infix to postfix form, most familiar to Hewlett Packard calculator users. In Chapter 9, you will see how the <queue> and <dequeue> STL templates perform similar logical data minipulations as stacks, only at both ends of the container.

NINE

The STL <queue> and <dequeue> Templates

The <queue> template, like the <stack> template, is implemented as an adaptor that wraps around an underlying container. As with the <stack>, the <queue> adaptor does not actually provide any new functionality, but simply modifies the interface. Operations are provided with their conventional queue-like names but are actually performed using operations on the underlying containers. Containers in the standard library that implement the necessary operations for the <queue> adaptor include the <list> and the <deque> data structure that we will introduce later in the chapter.

Unlike the <stack> template, the <queue> class in STL provides the ability to access both the front and back elements of the queue, whereas the conventional description of the queue data abstraction only permits access only to the front.

The <queue> Template Syntax

The following listing gives the syntax for the <queue> template.

```
template<class T,
    class Cont = deque<T> >
    class queue {
public:
    typedef Cont::allocator_type allocator_type;
    typedef Cont::value_type value_type;
    typedef Cont::size_type size_type;
    explicit queue(const allocator_type& al = allocator_type()) const;
    bool empty() const;
    size_type size() const;
    allocator_type get_allocator() const;
    value_type& top();
    const value_type& top() const;
    void push(const value_type& x);
    void pop();
protected:
    Cont c;
    };
```

The template class describes an object that controls a varying-length sequence of elements. The object allocates and frees storage for the sequence it controls through a protected object named `c`, of class `Cont`. The type `T` of elements in the controlled sequence must match `value_type`.

An object of class `Cont` must supply several public members defined the same as for `deque` and `list` (both of which are suitable candidates for class `Cont`). The required members are:

```
typedef T value_type;
typedef T0 size_type;
Cont(const allocator_type& al);
bool empty() const;
size_type size() const;
allocator_type get_allocator() const;
value_type& front();
const value_type& front() const;
value_type& back();
const value_type& back() const;
void push_back(const value_type& x);
void pop_front();
```

Here, `T0` is an unspecified type that meets the stated requirements.

<queue> Template Methods

The <queue> template provides the methods shown in Table 9.1.

Table 9.1 <queue> Template Methods and Descriptions

Method	Description
`explicit queue(const allocator_type& al = allocator_type());`	The constructor initializes the stored object with `c(al)`, to specify an empty initial controlled sequence.
`bool empty() const;`	The member function returns true for an empty controlled sequence.
`size_type size() const;`	The member function returns the length of the controlled sequence.
`allocator_type get_allocator() const;`	The member function returns `c.get_allocator()`.
`value_type& top();` `const value_type& top() const;`	The member function returns a reference to the first element of the controlled sequence, which must be non-empty.
`void push(const T& x);`	The member function inserts an element with value x at the end of the controlled sequence.
`void pop();`	The member function removes the last element of the controlled sequence, which must be non-empty.

The <deque> Template

The <deque> template provides one of the most interesting data structures in STL. Of all the STL code provided, the <deque> is the least conventional. The <deque> template represents a data type that is seldom considered to be one of the classic data abstractions, such as vectors, lists, sets, or trees.

Upon close examination, you will discover that the operations provided by <deque> are a combination of those provided by the classes <vector> and <list>. For example, like a vector, the deque is randomly accessible, meaning that instances of the class deque can be used in many of the same situations as a vector. Similarly, like a list, elements may be inserted into the middle of a deque, although such insertions are not as efficient as in the list equivalent.

Officially, deque stands for double-ended queue, and defines the structure as well. The deque is a combination of stack and queue, allowing elements to be inserted at either end. Whereas a vector allows efficient insertion only at one end, the deque can perform insertions in constant time at either the front or the back of the container. Like a vector, a deque is a very space-efficient structure, using far less memory for a given size collection than will a list, for example. However, note that, as with a vector, insertions into the middle of the structure are permitted, but are not time-efficient. An insertion into a deque may require the movement of every element in the collection!

Typically, a deque is used as an underlying container for either a stack or a queue. The deque is the preferred container whenever the size of the collection remains relatively stable during the course of execution, although if the size varies widely, a list or vector is a better container choice. Ultimately, for time-critical applications, you will have to write the algorithm using the different forms and performing direct measurement of program size and runtime efficiency.

The <deque> Template Syntax

The following listing gives the syntax for the <deque> template:

```
template<class T, class A = allocator<T> >
    class deque {
public:
    typedef A allocator_type;
    typedef A::size_type size_type;
    typedef A::difference_type difference_type;
    typedef A::reference reference;
    typedef A::const_reference const_reference;
    typedef A::value_type value_type;
    typedef T0 iterator;
    typedef T1 const_iterator;
    typedef reverse_iterator<iterator, value_type,
        reference, A::pointer, difference_type>
            reverse_iterator;
    typedef reverse_iterator<const_iterator, value_type,
        const_reference, A::const_pointer, difference_type>
            const_reverse_iterator;
    explicit deque(const A& al = A());
    explicit deque(size_type n, const T& v = T(), const A& al = A());
    deque(const deque& x);
    deque(const_iterator first, const_iterator last,
        const A& al = A());
    iterator begin();
    const_iterator begin() const;
    iterator end();
    iterator end() const;
    reverse_iterator rbegin();
    const_reverse_iterator rbegin() const;
    reverse_iterator rend();
    const_reverse_iterator rend() const;
    void resize(size_type n, T x = T());
    size_type size() const;
    size_type max_size() const;
```

```
    bool empty() const;
    A get_allocator() const;
    reference at(size_type pos);
    const_reference at(size_type pos) const;
    reference operator[](size_type pos);
    const_reference operator[](size_type pos);
    reference front();
    const_reference front() const;
    reference back();
    const_reference back() const;
    void push_front(const T& x);
    void pop_front();
    void push_back(const T& x);
    void pop_back();
    void assign(const_iterator first, const_iterator last);
    void assign(size_type n, const T& x = T());
    iterator insert(iterator it, const T& x = T());
    void insert(iterator it, size_type n, const T& x);
    void insert(iterator it,
        const_iterator first, const_iterator last);
    iterator erase(iterator it);
    iterator erase(iterator first, iterator last);
    void clear();
    void swap(deque x);
protected:
    A allocator;
    };
```

The template class describes an object that controls a varying-length sequence of elements of type `T`. The sequence is represented in a way that permits insertion and removal of an element at either end with a single element copy (constant time). Such operations in the middle of the sequence require element copies and assignments proportional to the number of elements in the sequence (linear time).

The object allocates and frees storage for the sequence it controls through a protected object named `allocator`, of class `A`. Such an allocator object must have the same external interface as an object of template class `allocator`. Note that `allocator` is not copied when the object is assigned. Deque reallocation occurs when a member function must insert or erase elements of the controlled sequence.

<deque> Overloaded Operators

The <deque> template overloads the operators shown in Table 9.2

Table 9.2 Overloaded operators for <deque>

Overloaded Operators
`bool operator==( const deque <T, A>& lhs, const deque <T, A>& rhs);`
`bool operator!=( const deque <T, A>& lhs, const deque <T, A>& rhs);`
`bool operator<( const deque <T, A>& lhs, const deque <T, A>& rhs);`
`bool operator>( const deque <T, A>& lhs, const deque <T, A>& rhs);`
`bool operator<=( const deque <T, A>& lhs, const deque <T, A>& rhs);`
`bool operator>=( const deque <T, A>& lhs, const deque <T, A>& rhs);`

<deque> Template Methods

The <deque> template provides the methods shown in Table 9.3.

Table 9.3 <deque> Template Methods and Descriptions

Method	Description
`explicit deque(const A& al = A());` `explicit deque(size_type n, const T& v = T(), const A& al = A());` `deque(const deque& x);` `deque(const_iterator first, const_iterator last, const A& al = A());`	All constructors store the allocator object al (or, for the copy constructor, `x.get_allocator()`) in `allocator` and initialize the controlled sequence. The first constructor specifies an empty initial controlled sequence. The second constructor specifies a repetition of `n` elements of value `x`. The third constructor specifies a copy of the sequence controlled by `x`. The last constructor specifies the sequence `[first, last)`.
`const_iterator begin() const;` `iterator begin();`	The member function returns a random-access iterator that points at the first element of the sequence (or just beyond the end of an empty sequence).
`const_iterator end() const;` `iterator end();`	The member function returns a random-access iterator that points just beyond the end of the sequence.
`const_reverse_iterator rbegin() const;` `reverse_iterator rbegin();`	The member function returns a reverse iterator that points just beyond the end of the controlled sequence. Hence, it designates the beginning of the reverse sequence.
`const_reverse_iterator rend() const;` `reverse_iterator rend();`	The member function returns a reverse iterator that points at the first element of the sequence (or just beyond the end of an empty sequence). Hence, it designates the end of the reverse sequence.

Table 9.3 <deque> Template Methods and Descriptions *(continued)*

Method	Description
`void resize(size_type n, T x = T());`	The member function ensures that size() henceforth returns `n`. If it must lengthen the controlled sequence, it appends elements with value `x`.
`size_type size() const;`	The member function returns the length of the controlled sequence.
`size_type max_size() const;`	The member function returns the length of the longest sequence that the object can control.
`bool empty() const;`	The member function returns true for an empty controlled sequence.
	The member function returns `allocator`.
`const_reference at(size_type pos) const;` `reference at(size_type pos);`	The member function returns a reference to the element of the controlled sequence at position `pos`. If that position is invalid, the function throws an object of class `out_of_range`.
`const_reference operator[](size_type pos) const;` `reference operator[](size_type pos);`	The member function returns a reference to the element of the controlled sequence at position `pos`. If that position is invalid, the behavior is undefined.
`reference front();` `const_reference front() const;`	The member function returns a reference to the first element of the controlled sequence, which must be non-empty.
`reference back();` `const_reference back() const;`	The member function returns a reference to the last element of the controlled sequence, which must be non-empty.
`void push_front(const T& x);`	The member function inserts an element with value `x` at the beginning of the controlled sequence. Inserting the element invalidates all iterators, but no references, to existing elements.
`void pop_front();`	The member function removes the first element of the controlled sequence, which must be non-empty. Removing the element invalidates only iterators and references that designate the erased element.
`void push_back(const T& x);`	The member function inserts an element with value `x` at the end of the controlled sequence. Inserting the element invalidates all iterators, but no references, to existing elements.

Table 9.3 <deque> Template Methods and Descriptions *(continued)*

Method	Description
`void pop_back();`	The member function removes the last element of the controlled sequence, which must be non-empty. Removing the element invalidates only iterators and references that designate the erased element.
`void assign(const_iterator first, const_iterator last);` `void assign(size_type n, const T& x = T());`	The first member function replaces the sequence controlled by `*this` with the sequence `[first, last)`. The second member function replaces the sequence controlled by `*this` with a repetition of `n` elements of value `x`.

`iterator insert(iterator it, const T& x = T());`
`void insert(iterator it, size_type n, const T& x);`
`void insert(iterator it, const_iterator first, const_iterator last);`
	Each of the member functions inserts, before the element pointed to by `it` in the controlled sequence, a sequence specified by the remaining operands. The first member function inserts a single element with value `x` and returns an iterator that points to the newly inserted element. The second member function inserts a repetition of `n` elements of value `x`. The last member function inserts the sequence `[first, last)`.

`iterator erase(iterator it);` `iterator erase(iterator first, iterator last);`	The first member function removes the element of the controlled sequence pointed to by `it`. The second member function removes the elements of the controlled sequence in the range `[first, last)`. Both return an iterator that designates the first element remaining beyond any elements removed, or `end()` if no such element exists. Removing `N` elements causes `N` destructor calls and an assignment for each of the elements between the insertion point and the nearer end of the sequence. Removing an element at either end invalidates only iterators and references that designate the erased elements. Otherwise, erasing an element invalidates all iterators and references.
`void clear() const;`	The member function calls `erase( begin(), end())`.
`void swap(deque& str);`	The member function swaps the controlled sequences between `*this` and `str`. If `allocator == str.allocator`, it does so in constant time. Otherwise, it performs a number of element assignments and constructor calls proportional to the number of elements in the two controlled sequences.

Sample Code

The following sample applications illustrate various <queue> and <deque> methods and areas of caution when using these templates.

The queue.cpp Application

The following application illustrates the <queue> template's most frequently used methods, highlighting the actions of a logical queue's first-in-first-out (FIFO) algorithm. The <queue> is implemented as a <list> container. The queue.cpp application instantiates both an integer and character queue for comparison purposes.

```
// queue.cpp
// Testing <queue>
// push(), pop(), empty(), back(), front(), size()
// Chris H. Pappas and William H. Murray


#include <list> // access to front() template function
#include <queue>
#include <iostream>

using namespace std ;

// queue implemented as <list> container
typedef list<int > INT_LIST_TYPE;
typedef queue<int>  INT_QUEUE_TYPE;
typedef queue<char*> CHAR_QUEUE_TYPE;

#define SPACER cout << "\n\n"

void main( void )
{
  int queueSize;

  INT_QUEUE_TYPE intQ;
  CHAR_QUEUE_TYPE charQ;

  // Pushing elements onto the queue
  intQ.push(1);
  intQ.push(2);
  intQ.push(3);
  intQ.push(4);
  intQ.push(5);
  intQ.push(6);


  // Verify queue size
```

```
  queueSize = intQ.size();
  cout << "The intQ contains " << queueSize << " elements\n\n";

  // Print queue elements in order
  // Elements accessed using front()
  // Elements removed using pop()
  while( !intQ.empty() )
  {
    cout << intQ.front() << endl;
    intQ.pop();

  }

  // Insert items in the queue(uses deque)
  charQ.push("First  in Q");
  charQ.push("Second in Q");
  charQ.push("Third  in Q");
  charQ.push("Fourth in Q");
  charQ.push("Fifth  in Q");

  SPACER;

  // Output the item inserted last using back()
  cout << "The last item inserted into charQ: "
       << "\"" << charQ.back() << "\"" << endl;

  // Output the size of queue
  queueSize = charQ.size();
  cout << "\nThe size of charQ is:" << queueSize << endl;

  SPACER;

  // Output items in queue using front()
  // and use pop() to get to next item until
  // queue is empty
  while (!charQ.empty())
  {
    cout << charQ.front() << endl;
    charQ.pop();

  }
}
```

Both *intQ* and *charQ* use the push() template function to add items to the back of their respective queues. Notice that the size() template function reports the actual number of elements contained within each queue.

The empty() template function provides an easy, reliable way to traverse queue list elements and drives the **while** loop test conditions:

```
while( !intQ.empty() )
  {
    cout << intQ.front() << endl;
    intQ.pop();

  }
```

The <list> template class provides the underlying front() template function required by the <queue> adaptor class providing access to the containers front element. Note, however, that accessing the front element does not remove the element and explains the call to pop(), which officially deletes the front element after output.

The output from the program looks like:

```
The intQ contains 6 elements

1
2
3
4
5
6


The last item inserted into charQ: "Fifth  in Q"

The size of charQ is:5


First  in Q
Second in Q
Third  in Q
Fourth in Q
Fifth  in Q
```

The deque.cpp Application

For a slight change of pace, the deque.cpp application illustrates several of the overloaded deque operators—equality, less-than, and greater-than. The application also uses the assign() template function to copy the contents of *intDQ2* to *intDQ1*.

```
// intDQ.cpp
// Testing <intDQ>
// Overloaded operators ==, >, <,
// push_front(), begin(), end(), and assign()
// Chris H. Pappas and William H. Murray

#include <deque>
#include <iostream>
```

```
using namespace std;

typedef deque<int>  INT_DEQUEUE_TYPE;
void printDequeue (INT_DEQUEUE_TYPE  intDQ, char*);

void main( void )
{
  // intDQ1 initialized with 4 1s
  INT_DEQUEUE_TYPE  intDQ1(4,1);

  // a 2 pushed to the front of intDQ1
  intDQ1.push_front(2);

  // intDQ2's initialized with 3 0s
  INT_DEQUEUE_TYPE  intDQ2(3,0);

  // print current container elements
    printDequeue (intDQ1,"intDQ1");
    printDequeue (intDQ2,"intDQ2");

  // check equality of intDQ1 and intDQ2
  if( intDQ1 == intDQ2 )
    cout <<"intDQ1 is equal to intDQ2"<<endl;
  else if( intDQ1 > intDQ2 )
      cout <<"intDQ1 is greater than intDQ2"<<endl;
    else
      cout <<"intDQ1 is less than intDQ2" <<endl;

  //assign the contents of intDQ2 to intDQ1
  intDQ1.assign(intDQ2.begin(),intDQ2.end());
  printDequeue (intDQ1,"intDQ1");
  printDequeue (intDQ2,"intDQ2");

  //compare intDQ1 and intDQ2 again
  if( intDQ1 == intDQ2 )
    cout <<"intDQ1 is equal to intDQ2"<<endl;
  else if( intDQ1 < intDQ2 )
      cout <<"intDQ1 is less than intDQ2"<<endl;
    else
      cout <<"intDQ1 is greater than intDQ2" <<endl;

}

void printDequeue (INT_DEQUEUE_TYPE  intDQ, char *name)
{
  INT_DEQUEUE_TYPE::iterator pintDQ;

  cout << name <<" contains these elements: ";
  for(pintDQ = intDQ.begin(); pintDQ != intDQ.end();
```

```
        pintDQ++) {
      cout << *pintDQ <<" " ;
    }
    cout<<endl;
}
```

The first overloaded operator (==) compares two objects of template class deque. The function returns: intDQ1.size() == intDQ2.size(). For equality, the number of elements must be equal in both deque objects.

The second overloaded operator (>) compares two objects of template class deque. The function returns: lexicographical_compare(intDQ1.begin(), intDQ1.end(), intDQ2.begin(), intDQ2.end()). Because lexicographic (as in a dictionary) compare is used, the number of elements does not matter while using the overloaded operator > . For this reason *intDQ1* is greater than *intDQ2*, *not* because it has more elements, but because *2* is greater than *0*.

The output from the program looks like:

```
intDQ1 contains these elements: 2 1 1 1 1
intDQ2 contains these elements: 0 0 0
intDQ1 is greater than intDQ2
intDQ1 contains these elements: 0 0 0
intDQ2 contains these elements: 0 0 0
intDQ1 is equal to intDQ2
```

Summary

In this chapter, you explored both the <queue> and <deque> templates; both structures maintain collections of values in a linear sequence. In a queue, values are inserted at one end and removed from the other, unlike the <stack>, which inserts and removes elements from one end.

You learned that while queues can be built on top of list structures, the advantage of a vector or deque implementation is improved performance, while the advantage of a list implementation is greater flexibility, because the number of elements need not be known in advance.

The deque, or double-ended queue, is a data structure that provides a combination of features from both the vector and list types. Like a vector, a deque is a randomly accessible and indexed data structure. Like a list, elements can be efficiently inserted at either the front or the end of the structure. This possibility actually provides a deque with both the actions of either a stack-like or a queue-like behavior.

Chapter 10 discusses the <list> STL. After reading this next chapter, you may want to return to this one to further understand the operations of the two template requirements and use.

TEN

The STL <list> Template

A <list> container is your best choice when the number of elements in a collection cannot be bounded or varies widely during the course of execution. Like a vector, a list maintains values of uniform type. Unlike a vector, a list can hold any number of values. Lists are not indexed. Instead, elements must be examined one by one in sequence. For this reason, the amount of time required to access an element in a list depends upon the position the element holds in the list.
Using an iterator to denote a given location, insertion into or deletion from a list can be performed in constant time. As with a vector, to determine whether or not a specific value occurs in a list requires a sequential search. Although a list can be ordered, you cannot perform a binary search on a list, and therefore the sequential search time is generally the best that can be achieved.

<list> Template Syntax

The following listing gives the syntax for the <list> template:

```
template<class T, class A = allocator<T> >
    class list {
public:
    typedef A allocator_type;
    typedef A::size_type size_type;
    typedef A::difference_type difference_type;
    typedef A::reference reference;
    typedef A::const_reference const_reference;
    typedef A::value_type value_type;
    typedef T0 iterator;
    typedef T1 const_iterator;
    typedef reverse_bidirectional_iterator<iterator,
        value_type, reference, A::pointer,
            difference_type> reverse_iterator;
    typedef reverse_bidirectional_iterator<const_iterator,
        value_type, const_reference, A::const_pointer,
            difference_type> const_reverse_iterator;
    explicit list(const A& al = A());
    explicit list(size_type n, const T& v = T(), const A& al = A());
    list(const list& x);
    list(const_iterator first, const_iterator last,
        const A& al = A());
    iterator begin();
    const_iterator begin() const;
    iterator end();
    iterator end() const;
    reverse_iterator rbegin();
    const_reverse_iterator rbegin() const;
    reverse_iterator rend();
    const_reverse_iterator rend() const;
    void resize(size_type n, T x = T());
    size_type size() const;
    size_type max_size() const;
    bool empty() const;
```

```
A get_allocator() const;
reference front();
const_reference front() const;
reference back();
const_reference back() const;
void push_front(const T& x);
void pop_front();
void push_back(const T& x);
void pop_back();
void assign(const_iterator first, const_iterator last);
void assign(size_type n, const T& x = T());
iterator insert(iterator it, const T& x = T());
void insert(iterator it, size_type n, const T& x);
void insert(iterator it,
    const_iterator first, const_iterator last);
void insert(iterator it,
    const T *first, const T *last);
iterator erase(iterator it);
iterator erase(iterator first, iterator last);
void clear();
void swap(list x);
void splice(iterator it, list& x);
void splice(iterator it, list& x, iterator first);
void splice(iterator it, list& x, iterator first, iterator last);
void remove(const T& x);
void remove_if(binder2nd<not_equal_to<T> > pr);
void unique();
void unique(not_equal_to<T> pr);
void merge(list& x);
void merge(list& x, greater<T> pr);
void sort();
template<class Pred>
    void sort(greater<T> pr);
void reverse();
```

```
protected:
    A allocator;
    };
```

The <list> template class describes an object that controls a varying-length sequence of elements of type T. The sequence is stored as a bidirectional linked list of elements, each containing a member of type T. The object allocates and frees storage for the sequence it controls through a protected object named allocator, of class A.

List reallocation occurs when a method must insert or erase elements within the container. In all such cases, only iterators or references that point at erased portions of the list become invalid.

The <list> template uses the following ten **typedef**s:

allocator_type

The *allocator_type* is a synonym for the template parameter A and has the following syntax:

```
typedef A allocator_type;
```

size_type

The *size_type* is defined as an unsigned integer that can represent the length of any list type. The syntax looks like:

```
typedef A::size_type size_type;
```

difference_type

The *difference_type* is defined as a signed integer that can represent the difference between the addresses of any two elements in a list. The syntax looks like:

```
typedef A::difference_type difference_type;
```

reference

The *reference* type describes an object that can serve as a reference to an element of a list. The syntax looks like:

```
typedef A::reference reference;
```

const_reference

The *const_reference* describes an object that can serve as a constant reference to an element of the list. The syntax looks like:

```
typedef A::const_reference const_reference;
```

value_type

The *value_type* is a synonym for the template parameter `T`. The syntax looks like:

```
typedef A::value_type value_type;
```

iterator

The *iterator* type describes an object that can serve as a bidirectional iterator for the list. It is described here as a synonym for the unspecified type `T0`. The syntax looks like:

```
typedef T0 iterator;
```

const_iterator

The *const_iterator* describes an object that can serve as a constant bidirectional iterator for the list. It is described here as a synonym for the unspecified type `T1`. The syntax looks like:

```
typedef T1 const_iterator;
```

reverse_iterator

The *reverse_iterator* defines an object that can serve as a reverse bidirectional iterator for the list. The syntax looks like:

```
typedef reverse_bidirectional_iterator<iterator,
    value_type, reference, A::pointer,
        difference_type> reverse_iterator;
```

const_reverse_iterator

The *const_reverse_iterator* describes an object that can serve as a constant reverse bidirectional iterator for the list. The syntax looks like:

```
typedef reverse_bidirectional_iterator<const_iterator,
    value_type, const_reference, A::const_pointer,
        difference_type> const_reverse_iterator;
```

<list>Template Methods

The <list> template provides the methods shown in Table 10.1.

Table 10.1 <list> template methods and descriptions

Method	Description
`explicit list(const A& al = A());` `explicit list(size_type n, const T& v = T(), const A& al = A());` `list(const list& x);` `list(const_iterator first, const_iterator last, const A& al = A());`	All constructors store the allocator object `al` (or, for the copy constructor, `x.()`) in and initialize the list. The first constructor specifies an empty initial list. The second constructor specifies a repetition of `n` elements of value `x`. The third constructor specifies a copy of the sequence controlled by `x`. The last constructor specifies the sequence `[first, last)`. None of the constructors perform any interim reallocations.
`const_iterator begin() const;` `iterator begin();`	The method returns a bidirectional iterator that points at the first element of the sequence (or just beyond the end of an empty sequence).
`const_iterator end() const;` `iterator end();`	The method returns a bidirectional iterator that points just beyond the end of the sequence.
`const_reverse_iterator rbegin() const;` `reverse_iterator rbegin();`	The method returns a reverse bidirectional iterator that points just beyond the end of the list.
`const_reverse_iterator rend() const;` `reverse_iterator rend();`	The method returns a reverse bidirectional iterator that points at the first element of the sequence (or just beyond the end of an empty sequence).
`void resize(size_type n, T x = T());`	The method ensures that `()` henceforth returns `n`. If it must make the list longer, it appends elements with value `x`.
`size_type size() const;`	The method returns the length of the list.
`size_type max_size() const;`	The method returns the length of the longest sequence that the object can control.
`bool empty() const;`	The method returns true for an empty list.
`get_allocator() const;`	The member function returns allocator.
`reference front();` `const_reference front() const;`	The method returns a reference to the first element of the list, which must be non-empty.

Table 10.1 <list> template methods and descriptions *(continued)*

Method	Description
`reference back();` `const_reference back() const;`	The method returns a reference to the last element of the list, which must be non-empty.
`void push_front(const T& x);`	The method inserts an element with value `x` at the beginning of the list.
`void pop_front();`	The method removes the first element of the list, which must be non-empty.
`void push_back(const T& x);`	The method inserts an element with value `x` at the end of the list.
`void pop_back();`	The method removes the last element of the list, which must be non-empty.
`void assign(const_iterator first, const_iterator last);` `void assign(size_type n, const T& x = T());`	The first method replaces the sequence controlled by `*this` with the sequence `[first, last)`. The second method replaces the sequence controlled by `*this` with a repetition of `n` elements of value `x`.

`iterator insert(iterator it, const T& x = T());`
`void insert(iterator it, size_type n, const T& x);`
`void insert(iterator it, const_iterator first, const_iterator last);`
	Each of the methods inserts, before the element pointed to by `it` in the list, a sequence specified by the remaining operands. The first method inserts a single element with value `x` and returns an iterator that points to the newly inserted element. The second method inserts a repetition of `n` elements of value `x`. The last method inserts the sequence `[first, last)`.

`iterator erase(iterator it);` `iterator erase(iterator first, iterator last);`	The first method removes the element of the list pointed to by `it`. The second method removes the elements of the list in the range `[first, last)`. Both return an iterator that designates the first element remaining beyond any elements removed. Erasing `N` elements causes `N` destructor calls. No reallocation occurs, so iterators and references become invalid only for the erased elements.
`void clear() const;`	The method calls `erase( begin(), end())`.

Table 10.1 <list> template methods and descriptions *(continued)*

Method	Description
void swap(list& str);	The method swaps the lists between *this and str. If == str.allocator, it does so in constant time. Otherwise, it performs a number of element assignments and constructor calls proportional to the number of elements in the two lists.

void splice(iterator it, list& x);
void splice(iterator it, list& x, iterator first);
void splice(iterator it, list& x, iterator first, iterator last);
	The first method inserts the sequence controlled by x before the element in the list pointed to by it. It also removes all elements from x. (&x must not equal this.) The second method removes the element pointed to by first in the sequence controlled by x and inserts it before the element in the list pointed to by it. (If it == first || it == ++first, no change occurs.) The third method inserts the subrange designated by [first, last) from the sequence controlled by x before the element in the list pointed to by it. It also removes the original subrange from the sequence controlled by x. (If &x == this, the range [first, last) must not include the element pointed to by it.)

void remove(const T& x);	The method removes from the list all elements designated by the iterator P, for which *P == x.
void remove_if(binder2nd<not_equal_to<T> > pr);	The method removes from the list all elements, designated by the iterator P, for which pr(*P) is true.
void unique(); void unique(not_equal_to<T> pr);	The first method removes from the list every element that compares equal to its preceding element. For the iterators Pi and Pj designating elements at positions i and j, the second method removes every element for which i + 1 == j && pr(*Pi, *Pj).

<list> template methods and descriptions *(continued)*

Method	Description
`void merge(list& x);` `void merge(list& x, greater<T> pr);`	Both methods remove all elements from the sequence controlled by `x` and insert them into the list. Both sequences must be ordered by the same predicate, described below. The resulting sequence is also ordered by that predicate. For the iterators `Pi` and `Pj` designating elements at positions `i` and `j`, the first method imposes the order `!(*Pj < *Pi)` whenever `i < j`. (The elements are sorted in ascending order.) The second method imposes the order `!pr(*Pj, *Pi)` whenever `i < j`.

`void sort();`
`template<class Pred>`
`void sort(greater<T> pr);`
	Both methods order the elements in the list by a predicate, described below. For the iterators `Pi` and `Pj` designating elements at positions `i` and `j`, the first method imposes the order `!(*Pj < *Pi)` whenever `i < j`. (The elements are sorted in ascending order.) The member template function imposes the order `!pr(*Pj, *Pi)` whenever `i < j`. No pairs of elements in the original list are reversed in the resulting list.

`void reverse();`	The method reverses the order in which elements appear in the list.

In the next section, you'll learn how to apply many of these <list> methods in actual sample applications.

Sample Code

The list1.cpp Application

The first example demonstrates the use of four **char** type lists. *ListA* and *ListB* are initialized when they are instantiated, whereas *ListC* and *ListD* are initialized at run-time with the insert() method:

```
// list1.cpp
// Testing <list>
// insert(), begin(), end()
// Chris H. Pappas and William H. Murray

#include <list>
#include <iostream>

using namespace std ;

typedef list<char> CHAR_LIST_TYPE;

void main( void )
{
  char ListA[] = {'a','b','c'};
  char ListB[] = {'x','y','z','w'};

  CHAR_LIST_TYPE ListC;
  CHAR_LIST_TYPE ListD;
  CHAR_LIST_TYPE::iterator ListIterator;

  // After inserts ListC contains: m f q
  ListC.insert (ListC.begin(), 'f');
  ListC.insert (ListC.begin(), 'm');
  ListC.insert (ListC.end(), 'q');

  // Print m f q
  for (ListIterator = ListC.begin(); ListIterator != ListC.end();
       ++ListIterator)
    cout << *ListIterator << " ";
  cout << endl;

  // Insert 4 ks
  ListC.insert (ListC.end(), 4, 'k');

  // Print m f q k k k k
  for (ListIterator = ListC.begin(); ListIterator != ListC.end();
       ++ListIterator)
    cout << *ListIterator << " ";
  cout << endl;

  // Add a b c to ListC
  ListC.insert (ListC.end(), ListA, ListA + 3);
  // Print m f q k k k a b c
  for (ListIterator = ListC.begin(); ListIterator != ListC.end();
       ++ListIterator)
    cout << *ListIterator << " ";
  cout << endl;

  // ListD is appended with first two elements of ListB: x y
```

```
  ListD.insert (ListD.begin(), ListB, ListB+2);

  // ListC gets an entire copy of ListD from begin() to end()
  ListC.insert (ListC.end(), ListD.begin(), ListD.end());

  // Print ListC's copied contents of ListD
  for (ListIterator = ListC.begin(); ListIterator != ListC.end();
       ++ListIterator)
     cout << *ListIterator << " ";
  cout << endl;
}
```

The straightforward output from the program looks like:

```
m f q m f q k k k k m f q k k k a b c m f q k k k k a b c x y
```

The next application adds to your understanding of list manipulation by adding the methods push_front(), push_back(), assign(), and erase().

The list2.cpp Application

The following program highlights the stack capabilities of a list with push_front(), and the queue logic of push_back() or adding an element at the end of a list. *ListB* sees a lot of action with initializations and multiple element reassignments with the use of the assign() method. Finally, *ListB* is deleted entirely with a call to the erase() method:

```
// list2.cpp
// Testing <list>
// push_front(), push_back(), assign(), begin(0, end(), erase()
// Chris H. Pappas and William H. Murray

#include <list>
#include <iostream>

using namespace std ;

typedef list<int> INT_LIST_TYPE;

void main( void )
{
  INT_LIST_TYPE ListA;
  INT_LIST_TYPE ListB;
  INT_LIST_TYPE::iterator ListIterator;

  // Initialize ListA with 4 values: 11 12 40 44
  ListA.push_front(12);
  ListA.push_front(11);
  ListA.push_back(40);
  ListA.push_back(44);
```

```
  cout << "ListA contains: ";
  for (ListIterator = ListA.begin(); ListIterator != ListA.end();
       ++ListIterator)
    cout << *ListIterator << " ";
  cout << endl;

  // Initialize ListB with 5
  ListB.push_front(5);

  // Print ListB
  cout << "ListB contains: ";
  for (ListIterator = ListB.begin(); ListIterator != ListB.end();
       ++ListIterator)
    cout << *ListIterator << " ";
  cout << endl;

  // Reassign ListB to ListA's contents
  ListB.assign(ListA.begin(), ListA.end());

  // Reprint ListB
  cout << "ListB now looks like ListA: ";
  for (ListIterator = ListB.begin(); ListIterator != ListB.end();
       ++ListIterator)
    cout << *ListIterator << " ";
  cout << endl;

  ListB.assign(5,2);

  // Reassign ListB to 5 2s
  cout << "ListB reassigned 5 2s: ";
  for (ListIterator = ListB.begin(); ListIterator != ListB.end();
       ++ListIterator)
    cout << *ListIterator << " ";
  cout << endl;


  // Erase the first element in ListB
  ListB.erase(ListB.begin());

  // Reprint ListB minus first 2
  cout << "ListB minus the first element: ";
  for (ListIterator = ListB.begin(); ListIterator != ListB.end();
       ++ListIterator)
    cout << *ListIterator << " ";
  cout << endl;

  // Erase all of ListB and verify with if...empty()
  ListB.erase(ListB.begin(), ListB.end());
  if( ListB.empty() )
    cout << "ListB has been erased!";
}
```

Pay particular attention to the order in which *ListA* is initialized in the following four lines of source code:

```
ListA.push_front(12);
ListA.push_front(11);
ListA.push_back(40);
ListA.push_back(44);
```

The second call to push_front() inserts the *11* in front of the first value placed into the container, or *12*. The calls to push_back(), however, add list elements in the order you would expect. The output from the program looks like:

```
ListA contains: 11 12 40 44

ListB contains: 5

ListB now looks like ListA: 11 12 40 44

ListB reassigned 5 2s: 2 2 2 2 2

ListB minus the first element: 2 2 2 2

ListB has been erased!
```

The list3.cpp Application

This next application reverses *ListA*'s contents, displays the list's size() and max_size(), then sort()s the list and finally splices the middle of *ListB* after the first element in *ListA*:

```
// list3.cpp
// Testing <list>
// size(), max_size(), sort(), reverse(), splice(), begin(), end()
// Chris H. Pappas and William H. Murray

#include <list>
#include <iostream>

using namespace std ;

typedef list<int> INT_LIST_TYPE;

void main( void )
{
  INT_LIST_TYPE ListA;
  INT_LIST_TYPE ListB;
  INT_LIST_TYPE::iterator ListIterator;

  //Print size() and max_size() of ListA;
  cout << "ListA's size: " << ListA.size() << endl;
  cout << "ListA's max_size " << ListA.max_size() << endl;

  // Initialize ListA with 4 values: 10 11 12 13
```

```
ListA.push_front(11);
ListA.push_front(10);
ListA.push_back(12);
ListA.push_back(13);

//Print size() and max_size() of ListA;
cout << "ListA's size: " << ListA.size() << endl;
cout << "ListA's max_size " << ListA.max_size() << endl;

cout << "ListA contains: ";
for (ListIterator = ListA.begin(); ListIterator != ListA.end();
     ++ListIterator)
  cout << *ListIterator << " ";
cout << endl;

// Reverse ListA
ListA.reverse();

// Reversed ListA
cout << "ListA reversed: ";
for (ListIterator = ListA.begin(); ListIterator != ListA.end();
     ++ListIterator)
  cout << *ListIterator << " ";
cout << endl;

// Sort ListA
ListA.sort();

// ListA after a call to the method sort()
cout << "ListA sorted  : ";
for (ListIterator = ListA.begin(); ListIterator != ListA.end();
     ++ListIterator)
  cout << *ListIterator << " ";
cout << endl;

// Initialize Listb
ListB.insert(ListB.end(),1);
ListB.insert(ListB.end(),2);
ListB.insert(ListB.end(),3);
ListB.insert(ListB.end(),4);
ListB.insert(ListB.end(),5);

// ListB after being initialized
cout << "ListB contains: ";
for (ListIterator = ListB.begin(); ListIterator != ListB.end();
     ++ListIterator)
  cout << *ListIterator << " ";
cout << endl;

// Splicing ListB's 2 3 4, after ListA's 10
```

```
  ListA.splice(++ListA.begin(),ListB, ++ListB.begin(), --ListB.end());

  // ListA after splicing with subrange of ListB
  cout << "ListA reversed: ";
  for (ListIterator = ListA.begin(); ListIterator != ListA.end();
       ++ListIterator)
    cout << *ListIterator << " ";
  cout << endl;

// ListB after the splice()
  cout << "ListB contains: ";
  for (ListIterator = ListB.begin(); ListIterator != ListB.end();
       ++ListIterator)
    cout << *ListIterator << " ";
  cout << endl;
}
```

Of the methods used in list3.cpp, the one needing additional explanation is splice():

```
// Splicing ListB's 2 3 4, after ListA's 10
ListA.splice(++ListA.begin(),ListB, ++ListB.begin(), --ListB.end());
```

The splice() method has four arguments, the insertion point for the receiving list, the source list's location, where within the source list to begin transferring information, and wherre to end. These parameters are, in order: *++ListA.begin(), ListB, ++ListB.begin(), --ListB.end()*. Notice the use of the prefix increment ++ and decrement -- operators to shift these default starting and ending points.

You will notice from the program's output, seen below, that splice() doesn't just copy the source's subrange but transfers the elements:

```
ListA's size: 0
ListA's max_size 1073741823
ListA's size: 4
ListA's max_size 1073741823
ListA contains: 10 11 12 13
ListA reversed: 13 12 11 10
ListA sorted  : 10 11 12 13
ListB contains: 1 2 3 4 5
ListA reversed: 10 2 3 4 11 12 13
ListB contains: 1 5
```

Summary

In this chapter, we have examined the STL <list> template. A list is an unordered collection of values. Unlike a vector, a list has no fixed size, but instead grows or shrinks as elements are added or removed from the structure. In the basic list structure, elements can be added or removed only from the front or back of the list. By means of iterators, elements can be added or removed from the middle of a list as was the case with splice().

E L E V E N

The STL <map> Template

Many languages support the concept of a map, sometimes referred to as a table, dictionary, associative array, or vector, meaning an indexed collection of data. However, unlike a vector with integer indices, maps may be keyed on different data types. You can think of a map as a collection of associations of key and value pairs. Certainly a phone book meets this definition, with the phone number being the key and the associated value being the owner's name.

Containers Revisited

Since most people learn by way of repetition, the following **Cont** template is reproduced from an earlier chapter to remind you of those characteristics common to all containers:

```
namespace std {
template<class T, class A>
    class Cont;
//    TEMPLATE FUNCTIONS
template<class T, class A>
    bool operator==(
        const Cont<T, A>& lhs,
        const Cont<T, A>& rhs);
template<class T, class A>
    bool operator!=(
        const Cont<T, A>& lhs,
```

```
            const Cont<T, A>& rhs);
    template<class T, class A>
        bool operator<(
            const Cont<T, A>& lhs,
            const Cont<T, A>& rhs);
    template<class T, class A>
        bool "operator>(
            const Cont<T, A>& lhs,
            const Cont<T, A>& rhs);
    template<class T, class A>
        bool operator<=(
            const Cont<T, A>& lhs,
            const Cont<T, A>& rhs);
    template<class T, class A>
        bool ="operator>=(
            const Cont<T, A>& lhs,
            const Cont<T, A>& rhs);
    template<class T, class A>
        void swap(
            const Cont<T, A>& lhs,
            const Cont<T, A>& rhs);
        };
```

Remember that a container is an STL template class that manages a sequence of elements. These elements can be of any object type that supplies a default constructor, a destructor, and an assignment operator. Also, particular container template classes can have additional template parameters and additional methods. The STL template container classes are: deque, list, map, multimap, multiset, set, and vector. Even the Standard C++ library template class `string` meets the requirements for a template container class.

<map> Template Syntax

The following listing gives the syntax for the <map> template:

```
template<class Key, class T, class Pred = less<Key>, class A =
allocator<T> >
    class map {
public:
    typedef Key key_type;
    typedef T referent_type;
    typedef Pred key_compare;
    typedef A allocator_type;
    typedef pair<const Key, T> value_type;
    class value_compare;
    typedef A::size_type size_type;
    typedef A::difference_type difference_type;
    typedef A::rebind<value_type>::other::reference reference;
```

```
    typedef A::rebind<value_type>::other::const_reference
const_reference;
    typedef T0 iterator;
    typedef T1 const_iterator;
    typedef reverse_bidirectional_iterator<iterator,
        value_type, reference, A::pointer,
            difference_type> reverse_iterator;
    typedef reverse_bidirectional_iterator<const_iterator,
        value_type, const_reference, A::const_pointer,
            difference_type> const_reverse_iterator;
    explicit map(const Pred& comp = Pred(), const A& al = A());
    map(const map& x);
    map(const value_type *first, const value_type *last,
        const Pred& comp = Pred(),
            const A& al = A());
    iterator begin();
    const_iterator begin() const;
    iterator end();
    iterator end() const;
    reverse_iterator rbegin();
    const_reverse_iterator rbegin() const;
    reverse_iterator rend();
    const_reverse_iterator rend() const;
    size_type size() const;
    size_type max_size() const;
    bool empty() const;
    A get_allocator() const;
    A::reference operator[](const Key& key);
    pair<iterator, bool> insert(const value_type& x);
    iterator insert(iterator it, const value_type& x);
    void insert(const value_type *first, const value_type *last);
    iterator erase(iterator it);
    iterator erase(iterator first, iterator last);
    size_type erase(const Key& key);
    void clear();
    void swap(map x);
    key_compare key_comp() const;
    value_compare value_comp() const;
    iterator find(const Key& key);
    const_iterator find(const Key& key) const;
    size_type count(const Key& key) const;
    iterator lower_bound(const Key& key);
    const_iterator lower_bound(const Key& key) const;
    iterator upper_bound(const Key& key);
    const_iterator upper_bound(const Key& key) const;
    pair<iterator, iterator> equal_range(const Key& key);
    pair<const_iterator, const_iterator>
        equal_range(const Key& key) const;
protected:
    A allocator;
    };
```

Officially, the template class defines a container that controls a varying-length sequence of elements of **pair** (see the typedef later in this chapter). The first element of each pair is the sort key and the second is its associated value. A map container allows the operations of lookup, insertion, and removal of an arbitrary element with a number of operations proportional to the logarithm of the number of elements in the sequence.

<map> Template Methods

The <map> template provides the methods shown in Table 11.1.

Table 11.1 <map> template methods and descriptions

Method	Description

`explicit map(const Pred& comp = Pred(), const A& al = A());`
`map(const map& x);`
`map(const value_type *first, const value_type *last, const Pred& comp = Pred(), const A& al = A());`
	The constructors with an argument named `comp` store the function object so that it can be later returned by calling `key_comp()`. All constructors also store the allocator object `al` (or, for the copy constructor, `x.get_allocator()`) in `allocator` and initialize the controlled container. The first constructor defines an empty initial controlled container. The second constructor defines a copy of the container controlled by `x`. The last constructor defines the container of element values `[first, last)`.

`const_iterator begin() const;` `iterator begin();`	The method returns a bidirectional iterator that points at the first element of the container (or just beyond the end of an empty container).
`const_iterator end() const;` `iterator end();`	The method returns a bidirectional iterator that points just beyond the end of the container.
`const_reverse_iterator rbegin() const;` `reverse_iterator rbegin();`	The method returns a reverse bidirectional iterator that points just beyond the end of the container. Therefore, it identifies the beginning of the reverse container.
`const_reverse_iterator rend() const;` `reverse_iterator rend();`	The method returns a reverse bidirectional iterator that points at the first element of the container (or just beyond the end of an empty container). Therefore, it identifies the end of the reverse container.

Table 11.1 <map> template methods and descriptions *(continued)*

Method	Description
`size_type size() const;`	The method returns the length of the container.
`size_type max_size() const;`	The method returns the length of the longest container that the object can control.
`bool empty() const;`	The method returns true for an empty container.
`A get_allocator() const;`	The method returns allocator.
`A::reference operator[](const Key& key);`	The method determines the iterator `it` as the return value of `insert( value_type(key, T())`. (It inserts an element with the specified key if no such element exists.) It then returns a reference to `(*it). second`.
`pair<iterator, bool> insert(const value_type& x);` `iterator insert(iterator it, const value_type& x);` `void insert(const value_type *first, const value_type *last);`	The first method determines whether an element `y` exists in the container whose key matches that of `x`. (The keys match if `!key_comp()(x. first, y.first) && !key_comp()(y.first, x.first)`.) If not, it creates such an element `y` and initializes it with `x`. The function then determines the iterator `it` that identifies `y`. If an insertion occurred, the function returns `pair(it, true)`. Otherwise, it returns `pair(it, false)`. The second method returns `insert(x)`, using `it` as a starting place within the container to search for the insertion point. (Insertion can occur in amortized constant time, instead of logarithmic time, if the insertion point immediately follows `it`.) The third method inserts the container of element values in the range `[first, last)`.
`iterator erase(iterator it);` `iterator erase(iterator first, iterator last);` `size_type erase(const Key& key);`	The first method removes the element of the container pointed to by `it`. The second method removes the elements in the interval `[first, last)`. Both return an iterator that identifies the first element remaining beyond any elements removed, or `end()` if no such element exists. The third method removes the elements with sort keys in the range `[lower_bound(key), upper_bound(key))`. It returns the number of elements removed.

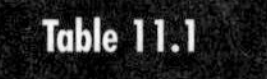
<map> template methods and descriptions *(continued)*

Method	Description
void clear() const;	The method calls erase(begin(), end()).
void swap(map& str);	The method swaps the containers between *this and str. If allocator == str.allocator, it does so in constant time. Otherwise, it performs a number of element assignments and constructor calls proportional to the number of elements in the two containers.
key_compare key_comp() const;	The method returns the stored function object that determines the order of elements in the container.
value_compare value_comp() const;	The method returns a function object that determines the order of elements in the container.
iterator find(const Key& key); const_iterator find(const Key& key) const;	The method returns an iterator that identifies the earliest element in the container whose sort key equals key. If no such element exists, the iterator equals end().
size_type count(const Key& key) const;	The method returns the number of elements x in the range [lower_bound(key), upper_bound(key)).
iterator lower_bound(const Key& key); const_iterator lower_bound(const Key& key) const;	The method returns an iterator that identifies the earliest element x in the container for which key_comp()(x. first, key) is false, otherwise the function returns end().
iterator upper_bound(const Key& key); const_iterator upper_bound(const Key& key) const;	The method returns an iterator that identifies the earliest element x in the container for which key_comp()(key, x.first) is true, otherwise, the function returns end().
pair<iterator, iterator> equal_range(const Key& key); pair<const_iterator, const_iterator> equal_range(const Key& key) const;	The method returns a pair of iterators x such that x.first == lower_bound(key) and x.second == upper_bound(key).

Sample Code

The declaration of a map follows the pattern we have seen repeatedly throughout the use of other Standard Template Libraries. A map is a template data structure, specialized by the type of the key elements and the type of the associated values. An optional third template argument defines the function to be used in comparing key values. Like dynamic <vector> containers, a map initially contains no elements. Some example definitions look like:

```
map<double, string> a_string_map;
map<int, float> a_float_map;
map<int, int> an_int_map;
```

The <map> STL also defines several container-specific type definitions. These are most commonly used in declaration statements. For example, an iterator for a map of integers to floats can be defined as:

```
map<int, float>::iterator it;
```

In addition to iterator, the following other types are defined: *key_type*, the type associated with the keys used to index the map, and *value_type*, the type of the pair used to store entries in the map. The constructor for this type is used to create new container entries.

You insert entries into a map using the insert() method. Notice that the actual arguments must be a key-value pair. This pair is easily generated using the constructor for the value_type specification, as in:

```
a_float_map.insert(a_float_map::value_type(1, 1.1));
```

Of course, values can be removed from a map by providing the key_value. The following example erases element 3:

```
an_int_map.erase(3);
```

Also, elements being removed can be referenced by means of an iterator, as, for example, the iterator yielded by a find() operation. The following two statements first locate the value 3 and then delete the container entry:

```
an_int_map::iterator it = an_int_map.find(3);

an_int_map.erase(it);
```

Entire subranges of container elements are removed by making a call to erase(). The next example erases all values between 3 and 5:

```
an_int_map::iterator start = an_int_map.find(3);

an_int_map::iterator end = an_int_map.find(5);

an_int_map.erase(start, end);
```

Remember from previous chapters that the methods begin() and end() represent bidirectional map iterators. Dereferencing a map iterator yields a map element pair of key and value. You can use the types *first_type* and *second_type* (seen below) to reference these values individually. The *first_type* is a constant that cannot be modified. The *second_type* field, however, can be used to change the value being held in association with a given key, and will modify the value being maintained in the container. Elements will be generated in container, based on the ordering of the key fields. The iterators generated by calls to rbegin() and rend() allow you to access container elements in reverse.

```
pair
template<class T, class U>
    struct pair {
    typedef T first_type;
    typedef U second_type
    T first;
    U second;
    pair();
    pair(const T& x, const U& y);
    template<class V, class W>
        pair(const pair<V, W>& pr);
    };
```

To traverse or count map elements, you use the find(), empty(), and size() methods. The method size() returns the number of elements held by the container, and empty() returns a Boolean true if the container is empty. This approach is faster than testing the value returned by size() with zero. The method find() takes a key_type argument, and returns an iterator denoting the associated key and value pair.

Advanced container element searches are possible with the methods lower_bound() and upper_bound(). The lower_bound() method yields the first entry that matches the argument key, whereas the method upper_bound() returns the first value past the last entry matching the argument. The method equal_range() returns a pair of iterators, holding both the lower and upper bounds. The count() method returns the number of elements that match the key value supplied as the argument.

The map.cpp Application

If you have been following all of the examples throughout the previous chapters, you should genuinely feel a sense of learned accomplishment as you scan the following program's STL syntax and logic. What you should begin discovering at this point is just how many of the earlier chapters' contents are beginning to congeal. For example, what once was an ethereal concept, iterators, is now a concrete, commonplace STL regular. You deserve some well-earned congratulations at this point for hanging in there!

First, take a look at map.cpp and prove to yourself just how much you have learned as you knowledgeably interpret each statement:

```
// map.cpp
// Testing <map>
// insert(), begin(), end(), size(), erase(),
// upper_bound(), lower_bound(), find(),
// rbegin(), rend(), empty(), count(), equal_range()
// Chris H. Pappas and William H. Murray, 1999

#pragma warning(disable:4786)
// "Microsoft has confirmed this to be a bug in the Microsoft
// products listed at the beginning of this article. We are
// researching this bug and will post new information here in
// the Microsoft Knowledge Base as it becomes available."

#include <map>
#include <string>
#include <iostream>

using namespace std;

typedef map<string, string, less<string> > STR2STR;
typedef pair<STR2STR::iterator,STR2STR::iterator> STR2STRPAIR;

void main( void )
{
  STR2STR phoneBook;
  STR2STR::iterator it, upperBound, lowerBound;


  // Inserting five pairs
  phoneBook.insert(STR2STR::value_type("111-111-1111",
                                       "Adam Smith"));
  phoneBook.insert(STR2STR::value_type("555-555-5555",
                                       "Tina Smith"));
  phoneBook.insert(STR2STR::value_type("222-222-2222",
                                       "Fred Smith"));
  phoneBook.insert(STR2STR::value_type("444-444-4444",
                                       "John Smith"));
  phoneBook.insert(STR2STR::value_type("333-333-3333",
                                       "Jane Smith"));

  // Print phoneBook
  cout << "phoneBook now contains:\n";
  for(it = phoneBook.begin(); it != phoneBook.end(); it++)
    cout << it->first << " " << it->second << endl;
```

```
// Print phoneBook's size
cout << "\n\nphoneBook size = " << phoneBook.size();

// Print phoneBook in reverse
cout << "\n\nphoneBook in reverse order:\n";

STR2STR::reverse_iterator rit;
for(rit = phoneBook.rbegin(); rit != phoneBook.rend(); rit++)
  cout << rit->first << " " << rit->second << endl;

// Find key value "333-333-3333"
cout << "\n\nName for phone number 333-333-3333 = ";
it = phoneBook.find("333-333-3333");
cout << it->second << endl;

// Find subrange of key_values
cout << "\n\nPairs between 222-222-222 and 444-444-444:\n";
lowerBound = phoneBook.lower_bound("222-222-2222");
upperBound = phoneBook.upper_bound("444-444-4444");
for(it = lowerBound; it!= upperBound; it++)
  cout << it->first << it->second << endl;

// Declare iterator pair
STR2STRPAIR itPair;
itPair = phoneBook.equal_range("444-444-4444");

// Print one equal_range() value
cout << "\n\nequal_range() = ";
for(it = itPair.first; it != itPair.second; it++)
  cout << it->first << endl;

// Find key value "333-333-3333" again
it = phoneBook.find("333-333-3333");
it->second = "New Name";
cout << "\n\n333-333-3333 with new paired name: ";
cout << it->second << endl;


// Counting key values matching "555-555-5555"
cout << "\n\nNumber of 555-555-5555s = "
     << phoneBook.count("555-555-5555");

// Erasing key value pair "111-111-1111"
cout << "\n\nphoneBook minus 111-111-1111:\n";
phoneBook.erase("111-111-1111");
for(it = phoneBook.begin(); it != phoneBook.end(); it++)
  cout << it->first << " " << it->second << endl;

// Erasing entire phoneBook
phoneBook.erase(phoneBook.begin(),phoneBook.end());
```

```
  if(phoneBook.empty())
    cout << "\n\nThe phoneBook is empty!";
}
```

The discussion of map.cpp begins with the Microsoft-specific need to include the **#pragma** pre-processor directive to avoid four screens of warning messages. Microsoft is working on this "bug" and therefore the statement may not be needed in the Microsoft Visual C++ studio you are using:

```
#pragma warning(disable:4786)
```

The program code continues with an STL style of declaring appropriate types needed by map.cpp:

```
typedef map<string, string, less<string> > STR2STR;
typedef pair<STR2STR::iterator,STR2STR::iterator> STR2STRPAIR;
```

Remember that <map> by definition creates a container of paired elements. The identifier *STR2STR* represents a map container keyed on strings and containing string elements. This is ideal for our *phoneBook*, with the key being the phone number in string format and the value_type being a string representing the name associated with the phone number.

Later on in the program, a call is made to equal_ranage(). This method returns a pair of iterators and therefore explains the need for the *STR2STRPAIR* typedef, which creates a pairing of two *STR2STR::iterators*.

These statements are logically followed by the instantiation of *phoneBook* and creation of three iterators—*it*, *upperBound*, and *lowerBound*:

```
  STR2STR phoneBook;
  STR2STR::iterator it, upperBound, lowerBound;
```

The actual *phoneBook* entries are added using the insert() method:

```
// Inserting five pairs
  phoneBook.insert(STR2STR::value_type("111-111-1111",
                                       "Adam Smith"));
  phoneBook.insert(STR2STR::value_type("555-555-5555",
                                       "Tina Smith"));
  phoneBook.insert(STR2STR::value_type("222-222-2222",
                                       "Fred Smith"));
  phoneBook.insert(STR2STR::value_type("444-444-4444",
                                       "John Smith"));
  phoneBook.insert(STR2STR::value_type("333-333-3333",
                                       "Jane Smith"));
```

Using a now-familiar iterator controlled **for** loop map.cpp outputs the current container's contents:

```
// Print phoneBook
  cout << "phoneBook now contains:\n";
  for(it = phoneBook.begin(); it != phoneBook.end(); it++)
    cout << it->first << " " << it->second << endl;
```

Although the calls to begin() and end(), and the reason **why** *it* is not tested with < and is appropriately tested using != are all old news by now (you do not know any relationship to container addresses, so testing against a pointer <, >, <=, or >= makes no sense), the **cout** statement needs some clarification.

Since map elements are **pair**s, you access their individual components using their respective data member names *first* and *second* (see definition of **pair** earlier in the chapter). In previous chapters accessing container elements with an iterator, i.e., *it*, required only the use of the dereference operator, as in:

```
*it
```

However, now *it* points to more complex data type. You could actually write the syntax out longhand, as in:

```
*it.first
*it.second
```

But this syntax presents an operator precedence-level nightmare since the period member-operator, ., binds or has a higher-precedence, than the dereference operator, *. A knowledgeable and syntactically legal fix uses a set of parentheses to raise the priority of the dereference operator, as in:

```
(*it).first
(*it).second
```

This approach is a kludgey, greasy, squeaky way to solve the problem, since C and C++ have a special operator designed to eliminate this syntax nightmare, namely the arrow, or pointer-operator, ->. This operator *requires* a pointer-type to its left and a **class** or **struct** member name to its right. The **for** loop's **cout** statement uses this syntactically cleaner style:

```
cout << it->first << "  " << it->second << endl;
```

The program then proceeds to demonstrate a method for determining the container's current number of entries, with a call to the size() method:

```
// Print phoneBook's size
  cout << "\n\nphoneBook size = " << phoneBook.size();
```

Next, map.cpp demonstrates the necessary syntax and logic necessary to access a map container in reverse:

```
// Print phoneBook in reverse
  cout << "\n\nphoneBook in reverse order:\n";

  STR2STR::reverse_iterator rit;
  for(rit = phoneBook.rbegin(); rit != phoneBook.rend(); rit++)
    cout << rit->first << "  " << rit->second << endl;
```

First, a **reverse_iterator** is declared and immediately initialized to the address to the *last* container element with a call to rbegin(). Once again, the **for** loop test condition for continued iteration is **not** *it* <, but *it* !=, and contrary what you might expect, the third statement in the **for** loop does not decrement *rit* but instead increments the **reverse_iterator** *rit*! Just when you think you can outguess STL, it humbles. . . .

With map.cpp, attempting to illustrate all of the common demands a program could put on a map container, the source code moves on to demonstrating how you would syntactically search a map container for a specific key using find():

```
// Find key value "333-333-3333"
  cout << "\n\nName for phone number 333-333-3333 = ";
  it = phoneBook.find("333-333-3333");
  cout << it->second << endl;
```

The **cout** statement in this case does not print the key but instead only the associated value.

Remembering that the map containers are sorted by the specified key makes scanning for subranges very easy. This next code segment does exactly that by searching for all pairs with keys >= "222-222-2222" and <= "444-444-4444", using calls to lower_bound() and upper_bound():

```
// Find subrange of key_values
  cout << "\n\nPairs between 222-222-222 and 444-444-444:\n";
  lowerBound = phoneBook.lower_bound("222-222-2222");
  upperBound = phoneBook.upper_bound("444-444-4444");
  for(it = lowerBound; it!= upperBound; it++)
    cout << it->first << it->second << endl;
```

Whereas map containers, by definition, have unique key values, multimap containers may contain duplicate keys. The following code segment uses the equal_range() to locate, in the case of map containers, a single matching pair, but could be used by multimap containers to locate key subranges. Notice the use of the typedef *STR2STRPAIR* to declare the variable *itPair*, which is equal_range()'s return type for this application:

```
// Declare iterator pair
  STR2STRPAIR itPair;
  itPair = phoneBook.equal_range("444-444-4444");

  // Print one equal_range() value
  cout << "\n\nequal_range() = ";
  for(it = itPair.first; it != itPair.second; it++)
    cout << it->first << endl;
```

itPair's two iterators are referenced using the data member names **first** and **second**, and preceded by the variable's name *itPair* and the period member operator, . . .

Of course, an applicataion using map containers could want to change a key's paired value so this next code segment uses a call to the method find() to first locate the key, and then using the returned iterator's address, points to the value member, *second*, and updates the name associated with the key phone number:

```
// Find key value "333-333-3333" again
  it = phoneBook.find("333-333-3333");
  it->second = "New Name";
  cout << "\n\n333-333-3333 with new paired name: ";
  cout << it->second << endl;
```

The count() method is used with both map and multimap containers and returns the number of container pairs that have a key (map) or keys (multimap) that match the search key:

```
// Counting key values matching "555-555-5555"
  cout << "\n\nNumber of 555-555-5555s = "
       << phoneBook.count("555-555-5555");
```

The map.cpp application next moves on to the syntax necessary to locate and then entirely delete an element pair with a call to erase() using only one actual argument, the key to delete:

```
// Erasing key value pair "111-111-1111"
  cout << "\n\nphoneBook minus 111-111-1111:\n";
  phoneBook.erase("111-111-1111");
  for(it = phoneBook.begin(); it != phoneBook.end(); it++)
    cout << it->first << " " << it->second << endl;
```

And finally, perform the step that many a programmer forgets—the professional and clean removal of the container from memory. Here again a call is made to erase(), only this time the overloaded method is passed two actual iterator arguments returned by begin() and end():

```
// Erasing entire phoneBook
  phoneBook.erase(phoneBook.begin(),phoneBook.end());
  if(phoneBook.empty())
    cout << "\n\nThe phoneBook is empty!";
```

The output from the program looks like:

```
phoneBook now contains:

111-111-1111 Adam Smith

222-222-2222 Fred Smith

333-333-3333 Jane Smith

444-444-4444 John Smith

555-555-5555 Tina Smith



phoneBook size = 5
```

```
phoneBook in reverse order:
555-555-5555 Tina Smith
444-444-4444 John Smith
333-333-3333 Jane Smith
222-222-2222 Fred Smith
111-111-1111 Adam Smith


Name for phone number 333-333-3333 = Jane Smith


Pairs between 222-222-222 and 444-444-444:
222-222-2222Fred Smith
333-333-3333Jane Smith
444-444-4444John Smith


equal_range() = 444-444-4444


333-333-3333 with new paired name: New Name


Number of 555-555-5555s = 1

phoneBook minus 111-111-1111:
222-222-2222 Fred Smith
333-333-3333 New Name
444-444-4444 John Smith
555-555-5555 Tina Smith


The phoneBook is empty!
```

Summary

In this chapter, you have learned that a map is like a vector except that it has a user-defined key field and an associated data value(s), or pair. Unlike a vector, the index key can be any ordered type, and the paired data member can be *any* data type. You also learned that, like vectors, methods such as find(), begin(), end(), and size() are used to give iterators legal starting, current, or ending pointer values to access container elements instead of the usual array[subscript] notation. And although array[subscript] notation is a legal syntax for map containers, it is a more antique, error-prone syntax, superceded by the more robust STL method approach. In Chapter 12, you will learn all about the <numeric> template library and its template functions useful for computing numeric values.

T W E L V E

The STL <numeric> Template

The <numeric> STL encompasses four template functions: accumulate(), inner_product(), partial_sum(), and adjacent_difference(). Although these four functions are part of the original STL release by HP, the ANSI C++/ISO committee standardized the template functions in the <numeric> section of the C++ standard. In the interests of completeness, this chapter will go ahead and document these four template functions. STL wasn't trying to be an all-inclusive library for every numeric operation. But the STL numeric functions do give you a glimpse of the kind of interface you could conceivably design for a template-based library of your own.

Of special import is the last sample program described in this chapter. This will be your first example of an STL being incorporated into a complete Windows application. If you are already familiar to Windows programming, after having looked at the first four procedural <numeric> sample programs, you will notice that incorporating STL technology is a straightforward process!

<numeric> Template Syntax

The following listing gives you the syntax for the <numeric> template.

```
namespace std {
template<class InIt, class T>
    T accumulate(InIt first, InIt last, T val);
template<class InIt, class T, class Pred>
    T accumulate(InIt first, InIt last, T val, Pred pr);
template<class InIt1, class InIt2, class T>
    T product(InIt1 first1, InIt1 last1,
        Init2 first2, T val);
template<class InIt1, class InIt2, class T,
    class Pred1, class Pred2>
    T product(InIt1 first1, InIt1 last1,
        Init2 first2, T val, Pred1 pr1, Pred2 pr2);
template<class InIt, class OutIt>
    OutIt partial_sum(InIt first, InIt last,
        OutIt result);
template<class InIt, class OutIt, class Pred>
    OutIt partial_sum(InIt first, InIt last,
        OutIt result, Pred pr);
template<class InIt, class OutIt>
    OutIt adjacent_difference(InIt first, InIt last,
        OutIt result);
template<class InIt, class OutIt, class Pred>
    OutIt adjacent_difference(InIt first, InIt last,
        OutIt result, Pred pr);
    };
```

The descriptions of these templates employ a number of conventions common to all algorithms.

<numeric> Template Methods

The <numeric> template provides the methods shown in Table 12.1.

Table 12.1 <numeric> template methods and descriptions

Method	Description

`template<class InIt, class T>`
`    T accumulate(InIt first, InIt last, T val);`
`template<class InIt, class T, class Pred>`
`    T accumulate(InIt first, InIt last, T val,`
`Pred pr);`
	The first method iterates replacing val with val + *I, for each value of the InIt iterator I in the interval [first, last). It then returns val. The second method iterates replacing val with pr(val, *I), for each value of the InIt iterator I in the interval [first, last). It then returns val.

`template<class InIt1, class InIt2, class T>`
`    T product(InIt1 first1, InIt1 last1,`
`        Init2 first2, T val);`
`template<class InIt1, class InIt2, class T,`
`    class Pred1, class Pred2>`
`    T product(InIt1 first1, InIt1 last1,`
`        Init2 first2, T val, Pred1 pr1, Pred2`
`pr2);`
	The first method repeatedly replaces val with val + (*I1 * *I2), for each value of the InIt1 iterator I1 in the interval [first1, last2). In each case, the InIt2 iterator I2 equals first2 + (I1 - first1). The method returns val. The second method iterates replacing val with pr1(val, pr2(*I1, *I2)), for each value of the InIt1 iterator I1 in the interval [first1, last2). In each case, the InIt2 iterator I2 equals first2 + (I1 - first1). The method returns val.

`template<class InIt, class OutIt>`
`    OutIt partial_sum(InIt first, InIt last,`
`        OutIt result);`
`template<class InIt, class OutIt, class Pred>`
`    OutIt partial_sum(InIt first, InIt last,`
`        OutIt result, Pred pr);`
	The first method stores successive values beginning at result, for each value of the InIt iterator I in the interval [first, last). The first value val stored (if any) is *I. Each subsequent value val stored is val + *I. The method returns result incremented last - first times. The second method stores successive values beginning at result, for each value of the InIt iterator I in the interval [first, last). The first value val stored (if any) is *I. Each subsequent value val stored is pr(val, *I). The method returns result incremented last - first times.

Table 12.1 <numeric> template methods and descriptions *(continued)*

Method	Description
`template<class InIt, class OutIt> OutIt adjacent_difference(InIt first, InIt last, OutIt result);` `template<class InIt, class OutIt, class Pred> OutIt adjacent_difference(InIt first, InIt last, OutIt result, Pred pr);`	The first method stores successive values, beginning at `result`, for each value of the `InIt` iterator `I` in the interval `[first, last)`. The first value `val` stored (if any) is `*I`. Each subsequent value stored is `*I - val`, and `val` is replaced by `*I`. The method returns `result` incremented `last - first` times. The second method stores successive values beginning at `result`, for each value of the `InIt` iterator `I` in the interval `[first, last)`. The first value `val` stored (if any) is `*I`. Each subsequent value stored is `pr(*I, val)`, and `val` is replaced by `*I`. The method returns `result` incremented `last - first` times.

Sample Code

The following sample applications illustrate the four <numeric> template functions. This section includes a super example combining the <numeric> STL with a complete Windows application generating a Fourier series!

The accum.cpp Application

This first sample program uses the <numeric> accumulate() template function. accumulate() repeatedly applies the template function to each member of a container, storing the result in a temporary location. The initial value of the result is determined by an input parameter to the template function itself. The template function is either the operator+() or a binary template function specified by the programmer.

First, a look at the complete program:

```
// accum.cpp
// Testing <numeric>
// accumulate(), char_traits< >, multiplies< >,
// copy(), begin(), end()
// Chris H. Pappas and William H. Murray, 1999
```

```
// "Symbols too long" warning disable #pragma
#pragma warning (disable : 4786)

#include <string>
#include <vector>
#include <numeric>
#include <iostream>
#include <iterator>
#include <functional>

using namespace std;

#define MAX_VALUES 5

typedef vector < float > FLOATVECTOR;
typedef vector < string > STRINGVECTOR;
typedef ostream_iterator <float, char,
                          char_traits <char> > OstreamFLOATit;

void main( void )
{
  // Naming convention for FVdfvVectorInstance
  // Instantiate FLOATVECTOR -  FV, dynamic float vector - dfv
  FLOATVECTOR FVdfvVectorInstance;

  // Ostream iterator that outputs value followed by a space and comma
  OstreamFLOATit OstreamIt(cout," ,");

  // Vector created with 1.0, 0.5, 0.33333, 0.25, 0.2
  for (int i=0; i < MAX_VALUES; i++)
    FVdfvVectorInstance.push_back(1.0f/(i+1));

  // Display FVdfvVectorInstance
```

```
copy(FVdfvVectorInstance.begin(),FVdfvVectorInstance.end(),OstreamIt);
  cout << "\n\n";

  // Sum FVdfvVectorInstance
  cout << "Accumulate generates the sum of      "
       << "1.0, 0.5, 0.33, 0.25, 0.2:\n"
       << accumulate(FVdfvVectorInstance.begin(),
                               FVdfvVectorInstance.end(),0.0f)
       << "\n\n";

  // Multiply FVdfvVectorInstance elements
  cout << "Accumulate generates the product of "
       << "1.0, 0.5, 0.33, 0.25, 0.2:\n"
       << accumulate(FVdfvVectorInstance.begin(),
                    FVdfvVectorInstance.end(),1.0f,
                         multiplies<float>())
       << "\n\n";

  // Naming convention for SV
  // Instantiate STRINGVECTOR -  SV, dynamic string vector - dsv.
  // with individual words
  STRINGVECTOR SVdsvVectorInstance;
  SVdsvVectorInstance.push_back("Build a"          );
  SVdsvVectorInstance.push_back("sentence "        );
  SVdsvVectorInstance.push_back("from string "     );
  SVdsvVectorInstance.push_back("vector elements!");

  // Using Accumulate() to concatenate SVdsvVectorInstance elements
  cout << "Accumulate used on string elements:\n"
       << accumulate(SVdsvVectorInstance.begin(),
                               SVdsvVectorInstance.end(),string(""))
       << endl;
}
```

When using accumulate(), the first formal argument is a copy of the current intermediate value of the result. The second formal argument is the next value from the container. The two are processed by the template function, and the result is stored in the intermediate result.

Since the sample programs use an **ostream_iterator** of **char_traits**:

```
typedef ostream_iterator <float, char,
                         char_traits <char> > OstreamFLOATit;
```

The following **struct char_traits** definition is included here for reference:

```
struct char_traits<E> {
    typedef E char_type;
    typedef T1 int_type;
    typedef T2 pos_type;
    typedef T3 off_type;
    typedef T4 state_type;
    static void assign(E& x, const E& y);
    static E *assign(E *x, size_t n, const E& y);
    static bool eq(const E& x, const E& y);
    static bool lt(const E& x, const E& y);
    static int compare(const E *x, const E *y, size_t n);
    static size_t length(const E *x);
    static E *copy(E *x, const E *y, size_t n);
    static E *move(E *x, const E *y, size_t n);
    static const E *find(const E *x, size_t n, const E& y);
    static E to_char_type(const int_type& ch);
    static int_type to_int_type(const E& c);
    static bool eq_int_type(const int_type& ch1, const int_type& ch2);
    static int_type eof();
    static int_type not_eof(const int_type& ch);
    };
```

The accum.cpp application also uses accumulate() in the form requiring a binary template function, so once again, the syntax for declaring a **binary_function** is included here for easy reference:

```
template<class T>
    struct multiplies : public binary_function<T, T, T> {
    T operator()(const T& x, const T& y) const;
    };
```

The binary_function() template defines its method as returning `x * y`.

By now, the <vector> typedefs, declarations, initializations, and element display coding should be "old hat." So the discussion begins by examining the use of accumulate():

```
// Sum FVdfvVectorInstance
  cout << "Accumulate generates the sum of      "
       << "1.0, 0.5, 0.33, 0.25, 0.2:\n"
       << accumulate(FVdfvVectorInstance.begin(),
                     FVdfvVectorInstance.end(),0.0f)
       << "\n\n";
```

The first actual argument to accumulate() is the STL syntax required to reference the pointer, or address, to the first vector element, FVdfvVectorInstance.begin(). The second actual argument uses the same logical approach provided by the .end() method syntax. The final, or third actual argument, *0.0*, represents the initial value required by the accumulate algorithm. For example, if you were using accumulate to add up a vector of integers, you would need to provide an **int** value of 0. Because the accumulate() method call resides within a **cout <<** statement, the method's return value is directly output.

The second call to accumulate():

```
// Multiply FVdfvVectorInstance elements
  cout << "Accumulate generates the product of "
       << "1.0, 0.5, 0.33, 0.25, 0.2:\n"
       << accumulate(FVdfvVectorInstance.begin(),
                     FVdfvVectorInstance.end(),1.0f,
                     multiplies<float>())
       << "\n\n";
```

uses the overloaded version of accumulate() requiring a binary_function(), in this case, multiplies< >(). Remember that the binary_function() must be an object that obeys function semantics. It should take two formal arguments, one of type T, and one of the type pointed to by the input iterators. The template function should also return an object of type T, which is updated to supply the new cumulative value. The preceding **cout <<** statement uses the multiplies< >() template function to generate the product of *FVdfvVectorInstance*.

The third significant code section in accum.cpp revisits the accumulate() template function, only this time using a binary_function() returning a concatenation of vector string elements:

```
// Using Accumulate() to concatenate SVdsvVectorInstance elements
  cout << "Accumulate used on string elements:\n"
       << accumulate(SVdsvVectorInstance.begin(),
                                    SVdsvVectorInstance.end(),string(""))
       << endl;
```

The program output looks like:

```
1 ,0.5 ,0.333333 ,0.25 ,0.2 ,

Accumulate generates the sum of     1.0, 0.5, 0.33, 0.25, 0.2:
2.28333

Accumulate generates the product of 1.0, 0.5, 0.33, 0.25, 0.2:
0.00833333

Accumulate used on string elements:
Build a sentence from string vector elements!
```

The product.cpp Application

The product.cpp application uses the <numeric> inner_product() template function along with familiar <vector> syntax:

```
// product.cpp
// Testing <numeric>
// product(), begin(), end(), copy(),
// inner_product(), char_traits< >, multiplies< >
// Chris H. Pappas and William H. Murray, 1999

#include <vector>
#include <numeric>
#include <iostream>
#include <iterator>
#include <functional>

#define MAX_VALUES 4
```

```
using namespace std;

typedef vector < float > FLOATVECTOR;
typedef ostream_iterator < float, char,
                           char_traits<char> > OstreamFLOATit;

void main( void )
{
  OstreamFLOATit itOstream(cout," ");

  // Instantiate and initialize
  //            FVdfvVectorInstance1 to iValue
  // Instantiate and initialize
  //            FVdfvVectorInstance2 to iValue squared
  FLOATVECTOR FVdfvVectorInstance1, FVdfvVectorInstance2;
  for(int iValue=1; iValue <= MAX_VALUES; iValue++) {
    FVdfvVectorInstance1.push_back(iValue);
    FVdfvVectorInstance2.push_back(iValue*iValue);
  };

  // Display both FVdfvVectorInstance1 and FVdfvVectorInstance2
  cout << "FVdfvVectorInstance1 : ";
  copy(FVdfvVectorInstance1.begin(),
       FVdfvVectorInstance1.end(),itOstream);
  cout << endl;
  cout << "FVdfvVectorInstance2 : ";
  copy(FVdfvVectorInstance2.begin(),
       FVdfvVectorInstance2.end(),itOstream);
  cout << endl;

  // Use inner_product() to calculate the Sum of Products
float fTheSumOfProducts=inner_product(FVdfvVectorInstance1.begin(),
                                          FVdfvVectorInstance1.end(),
FVdfvVectorInstance2.begin(),0);
```

```
  cout << "\n\ninner_product() -> Sum of Products: "
       << fTheSumOfProducts
       << endl;

  // Use inner_product() to calculate the Product of Sums
  float fTheProductOfSums = inner_product(FVdfvVectorInstance1.begin(),
                                        FVdfvVectorInstance1.end(),
                                   FVdfvVectorInstance2.begin(),1,
                             multiplies<float>(),plus<float>());
  cout << "\n\ninner_product() -> Product of Sums: "
       << fTheProductOfSums
       << endl;
}
```

The interesting portion of this application begins with the first call to inner_product():

```
// Use inner_product() to calculate the Sum of Products
floatfTheSumOfProducts=inner_product(FVdfvVectorInstance1.begin(),
                                        FVdfvVectorInstance1.end(),
FVdfvVectorInstance2.begin(),0);
  cout << "\n\ninner_product() -> Sum of Products: "
       << fTheSumOfProducts
       << endl;
```

The variable *fTheSumOfProducts* is assigned the return value generated by the call to inner_product() that accumulates the result of the operation on two input sequences, *FVdfvVectorInstance1* and *FVdfvVectorInstance2*. Notice that unlike the required ending point for the first vector, FVdfvVectorInstance1.end(), there is no related end point exists for the second vector because both vectors *must* must be of the same size.

The second call to inner_product() generates the *fTheProductOfSums* by supplying the two binary operation actual arguments, multiplies< >(), and plus< >():

```
// Use inner_product() to calculate the Product of Sums
  float fTheProductOfSums = inner_product(FVdfvVectorInstance1.begin(),
                                        FVdfvVectorInstance1.end(),
                                      FVdfvVectorInstance2.begin(),1,
                                  multiplies<float>(),plus<float>());
```

```
  cout << "\n\ninner_product() -> Product of Sums: "
       << fTheProductOfSums
       << endl;
```

This overloaded version of inner_product() applies the second specified binary operation, plus< >(), to the two elements from the input containers. It then uses the first specified binary operation, multiplies< >(), with the result to update the accumulated value.

The program output looks like:

```
FVdfvVectorInstance1 : 1 2 3 4
FVdfvVectorInstance2 : 1 4 9 16



inner_product() -> Sum of Products: 100



inner_product() -> Product of Sums: 2880
```

The partsum.cpp Application

The third sample program, partsum.cpp, uses the partial_sum() <numeric> template function:

```
// partsum.cpp
// Testing <numeric>
// begin(), end(), char_traits< >,
// partial_sum(), copy(), multiplies < >
// Chris H. Pappas and William H. Murray, 1999

#include <iostream>
#include <numeric>
#include <functional>
#include <vector>
#include <iterator>

#define MAX_VALUES 5

using namespace std;
```

```
typedef vector < float > FLOATVECTOR;
typedef ostream_iterator < float, char,
                           char_traits<char> > OstreamFLOATit;

void main( void )
{
  OstreamFLOATit itOstream(cout," ");

  // Instantiate and initialize FVdfvVectorInstance
  FLOATVECTOR FVdfvVectorInstance;
  for (int i=1; i <= MAX_VALUES; i++)
    FVdfvVectorInstance.push_back(i);

  // Display FVdfvVectorInstance
  cout << "FvdfvVectorInstance contains: ";
  copy(FVdfvVectorInstance.begin(),
       FVdfvVectorInstance.end(),itOstream);
  cout << endl;

  // Declare and initialize FVdfvVectorResultInstance
  FLOATVECTOR FVdfvVectorResultInstance(FVdfvVectorInstance.size());

  // Use partial_sum on FVdfvVectorInstance elements
  partial_sum(FVdfvVectorInstance.begin(),
              FVdfvVectorInstance.end(),
                       FVdfvVectorResultInstance.begin());

  // Display FVdfvVectorResultInstance partial_sum()s
  cout << "\n\nFVdfvVectorResultInstance sum    : ";
  copy(FVdfvVectorResultInstance.begin(),
       FVdfvVectorResultInstance.end(),itOstream);
  cout << endl;
```

```
  // Use partial_sum to calculate partial product
  partial_sum(FVdfvVectorInstance.begin(),
              FVdfvVectorInstance.end(),

FVdfvVectorResultInstance.begin(),multiplies<float>());

  // Display FVdfvVectorResultInstance partial product
  cout << "\n\nFVdfvVectorResultInstance product : ";
  partial_sum(FVdfvVectorResultInstance.begin(),
              FVdfvVectorResultInstance.end(),itOstream);
  cout << endl;
}
```

The interesting portion of the application begins with the call to partial_sum():

```
// Use partial_sum on FVdfvVectorInstance elements
  partial_sum(FVdfvVectorInstance.begin(),
              FVdfvVectorInstance.end(),
                 FVdfvVectorResultInstance.begin());
```

Here the template function creates a sequence of elements that represent a running total of the container's elements. The second use of partial_sum():

```
// Use partial_sum to calculate partial product
  partial_sum(FVdfvVectorInstance.begin(),
              FVdfvVectorInstance.end(),
                FVdfvVectorResultInstance.begin(),multiplies<float>());
```

uses its overloaded form where the fourth actual argument is a binary operation, in this case *multiples< >()*, which in turn generates the partial product.

The program output looks like:

```
FvdfvVectorInstance contains: 1 2 3 4 5


FVdfvVectorResultInstance sum     : 1 3 6 10 15


FVdfvVectorResultInstance product : 1 3 9 33 153
```

The adjacent.cpp Application

The adjacent.cpp application uses the adjacent_difference <numeric> template function to return an output sequence containing the difference between adjacent container elements, in this case telephone trunk lines:

```
// adjacent.cpp
// Testing <numeric>
// adjacent_difference(), begin(), end()
// copy()
// Chris H. Pappas and William H. Murray

#include <vector>
#include <numeric>
#include <iterator>
#include <iostream>
#include <functional>

#define MAX_VALUES 5

using namespace std;


typedef vector < int > INTVECTOR;
typedef ostream_iterator < int, char,
                           char_traits<char> > OstreamINTit;

void main( void )
{
  OstreamINTit itOstream(cout," ");

  // Declare and initialize IVdivVectorInstance
  // containing trunk line lenghts in kilometers
  // with routing origin New York
  INTVECTOR IVdivVectorInstance;
  IVdivVectorInstance.push_back( 2786); // San Francisco to Berlin
```

```
  IVdivVectorInstance.push_back(11554); // to Cairo
  IVdivVectorInstance.push_back(13802); // to Calcutta
  IVdivVectorInstance.push_back(40021); // to Cape Town
  IVdivVectorInstance.push_back(75722); // to Hong Kong

  // Display IVdivVectorInstance trunk line entries
  cout << "IVdivVectorInstance contains    : ";
  copy(IVdivVectorInstance.begin(),
       IVdivVectorInstance.end(),itOstream);
  cout << endl;

  // Declare and initialize IVdivVectorDifferenceInstance
  // with the calculated distance between each trunk line
  INTVECTOR IVdivVectorDifferenceInstance(MAX_VALUES);
  INTVECTOR::iterator Difference_it =
                    IVdivVectorDifferenceInstance.begin();
  adjacent_difference(IVdivVectorInstance.begin(),
                    IVdivVectorInstance.end(),Difference_it);

  // Display IVdivVectorDifferenceInstance differences
  cout << "\n\nIVdivVectorInstance differences : ";
  copy(IVdivVectorDifferenceInstance.begin()+1,
       IVdivVectorDifferenceInstance.end(),itOstream);
  cout << endl;
}
```

The first call to adjacent_difference() looks like:

```
// Declare and initialize IVdivVectorDifferenceInstance
  // with the calculated distance between each trunk line
  INTVECTOR IVdivVectorDifferenceInstance(MAX_VALUES);
  INTVECTOR::iterator Difference_it =
                    IVdivVectorDifferenceInstance.begin();
  adjacent_difference(IVdivVectorInstance.begin(),
                    IVdivVectorInstance.end(),Difference_it);
```

Notice that the template function requires the definition of a bidirectional iterator in the form vector::iterator it. The generated results are then simply output with a call to copy(), using the ostream iterator *itOstream*:

```
copy(IVdivVectorDifferenceInstance.begin()+1,
       IVdivVectorDifferenceInstance.end(),itOstream);
```

The program output looks like:

```
IVdivVectorInstance contains    : 2786 11554 13802 40021 75722



IVdivVectorInstance differences : 8768 2248 26219 35701
```

Windows Application Using <numeric>

The previous examples can be easily expanded into a full-blown Windows plotting example involving Fourier series calculations. The French mathematician Baron Jean Baptiste Joseph Fourier (1768-1830) found that any periodic waveform could be constructed by simply adding the correct combinations of sine wave harmonics together. Using his techniques, a wide variety of waveforms, from square to triangular, can be created. Electrical engineers are often interested in square wave reproduction, because square waves are made from a fundamental sine wave and its associated overtones. The quality of amplifiers and other communication devices depends on how well they can reproduce these signals. (For a more detailed treatment of the Fourier series, refer to college-level physics or electrical engineering textbooks.) Fourier's formal equation is usually expressed as:

```
y = A + A1(sin wt) + A2(sin 2wt) + A3(sin 3wt) +
    A4(sin 4wt)...
```

Some periodic waveforms include just the odd or even harmonics only. In others, all terms are included. Also, in some periodic waveforms, the signs alternate between + and - for adjacent terms. This example constructs a square wave by adding the odd harmonic terms in a Fourier series together. The more terms that are used in the series, the more the final result will approach a precise square wave. For a square wave, the general Fourier series equation becomes:

```
y = (sin wt) + (1/3)(sin 3wt) + (1/5)(sin 5wt) +
    (1/7)(sin 7wt)...
```

You can now see that the work done in the previous example is ideal for calculating a Fourier series of terms. Notice that only odd harmonics will contribute to the final result. Can you see from the equation that if only one harmonic is chosen, the result will be a sine wave? Notice also that each successive term uses a fractional multiplier—in other words, each successively higher harmonic affects the waveform less and less.

To fully appreciate what this application is about to accomplish, remember that each term in a Fourier series will be calculated separately by the program, for each angle. Individual values will be saved in an array by using the vector push_back() member function. The sum of the individual calculations, for a given angle, is then found by using the accumulate() member function to sum each value in the array. Before going on to the next angle, the values are removed from the array by using the pop_back() member function.

If you ask the application to use 1000 harmonic terms, then 1000 separate sine values will be scaled, calculated, and saved to the array for each angle. When the array values are accumulated (summed together), the value will represent one point on the Fourier series plot. This procedure must be repeated for each point that is to be plotted on the window. Therefore, 1000 calculations times 400 points (along the horizontal) = 400,000 calculations.

To create this project, use the MFC Application Wizard to create a project named Fourier. Accept the defaults offered by the Application Wizard to create the base code. To this code, you will need to add a data entry dialog box and associated member variables.

Modify the FourierView.cpp code to reflect the changes shown in a bold font in the following listing. These modifications will provide the code necessary to include the Fourier series calculations.

```
// FourierView.cpp : implementation of the CFourierView class
//

#include "stdafx.h"
#include "Fourier.h"

#include "FourierDoc.h"
#include "FourierView.h"
#include "FourierDlg.h"
#include "FourierDlg2.h"
#include <iostream>
#include <numeric>
#include <functional>
#include <vector>
#include <iterator>
#include <string>
#include <math.h>

// turn off warning for symbols
// too long for debugger
#pragma warning (disable : 4786)

using namespace std;

typedef vector <float> FourierArray;
```

```
#ifdef _DEBUG
#define new DEBUG_NEW
#undef THIS_FILE
static char THIS_FILE[] = __FILE__;
#endif

///////////////////////////////////////////////////////////////////////////
//////
// CFourierView

IMPLEMENT_DYNCREATE(CFourierView, CView)

BEGIN_MESSAGE_MAP(CFourierView, CView)
    //{{AFX_MSG_MAP(CFourierView)
    ON_WM_SIZE()
    ON_COMMAND(IDM_FOURIER, OnFourier)
    //}}AFX_MSG_MAP
END_MESSAGE_MAP()

///////////////////////////////////////////////////////////////////////////
//////
// CFourierView construction/destruction

CFourierView::CFourierView()
{
}

CFourierView::~CFourierView()
{
}

BOOL CFourierView::PreCreateWindow(CREATESTRUCT& cs)
{
    return CView::PreCreateWindow(cs);
}

///////////////////////////////////////////////////////////////////////////
//////
// CFourierView drawing

void CFourierView::OnDraw(CDC* pDC)
{
    CFourierDoc* pDoc = GetDocument();
    ASSERT_VALID(pDoc);

    int ltitle;
    double y, yp;
    double vertscale, horzscale;
```

```
    // vertical plotting scaling factor
    vertscale = 180.0;
    // convert degrees to radians and scale
    // horozontal for 360 degrees in 400 points
    horzscale = 3.1415927 * 360 / (180 * 400);

    // define a vector of floats
    FourierArray rgFA;

    // set mapping mode, viewport, and so on
    pDC->SetMapMode(MM_ISOTROPIC);
    pDC->SetWindowExt(500,500);
    pDC->SetViewportExt(m_cxClient,-m_cyClient);
    pDC->SetViewportOrg(m_cxClient/20,m_cyClient/2);

    // draw x & y coordinate axes
    pDC->MoveTo(0,240);
    pDC->LineTo(0,-240);
    pDC->MoveTo(0,0);
    pDC->LineTo(400,0);
    pDC->MoveTo(0,0);

    // i represents a given angle for the series
    for (int i = 0; i <= 400; i++) {
        // calculate Fourier terms for the angle
        // place each term in the array
        for (int j=1; j<=pDoc->myterms; j++) {
            y = (vertscale / ((2.0 * j) - 1.0)) * \
                 sin(((j *  2.0) - 1.0) * horzscale * i);
            rgFA.push_back(y);
        }
        // accumulate the individual array terms
        // for the angle
        yp = accumulate(rgFA.begin(),rgFA.end(),0.0f);
        // draw the scaled point in the client area
        pDC->LineTo(i, (int)yp);
        yp-=yp;

        // clean out the array and prepare for
        // with next angle's values.
        for (j=1; j<=pDoc->myterms; j++) {
            rgFA.pop_back();
        }
    }

    // print waveform title
    ltitle=strlen(pDoc->mytext);
    pDC->TextOut(200-(ltitle*8/2),200,pDoc->mytext,ltitle);
}
```

```
////////////////////////////////////////////////////////////////////////
//////
// CFourierView diagnostics

#ifdef _DEBUG
void CFourierView::AssertValid() const
{
    CView::AssertValid();
}

void CFourierView::Dump(CDumpContext& dc) const
{
    CView::Dump(dc);
}

CFourierDoc* CFourierView::GetDocument() // non-debug version is inline
{
    ASSERT(m_pDocument->IsKindOf(RUNTIME_CLASS(CFourierDoc)));
    return (CFourierDoc*)m_pDocument;
}
#endif //_DEBUG

////////////////////////////////////////////////////////////////////////
//////
// CFourierView message handlers

void CFourierView::OnSize(UINT nType, int cx, int cy)
{
    CView::OnSize(nType, cx, cy);
    // TODO: Add your message handler code here

    // WHM: added for sizing and scaling window
    m_cxClient = cx;
    m_cyClient = cy;
}

void CFourierView::OnFourier()
{
    // TODO: Add your command handler code here

    // WHM: added to process dialog information
    FourierDlg dlg (this);
    int result = dlg.DoModal();

    if(result==IDOK) {
        CFourierDoc* pDoc = GetDocument();
        ASSERT_VALID(pDoc);

        pDoc->mytext=dlg.m_text;
        pDoc->myterms=dlg.m_terms;
```

```
        Invalidate();
    }
}
```

MFC Windows applications built with the Application Wizard are quite intimidating. Although covering the details of MFC applications is beyond the scope of this book, we hope that you'll appreciate the practical use of the material developed in the previous example in this practical application.

A CLOSER LOOK AT THE CODE

The actual Fourier calculations are made within two **for** loops and drawn with the LineTo() function.

```
// i represents a given angle for the series
    for (int i = 0; i <= 400; i++) {
        // calculate Fourier terms for the angle
        // place each term in the array
        for (int j=1; j<=pDoc->myterms; j++) {
            y = (vertscale / ((2.0 * j) - 1.0)) * \
                 sin(((j *  2.0) - 1.0) * horzscale * i);
            rgFA.push_back(y);
        }
        // accumulate the individual array terms
        // for the angle
        yp = accumulate(rgFA.begin(),rgFA.end(),0.0f);
        // draw the scaled point in the client area
        pDC->LineTo(i, (int)yp);
        yp-=yp;

        // clean out the array and prepare for
        // with next angle's values
        for (j=1; j<=pDoc->myterms; j++) {
            rgFA.pop_back();
        }
    }
```

The outer loop, using the *i* index, increments the horizontal plotting position across the window. This value represents the scaled angle for one set of Fourier series of terms. The inner loop, using the *j* index, calculates the appropriate number of Fourier values for the given angle. For example, if *i* is pointing to a value representing 45 degrees and if the number of Fourier terms is 10, then 10 calculations will be made in the inner loop for each *i* value and pushed on to the array. Outside this loop, the individual array values are accumulated (added together) to form a single point that will be scaled and drawn to the window.

Figure 12.1 is the default waveform created by calculating four terms in the Fourier series for each point on the plot.

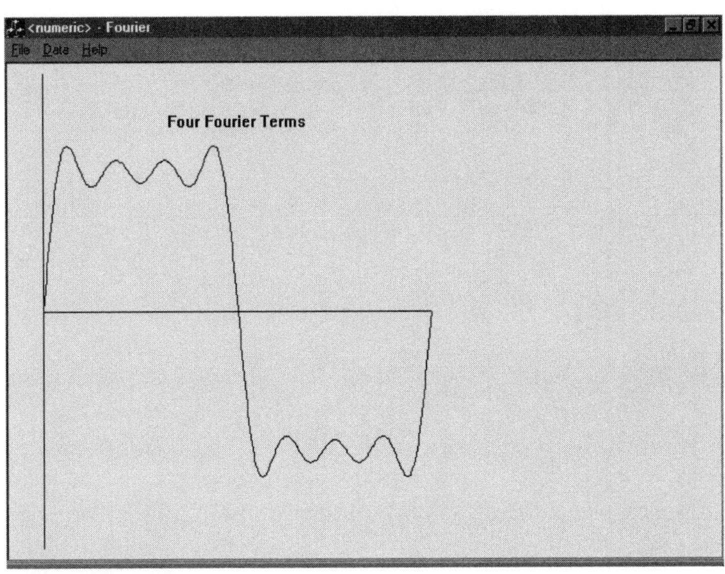

Figure 12.1 *The default Fourier series showing four harmonics.*

Figure 12.2 shows a plot created by opening the dialog box and requesting one harmonic.

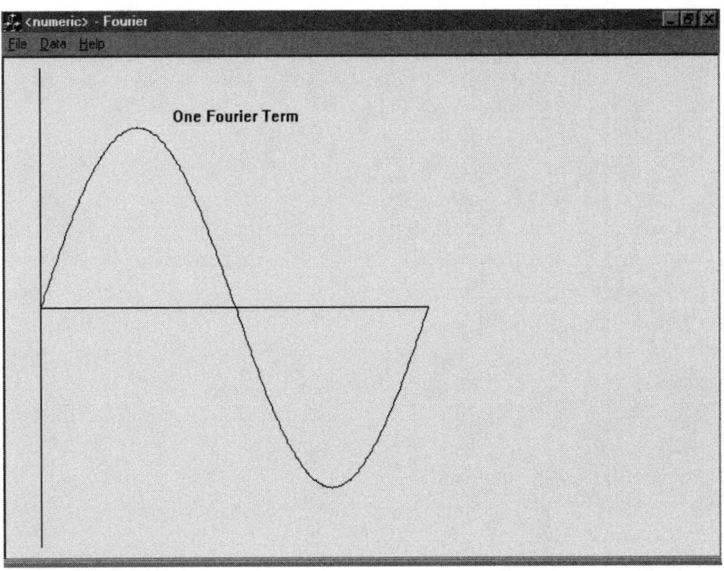

Figure 12.2 *A Fourier series created by requesting one harmonic.*

Figure 12.3 shows a plot created by requesting forty harmonics.

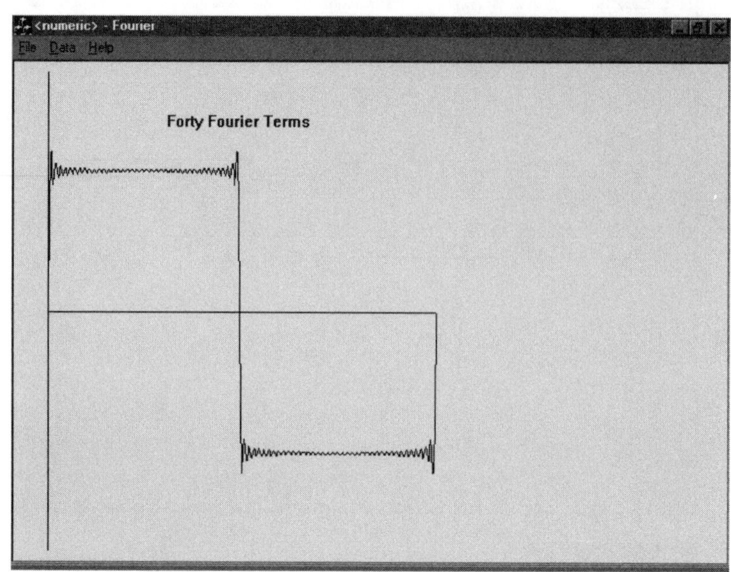

Figure 12.3 *A Fourier series created by requesting forty harmonics.*

If you increase the number of harmonics to 1000 or 5000, you'll end up with a pretty good square wave.

Summary

In this chapter, you have discovered just how easily you can use the <numeric> template functions accumulate(), inner_product(), partial_sum(), and adjacent_difference(). In addition, you have seen your first STL-ready Windows application using accumulate() to generate a Fourier series. Chapters 13 and 14, describing the STL <set> and <memory> templates, will complete your formal introduction to and use of the most significant addition to C++ by the ANSI C++/ISO Committee—namely STL!

T H I R T E E N

The <set> and <multiset> Templates

These template classes describe the associative container template classes <set> and <multiset>. The template classes show how an object can control a sequence of elements. The elements can vary in length but must be of type const Key. The sequence of elements allows lookup, insertion, and removal of an individual element, since each element can function as a sort key and a value. Elements invalidate iterators that point at the removed elements, but no invalidation occurs for element insertions.

The sequence is ordered with a call to a stored function object. This stored function must be of type Pred and is accessed by calling the key_comp() method. For any element `x` *that precedes element* `y` *in the sequence, key_comp()(y,x) is false. With the template class multiset, an object of the template class* `set` *insists that key_comp()(y,x) is true.*

The protected object named allocator, of class A, is used to assign and free storage for the sequence. The allocator object and the object of the template class allocator must have the same external interface.

<set> and <multiset> Template Syntax

This section will examine the syntax used to support both the <set> and <multiset> templates. The following listing shows the template prototypes and the related template functions.

```
namespace std {
template<class Key, class Pred, class A>
  class set;
template<class Key, class Pred, class A>
  class multiset;
// Template Functions
template<class Key, class Pred, class A>
  bool operator==(
  const <Key, Pred, A>& lhs,
  const <Key, Pred, A>& rhs);
template<class Key, class Pred, class A>
  bool operator==(
  const multiset<Key, Pred, A>& lhs,
  const multiset<Key, Pred, A>& rhs);
template<class Key, class Pred, class A>
  bool operator!=(
  const <Key, Pred, A>& lhs,
  const <Key, Pred, A>& rhs);
template<class Key, class Pred, class A>
  bool operator!=(
  const multiset<Key, Pred, A>& lhs,
  const multiset<Key, Pred, A>& rhs);
template<class Key, class Pred, class A>
  bool operator<(
  const <Key, Pred, A>& lhs,
  const <Key, Pred, A>& rhs);
template<class Key, class Pred, class A>
  bool operator<(
  const multiset<Key, Pred, A>& lhs,
  const multiset<Key, Pred, A>& rhs);
template<class Key, class Pred, class A>
  bool "operator>(
  const <Key, Pred, A>& lhs,
  const <Key, Pred, A>& rhs);
template<class Key, class Pred, class A>
  bool "operator>(
  const multiset<Key, Pred, A>& lhs,
  const multiset<Key, Pred, A>& rhs);
template<class Key, class Pred, class A>
  bool operator<=(
  const <Key, Pred, A>& lhs,
  const <Key, Pred, A>& rhs);
template<class Key, class Pred, class A>
  bool operator<=(
  const multiset<Key, Pred, A>& lhs,
  const multiset<Key, Pred, A>& rhs);
template<class Key, class Pred, class A>
  bool ="operator>=(
  const <Key, Pred, A>& lhs,
  const <Key, Pred, A>& rhs);
```

```
template<class Key, class Pred, class A>
  bool ="operator>=(
  const multiset<Key, Pred, A>& lhs,
  const multiset<Key, Pred, A>& rhs);
template<class Key, class Pred, class A>
  void swap(
  const <Key, Pred, A>& lhs,
  const <Key, Pred, A>& rhs);
template<class Key, class Pred, class A>
  void swap(
  const multiset<Key, Pred, A>& lhs,
  const multiset<Key, Pred, A>& rhs);
  };
```

The following listing is for the set template class. Note that some long listing lines are wrapped due to page limitations.

```
template<class Key, class Pred = less<Key>,
         class A = allocator<Key> >
  class set {
public:
  typedef Key key_type;
  typedef Pred key_compare;
  typedef Key value_type;
  typedef Pred value_compare;
  typedef A allocator_type;
  typedef A::size_type size_type;
  typedef A::difference_type difference_type;
  typedef A::rebind<value_type>::other
                               ::const_reference reference;
  typedef A::rebind<value_type>::other
                               ::const_reference const_reference;
  typedef T0 iterator;
  typedef T1 const_iterator;
  typedef reverse_bidirectional_iterator<iterator, value_type,
                                          reference,
                                          A::pointer,
                                          difference_type>
                                          reverse_iterator;
  typedef reverse_bidirectional_iterator<const_iterator,
                                          value_type,
                                          const_reference,
                                          A::const_pointer,
                                          difference_type>
                                          const_reverse_iterator;
  explicit set(const Pred& comp = Pred(), const A& al = A());
  set(const set& x);
  set(const value_type *first, const value_type *last,
      const Pred& comp = Pred(), const A& al = A());
  const_iterator begin() const;
  iterator end() const;
```

```
    const_reverse_iterator rbegin() const;
    const_reverse_iterator rend() const;
    size_type size() const;
    size_type max_size() const;
    bool empty() const;
    A get_allocator() const;
    pair<iterator, bool> insert(const value_type& x);
    iterator insert(iterator it, const value_type& x);
    void insert(InIt first, InIt last);
    iterator erase(iterator it);
    iterator erase(iterator first, iterator last);
    size_type erase(const Key& key);
    void clear();
    void swap(set x);
    key_compare key_comp() const;
    value_compare value_comp() const;
    const_iterator find(const Key& key) const;
    size_type count(const Key& key) const;
    const_iterator lower_bound(const Key& key) const;
    const_iterator upper_bound(const Key& key) const;
    pair<const_iterator, const_iterator>
      equal_range(const Key& key) const;
protected:
  A allocator;
  };
```

The following listing is for the template class multiset. Note that some long listing lines are wrapped due to page limitations.

```
template<class Key, class Pred = less<Key>,
      class A = allocator<Key> >
  class multiset {
public: typedef Key key_type;
  typedef Pred key_compare;
  typedef Key value_type;
  typedef Pred value_compare;
  typedef A allocator_type;
  typedef A::size_type size_type;
  typedef A::difference_type difference_type;
  typedef A::rebind<value_type>::other
                           ::const_reference reference;
  typedef A::rebind<value_type>::other
                           ::const_reference const_reference;
  typedef T0 iterator;
  typedef T1 const_iterator;
  typedef reverse_bidirectional_iterator<iterator,
    value_type,
    reference, A::const_pointer, difference_type>
   reverse_iterator;
  typedef reverse_bidirectional_iterator<const_iterator,
    value_type,
```

```
    const_reference, A::pointer, difference_type>
  const_reverse_iterator;
  explicit multiset(const Pred& comp = Pred(),
  const A& al = A());
  multiset(const multiset& x);
  multiset(const value_type *first,
    const value_type *last,
    const Pred& comp =  Pred(), const A& al = A());
  const_iterator begin() const;
  iterator end() const;
  const_reverse_iterator rbegin() const;
  const_reverse_iterator rend() const;
  size_type size() const;
  size_type max_size() const;
  bool empty() const;
  A get_allocator() const;
  iterator insert(const value_type& x);
  iterator insert(iterator it, const value_type& x);
  void insert(const value_type *first,
    const value_type *last);
  iterator erase(iterator it);
  iterator erase(iterator first, iterator last);
  size_type erase(const Key& key);
  void clear();
  void swap(multiset x);
  key_compare key_comp() const;
  value_compare value_comp() const;
  const_iterator find(const Key& key) const;
  size_type count(const Key& key) const;
  const_iterator lower_bound(const Key& key) const;
  const_iterator upper_bound(const Key& key) const;
  pair<const_iterator, const_iterator>
    equal_range(const Key& key) const;
protected:
  A allocator;
  };
```

In the next sections, you will learn the meaning of each <set> and <multiset> member function and template function.

<set> and <multiset> Template Functions

Template functions that are used with both set and multiset are shown in Table 13.1, along with a brief description of their purpose and return values.

Table 13.1 Template functions used by set and multiset

Template Function	Description
bool operator!=	Returns !(lhs == rhs).
bool operator==	The <set> template uses this function, overloads the operator==, and compares two objects of template class set. The <multiset> template uses this function, overloads the operator==, and compares two objects of template class multiset. The template functions return lhs.size() == rhs.size() && equal(lhs.begin(), lhs.end(), and rhs.begin()).
bool operator<	The <set> template uses this function, overloads the operator<, and compares two objects of template class set. The <multiset> template uses this function, overloads the operator<, and compares two objects of template class multiset. The template functions return lexicographical compare(lhs.begin(), lhs.end(), rhs.begin(), and rhs.end()).
bool operator<=	Returns !(rhs < lhs).
bool operator>	Returns rhs < lhs.
bool operator>=	Returns !(lhs < rhs).
bool swap	This template function executes a lhs.swap(rhs). Here, the swap member function switches between *this and str. When allocator == str.allocator, the swapping occurs in constant time. For all other cases, swap() executes a number of element assignments and constructor calls. The number of executions is proportional to the number of elements in the controlled sequences.

An example that uses the swap() template function is included in the sample code section of this chapter.

<set> Template Methods

The set and multiset templates provide the methods shown in Table 13.2. This table lists the template methods, along with a short description of each method and returned values.

Table 13.2 The set and multiset template methods and descriptions

Template Method	Description
const_iterator begin() const	Returns a const_iterator to the first object in the container. The const_iterator will equal the iterator returned by end() if the container is empty.
iterator end() const	Returns a const iterator. This iterator points beyond the last object in the container. The result is undefined when the container is empty.
const_reverse_iterator rbegin() const	Returns a const_reverse_iterator. This iterator points to the last location used in the container. rbegin() returns a value that must be stored in a set&lT, A>::const_reverse_iterator. A standard iterator should not be used.
const_reverse_iterator rend() const	Returns a const_reverse_iterator. This iterator points to a location just prior to the first element of the set container. rend() returns a value that must not be dereferenced.
size_type size() const	Returns the number of objects stored in the set container.
size_type max_size() const	Returns the maximum number of objects that can fit in the set container.
bool empty() const	Returns a true when the set container is empty. A false is returned for all other cases.
A get_allocator() const	Returns allocator.
pair<iterator, bool> insert(const value_type& x) iterator insert(iterator it, const value_type& x) void insert(InIt first, InIt last)	Inserts object x in the set if and only if x is not already present in the set and returns a pair. The bool value shows when the object is inserted in the set. (or) The iterator gives the object's position in the set when the object is inserted in the set. If the object is not inserted, it gives the position of the element x that is present in the set. (or) Inserts the objects given in the range (first, last) in the set. The range must be valid and consist of elements of type value_type.

Table 13.2 The set and multiset template methods and descriptions *(continued)*

Template Method	Description
iterator erase(iterator it)	The element as positioned is removed from the set container. (or)
iterator erase(iterator first, iterator last)	The elements given in the range (first, last) are removed from the set container. Note: The iterators returned by the first two cases give the first element beyond the erased elements. If the element does not exist, end() is returned. (or)
size_type erase(const Key& key)	Removes the set elements that match the key. Returns the number of elements removed. Returns a 0 if no elements match the key.
void clear()	The elements of the set container are erased. This function calls erase(begin(), end()).
void swap(set x)	The elements of the set container are swapped with the elements of x.
key_compare key_comp() const	Returns the function object that set uses to order elements.
value_compare value_comp() const	Returns an object of type value_compare. This object is created from the function object used to order the elements of set.
const_iterator find(const Key& key) const	Returns a const_iterator. This iterator points to an element key if key is found in the set. If the element does not exist, an end() is returned.
size_type count(const Key& key) const	Returns the number of elements in the set that match key. If key is present, the function returns 1; otherwise, it returns 0.
const_iterator lower_bound(const Key& key) const	Returns a const_iterator. This iterator points to the first element that is not less than key. Returns end() if all the elements in the set are less than key.
const_iterator upper_bound(const Key& key) const	Returns a const_iterator. The iterator is for the first element greater than key. Returns end() if no element is greater than key.
pair<const_iterator, const_iterator> equal_range(const Key& key) const	Returns a pair provided by: pair(lower_bound(key), upper_bound(key)).

In the next section, you'll learn how to apply many of these set and multiset methods in actual sample applications.

Sample Code

The following sample applications illustrate various set and multisets methods. The first example illustrates the use of the insert(), swap(), begin(), and end() methods. The second example continues by illustrating the size(), erase(), and clear() methods. The third example uses many of the methods introduced in the first two examples and includes the use of the unique_copy() method.

The set1.cpp Application

The first example application, set1.cpp, shows how the insert(), swap(), begin(), and end() methods can be used to control elements in the sequence.

```
// set1.cpp
// Testing <set>
// insert(), swap(), begin(), and end()
// Chris H. Pappas and William H. Murray, 1999

#include <set>
#include <iostream>
#pragma warning(disable:4786)

using namespace std ;

typedef set<char> SET_CHAR;

void main() {
  SET_CHAR set1;
  SET_CHAR set2;
  SET_CHAR::iterator it;

  // insert elements into first set
  cout << "insert a Z in set1" << endl;
  set1.insert(90);
  cout << "insert an A in set1" << endl;
  set1.insert(65);
  cout << "insert a F in set1" << endl;
  set1.insert(70);
  // set1 now holds Z, A and F

  // insert elements into second set
  cout << "insert a S in set2" << endl;
  set2.insert(83);
  cout << "insert a T in set2" << endl;
  set2.insert(84);
  cout << "insert a C in set2" << endl;
  set2.insert(67);
  // set2 now holds S, T and C
```

```
  // illustrate swap()
  cout << "swap set1 and set2" << endl;
  swap(set1,set2);

  // illustrates begin(), end(), and results of
  // previous swap()
  // set1 now holds the ordered elements C, S, T
  for (it=set1.begin();it!=set1.end();it++)
     cout << "set1 holds the following elements: "
        << *it << endl;

  // set2 now holds the ordered elements A, F, Z
  for (it=set2.begin();it!=set2.end();it++)
     cout << "set2 holds the following elements: "
        << *it << endl;
}
```

The output from this program shows each element as it is added to the appropriate sequence, the swapping operation, and the elements as they are ordered in the swapped sequences.

```
insert a Z in set1
insert an A in set1
insert a F in set1
insert a S in set2
insert a T in set2
insert a C in set2
swap set1 and set2
set1 holds the following elements: C
set1 holds the following elements: S
set1 holds the following elements: T
set2 holds the following elements: A
set2 holds the following elements: F
set2 holds the following elements: Z
```

In this example, the swap() function is used to swap the two sequences. The begin() function shows how to obtain an iterator that points to the first element in a sequence. The end() function shows how to obtain an iterator that points "just beyond" the last element in a sequence. Both begin() and end() return bidirectional iterators.

The set2.cpp Application

The second example application, set2.cpp, shows how the size(), erase(), and clear() methods can be used to control elements in the sequence.

```
// set2.cpp
// Testing <set>
// insert(), size(), clear(), erase(), begin(), and end()
// Chris H. Pappas and William H. Murray, 1999
```

```
#pragma warning(disable:4786)
#include <set>
#include <iostream>

using namespace std ;

typedef set<int> SET_INT;

void main()
{
  SET_INT set1;
  SET_INT::iterator it;

  // insert elements into first set
  cout << "insert a 10 in set1" << endl;
  set1.insert(10);
  cout << "insert a 70 in set1" << endl;
  set1.insert(70);
  cout << "insert a 30 in set1" << endl;
  set1.insert(30);
  cout << "insert a 90 in set1" << endl;
  set1.insert(90);
  cout << "insert a 45 in set1" << endl;
  set1.insert(45);
  // set1 now holds 10, 70, 30, 90 and 45

  // illustrate size()
  cout << "\nThe size of the sequence: "
     << set1.size() << endl;
  // use begin() and end() to show current sequence
  for (it=set1.begin();it!=set1.end();it++)
     cout << "set1 holds the following elements: "
        << *it << endl;

  // illustrate erase()
  set1.erase(45);  // erase any 45
  set1.erase(5);   // erase any 5
  set1.erase(70);  // erase any 70
  cout << "\nThe size of the sequence: "
     << set1.size() << endl;
  // use begin() and end() to show current sequence
  for (it=set1.begin();it!=set1.end();it++)
     cout << "set1 holds the following elements: "
        << *it << endl;

  // illustrate clear()
  set1.clear();     // clear all elements
  cout << "\nThe size of the sequence: "
     << set1.size() << endl;
}
```

The output from this program shows each element as it is added to the appropriate sequence. The size of the sequence is checked and then elements are erased. Finally, the entire sequence is cleared.

```
insert a 10 in set1
insert a 70 in set1
insert a 30 in set1
insert a 90 in set1
insert a 45 in set1

The size of the sequence: 5
set1 holds the following elements: 10
set1 holds the following elements: 30
set1 holds the following elements: 45
set1 holds the following elements: 70
set1 holds the following elements: 90

The size of the sequence: 3
set1 holds the following elements: 10
set1 holds the following elements: 30
set1 holds the following elements: 90

The size of the sequence: 0
```

In this example, the size() function is used to report the number of elements in the sequence. Initially, the sequence contains five elements. The erase() function is called three times to search the sequence for a 45, 5, and 70. The original sequence contains a 45 and 70, but not a 5. After eliminating the 45 and 70, the new sequence is printed. Finally, the entire sequence is cleared with a call to clear(). The sequence is now empty.

The set3.cpp Application

The third example application, set3.cpp, uses insert(), begin(), and end() as in the previous examples. However, this application also illustrates how the unique_copy() method can be used to help eliminate duplicate elements in a set.

```
// set3.cpp
// Testing <multiset>
// insert(), begin(), and end()
// with additional unique features
// Chris H. Pappas and William H. Murray, 1999

#pragma warning(disable:4786)
#include <iostream>
#include <set>
#include <list>
#include <algorithm>
```

```
using namespace std ;

typedef set<int> SET_INT;

void main() {
  SET_INT set1;
  SET_INT::iterator it;

  // insert elements into set
  cout << "insert a 10 in set1" << endl;
  set1.insert(10);
  cout << "insert a 70 in set1" << endl;
  set1.insert(70);
  cout << "insert a 30 in set1" << endl;
  set1.insert(30);
  cout << "insert a 70 in set1" << endl;
  set1.insert(70);
  cout << "insert a 30 in set1" << endl;
  set1.insert(30);
  cout << "insert a 40 in set1" << endl;
  set1.insert(40);
  // set1 now holds 10, 70, 30, 70, 30, and 40

  // remove duplicates in set
  list<int> base;
  back_insert_iterator<list<int> > i(base);
  unique_copy(set1.begin(), set1.end(), i);

  for (it=set1.begin();it!=set1.end();it++)
     cout << "set1 holds only unique elements: "
        << *it << endl;
}
```

The output from this program shows each element as it is added to the appropriate sequence. Next, duplicates are removed with a small portion of code:

```
list<int> base;
back_insert_iterator<list<int> > i(base);
unique_copy(set1.begin(), set1.end(), i);
```

The <list> template class is used to describe an object that controls a varying-length sequence of elements of type T. Just what we need! Recall that this sequence is stored as a bidirectional linked list of elements. Each element in the linked list contains a member of type T.

Next, the back_insert_iterator template class used to describe an output iterator object is used to insert elements into a container of type Cont. The container provides the member type and value_type, that is, the type of element being used in the sequence. A member function push_back(value_type

c) can be used to append a new element to the end of a sequence. It then returns x.

The unique_copy() function is used to remove duplicate elements. It removes from the sequence any duplicates without altering the relative order of remaining elements. It does so repeatedly and finally returns the iterator value that designates the end of the new sequence.

For this example, the output takes the following form:

```
insert a 10 in set1
insert a 70 in set1
insert a 30 in set1
insert a 70 in set1
insert a 30 in set1
insert a 40 in set1
set1 holds only unique elements: 10
set1 holds only unique elements: 30
set1 holds only unique elements: 40
set1 holds only unique elements: 70
```

Experiment with this application by inserting elements all with the same value. What happens then?

Summary

The set and multiset templates provide a number of useful template functions and methods that allow control over a sequence of elements.

You may want to experiment with other template methods, such as lower_bound() and upper_bound().

F O U R T E E N

The <memory> Template

The STL standard header <memory> is used to define a class, an operator, and several templates that help allocate and free storage for a sequence of elements.

<memory> Template Syntax

This section will examine the code used to support the memory template. The following listing shows the syntax for the template classes, operators, and functions:

```
namespace std {

//  Template Classes
template<class T>
    class allocator;
class "allocator<void>;
template<class FwdIt, class T>
    class raw_storage_iterator;
template<class T>
    class auto_ptr;

//  Template Operators
template<class T>
    bool operator==(allocator<T>& lhs,
        allocator<T>& rhs);
template<class T>
    bool operator!=(allocator<T>& lhs,
        allocator<T>& rhs);
template<class T>
    void operator delete(void *p, size_t n, allocator& al);
template<class T>
    void *operator new(size_t n, allocator& al);

//  Template Functions
template<class T>
    pair<T *, ptrdiff_t> get_temporary_buffer(ptrdiff_t n, T *);
template<class T>
    void return_temporary_buffer(T *p);
template<class InIt, class FwdIt>
    FwdIt uninitialized_copy(InIt first, InIt last, FwdIt result);
template<class FwdIt, class T>
    void uninitialized_fill(FwdIt first, FwdIt last, const T& x);
template<class FwdIt, class Size, class T>
    void uninitialized_fill_n(FwdIt first, Size n, const T& x);
};
```

In the next sections you will learn the meaning of each memory member function and template function.

<memory> Template Operators

The memory template operators are shown in Table 14.1, along with a brief description of their purpose and return values.

Table 14.1 Template operators for memory

Template Operator Functions	Description
bool operator==(allocator<T>& lhs,allocator<T>& rhs);	This operator will return a true when both allocator objects compare equal and when one allocated object can be deallocated through the other object. The two allocator objects will compare equal if the value of one object is derived from another by assignment or construction.
bool operator!=(allocator<T>& lhs,allocator<T>& rhs);	This operator returns false. See above.
void operator delete(void *p, size_t n, allocator& al);	This operator function permits a placement delete expression. This expression can be used to deallocates storage using the allocator object. For example: delete(n,al) p; In effect, the operation is: al.deallocate(p,n);
void *operator new(size_t n, allocator& al);	This operator function permits a placement new expression. This expression can be used to allocates storage using the allocator object that allocates and constructs a new object of type U. For example: new(al) U; In effect, the operation is: allocator<T>::rebind<char>::other(al).allocate(n,(void *)0).

An example that uses the new() template operator is included in the sample code section of this chapter.

<memory> Template Methods

The memory template provides the methods shown in Table 14.2. This table lists the template methods, along with a short description of each method and returned values.

Table 14.2 The memory template methods and descriptions

Template Methods	Description
pair<T *, ptrdiff_t> get_temporary_buffer(ptrdiff_t n, T *);	The get_temporary_buffer() template function is used to allocate storage for a sequence of a maximum of n elements. The elements are from an unspecified source and are of type T. They could, for example, be from the standard heap. The function returns a value, pr, of type pair<T *, ptrdiff_t>. When storage is allocated, pr.first indicates the allocated storage, and pr.second indicates the number of elements in the longest sequence that the allocated storage can hold. When these conditions do not occur, pr.first is a null pointer. When a translator does not support member template functions, this function replaces the template with: template<class T> pair<T *, ptrdiff_t> get_temporary_buffer(ptrdiff_t n);
void return_temporary_buffer(T *p);	The return_temporary_buffer() template function is used to free the storage specified by p. The storage was allocated earlier by a call to get_temporary_buffer().

FwdIt uninitialized_copy(InIt first,
InIt last,FwdIt result);
	The uninitialized_copy() template function is used to perform the equivalent of the following operation:
	while (first != last)
	new ((void *)&*result++) T(*first++);
	In this case, T is of the type *first.

void uninitialized_fill(FwdIt first,
FwdIt last, const T& x);
	The uninitialized_fill() template function is used to perform the equivalent of the following operation:
	while (first != last)
	new ((void *)&*first++) T(x);

void uninitialized_fill_n(FwdIt first,
Size n, const T& x);
	The template function effectively executes:
	while (0 < n--)
	new ((void *)&*first++) T(x);

Note that the get_temporary_buffer() template function, used to allocate storage for a sequence of a maximum of n elements, returns a value, pr, of type pair<T *, ptrdiff_t>.

Here is the pair syntax:

```
template<class T, class U>
    struct pair {
    typedef T first_type;
    typedef U second_type
    T first;
    U second;
    pair();
    pair(const T& x, const U& y);
    template<class V, class W>
        pair(const pair<V, W>& pr);
    };
```

Table 14.2 indicates that when storage is successfully allocated, pr.first indicates the allocated storage. Then pr.second is used to indicate the number of elements in the longest sequence that the allocated storage can hold. A null pointer is returned when these conditions do not occur.

In the next section, you'll learn how to return the number of elements in the longest sequence that the allocated storage can hold.

Sample Code

The following sample applications illustrate a sample template operator and template method for the memory template. The first example illustrates the use of the new() operator, and the second example illustrates the use of the get_temporary_buffer() method.

The new1.cpp Application

The first example application, new1.cpp, shows how the new() operator is used to allocate storage. The following code was described in Table 14.1:

```
void *operator new(size_t n,  allocator& al);
```

In this example, the storage allocation is separated from the constructor of the my_storage class. (Remember that constructors are frequently used for storage allocation.) It is an allocator class (see Table 14.1 again) that actually performs the allocation. The class syntax for the allocator class is:

```
class allocator<void> {
  typedef void *pointer;
  typedef const void *const_pointer;
  typedef void value_type;
  allocator();
  template<class U>
    allocator(const allocator<U>);
  template<class U>
    operator=(const allocator<U>);
};
```

This class explicitly makes the template class allocator for type *void* and defines the const_pointer, pointer, and value_type types.

The allocator class uses placement syntax to force **new** into using user-specified memory locations, as you'll see in the following listing:

```
// new1.cpp
// Testing void* operator new()
// Chris H. Pappas and William H. Murray, 1999

#include <iostream.h>
#include <memory>

using namespace std;

class my_storage {
  char a1,a2,a3,a4,a5,a6,a7,a8;
public:
  my_storage() : a1('a'),
                 a2('b'),
                 a3('c'),
                 a4('d'),
                 a5('e'),
                 a6('f'),
                 a7('g'),
                 a8('h') {}
  ~my_storage() {a1 = 'i';
                 a2 = 'j';
                 a3 = 'k';
                 a4 = 'l';
                 a5 = 'm';
                 a6 = 'n';
                 a7 = 'o';
                 a8 = 'p';
  }
};

void main() {
  char ar[8];
  int i;

  // create object
  my_storage *p = new(ar) my_storage;
  for (i=0;i<8;i++)
    cout << ar[i] << endl;

  // insert a few lines
  cout << endl << endl;

  // delete object
  p->my_storage::~my_storage();
```

```
  for (i=0;i<8;i++)
    cout << ar[i] << endl;
}
```

The output from this program shows that a storage object was created and destroyed:

```
a
b
c
d
e
f
g
h


i
j
k
l
m
n
o
p
```

In this example, the constructor fills the object with a set of characters. This will be the evidence that the object was created. The destructor replaces the original characters with different characters. These will be the evidence that the original object was deleted.

The size2.cpp Application

The second example application, size2.cpp, shows how the get_temporary_buffer() method can be used to allocate storage for a sequence of elements. In this example, the storage is allocated and information is returned on the number of elements in the longest sequence that the allocated storage can hold.

```
// size2.cpp
// Testing get_temporary_buffer()
// Chris H. Pappas and William H. Murray, 1999

#include <iostream.h>
#include <memory>

using namespace std;

int mydata[] = {1,2,3,10,20,30,100,200,300};
int count = sizeof(mydata)/sizeof(int);
```

```
void main() {

  pair<int *, int> pr;
  pr = get_temporary_buffer(count, mydata);

  cout << "The number of elements returned is: "
     << pr.second << endl;
}
```

The output from this simple program displays the number of elements returned when the storage is actually allocated.

```
The number of elements returned is: 9
```

In this example, the get_temporary_buffer() method allocates storage for the integer elements contained in *mydata[]*. Here, the number of elements are calculated and returned to *count*. If the allocation is successful, get_temporary_buffer() will return a value *pr*, of type pair(T*, ptrdiff_t). The allocated storage is indicated by *pr.first* and the number of elements in the longest sequence that the allocated storage can hold in *pr.second*.

The fact that *pr.second* returns a 9, in this example, indicates the success of the allocated storage.

Summary

The memory templates provide a number of useful template operators and methods that allow for the allocation of storage over a sequence of elements.

You may want to experiment with other element sequences, such as sequences of characters and so on.

F I F T E E N

The <bitset> Template

This standard header <bitset> defines a template class that is used to describe objects that store sequences of bits (N). The bits can be set (1) or reset (0). An individual bit value can also be complemented or flipped. The bit position (j) of an object class bitset <N> corresponds to a bit value of 1 << j when converting to an object of some integral type. In this case, an integral value that corresponds to multiple bits is the sum of their bit values.

<bitset> Template Syntax

The following listing gives the syntax for the bitset template:

```
template<size_t N>
  class bitset {
public:
  typedef bool element_type;
  class reference;
  bitset();
  bitset(unsigned long val);
  template<class E, class T, class A>
    explicit bitset(const string<E, T, A>&  str,
      string<E, T, A>size_type pos = 0,
      string<E, T, A>size_type n = string<E, T, A>::npos);
  bitset<N>& operator&=(const bitset<N>& rhs);
  bitset<N>& operator|=(const bitset<N>& rhs);
  bitset<N>& operator^=(const bitset<N>& rhs);
  bitset<N>& operator<<=(const bitset<N>& pos);
  bitset<N>& ="operator>>=(const bitset<N>& pos);
  bitset<N>& set();
  bitset<N>& set(size_t pos, bool val = true);
  bitset<N>& reset();
  bitset<N>& flip();
  bitset<N>& flip(size_t pos);
  reference operator[](size_t pos);
  bool operator[](size_t pos) const;
  reference at(size_t pos);
  bool at(size_t pos) const;
  unsigned long to_ulong() const;
  template<class E, class T, class A> string to_string() const;
  size_t count() const;
  size_t size() const;
  bool operator==(const bitset<N>& rhs) const;
  bool operator!=(const bitset<N>& rhs) const;
  bool test(size_t pos) const;
  bool any() const;
  bool none() const;
  bitset<N> operator<<(size_t pos) const;
  bitset<N> operator>>(size_t pos) const;
  bitset<N> operator~();
  static const size_t bitset_size = N;
  };
```

Here element_type is a synonym for `bool`. The const static member, bitset_size, is initialized to the template parameter N.

The class reference has the following syntax:

```
class reference {
public:
    reference& operator=(bool b};
    reference& operator=(const reference& x);
    bool operator~() const;
    operator bool() const;
    reference& flip();
    };
```

The reference member class is used to describe an object that identifies a single bit in a sequence of bits. For example, assume that *bvalue* is an object of type **bool** and x is an object of type bitset<N>. If x[i] = bvalue, then *bvalue* will be stores at bit position *i* in x. Likewise, if *bvalue* = ~x[i], then `bvalue` holds the flipped value of the bit x[i].

To flip a bit in x, use:

```
bvalue = ~x[i];
x[i] = bvalue;
```

Or better yet:

```
x[i].flip();
```

You'll see how to use additional bitset methods in the sample code section of this chapter.

<bitset> Template Overloaded Operators

The bitset template overloads the operators shown in Table 15.1.

Table 15.1 Overloaded operators for bitset

Overloaded Operators
`bitset<N> operator~();`
`bitset<N> operator<<(size_t pos) const;`
`bitset<N> operator>>(size_t pos) const;`
`bitset<N>& operator&=(const bitset<N>& rhs);`
`bitset<N>& operator^=(const bitset<N>& rhs);`
`bitset<N>& operator|=(const bitset<N>& rhs);`
`bitset<N>& operator<<=(const bitset<N>& pos);`
`bitset<N>& operator>>=(const bitset<N>& pos);`
`bool operator!=(const bitset<N>& rhs) const;`
`bool operator[](size_t pos) const;`
`bool operator==(const bitset<N>& rhs) const;`
`reference operator[] (size_t pos);`

An example using overloaded operators is included in the sample code section of this chapter.

<bitset> Template Methods

The bitset template provides the methods shown in Table 15.2.

Table 15.2 bitset template methods and descriptions

Method	Description
bitset()	This constructor resets all bits in the sequence of bits.
bitset(unsigned long val)	This constructor sets just those bits at position j when val & 1 << j is nonzero.
template<class E, class T, class A> explicit bitset(const string<E, T, A>& str, string<E, T, A>size_type pos = 0, string<E, T, A>size_type n = string<E, T, A>::npos)	This template finds the initial bit values from elements of a string found in str. When str.size() < pos, an out_of_range is thrown. In all other cases, the string length, rlen, is selected to be the smaller of n and str.size() - pos. An invalid_argument will be thrown when any rlen elements starting at position pos are other than 0 or 1. In all other cases, bits will be set at position j when the element at position pos + j is 1.
bitset<N>& set()	Resets all bits in the bit sequence. Returns *this.
bitset<N>& set(size_t pos, bool val = true)	Stores val in the bit at position pos, and then returns *this. When size()<=pos, throws out_of_range.
bitset<N>& reset()	Resets all bits in the bit sequence. Returns *this.
bitset<N>& reset(size_t pos)	Resets the bit at position pos, and then returns *this. When size()<=pos, throws out_of_range.
bitset<N>& flip()	Flips all bits in the bit sequence. Returns *this.
bitset<N>& flip(size_t pos)	Throws an out_of_range for cases where size() <= pos. In all other cases, it flips the bit at position pos. Returns *this.
reference at(size_t pos) bool at(size_t pos) const	Returns an object of class reference. This object designates the bit at position pos when the object can be modified. For all other cases, it will return the value of the bit at position pos in the sequence of bits. When that bit position is invalid, it will throw an object of class out_of_range.
unsigned long to_ulong() const	Returns the sum of the bit values in the sequence of bits. It will throw an overflow_error if any bit in the sequence cannot be a type unsigned long.

Table 15.2 bitset template methods and descriptions *(continued)*

Method	Description
`template<class E, class T, class A> string to_string() const;`	The template constructs str, which is an object of class string. The method appends a 1 if the bit is set in the bit sequence. Bit position zero is appended last. Returns str. If templates are not supported, the template is is replaced with: string to_string() const;
`size_t count() const`	Returns the number of bits that are set in the sequence of bits.
`size_t size() const`	Returns the size, N.
`bool test(size_t pos) const`	Returns true iff the bit at position pos is set. Throws out_of_range when size() <= pos.
`bool any() const`	Returns true if any bit is set in the sequence of bits.
`bool none() const`	Returns true if none of the bits are set in the sequence of bits.

In the next section, you'll learn how to apply many of these bitset methods in actual sample applications.

Sample Code

The following sample applications illustrate various bitset methods, overloaded operators, and areas of caution when using this template. You find many interesting features in the following example programs.

The bitset1.cpp Application

The first example application, bitset1.cpp, shows how the set(), reset(), and flip() methods can be used to control all or individual bits.

```
// bitset1.cpp
// Testing <bitset>
// set(), reset(), and flip()
// Chris H. Pappas and William H. Murray, 1999

#include <iostream>
#include <bitset>
```

```
using namespace std;

void main()
{
    bitset<8*sizeof(int)> x;
    int i;

    x = 0;

    // starting with bits set to 0
    for(i=0;i<=31;i++) {
      x.flip(i);
      cout << x  << " the bit flipped is " << i << "\n";
    }

    x.reset();
    cout << "\nnew reset value equals " << x << "\n";

    x.set();
    cout << "\nnew set value equals " << x << "\n\n";

    // starting with bits set to 1
    for(i=0;i<=31;i++) {
      x.flip(i);
      cout << x << " the bit flipped is " << i  << "\n";
    }
}
```

The output from this program shows a series of bits as they are flipped from right to left:

```
00000000000000000000000000000001 the bit flipped is 0
00000000000000000000000000000011 the bit flipped is 1
00000000000000000000000000000111 the bit flipped is 2
00000000000000000000000000001111 the bit flipped is 3
00000000000000000000000000011111 the bit flipped is 4
00000000000000000000000000111111 the bit flipped is 5
00000000000000000000000001111111 the bit flipped is 6
00000000000000000000000011111111 the bit flipped is 7
00000000000000000000000111111111 the bit flipped is 8
00000000000000000000001111111111 the bit flipped is 9
00000000000000000000011111111111 the bit flipped is 10
00000000000000000000111111111111 the bit flipped is 11
00000000000000000001111111111111 the bit flipped is 12
00000000000000000011111111111111 the bit flipped is 13
00000000000000000111111111111111 the bit flipped is 14
00000000000000001111111111111111 the bit flipped is 15
00000000000000011111111111111111 the bit flipped is 16
00000000000000111111111111111111 the bit flipped is 17
00000000000001111111111111111111 the bit flipped is 18
00000000000011111111111111111111 the bit flipped is 19
```

```
00000000000111111111111111111111 the bit flipped is 20
00000000001111111111111111111111 the bit flipped is 21
00000000011111111111111111111111 the bit flipped is 22
00000000111111111111111111111111 the bit flipped is 23
00000001111111111111111111111111 the bit flipped is 24
00000011111111111111111111111111 the bit flipped is 25
00000111111111111111111111111111 the bit flipped is 26
00001111111111111111111111111111 the bit flipped is 27
00011111111111111111111111111111 the bit flipped is 28
00111111111111111111111111111111 the bit flipped is 29
01111111111111111111111111111111 the bit flipped is 30
11111111111111111111111111111111 the bit flipped is 31

new reset value equals 00000000000000000000000000000000

new set value equals 11111111111111111111111111111111

11111111111111111111111111111110 the bit flipped is 0
11111111111111111111111111111100 the bit flipped is 1
11111111111111111111111111111000 the bit flipped is 2
11111111111111111111111111110000 the bit flipped is 3
11111111111111111111111111100000 the bit flipped is 4
11111111111111111111111111000000 the bit flipped is 5
11111111111111111111111110000000 the bit flipped is 6
11111111111111111111111100000000 the bit flipped is 7
11111111111111111111111000000000 the bit flipped is 8
11111111111111111111110000000000 the bit flipped is 9
11111111111111111111100000000000 the bit flipped is 10
11111111111111111111000000000000 the bit flipped is 11
11111111111111111110000000000000 the bit flipped is 12
11111111111111111100000000000000 the bit flipped is 13
11111111111111111000000000000000 the bit flipped is 14
11111111111111110000000000000000 the bit flipped is 15
11111111111111100000000000000000 the bit flipped is 16
11111111111111000000000000000000 the bit flipped is 17
11111111111110000000000000000000 the bit flipped is 18
11111111111100000000000000000000 the bit flipped is 19
11111111111000000000000000000000 the bit flipped is 20
11111111110000000000000000000000 the bit flipped is 21
11111111100000000000000000000000 the bit flipped is 22
11111111000000000000000000000000 the bit flipped is 23
11111110000000000000000000000000 the bit flipped is 24
11111100000000000000000000000000 the bit flipped is 25
11111000000000000000000000000000 the bit flipped is 26
11110000000000000000000000000000 the bit flipped is 27
11100000000000000000000000000000 the bit flipped is 28
11000000000000000000000000000000 the bit flipped is 29
10000000000000000000000000000000 the bit flipped is 30
00000000000000000000000000000000 the bit flipped is 31
```

First, the number of bits is set in this example with:

```
bitset<8*sizeof(int)> x;
```

The sizeof() function returns 4 bytes for the size of an integer. This number is multiplied by 8 to obtain the number of bits.

The value of all bits is set to 0 with:

```
x = 0;
```

Then bits are flipped starting with the LSB to the MSB using a simple **for** loop.

```
// starting with bits set to 0
for(i=0;i<=31;i++) {
  x.flip(i);
  cout << x  << " the bit flipped is " << i << "\n";
}
```

Since all of the bits were initially 0, they will each be set to 1 when they are flipped. The bits could have all been reset to 0 by using the reset() method.

```
x.reset();
cout << "\nnew reset value equals " << x << "\n";
```

The set() method is used to initially set all of the bits to 1, and the remaining program code flips the individual bits back to a 0 value.

The bitset2.cpp Application

The second application, bitset2.cpp, shows how the count(), size(), test(), any(), and none() methods can be used.

```
// bitset2.cpp
// Testing <bitset>
// count(), size(), test(), any(), none()
// Chris H. Pappas and William H. Murray, 1999

#include <iostream>
#include <bitset>

using namespace std;

void main()
{
    bitset<8*sizeof(int)> x;

    x = 87654321;   // 5397FB1 hexadecimal
                    // 0101001110010111111110110001 binary

    cout << x.count() << " is the count of all set bits\n";
```

```
    cout << x.size() << " is the size (in bits)\n";

    cout << x.test(0) << " -> a 1 means the particular bit is set\n";

    cout << x.any() << " -> a 1 means at least one bit is set\n";

    cout << x.none() << " -> a 1 means no bits are set\n";
}
```

The output from this program shows the information returned by each of the five methods when applied to a value of 87654321. Since we are working with individual bits, a hexadecimal or binary representation would be more useful. The decimal number 87654321 is equivalent to 5397FB1 in hexadecimal or 0101001110010111111110110001 in binary.

```
17 is the count of all set bits
32 is the size (in bits)
1 -> a 1 means that the particular bit is set
1 -> a 1 means that at least one bit is set
0 -> a 1 means  that no bits are set
```

The count() method returns a total of all bits set to one. In this example, count() returns a 17. The size() method returns the total size of the value in bits. With these two methods and simple subtraction, you could calculate the number of bits set to 0, if desired. The test() method can test any particular bit to see whether it is set or reset. In this example, the first bit (position 0) is tested. The test() method returns a 1 if the bit is set and a 0 if the bit is reset. The any() method is useful if you want to check to see whether any bits are set. The any() method will return a 1 if at least one bit in the sequence is 1, and a 0 otherwise. Likewise, the none() method can be used to check to see whether none of the bits are set. The none() method will return a 1 if none of the bits are set and a 0 if at least one bit is set in the sequence.

The bitset3.cpp Application

The third application, bitset3.cpp, shows how the overloaded operators ~ and == can be used with the <bitset> template.

```
// bitset3.cpp
// Testing <bitset>
// evaluating the ~ and == operators
// Chris H. Pappas and William H. Murray, 1999

#include <iostream>
#include <bitset>

using namespace std;

void main()
{
```

```
    bitset<8*sizeof(int)> x;
    x = 87654321;   // 5397FB1 hexadecimal
                    // 0101001110010111111110110001 binary

    cout << x << " -> represents the original bits.\n";
    cout << ~x << " -> represents the compliment of the bits.\n";

    if (x == ~x)
        cout << "The numbers are equal.\n";
    else
        cout << "The numbers are not equal.\n";
}
```

The output from this program shows the information returned by using the operators mentioned. The original sequence of bits is given by the decimal number 87654321. This, as you may recall, is equivalent to 5397FB1 in hexadecimal or 0101001110010111111110110001 in binary.

```
00000101001110010111111110110001 -> represents the original bits.
11111010110001101000000001001110 -> represents the compliment of the bits.
The numbers are not equal.
```

The original number is printed first, followed by the compliment of the number generated with the ~ operator.

A simple test for equality is then done on x and ~x. They are, of course, not equal. However, if the test for equality is done on x and x, the reported results will show that they are equal.

The bitset4.cpp Application

The fourth application, bitset4.cpp, shows how the to_long() method can be used to convert the sequence of bits to an unsigned long. You'll also see an interesting case of accidentally using a signed number where only an unsigned number should be supplied.

```
// bitset4.cpp
// Testing <bitset>
// signed and unsigned values
// Chris H. Pappas and William H. Murray, 1999

#include <iostream>
#include <bitset>

using namespace std;

void main()
{
    bitset<8*sizeof(char)> x;
```

```
    cout << "expected results using an unsigned number\n";
    x = 135;
    cout << x << " -> represents the original bits.\n";
    cout << x.to_ulong() << " -> bits represented as an unsigned
long.\n";

    cout << "\nunexpected results using a signed number\n";
    x = -135;
    cout << x << " -> represents the original bits.\n";
    cout << x.to_ulong() << " -> bits represented as an unsigned
long.\n";
}
```

The first two three lines of output from this program correctly show the expected results. The second line of output shows the sequence of bits and the third line uses the to_long() method to correctly convert that sequence to an unsigned long.

The second portion of code attempts to duplicate the same feats using a negative number. Since an unsigned number is expected by bitset, you can anticipate unpredictable results.

```
expected results using an unsigned number
10000111 -> represents the original bits.
135 -> bits represented as an unsigned long.

unexpected results using a signed number
01111001 -> represents the original bits.
121 -> bits represented as an unsigned long.
```

If you are good at 1's and 2's compliment arithmetic, you may be able to figure out what happened to each of the bits. (Hint: Even though you supplied a negative number, <bitset> treated the number as an unsigned sequence of bits.)

Summary

The bitset template provides a number of useful overloaded operators and methods that allow control over individual bits in a sequence of bits.

You may want to consider the use of this template when creating applications that encrypt or encode sequences of bits.

SIXTEEN

The <cassert>, <cerrno>, <exception>, and <stdexcept> Standard C++ Headers

This chapter describes the Standard C++ library headers <cassert>, <cerrno>, <exception> and <stdexcept>. In this chapter, you'll learn the new ANSI standard header syntax for these headers, investigate features for implementing the header code, and see several working examples illustrating various features of these standard header files.

The <cassert> Header Syntax

The following listing gives the syntax for using the <cassert> standard header file:

```
namespace std {#include <assert.h> };
```

The <cassert> standard header is used to include the <assert.h> header within the *std* namespace.

The <assert.h> header provides the assert macro that is used to identify logic errors when creating programs. Usually the assert macro implements an *expression* argument that evaluates to false when the program is not operating correctly. The assert macro can be used to print a message, including the source file name and the line number where the assertion failed, when the *expression* evaluates to false. A call to abort terminates the application.

The syntax for using the assert macro is

```
void assert( int expression );
```

The expression parameter is an expression, including pointers, that evaluates to a non-zero or zero values.

The first example in the sample code section of this chapter illustrates the use of the <cassert> header.

The <cerrno> Header Syntax

The following listing gives the syntax for using the <cerrno> standard header file:

```
namespace std {#include <errno.h> };
```

The <cerrno> standard header is used to include the **<**errno.h**>** header file within the *std* namespace.

The int _doserrno, int errno, char *_sys_errlist[ ], and int _sys_nerr are global variables, of type **extern**, that hold the error codes used by both the perror() and strerror() functions. The variables are declared in the stdlib.h header file.

An errno value is set in a system-level call when an error occurs. The errno value should be checked before and after succeeding calls, since errno retains the value for the last call that set it. The errno.h header file defines all UNIX compatible constants, as shown in Table 16.1. Every errno value is associated with an error message. This message can be printed or stored as a string using perror or strerror appropriately.

Table 16.1 Operating system error codes and constants found in errno.h

Error Code	Constant
EPERM	1
ENOENT	2
ESRCH	3
EINTR	4
EIO	5
ENXIO	6
E2BIG	7
ENOEXEC	8
EBADF	9
ECHILD	10
EAGAIN	11
ENOMEM	12

Table 16.1 Operating system error codes and constants found in errno.h

Error Code	Constant
EACCES	13
EFAULT	14
EBUSY	16
EEXIST	17
EXDEV	18
ENODEV	19
ENOTDIR	20
EISDIR	21
EINVAL	22
ENFILE	23
EMFILE	24
ENOTTY	25
EFBIG	27
ENOSPC	28
ESPIPE	29
EROFS	30
EMLINK	31
EPIPE	32
EDOM (ANSI)	33
ERANGE (ANSI)	34
EDEADLK	36
ENAMETOOLONG	38
ENOLCK	39
ENOSYS	40
ENOTEMPTY	41
EILSEQ	42

The following sections will examine errno values that are compatible with 32-bit Windows applications. Of these values, ERANGE and EDOM are the only constants described in the ANSI standard. To access the actual operating system error code under Windows NT (2000) or Windows 98, use the _doserrno variable, which contains the value.

ECHILD

Indicates that no spawned processes exist.

EAGAIN

Indicates that no more processes exist. This value may result from an attempt to create a new process due when not enough memory is available, when no more process slots are available, or when the maximum nesting level has been reached.

E2BIG

Indicates that the argument list is too big.

EACCES

Indicates that permission is denied when the file's permission setting will not allow a specific type of access. This error indicates an attempted file access that is contrary to the file's attribute settings.

EBADF

Indicates a bad file number. Bad file numbers usually result from invalid file handles or attempts to write to read-only files.

EDEADLOCK

Indicates that a potential resource deadlock can occur. Math function arguments are not included in this consideration.

EDOM

Indicates a math argument domain error.

EEXIST

Indicates that a file exists or that an attempt is made to create an existing file.

EINVAL

Indicates that an invalid argument is supplied to a function's argument list. For example, a file read or write is attempted before a file handle is retrieved.

EMFILE

Indicates that too many files are opened, usually because no more file handles are available for subsequent opened files.

ENOENT

Indicates that no file or directory of the name specified exists. For a file, this value may mean that the file doesn't exist or that the path is not correct.

ENOEXEC

Indicates an executable format error that results when attempting to execute either a file with a non-executable file format or a file with an invalid executable file format.

ENOMEM

Indicates that not enough memory is available to perform the operation.

ENOSPC

Indicates that insufficient space is left on a device, for example, attempting to write to an almost full or full 3.5" floppy disk.

ERANGE

Indicates that the result for an operation is too large. This message is frequently encountered when math functions are passed arguments that are too large and would result in loss of precision of returned results.

EXDEV

Indicates the presence of a cross-device link, a result of trying to move a file from one device to another using the rename function.

The <exception> Header Syntax

The following listing gives the syntax for the <exception> header:

```
namespace std {
    class exception;
    class bad_exception;
    typedef void (*terminate_handler)();
    typedef void (*unexpected_handler)();
    terminate_handler set_terminate(terminate_handler ph) throw();
    unexpected_handler set_unexpected(unexpected_handler ph) throw();
    void terminate();
    void unexpected();
    bool uncaught_exception();
    };
```

The standard header `<exception>` is included in order to define several types and methods related to the handling of exceptions.

In the following sections, we'll examine each class and typedef in more detail.

exception

The syntax for the exception class follows:

```
class exception {
public:
    exception() throw();
    exception(const exception& rhs) throw();
    exception& operator=(const exception& rhs) throw();
    virtual ~exception() throw();
    virtual const char *what() const throw();
    };
```

The exception class is the parent class for all exceptions thrown by specific expressions and the Standard C++ library. The member functions of the exception class do not throw any exceptions. The string value returned by `what()` is not specified by the default constructor. It may, however, be defined by constructors for specific derived classes.

The operand of throw is syntactically similar to the operand of a return statement. Currently, Visual C++ does not support *exception-specifications*, as described in section 15.4 of the ANSI C++ draft or *function-try-block* described in section 15.

bad_exception

The syntax for the bad_exception class follows:

```
class bad_exception : public exception {
    };
```

The bad_exception class describes an exception that can be thrown from an unexpected handler. The class methods do not themselves throw exceptions. The value returned by what(), in this case, is implementation-specific.

terminate_handler

The syntax for terminate_handler follows:

```
typedef void (*terminate_handler)();
```

This **typedef** creates a pointer to a function that can be used as a terminate handler.

unexpected_handler

The syntax for unexpected_handler follows:

```
typedef void (*unexpected_handler)();
```

This **typedef** creates a pointer to a function that can be used as an unexpected handler.

set_terminate

The syntax for set_terminate follows:

```
terminate_handler set_terminate(terminate_handler ph) throw();
```

The set_terminate() function identifies a terminate handler function pointed to by `*ph`. The function returns the address of the previous terminate handler. When no previous function exists, the return value can be used to restore the default behavior. This value can be NULL. `*ph` cannot be a null pointer. When multiple thread environments are encountered, use separate terminate functions for each thread.

The terminate_function type, for user-defined functions, is defined in the eh.h header file. This function should take no arguments and should not return to its caller.

set_unexpected

The syntax for the set_unexpected() function follows:

```
unexpected_handler set_unexpected(unexpected_handler ph) throw();
```

The set_unexpected() function is used to create an unexpected_handler named *ph. The function returns the address of the former unexpected handler. The unexpected_handler function cannot be a null pointer.

terminate()

The syntax for the terminate() function follows:

```
void terminate();
```

The terminate() method is used to call abort() at program startup or the terminate handler, if one is written. The terminate handler is used when exception handling is to be aborted. A terminate handler is of type void. Terminate handlers do not return to the calling routine.

An example of the use of the terminate() method is shown in the sample code section of this chapter.

unexpected()

The syntax for the unexpected() function follows:

```
void unexpected();
```

The unexpected() function calls the unexpected handler. The terminate handler is used when control leaves a function by a thrown exception. This exception is a type not allowed by the function. A terminate handler is of type void. Terminate handlers do not return to the calling routine. The terminate handler can terminate execution by throwing an object of type bad_exception or by throwing an object listed in the exception specification. Termination can also occur by calling abort(), exit(), or terminate().

uncaught_exception

The syntax for the uncaught_exception() function follows:

```
bool uncaught_exception();
```

The uncaught_exception() function returns a type **bool**. It returns true only when a thrown exception is being processed. False is returned for all other cases.

The <stdexcept> Header Syntax

The following listing gives the syntax for the <stdexcept> header:

```
namespace std {
class logic_error;
    class domain_error;
    class invalid_argument;
    class length_error;
    class out_of_range;
class runtime_error;
    class range_error;
    class overflow_error;
    class underflow_error;
    };
```

The standard header `<stdexcept>` is used for defining classes that report exceptions. All the classes are derived from exception class exception. In the following sections, we'll examine each class in this group.

logic_error class

The logic_error class serves as the parent class for exceptions thrown in order to report errors before program execution. The syntax for the logic_error class follows:

```
class logic_error : public exception {
public:
    logic_error(const string& what_arg);
    };
```

The value returned by what() is `what_arg.data()`.

domain_error class

The domain_error class, derived from the logic_error parent class, is the parent class for exceptions thrown when reporting domain errors. The syntax for the domain_error class follows:

```
class domain_error : public logic_error
public:
    domain_error(const string& what_arg);
    };
```

The value returned by what() is `what_arg.data()`.

invalid_argument class

The invalid_argument class, derived from the logic_error parent class, is the parent class for exceptions thrown when reporting invalid argument errors. The syntax for the invalid_argument class follows:

```
class invalid_argument : public logic_error {
public:
    invalid_argument(const string& what_arg);
    };
```

The value returned by what() is `what_arg.data()`.

length_error class

The length_error class, derived from the logic_error parent class, is the parent class for exceptions thrown when an attempt is made to generate an object that is too long. The syntax for the length_error class follows:

```
class length_error : public logic_error {
public:
    length_error(const string& what_arg);
    };
```

The value returned by what() is `what_arg.data()`.

out_of_range class

The out_of_range class, derived from the logic_error parent class, is the parent class for exceptions thrown when reporting an argument that is out of range. The syntax for the out_of_range class follows:

```
class out_of_range : public logic_error {
public:
    out_of_range(const string& what_arg);
    };
```

The value returned by what() is `what_arg.data()`.

runtime_error class

The class serves as the parent class for all exceptions thrown to report errors that are generated when the program executes. The syntax for the runtime_error class follows:

```
class runtime_error : public exception {
public:
    runtime_error(const string& what_arg);
    };
```

The value returned by what() is `what_arg.data()`.

range_error class

The range_error class, derived from the runtime_error parent class, is the parent class for exceptions thrown when reporting a range error. The syntax for the range_error class follows:

```
class range_error : public runtime_error {
public:
    range_error(const string& what_arg);
    };
```

The value returned by what() is `what_arg.data()`.

overflow_error class

The overflow_error class, derived from the runtime_error parent class, is the parent class for exceptions thrown when reporting an arithmetic overflow. The syntax for the overflow_class follows:

```
class overflow_error : public runtime_error {
public:
    overflow_error(const string& what_arg);
    };
```

The value returned by what() is `what_arg.data()`.

underflow_error class

The underflow_error class, derived from the runtime_error parent class, is the parent class for exceptions thrown when reporting an arithmetic underflow error. The syntax for the underflow_error class follows:

```
class underflow_error : public runtime_error{
public:
    underflow_error(const string& what_arg);
    };
```

The value returned by what() is `what_arg.data()`.

Sample Code

In the following sections, two sample applications illustrate how to implement the <cassert> and <terminate> standard headers.

A <cassert> Application

The first example application, assert1.cpp, shows how the assert macro can be used to test for a NULL condition.

```
// assert1.cpp
// The check_string function uses
// the assert macro and tests for a NULL condition.
// Chris H. Pappas and William H. Murray, 1999

#include <iostream>
#include <cassert>
#include <string>

using namespace std;

void check_string(char *string );

void main()
{
   char  str1[] = "non-NULL string";
   char  *str2 = NULL;

   cout << "Checking first string\n";
   check_string(str1);

   cout << "Checking second string\n";
   check_string(str2);
}

void check_string(char * string)
{
   assert(string != NULL);
}
```

The output from this program shows how an assert() function reports an error to the screen.

```
Checking first string
Checking second string
Assertion failed: string != NULL, file c:\assert1.cpp, line
28

abnormal program termination
Press any key to continue
```

In this example, a check is made for a NULL string. Two strings are checked, with the assertion error being reported for the second string.

The termin2.cpp Application

The second application, termin2.cpp, shows how to invoke set_terminate provided in the <exception> header.

```
// termin2.cpp
// illustrates set_terminate() function
// Chris H. Pappas and William H. Murray, 1999

#include <iostream>
#include <math.h>
#include <process.h>
#include <eh.h>

using namespace std;

void notify_me();

void main()
{
    double i = 0;  // test value
    double j;

    set_terminate(notify_me);

    try {
        if( i == 0 )
            throw "Can't find log(0)!";
        else
            j = log(i);
    }

    catch(double) {
        cout << "Found an exception.\n";
    }

    cout << "log = " << j << "\n";
}

void notify_me()
{
    cout << "terminate called notify_me().\n";
    exit(-1);
}
```

The output for this program for i = 0 reports:

```
terminate called notify_me().
```

In this application, set_terminate() uses the terminate_handler notify_me() to report an exception. You cannot obtain the logarithm of the number 0. Once the message is printed, the routine calls exit() to terminate without returning to the calling routine.

Change the test number to a non-zero value and satisfy yourself that the exception will not be generated.

Summary

The <cassert>, <cerrno>, <exception>, and <stdexcept> Standard C++ headers provide an effective means of handling assertion, error and exceptions.

The previous examples illustrate how easily you can include these Standard C++ headers into simple applications.

SEVENTEEN

The <cctype> and <cstring> Standard C++ Headers and <string> Template Class

This chapter describes the <cctype> and <cstring> standard C++ Headers as well as the header for the <string> template class. In this chapter, you'll learn the new ANSI Standard C++ header syntax for these headers, investigate features for implementing the header code, and see several working examples illustrating various features of these standard header files. Several examples will also be included to show features common to the <string> template class.

The <cctype> Standard C++ Header Syntax

The following listing gives the syntax for using the <cctype> Standard C++ header file:

```
namespace std {#include <ctype.h> };
```

The <cctype> Standard C++ header is used to include the <ctype.h> header within the *std* namespace. The ctype.h header file defines macros for character classification and/or conversion.

For example, the following portion of the ctype.h header file sets the bit masks for various character types:

```
#define _UPPER          0x1     // upper case letter
#define _LOWER          0x2     // lower case letter
#define _DIGIT          0x4     // digit[0-9]
#define _SPACE          0x8     // tab, carriage return, newline,
                                //vertical tab or form feed
#define _PUNCT          0x10    // punctuation character
#define _CONTROL        0x20    // control character
#define _BLANK          0x40    // space char
#define _HEX            0x80    // hexadecimal digit

#define _LEADBYTE       0x8000                  // multibyte
#define _ALPHA          (0x0100|_UPPER|_LOWER)  // alphabetic
```

You'll also find the function prototypes for a variety of familiar character handling functions. The following partial listing is also from ctype.h:

```
_CRTIMP int __cdecl _isctype(int, int);
_CRTIMP int __cdecl isalpha(int);
_CRTIMP int __cdecl isupper(int);
_CRTIMP int __cdecl islower(int);
_CRTIMP int __cdecl isdigit(int);
_CRTIMP int __cdecl isxdigit(int);
_CRTIMP int __cdecl isspace(int);
_CRTIMP int __cdecl ispunct(int);
_CRTIMP int __cdecl isalnum(int);
_CRTIMP int __cdecl isprint(int);
_CRTIMP int __cdecl isgraph(int);
_CRTIMP int __cdecl iscntrl(int);
_CRTIMP int __cdecl toupper(int);
_CRTIMP int __cdecl tolower(int);
_CRTIMP int __cdecl _tolower(int);
_CRTIMP int __cdecl _toupper(int);
_CRTIMP int __cdecl __isascii(int);
_CRTIMP int __cdecl __toascii(int);
_CRTIMP int __cdecl __iscsymf(int);
_CRTIMP int __cdecl __iscsym(int);
```

Table 17.1 lists the most frequently used functions from ctype.h and gives a brief description of their use.

Table 17.1 <cctype> functions and meanings

Function	Meaning
`isalpha(int)`	Returns nonzero if character being passed is a letter. For all other cases, a zero is returned.
`isupper(int)`	Returns nonzero if character being passed is uppercase. For all other cases, a zero is returned.
`islower(int)`	Returns nonzero if character being passed is lowercase. For all other cases, a zero is returned.
`isdigit(int)`	Returns nonzero if character being passed is a digit (0-9). For all other cases, a zero is returned.
`isxdigit(int)`	Returns nonzero if character being passed is a hexadecimal digit (0-F) or (0-f). For all other cases, a zero is returned.
`isspace(int)`	Returns nonzero if character being passed is a space, vertical or horizontal tab, formfeed or carriage return, or a newline character. For all other cases, a zero is returned.
`ispunct(int)`	Returns nonzero if character being passed is punctuation. (These are printable characters that are not alphanumeric or a space. For all other cases, a zero is returned.
`isalnum(int)`	Returns nonzero if character being passed is a letter or a digit. For all other cases, a zero is returned.
`isprint(int)`	Returns nonzero if character being passed is printable. A space is included in the list of printable characters. See isgraph(). For all other cases, a zero is returned.
`isgraph(int)`	Returns nonzero if character being passed is printable. A space is excluded from the list of printable characters. See isprint(). For all other cases, a zero is returned.
`iscntrl(int)`	Returns nonzero if character being passed is a printable character excluding a space. For all other cases, a zero is returned.
`toupper(int)`	Returns the uppercase equivalent to the character being passed. If a letter (a-z) is not passed, the character remains unchanged.
`tolower(int)`	Returns the lowercase equivalent to the character being passed. If a letter (A-Z) is not passed, the character remains unchanged.

You'll also find the function prototypes for wide character handling functions, such as those in the following partial listing:

```
_CRTIMP int __cdecl iswalpha(wint_t);
_CRTIMP int __cdecl iswupper(wint_t);
```

```
_CRTIMP int __cdecl iswlower(wint_t);
_CRTIMP int __cdecl iswdigit(wint_t);
_CRTIMP int __cdecl iswxdigit(wint_t);
_CRTIMP int __cdecl iswspace(wint_t);
_CRTIMP int __cdecl iswpunct(wint_t);
_CRTIMP int __cdecl iswalnum(wint_t);
_CRTIMP int __cdecl iswprint(wint_t);
_CRTIMP int __cdecl iswgraph(wint_t);
_CRTIMP int __cdecl iswcntrl(wint_t);
_CRTIMP int __cdecl iswascii(wint_t);
_CRTIMP int __cdecl isleadbyte(int);

_CRTIMP wchar_t __cdecl towupper(wchar_t);
_CRTIMP wchar_t __cdecl towlower(wchar_t);

_CRTIMP int __cdecl iswctype(wint_t, wctype_t);

// OBSOLETE
_CRTIMP int __cdecl is_wctype(wint_t, wctype_t);
// OBSOLETE
```

You'll see an example of using the <cctype> Standard C++ header file in the example portion of this chapter.

The <cstring> standard C++ Header Syntax

The following listing gives the syntax for using the <cstring> Standard C++ header file:

```
namespace std {#include <string.h> };
```

The <cstring> Standard C++ header is used to include the <string.h> header within the *std* namespace. The string.h header file contains a variety of items, including the function declarations for various string manipulation functions.

For example, the following portion of the string.h header defines size_t as a type unsigned:

```
#ifndef _SIZE_T_DEFINED
  typedef unsigned int size_t;
  #define _SIZE_T_DEFINED
#endif
```

The following listing represents a portion of the string.h header file used to declare various string functions:

```
_CRTIMP void *  __cdecl memcpy(void *, const void *, size_t);
_CRTIMP int     __cdecl memcmp(const void *, const void *,
                              size_t);
_CRTIMP void *  __cdecl memset(void *, int, size_t);
```

```
_CRTIMP char *   __cdecl _strset(char *, int);
_CRTIMP char *   __cdecl strcpy(char *, const char *);
_CRTIMP char *   __cdecl strcat(char *, const char *);
_CRTIMP int      __cdecl strcmp(const char *, const char *);
_CRTIMP size_t   __cdecl strlen(const char *);
#if
  void *   __cdecl memcpy(void *, const void *, size_t);
  int      __cdecl memcmp(const void *, const void *, size_t);
  void *   __cdecl memset(void *, int, size_t);
  char *   __cdecl _strset(char *, int);
  char *   __cdecl strcpy(char *, const char *);
  char *   __cdecl strcat(char *, const char *);
  int      __cdecl strcmp(const char *, const char *);
  size_t   __cdecl strlen(const char *);
#endif
_CRTIMP void *   __cdecl _memccpy(void *, const void *, int,
                                 unsigned int);
_CRTIMP void *   __cdecl memchr(const void *, int, size_t);
_CRTIMP int      __cdecl _memicmp(const void *, const void *,
                                 unsigned int);

#ifdef  _M_ALPHA
  //memmove as an intrinsic in the Alpha compiler
  void *   __cdecl memmove(void *, const void *, size_t);
#else
_CRTIMP void *   __cdecl memmove(void *, const void *, size_t);
#endif

_CRTIMP char *   __cdecl strchr(const char *, int);
_CRTIMP int      __cdecl _strcmpi(const char *, const char *);
_CRTIMP int      __cdecl _stricmp(const char *, const char *);
_CRTIMP int      __cdecl strcoll(const char *, const char *);
_CRTIMP int      __cdecl _stricoll(const char *, const char *);
_CRTIMP int      __cdecl _strncoll(const char *, const char *,
                                  size_t);
_CRTIMP int      __cdecl _strnicoll(const char *, const char *,
                                   size_t);
_CRTIMP size_t   __cdecl strcspn(const char *, const char *);
_CRTIMP char *   __cdecl _strdup(const char *);
_CRTIMP char *   __cdecl _strerror(const char *);
_CRTIMP char *   __cdecl strerror(int);
_CRTIMP char *   __cdecl _strlwr(char *);
_CRTIMP char *   __cdecl strncat(char *, const char *, size_t);
_CRTIMP int      __cdecl strncmp(const char *, const char *,
                                size_t);
_CRTIMP int      __cdecl _strnicmp(const char *, const char *,
                                  size_t);
_CRTIMP char *   __cdecl strncpy(char *, const char *, size_t);
_CRTIMP char *   __cdecl _strnset(char *, int, size_t);
_CRTIMP char *   __cdecl strpbrk(const char *, const char *);
```

```
_CRTIMP char *   __cdecl strrchr(const char *, int);
_CRTIMP char *   __cdecl _strrev(char *);
_CRTIMP size_t   __cdecl strspn(const char *, const char *);
_CRTIMP char *   __cdecl strstr(const char *, const char *);
_CRTIMP char *   __cdecl strtok(char *, const char *);
_CRTIMP char *   __cdecl _strupr(char *);
_CRTIMP size_t   __cdecl strxfrm (char *, const char *, size_t);
```

Table 17.2 lists the most frequently used functions from string.h and gives a brief description of their use.

Table 17.2 <cstring> functions and meanings

Function	Meaning
`void * memcpy(void *, const void *, size_t)`	Copies number of characters specified by size_t parameter from const void * array to void * array. Undefined results if arrays overlap. Returns a pointer to void * array.
`int memcmp(const void *, const void *, size_t)`	Compares number of characters specified by size_t parameter from second const void * array to first const void * array. Returns an integer less than zero when array1 < array2. Returns a zero when array1 = array2. Returns an integer greater than zero when array1 > array2.
`void * memset(void *, int, size_t)`	Copies number of characters specified by size_t parameter as low-order byte given in int parameter into void * array. The void * array will be returned.
`char * strcpy(char *, const char *)`	Copies contents of second parameter into first parameter. The string specified in the second parameter must be a null-terminated string. Returns a pointer to the string specified in the first parameter.
`char * strcat(char *, const char *)`	Concatenates the string given by the second parameter to the string given by the first parameter. The first string is terminated with a null terminator. The second string remains unchanged. Returns the first string. No bounds checking is employed.
`int strcmp(const char *, const char *)`	Compares the string specified by parameter two with the string specified by parameter one. Returns an integer less than zero when string1 < string2. Returns a zero when string1 = string2. Returns an integer greater than zero when string1 > string2.

Table 17.2 <cstring> functions and meanings *(continued)*

Function	Meaning
`size_t strlen(const char *)`	Returns the length of the string given as parameter one. The string must be null-terminated.
`void * memchr(const void *, int, size_t)`	For a given number of characters specified by the size_t parameter, a search is made for the first occurrence of the int parameter (character) in the const void * array. A pointer to the first occurrence is returned. If no match is found, a null pointer is returned.
`void * memmove(void *, const void *, size_t)`	Moves number of characters specified by size_t parameter from const void * array to void * array. If arrays overlap, copy of characters is valid with const void * parameter unchanged. Returns a pointer to void * array.
`char * strchr(const char *, int)`	For a given number of characters specified by the size_t parameter, a search is made for the first occurrence of the int parameter (character) in the const char * array. A pointer to the first occurrence is returned. If no match is found, a null pointer is returned.
`int strcoll(const char *, const char *)`	Compares the string given by the first const char * parameter with the string specified by the second const char * parameter. Returns an integer less than zero when string1 < string2. Returns a zero when string1 = string2. Returns an integer greater than zero when string1 > string2.
`size_t strcspn(const char *, const char *)`	Returns the length of the string specified by the first const char * parameter made from those characters **not** contained in the string specified by the second const char * parameter. Returns an integer giving the position of the first match, or a null if no match occurs.
`char * strerror(int)`	A pointer is returned to an implement-defined string that correlates with the error value specified by the int parameter.
`char * strncat(char *, const char *, size_t)`	Concatenates up to size_t parameter the string given by the second parameter to the string given by the first parameter. The first string is terminated with a null terminator. The second string remains unchanged. Returns the first string. No bounds checking is employed.

Table 17.2 <cstring> functions and meanings *(continued)*

Function	Meaning
`int strncmp(const char *, const char *, size_t)`	Compares up to size_t parameter of the string specified by parameter two with the string specified by parameter one. Returns an integer less than zero when string1 < string2. Returns a zero when string1 = string2. Returns an integer greater than zero when string1 > string2.
`char * strncpy(char *, const char *, size_t)`	Copies number of characters specified by size_t parameter from string given by the const char * string2 to the string given by the char * string1. The const char * string2 is null terminated. Undefined results if strings overlap. If string2 (second parameter) has fewer characters than string1 (first parameter), nulls are appended. If string2 has more characters than string 1, the string will not be null terminated. Returns a pointer to char * string1.
`char * strpbrk(const char *, const char *)`	Returns a pointer to the first character of const char * string1 matching a character in const char * string2. Null terminators are not considered. If no match occurs, a null pointer is returned.
`char * strrchr(const char *, int)`	Returns a pointer to the last occurrence of the low-order byte of the int parameter found in the const char * string. A null pointer is returned when no match is found.
`size_t strspn(const char *, const char *)`	Returns the length of the const char * string1 (parameter 1) made up of the characters contained in const char * string2 (parameter 2). The length returned is an index value to the first non-matched character in string1.
`char * strstr(const char *, const char *)`	Returns a pointer to the first occurrence in the const char * string1 (first parameter) of the string given by const char * string2 (second parameter). A null pointer is returned when no match is found.
`char * strtok(char *, const char *)`	Returns a pointer to the next token in the string given by char * string1 (first parameter). The characters of const char * string2 (second parameter) serve as the delimiters that make up the token. A null pointer is returned when no tokens are found.

Table 17.2 <cstring> functions and meanings *(continued)*

Function	Meaning
`size_t strxfrm (char *, const char *, size_t)`	Transforms size_t parameter characters in const char * string2 (second parameter) for use by the strcmp() function, placing the results in to the char * string1 (first parameter). Returns the length of the transforming string.

You'll also find the function prototypes for wide character strings, such as those in the following partial listing:

```
_CRTIMP wchar_t * __cdecl wcscat(wchar_t *, const wchar_t *);
_CRTIMP wchar_t * __cdecl wcschr(const wchar_t *, wchar_t);
_CRTIMP int __cdecl wcscmp(const wchar_t *, const wchar_t *);
_CRTIMP wchar_t * __cdecl wcscpy(wchar_t *, const wchar_t *);
_CRTIMP size_t __cdecl wcscspn(const wchar_t *, const wchar_t *);
_CRTIMP size_t __cdecl wcslen(const wchar_t *);
_CRTIMP wchar_t * __cdecl wcsncat(wchar_t *, const wchar_t *,
                                   size_t);
_CRTIMP int __cdecl wcsncmp(const wchar_t *, const wchar_t *,
                            size_t);
_CRTIMP wchar_t * __cdecl wcsncpy(wchar_t *, const wchar_t *,
                                   size_t);
_CRTIMP wchar_t * __cdecl wcspbrk(const wchar_t *,
                                   const wchar_t *);
_CRTIMP wchar_t * __cdecl wcsrchr(const wchar_t *, wchar_t);
_CRTIMP size_t __cdecl wcsspn(const wchar_t *, const wchar_t *);
_CRTIMP wchar_t * __cdecl wcsstr(const wchar_t *,
                                  const wchar_t *);
_CRTIMP wchar_t * __cdecl wcstok(wchar_t *, const wchar_t *);

_CRTIMP wchar_t * __cdecl _wcsdup(const wchar_t *);
_CRTIMP int __cdecl _wcsicmp(const wchar_t *, const wchar_t *);
_CRTIMP int __cdecl _wcsnicmp(const wchar_t *, const wchar_t *,
                              size_t);
_CRTIMP wchar_t * __cdecl _wcsnset(wchar_t *, wchar_t, size_t);
_CRTIMP wchar_t * __cdecl _wcsrev(wchar_t *);
_CRTIMP wchar_t * __cdecl _wcsset(wchar_t *, wchar_t);

_CRTIMP wchar_t * __cdecl _wcslwr(wchar_t *);
_CRTIMP wchar_t * __cdecl _wcsupr(wchar_t *);
_CRTIMP size_t __cdecl wcsxfrm(wchar_t *, const wchar_t *,
                               size_t);
_CRTIMP int __cdecl wcscoll(const wchar_t *, const wchar_t *);
_CRTIMP int __cdecl _wcsicoll(const wchar_t *, const wchar_t *);
_CRTIMP int __cdecl _wcsncoll(const wchar_t *, const wchar_t *,
                              size_t);
_CRTIMP int __cdecl _wcsnicoll(const wchar_t *, const wchar_t *,
                               size_t);
```

In the example portion of this chapter, you'll see an example of using the <cstring> Standard C++ header file.

<string> Template Syntax

The Standard C++ header <string> is used to define a container template class that uses the basic_string template class and a variety of additional supporting templates. The basic_string template class will be discussed in more detail later in this section. The following listing gives the syntax for the <string> template:

```
namespace std {
// TEMPLATE CLASSES
template<class E>
  struct char_traits;
struct "char_traits<char>;
struct "char_traits<wchar_t>;
template<class E,
  class T = char_traits<E>,
  class A = allocator<E> >
  class basic_string;
typedef basic_string<char> string;
typedef basic_string>wchar_t> wstring;
// TEMPLATE FUNCTIONS
template<class E, class T, class A>
  basic_string<E, T, A> operator+(
    const basic_string<E, T, A>& lhs,
    const basic_string<E, T, A>& rhs);
template<class E, class T, class A>
  basic_string<E, T, A> operator+(
    const basic_string<E, T, A>& lhs,const E *rhs);
template<class E, class T, class A>
  basic_string<E, T, A> operator+(
    const basic_string<E, T, A>& lhs, E rhs);
template<class E, class T, class A>
  basic_string<E, T, A> operator+(
    const E *lhs, const basic_string<E, T, A>& rhs);
template<class E, class T, class A>
  basic_string<E, T, A> operator+(
    E lhs, const basic_string<E, T, A>& rhs);
template<class E, class T, class A>
  bool operator==(
    const basic_string<E, T, A>& lhs,
    const basic_string<E, T, A>& rhs);
template<class E, class T, class A>
  bool operator==(
    const basic_string<E, T, A>& lhs, const E *rhs);
template<class E, class T, class A>
```

```
  bool operator==( const E *lhs,
    const basic_string<E, T, A>& rhs);
template<class E, class T, class A>
  bool operator!=( const basic_string<E, T, A>& lhs,
    const basic_string<E, T, A>& rhs);
template<class E, class T, class A>
  bool operator!=( const basic_string<E, T, A>& lhs,
    const E *rhs);
template<class E, class T, class A>
  bool operator!=( const E *lhs,
    const basic_string<E, T, A>& rhs);
template<class E, class T, class A>
  bool operator<( const basic_string<E, T, A>& lhs,
    const basic_string<E, T, A>& rhs);
template<class E, class T, class A>
  bool operator<( const basic_string<E, T, A>& lhs,
    const E *rhs);
template<class E, class T, class A>
  bool operator<( const E *lhs,
    const basic_string<E, T, A>& rhs);
template<class E, class T, class A>
  bool "operator>( const basic_string<E, T, A>& lhs,
    const basic_string<E, T, A>& rhs);
template<class E, class T, class A>
  bool "operator>( const basic_string<E, T, A>& lhs,
    const E *rhs);
template<class E, class T, class A>
  bool "operator>( const E *lhs,
    const basic_string<E, T, A>& rhs);
template<class E, class T, class A>
  bool operator<=( const basic_string<E, T, A>& lhs,
    const basic_string<E, T, A>& rhs);
template<class E, class T, class A>
  bool operator<=( const basic_string<E, T, A>& lhs,
    const E *rhs);
template<class E, class T, class A>
  bool operator<=( const E *lhs,
    const basic_string<E, T, A>& rhs);
template<class E, class T, class A>
  bool ="operator>=( const basic_string<E, T, A>& lhs,
    const basic_string<E, T, A>& rhs);
template<class E, class T, class A>
  bool ="operator>=( const basic_string<E, T, A>& lhs,
    const E *rhs);
template<class E, class T, class A>
  bool ="operator>=( const E *lhs,
    const basic_string<E, T, A>& rhs);
template<class E, class T, class A>
  void swap( const basic_string<E, T, A>& lhs,
    const basic_string<E, T, A>& rhs);
```

```
template<class E, class T, class A>
  basic_ostream<E>& operator<<( basic_ostream <E>& os,
    const basic_string<E, T, A>& str);
template<class E, class T, class A>
  basic_istream<E>& "operator>>( basic_istream <E>& is,
    basic_string<E, T, A>& str);
template<class E, class T, class A>
  basic_istream<E, T>& getline( basic_istream <E, T>& is,
    basic_string<E, T, A>& str);
template<class E, class T, class A>
  basic_istream<E, T>& getline( basic_istream <E, T>& is,
    basic_string<E, T, A>& str, E delim);
};
```

In the following section, we'll list the important template functions of the <string> template.

<string> Template Functions

Table 17.3 provides a list of the important template functions for <string> extracted from the template syntax.

Table 17.3 Template functions for <string>

Template Functions
`basic_string<E, T, A> operator+( const basic_string<E, T, A>& lhs,const E *rhs);`
`basic_string<E, T, A> operator+( const basic_string<E, T, A>& lhs,E rhs);`
`basic_string<E, T, A> operator+( const E *lhs,const basic_string<E, T, A>& rhs);`
`basic_string<E, T, A> operator+( E lhs,const basic_string<E, T, A>& rhs);`
`bool operator==( const basic_string<E, T, A>& lhs,const basic_string<E, T, A>& rhs);`
`bool operator==( const basic_string<E, T, A>& lhs,const E *rhs);`
`bool operator==( const E *lhs,const basic_string<E, T, A>& rhs);`
`bool operator!=( const basic_string<E, T, A>& lhs,const basic_string<E, T, A>& rhs);`

Table 17.3 Template functions for <string> *(continued)*

Template Functions
`bool operator!=( const basic_string<E, T, A>& lhs,const E *rhs);`
`bool operator!=( const E *lhs,const basic_string<E, T, A>& rhs);`
`bool operator<( const basic_string<E, T, A>& lhs,const basic_string<E, T, A>& rhs);`
`bool operator<( const basic_string<E, T, A>& lhs,const E *rhs);`
`bool operator<( const E *lhs,const basic_string<E, T, A>& rhs);`
`bool "operator>( const basic_string<E, T, A>& lhs,const basic_string<E, T, A>& rhs);`
`bool "operator>( const basic_string<E, T, A>& lhs,const E *rhs);`
`bool "operator>( const E *lhs,const basic_string<E, T, A>& rhs);`
`bool operator<=( const basic_string<E, T, A>& lhs,const basic_string<E, T, A>& rhs);`
`bool operator<=( const basic_string<E, T, A>& lhs,const E *rhs);`
`bool operator<=( const E *lhs,const basic_string<E, T, A>& rhs);`
`bool ="operator>=( const basic_string<E, T, A>& lhs,const basic_string<E, T, A>& rhs);`
`bool ="operator>=( const basic_string<E, T, A>& lhs,const E *rhs);`
`bool ="operator>=( const E *lhs,const basic_string<E, T, A>& rhs);`
`basic_ostream<E>& operator<<( basic_ostream <E>& os,const basic_string<E, T, A>& str);`
`basic_istream<E>& "operator>>( basic_istream <E>& is,basic_string<E, T, A>& str);`

For more information on the E, T, and A classes described in Table 17.3, see the next section of this chapter, dealing with the basic_string template class.

The basic_string class

As you'll see from the following listing, the basic_string class provides many member functions. Many of the functions you'll find in the basic_string class come in multiples in order to provide support for single characters, repeating characters with a repetition count, pointers to null-terminated character strings, pointers to a character sequence with a sequence length provided, and so on.

```
template<class E,
    class T = char_traits<E>,
    class A = allocator<T> >
    class basic_string {
public:
    typedef T traits_type;
    typedef A allocator_type;
    typedef T::char_type char_type;
    typedef A::size_type size_type;
    typedef A::difference_type difference_type;
    typedef A::pointer pointer;
    typedef A::const_pointer const_pointer;
    typedef A::reference reference;
    typedef A::const_reference const_reference;
    typedef A::value_type value_type;
    typedef T0 iterator;
    typedef T1 const_iterator;
    typedef reverse_iterator<iterator, value_type,
        reference, pointer, difference_type>
            reverse_iterator;
    typedef reverse_iterator<const_iterator, value_type,
        const_reference, const_pointer, difference_type>
            const_reverse_iterator;
    static const size_type npos = -1;
    explicit basic_string(const A& al = A());
    basic_string(const basic_string& rhs);
    basic_string(const basic_string& rhs, size_type pos, size_type n,
        const A& al = A());
    basic_string(const E *s, size_type n, const A& al = A());
    basic_string(const E *s, const A& al = A());
    basic_string(size_type n, E c, const A& al = A());
    basic_string(const_iterator first, const_iterator last,
        const A& al = A());
    basic_string& operator=(const basic_string& rhs);
    basic_string& operator=(const E *s);
    basic_string& operator=(E c);
```

```
iterator begin();
const_iterator begin() const;
iterator end();
const_iterator end() const;
reverse_iterator rbegin();
const_reverse_iterator rbegin() const;
reverse_iterator rend();
const_reverse_iterator rend() const;
const_reference at(size_type pos) const;
reference at(size_type pos);
const_reference operator[](size_type pos) const;
reference operator[](size_type pos);
const E *c_str() const;
const E *data() const;
size_type length() const;
size_type size() const;
size_type max_size() const;
void resize(size_type n, E c = E());
size_type capacity() const;
void reserve(size_type n = 0);
bool empty() const;
basic_string& operator+=(const basic_string& rhs);
basic_string& operator+=(const E *s);
basic_string& operator+=(E c);
basic_string& append(const basic_string& str);
basic_string& append(const basic_string& str,
    size_type pos, size_type n);
basic_string& append(const E *s, size_type n);
basic_string& append(const E *s);
basic_string& append(size_type n, E c);
basic_string& append(const_iterator first, const_iterator last);
basic_string& assign(const basic_string& str);
basic_string& assign(const basic_string& str,
    size_type pos, size_type n);
basic_string& assign(const E *s, size_type n);
basic_string& assign(const E *s);
basic_string& assign(size_type n, E c);
basic_string& assign(const_iterator first, const_iterator last);
basic_string& insert(size_type p0,
    const basic_string& str);
basic_string& insert(size_type p0,
    const basic_string& str, size_type pos, size_type n);
basic_string& insert(size_type p0,
    const E *s, size_type n);
basic_string& insert(size_type p0, const E *s);
basic_string& insert(size_type p0, size_type n, E c);
iterator insert(iterator it, E c);
void insert(iterator it, size_type n, E c);
void insert(iterator it,
    const_iterator first, const_iterator last);
```

```
basic_string& erase(size_type p0 = 0, size_type n = npos);
iterator erase(iterator it);
iterator erase(iterator first, iterator last);
basic_string& replace(size_type p0, size_type n0,
    const basic_string& str);
basic_string& replace(size_type p0, size_type n0,
    const basic_string& str, size_type pos, size_type n);
basic_string& replace(size_type p0, size_type n0,
    const E *s, size_type n);
basic_string& replace(size_type p0, size_type n0,
    const E *s);
basic_string& replace(size_type p0, size_type n0,
    size_type n, E c);
basic_string& replace(iterator first0, iterator last0,
    const basic_string& str);
basic_string& replace(iterator first0, iterator last0,
    const E *s, size_type n);
basic_string& replace(iterator first0, iterator last0,
    const E *s);
basic_string& replace(iterator first0, iterator last0,
    size_type n, E c);
basic_string& replace(iterator first0, iterator last0,
    const_iterator first, const_iterator last);
size_type copy(E *s, size_type n, size_type pos = 0) const;
void swap(basic_string& str);
size_type find(const basic_string& str,
    size_type pos = 0) const;
size_type find(const E *s, size_type pos, size_type n) const;
size_type find(const E *s, size_type pos = 0) const;
size_type find(E c, size_type pos = 0) const;
size_type rfind(const basic_string& str,
    size_type pos = npos) const;
size_type rfind(const E *s, size_type pos,
    size_type n = npos) const;
size_type rfind(const E *s, size_type pos = npos) const;
size_type rfind(E c, size_type pos = npos) const;
size_type find_first_of(const basic_string& str,
    size_type pos = 0) const;
size_type find_first_of(const E *s, size_type pos,
    size_type n) const;
size_type find_first_of(const E *s, size_type pos = 0) const;
size_type find_first_of(E c, size_type pos = 0) const;
size_type find_last_of(const basic_string& str,
    size_type pos = npos) const;
size_type find_last_of(const E *s, size_type pos,
    size_type n = npos) con/t;
size_type find_last_of(const E *s, size_type pos = npos) const;
size_type find_last_of(E c, size_type pos = npos) const;
size_type find_first_not_of(const basic_string& str,
    size_type pos = 0) const;
```

```
    size_type find_first_not_of(const E *s, size_type pos,
        size_type n) const;
    size_type find_first_not_of(const E *s, size_type pos = 0) const;
    size_type find_first_not_of(E c, size_type pos = 0) const;
    size_type find_last_not_of(const basic_string& str,
        size_type pos = npos) const;
    size_type find_last_not_of(const E *s, size_type pos,
         size_type n) const;
    size_type find_last_not_of(const E *s,
        size_type pos = npos) const;
    size_type find_last_not_of(E c, size_type pos = npos) const;
    basic_string substr(size_type pos = 0, size_type n = npos) const;
    int compare(const basic_string& str) const;
    int compare(size_type p0, size_type n0,
        const basic_string& str);
    int compare(size_type p0, size_type n0,
        const basic_string& str, size_type pos, size_type n);
    int compare(const E *s) const;
    int compare(size_type p0, size_type n0,
        const E *s) const;
    int compare(size_type p0, size_type n0,
        const E *s, size_type pos) const;
    A get_allocator() const;
protected:
    A allocator;
    };
```

When you examine this listing, you'll note that the template class provides a description of an object that controls a sequence of elements of type E. This sequence can vary in length. Support is provided by the Standard C++ library, using string for elements of type char and wstring for elements of type wchar_t. Elements of type E must be acceptable as parameters to basic_istream and basic_ostream.

Class T provides support for properties of the various basic_string elements. This class has the same external interface as an object of template class char_traits.

Class A provides a protected allocator object that allocates and frees storage for the sequence it controls. This class has the same external interface as an object of template class allocator.

The template class basic_string is used to control sequences referred to as strings. These objects are not the same as the frequently used null-terminate strings of C and C++. To operate on basic_string sequences, most basic_string member functions require the use of an operation sequence of elements of type E. Table 17.4 shows various operations sequences that you'll encounter.

Table 17.4 Operation sequences for basic_string member functions

Sequence	Description
c	Represents a sequence with one element of value c.
n, c	Represents a repetition of n elements of value c.
s	Represents a null-terminated sequence that begins at s and terminates at an element whose value is E(0) and that is not part of the operand sequence. The null-terminated sequence can be a C string for an E of type char.
s, n	Represents a sequence of n elements that begins at s. This cannot be a null pointer.
str	Represents a sequence described with the basic_string object str.
str, pos, n	Represents a substring of the basic_string object str. The substring has a maximum of n elements and begins at position pos. If pos is beyond the number of elements in the sequence, an out-of-range error is reported.
first, last	Represents a sequence of elements that is delimited using the iterators first and last for the range.

The operation sequences are used by the member functions of basic_string to provide support for a wide variety of string manipulations. Table 17.5 provides a list of the member functions and a brief description of their use.

Table 17.5 Important basic_string methods and descriptions

Function	Description
append	Appends elements to the end of the string. Each function form allows alternate ways to specify the source of the elements to be appended. Returns a reference to the string where the elements were appended.
assign	Replaces the sequence controlled by *this with the operand sequence. Returns *this.
at	Returns a reference to the element of the controlled sequence at position pos, or reports an out-of-range error.
begin	Returns a random-access iterator pointing to the first element of the sequence. If the sequence is empty, it will point just beyond the sequence.
c_str	Returns a pointer to a C string constructed by adding a terminating null element (E(0)) to the controlled sequence. This C string is not modifiable. The pointer can be invalidated by calling any non-const member function for *this.
capacity	Returns the storage allocated to hold the controlled sequence. The minimum value will be equal to that of size().

Table 17.5 Important basic_string methods and descriptions *(continued)*

Function	Description
compare	Compares a maximum of n0 elements of the controlled sequence starting at position p0. If these elements are not supplied to the argument, the entire controlled sequence will be compared. Returns a negative value when the first differing element in the controlled sequence compares to less than the corresponding element in the operand sequence (using T::compare) or when both have a common prefix but the operand sequence is longer. Returns a zero when the two compare equal element by element and are the same length. All other cases return a positive value.
copy	Copies up to n elements from the controlled sequence, starting at position pos, to the array of E, starting at s. Returns the number of elements copied.
data	Returns a pointer to the first element of the sequence. If the sequence is empty, a non-null pointer is returned. This pointer cannot be dereferenced.
empty	Returns true for an empty controlled sequence.
end	Returns a random-access iterator that points just beyond the end of the sequence.
erase	Depending on the invocation, the function can remove the elements of the controlled sequence in the range [first, last) or remove the element of the controlled sequence pointed to by it. In these cases, an iterator is returned designating the first element remaining beyond the elements removed. If the element does not exist, end() is returned. Another invocation removes up to n elements of the controlled sequence starting at position p0. In this case, *this is returned.
find	Locates the first subsequence in the controlled sequence, starting at or after position pos, matching the operand sequence given by the remaining operands. Returns the position where the matching subsequence starts. If not found, returns npos.
find_first_not_of	Locates the first element of the controlled sequence, starting at or after position pos, matching none of the elements in the operand sequence given by the remaining operands. Returns the position where the matching subsequence starts. If not found, returns npos.
find_first_of	Locates the first element of the controlled sequence, starting at or after position pos, matching any of the elements in the operand sequence given by the remaining operands. Returns the position where the matching subsequence starts. If not found, returns npos.

Table 17.5 Important basic_string methods and descriptions *(continued)*

Function	Description
find_last_not_of	Locates the last element of the controlled sequence, starting at or before position pos, matching none of the elements in the operand sequence given by the remaining operands. Returns the position where the matching subsequence starts. If not found, returns npos.
find_last_of	Locates the last element of the controlled sequence, starting at or before position pos, matching any of the elements in the operand sequence given by the remaining operands. Returns the position where the matching subsequence starts. If not found, returns npos.
get_allocator	Returns the allocator.
insert	Inserts, prior to position p0 or before the element pointed to by it in the controlled sequence, the operand sequence given by the remaining operands. Returns *this.
length	Returns the length of the controlled sequence.
max_size	Returns the length of the longest sequence that the object can control.
operator[]	Returns a reference to the element of the controlled sequence at position pos. When that position is invalid, the behavior is not defined.
rbegin	Returns a reverse iterator pointing just beyond the end of the controlled sequence. This represents the start of the reverse sequence.
rend	Returns a reverse iterator pointing to the first element of the sequence. This represents the end of the reverse sequence.
replace	Used to replace a maximum of n0 elements of the controlled sequence starting at p0, or the elements of the sequence starting at the one pointed to by first, up to but not including last. The replacement becomes the operand sequence given by the remaining operands. Returns *this.
reserve	Makes certain that capacity() will return at least n.
resize	Makes certain that size() will return n. When the control sequence is lengthened, it will append elements with value c.
rfind	Locates the last subsequence in the controlled sequence, starting at or before position pos, matching the operand sequence given by the remaining operands. Returns the position where the matching subsequence starts. If not found, returns npos.
size	Returns the length of the controlled sequence.
substr	Returns an object where the controlled sequence is a copy of a maximum of n elements of the controlled sequence starting at position pos.

If you are still wondering how to implement these methods, you'll find many of them illustrated with clear, straightforward code in the sample code section that follows.

Sample Code

In the following sections, six sample applications illustrate how to implement the <cctype>, <cstring>, and <string> Standard C++ header files.

A <cctype> Application

The first example application, cctype1.cpp, uses values that can represent ASCII characters to test various <cctype> methods. Here is the complete listing for this example:

```
// cctype1.cpp
// Testing <cctype> method on a range of
// character values.
// Chris H. Pappas and William H. Murray, 1999

#include <iostream>
#include <cctype>

using namespace std;

void main()
{
 // int ch;
  for (int ch=0;ch<=127;ch++) {
    cout << "The ASCII digit " << ch  << " is a(n):\n";
    if (isprint(ch)) cout << " printable char\n";
    if (islower(ch)) cout << " lowercase char\n";
    if (isupper(ch)) cout << " uppercase char\n";
    if (ispunct(ch)) cout << " punctuation char\n";
    if (isspace(ch)) cout << " space char\n";
    if (isdigit(ch)) cout << " char digit\n";
    if (isgraph(ch)) cout << " graphics char\n";
    if (iscntrl(ch)) cout << " control char\n";
    if (isxdigit(ch)) cout << " hexadecimal char\n";
    cout << "\n\n";
  }
}
```

Study the listing and note that the isprint(), islower(), isupper(), ispunct(), isspace(), isdigit(), isgraph(), iscntrl(), and isxdigit() methods will return information on a character whose value can change from 0 to 127.

The following listing is an abbreviated output from the program showing various groups of character information:

```
The ASCII digit 0 is a(n):
 control char


The ASCII digit 1 is a(n):
 control char
      .
      .
      .
The ASCII digit 32 is a(n):
 printable char
 space char


The ASCII digit 33 is a(n):
 printable char
 punctuation char
 graphics char


The ASCII digit 34 is a(n):
 printable char
 punctuation char
 graphics char
      .
      .
      .
The ASCII digit 48 is a(n):
 printable char
 char digit
 graphics char
 hexadecimal char


The ASCII digit 49 is a(n):
 printable char
 char digit
 graphics char
 hexadecimal char
      .
      .
      .
 The ASCII digit 101 is a(n):
 printable char
 lowercase char
 graphics char
 hexadecimal char


The ASCII digit 102 is a(n):
```

```
 printable char
 lowercase char
 graphics char
 hexadecimal char
      .
      .
      .
The ASCII digit 126 is a(n):
 printable char
 punctuation char
 graphics char


The ASCII digit 127 is a(n):
 control char
```

Recall that the decimal range of numbers from 65 to 90 represents the ASCII characters "A..Z" while the decimal range of numbers from 97 to 122 represents the ASCII characters "a..z". Numeric digits, "0..9" are represented with the decimal values 48 to 57.

A <cstring> Application

The second application, cstring1.cpp, shows how to invoke a number of <cstring> methods on a few null-terminated test strings.

```
// cstring1.cpp
// Testing <cstring> methods on a variety of
// strings.
// Chris H. Pappas and William H. Murray, 1999

#include <iostream>
#include <cstring>

using namespace std;

void main()
{
  const char str1[] = "This is my story, this is my song.";
  const char str2[] = "my";
  char str3[] = "abcdefghijklmnop";
  const char str4[] = "wxyz";
  const char str5[] = "abcd";
  const char str6[] = "abcde";

  // testing strstr()
  cout << "Print from first 'my' in str1:\n";
  cout << strstr(str1, str2) << "\n\n";

  // testing strncpy()
```

```
  cout << "Replace first 4 characters in str3 with\n"
       << "those from str4:\n";
  cout << strncpy(str3, str4, 4) << "\n\n";

  // testing strlen()
  cout << "The length of str3 is: " << strlen(str3) << "\n\n";

  // testing strcmp()
  int test = strcmp(str5, str6);
  cout << "test is equal to " << test << "\n";
  if (test < 0)
    cout << "str5 is less than str6\n\n";
    else
      if (test == 0)
        cout << "str5 is equal to str6\n\n";
        else
          cout << "str5 is greater than str6\n\n";
}
```

This example uses the strstr(), strncpy(), strlen(), and strcmp() methods to manipulate standard null-terminated strings. The output for this program reports:

```
Print from first 'my' in str1:
my story, this is my song.

Replace first 4 characters in str3 with
those from str4:
wxyzefghijklmnop

The length of str3 is: 16

test is equal to -1
str5 is less than str6
```

If you have worked with C and C++ string functions, you are probably familiar with the operation of these <cstring> methods.

However, in the remaining examples in this chapter, you'll learn how to invoke <string> methods on both null-terminated and non null-terminated strings.

The First <string> Application

The first <string> application, string1.cpp, shows how to invoke the append() and c_str() methods as well as the begin() and end() iterators.

```
// string1.cpp
// Testing the append() <string> methods on a variety of
// strings.
// Chris H. Pappas and William H. Murray, 1999
```

```
#include <iostream>
#include <string>

using namespace std;

void main()
{
  string str1("ABCDEFG");
  string str2("HIJKLMN");
  string str3("OPQRSTU");
  string str4("*******");

  // print str1
  cout << "The original string is: " << str1.c_str() << endl;

  // append str2 to str1 and print
  str1.append(str2);
  cout << "The new string is: " << str1.c_str() << endl;

  // append three characters from str3 to str1.
  // start at first character 'P' and end at 'R'
  // print results
  str1.append(str3, 1, 3);
  cout << "The modified string is now: " << str1.c_str() << endl;

  // append one character of the element type to str1 and print
  str1.append(1, 'Z');
  cout << "Appending a single element: " << str1.c_str()
       << endl;

  // append str4 to str1 using iterators
  str1.append (str4.begin(), str4.end());
  cout << "Appending with iterators: " << str1.c_str() << endl;

  cout << endl;
}
```

This example illustrates how to use the append() method to append portions of one string to another string. Of particular importance is the fact that the strings are not null-terminated!

```
The original string is: ABCDEFG
The new string is: ABCDEFGHIJKLMN
The modified string is now: ABCDEFGHIJKLMNPQR
Appending a single element: ABCDEFGHIJKLMNPQRZ
Appending with iterators: ABCDEFGHIJKLMNPQRZ*******
```

The application is fairly simple, so you should have no trouble understanding how these methods and iterators can be applied.

What do you think would happen to the output if the second string were declared in the following manner?

```
char str2[]="HIJKLMN";
```

If you made your educated guess, now is the time to try the replacement code and see whether you are right.

The Second <string> Application

The second <string> application, string2.cpp, shows how to invoke set_terminate provided in the <exception> header.

```
// string2.cpp
// Testing the find_first_of() <string> method on a variety of
// strings.
// Chris H. Pappas and William H. Murray, 1999

#include <iostream>
#include <string>

using namespace std;

void main()
{
  string str1("There is no other name...");
  string str2("abcde");
  int iLoc = 0;

  // Print the string that will be searched.
  cout << "The string that will be searched is: "
       << str1.c_str() << endl;

  // Print the string with search elements
  cout << "The string containing search elements is: "
       << str2.c_str() << endl << endl;

  // Find the first location of an a, b, or c in str1
  // start at beginning (index is 0)
  iLoc = str1.find_first_of(str2, 0);
  cout << "Start the search at the beginning position."
       << endl;
  cout << "An element in str2 was found in str1 at location: "
       << iLoc << endl << endl;

  // Find the first location of an a, b, or c in str1
  // but start at the 10th position (index is 9)
  iLoc = str1.find_first_of(str2, 9);
  cout << "Start the search at the 10th position." << endl;
  cout << "An element in str2 was found in str1 at location: "
       << iLoc << endl << endl;
}
```

The find_first_of() method is great for locating the first occurrence of an element, specified in another string and searched for in the specified string:

```
The string that will be searched is: There is no other name...
The string containing search elements is: abcde

Start the search at the beginning position.
An element in str2 was found in str1 at location: 2

Start the search at the 10th position.
An element in str2 was found in str1 at location: 15
```

From the comments in the application's code, we're sure that you've figured out how this method works. However, you may want to examine some close cousins to the find_first_of() method. Methods, such as find_first_not_of(), find_last_of(), and find_last_not_of(), will allow you to hone your skills for this useful group of <string> methods.

The Third <string> Application

The third <string> application, string3.cpp, shows how to invoke the size() and resize() methods.

```
// string3.cpp
// Testing the size() and resize() <string> methods.
// Chris H. Pappas and William H. Murray, 1999

#include <iostream>
#include <string>

using namespace std;

void main()
{
  string str1("There is no other name...");
  string str2("Once I was lost...");

  // Print the original str1
  cout << "The original strings are: "
       << endl << endl;
  cout << str1 << endl;
  // Print the original str2
  cout << str2 << endl << endl;
  // Print the original size of each string
  cout << "str1's size is: " << str1.size()
       << endl;
  cout << "str2's size is: " << str2.size()
       << endl << endl;

  // Now, resize each string
```

```
  str1.resize(10);
  str2.resize(25,'*');
  cout << endl  << endl;

  // Print each resized string
  cout << "Resizing each string: "
       << endl << endl;
  cout << str1 << endl;
  cout << str2 << endl << endl;
 // Print the size of each string
  cout << "str1's size is now: " << str1.size()
       << endl;
  cout << "str2's size is now: " << str2.size()
       << endl << endl;
}
```

Of particular importance here is how two different invocations of resize are used to resize the strings.

```
// Now, resize each string
str1.resize(10);
str2.resize(25,'*');
```

In the first case, the string is simply resized to hold 10 elements. In the second case, the string is resized to 25 elements, with new elements being added as '*' characters.

The output for this program reports:

```
The original strings are:

There is no other name...
Once I was lost...

str1's size is: 25
str2's size is: 18



Resizing each string:

There is n
Once I was lost...*******

str1's size is now: 10
str2's size is now: 25
```

The size() and resize() methods should add a lot of flexibility to your application's string manipulations.

What do you think would happen if the '*' element was changed to a space, ' '?

The Fourth <string> Application

The final <string> application, string4.cpp, shows how to invoke operator+ template function to concatenate two strings. However, as you examine the following listing, you'll notice something interesting about those two strings.

```
// string4.cpp
// Testing the operator+ from the <string> template.
// Chris H. Pappas and William H. Murray, 1999

#include <iostream>
#include <string>

using namespace std;

void main()
{
  string str1("Strings and characters ");
  char str2[]="are within your grasp.";
  string temp;

  // Print the original str1
  cout << "The original strings are: "
       << endl << endl;
  cout << str1 << endl;
  // Print the original str2
  cout << str2 << endl << endl << endl;

  // Concatenate the strings with operator+
  temp=str1+str2;
  cout << "Concatenate Str1+Str2: " << temp << endl << endl;
}
```

You probably noticed right away that one of the strings was a standard null-terminated string. This template function will allow us to work with either type.

The output for this program reports:

```
The original strings are:

Strings and characters
are within your grasp.

Concatenate Str1+Str2: Strings and characters are within your grasp.
```

We're sure that you were able to predict the results of this application. However, you may want to experiment with other template functions such as operator>, operator>=, operator!=, and so on.

Summary

The <cctype>, <cstring>, and <string> Standard C++ header files provide powerful new options to the programmer when working with characters, null-terminate strings, and the new string class template methods.

The <string> template class is so large that you will need to take time to experiment with the various methods provided.

EIGHTEEN

The <cfloat> and <cmath> Standard C++ Headers and <complex> Template Class

This chapter describes the <cfloat> and <cmath> standard C++ Headers as well as the header for the <complex> template class. In this chapter, you'll learn the new ANSI Standard C++ header syntax for these headers, investigate features for implementing the header code, and see several working examples illustrating various features of these standard header files. Three examples will also be included to show features common to the <complex> template class.

The <cfloat> Standard C++ Header Syntax

The following listing gives the syntax for using the <cfloat> Standard C++ header file:

```
namespace std {#include <float.h> };
```

The <cfloat> Standard C++ header is used to include the <float.h> header within the *std* namespace. The float.h header file is used for testing floating-point type properties and contains constants for numerous floating point values. Many of the #defines found in float.h are implementation-specific and are used for complex numeric calculations. As such, you'll find #defines for i386, PowerMac, RISC and so on.

Table 18.1 is derived from the information found in the float.h header file and provides a rich source of floating-point constants.

Table 18.1 Floating-point constants defined in <float.h>

Define	Value	Description
DBL_DIG	15	number of decimal digits of precision
DBL_EPSILON	2.2204460492503131e-016	smallest such that 1.0+DBL_EPSILON != 1.0
DBL_MANT_DIG	53	number of bits in mantissa
DBL_MAX	1.7976931348623158e+308	max value
DBL_MAX_10_EXP	308	max decimal exponent
DBL_MAX_EXP	1024	max binary exponent
DBL_MIN	2.2250738585072014e-308	min positive value
DBL_MIN_10_EXP	(-307)	min decimal exponent
DBL_MIN_EXP	(-1021)	min binary exponent
_DBL_RADIX	2	exponent radix
_DBL_ROUNDS	1	addition rounding: near
FLT_DIG	6	number of decimal digits of precision
FLT_EPSILON	1.192092896e-07F	smallest such that 1.0+FLT_EPSILON != 1.0
FLT_GUARD	0	guard value
FLT_MANT_DIG	24	number of bits in mantissa
FLT_MAX	3.402823466e+38F	max value
FLT_MAX_10_EXP	38	max decimal exponent
FLT_MAX_EXP	128	max binary exponent
FLT_MIN	1.175494351e-38F	min positive value
FLT_MIN_10_EXP	(-37)	min decimal exponent
FLT_MIN_EXP	(-125)	min binary exponent
FLT_NORMALIZE	0	normalized value
FLT_RADIX	2	exponent radix
FLT_ROUNDS	1	addition rounding: near
LDBL_DIG	DBL_DIG	number of decimal digits of precision
LDBL_EPSILON	DBL_EPSILON	smallest such that 1.0+LDBL_EPSILON != 1.0
LDBL_MANT_DIG	DBL_MANT_DIG	number of bits in mantissa
LDBL_MAX	DBL_MAX	max value
LDBL_MAX_10_EXP	DBL_MAX_10_EXP	max decimal exponent
LDBL_MAX_EXP	DBL_MAX_EXP	max binary exponent

Table 18.1 Floating-point constants defined in <float.h> *(continued)*

Define	Value	Description
LDBL_MIN	DBL_MIN	min positive value
LDBL_MIN_10_EXP	DBL_MIN_10_EXP	min decimal exponent
LDBL_MIN_EXP	DBL_MIN_EXP	min binary exponent
_LDBL_RADIX	DBL_RADIX	exponent radix
_LDBL_ROUNDS	DBL_ROUNDS	addition rounding: near
LDBL_DIG	18	number of decimal digits of precision
LDBL_EPSILON	1.084202172485504434 12e-019L	smallest such that 1.0+LDBL_EPSILON != 1.0
LDBL_MANT_DIG	64	number of bits in mantissa
LDBL_MAX	1.189731495357231765e+4932L	max value
LDBL_MAX_10_EXP	4932	max decimal exponent
LDBL_MAX_EXP	16384	max binary exponent
LDBL_MIN	3.3621031431120935063e-4932L	min positive value
LDBL_MIN_10_EXP	(-4931)	min decimal exponent
LDBL_MIN_EXP	(-16381)	min binary exponent
_LDBL_RADIX	2	exponent radix
_LDBL_ROUNDS	1	addition rounding: near

Many floating-point control and status values can be set with just a few functions, also prototyped in <float.h>. Table 18.2 lists these function prototypes.

Table 18.2 <float.h> function prototypes

Function Prototypes	Description
unsigned int _clearfp(void);	clear the floating-point processor
unsigned int _controlfp(unsigned int,unsigned int);	set the floating-point control register
unsigned int _statusfp(void);	set the floating-point status register
void _fpreset(void);	reset the floating-point processor
_clear87	same as _clearfp but for MAC
_status87	same as _statusfp but for MAC

The float.h header file also contains a variety of abstract user control word mask and bit definitions. Table 18.3 shows these definitions along with their mask values and description.

Table 18.3 Abstract user control word mask and bit definitions

Mask	Mask Value	Description
_MCW_EM	0x0008001f	MAC interrupt exception masks
_MCW_EM	0x0000001f	interrupt exception masks
_EM_INEXACT	0x00000001	inexact (precision)
_EM_UNDERFLOW	0x00000002	underflow
_EM_OVERFLOW	0x00000004	overflow
_EM_ZERODIVIDE	0x00000008	zero divide
_EM_INVALID	0x00000010	invalid
_MCW_RC	0x00000300	rounding control
_RC_NEAR	0x00000000	near
_RC_DOWN	0x00000100	down
_RC_UP	0x00000200	up
_RC_CHOP	0x00000300	chop

Five status word bit definitions are included in this header file and are shown in Table 18.4.

Table 18.4 Abstract user status word bit definitions

Mask	Mask Value	Description
_SW_INEXACT	0x00000001	inexact (precision)
_SW_UNDERFLOW	0x00000002	underflow
_SW_OVERFLOW	0x00000004	overflow
_SW_ZERODIVIDE	0x00000008	zero divide
_SW_INVALID	0x00000010	invalid

Hardware-specific control values can be found for the Intel family, PowerMac, and RISC processors. Table 18.5 lists the masks, values, and descriptions.

Table 18.5 Hardware-specific control values

Mask	Mask Value	Description
_MCW_PC	0x00030000	i386 Precision Control
_PC_64	0x00000000	PowerMac 64 bits
_PC_53	0x00000000	PowerMac 53 bits
_PC_24	0x00000000	PowerMac 24 bits
_MCW_IC	0x00040000	Infinity Control
_IC_AFFINE	0x00040000	affine
_IC_PROJECTIVE	0x00000000	projective
_EM_DENORMAL	0x00080000	denormal exception mask (_control87 only)
_SW_DENORMAL	0x00080000	denormal status bit
_CRTIMP		unsigned int __cdecl _control87(unsigned int,unsigned int);
_MCW_DN	0x03000000	RISC Denormal Control
_DN_SAVE	0x00000000	RISC save denormal results and operands
_DN_FLUSH	0x01000000	RISC flush denormal results and operands to zero
_DN_FLUSH_OPERANDS_SAVE_RESULTS	0x02000000	RISC flush operands to zero and save results
_DN_SAVE_OPERANDS_FLUSH_RESULTS	0x03000000	RISC save operands and flush results to zero

Error codes for floating-point operations can be retrieved after various operations. A global variable returns a floating-point error code using one of the following formats:

```
extern int * __fpecode(void);
extern int _fpecode;
```

Table 18.6 lists invalid sub-conditions and floating-point error codes for a variety of situations.

Table 18.6 Invalid sub-conditions and floating-point error codes

Mask	Mask Value	Description
_SW_UNEMULATED	0x0040	unemulated instruction
_SW_SQRTNEG	0x0080	square root of a neg number
_SW_STACKOVERFLOW	0x0200	floating-point stack overflow
_SW_STACKUNDERFLOW	0x0400	floating-point stack underflow
_FPE_INVALID	0x81	floating-point invalid operation
_FPE_DENORMAL	0x82	floating-point denormalized result
_FPE_ZERODIVIDE	0x83	floating-point divide by zero
_FPE_OVERFLOW	0x84	floating-point overflow
_FPE_UNDERFLOW	0x85	floating-point underflow
_FPE_INEXACT	0x86	floating-point inexact result
_FPE_UNEMULATED	0x87	floating-point unemulated result
_FPE_SQRTNEG	0x88	floating-point square root of negative number
_FPE_STACKOVERFLOW	0x8a	floating-point stack overflow
_FPE_STACKUNDERFLOW	0x8b	floating-point stack underflow
_FPE_EXPLICITGEN	0x8c	raise SIGFPE

The float.h header file also prototypes several recommended IEEE functions. These functions include _copysign(), _chgsign(), _logb(), _isnan(), and so on. Table 18.7 provides a list of these function prototypes and a brief description of their use.

Table 18.7 IEEE recommended functions

IEEE Function	Description
double _copysign (double, double);	copy sign
double _chgsign (double);	change sign
double _scalb(double, long);	convert
double _logb(double);	logarithm
double _nextafter(double, double);	next after
int _finite(double);	finite
int _isnan(double);	is number
int _fpclass(double);	floating point class

Table 18.8 provides a list of various floating-point class constants and a short description of their use.

Table 18.8 Floating-point class constants

Mask	Mask Value	Description
_FPCLASS_SNAN	0x0001	signaling NaN
_FPCLASS_QNAN	0x0002	quiet NaN
_FPCLASS_NINF	0x0004	negative infinity
_FPCLASS_NN	0x0008	negative normal
_FPCLASS_ND	0x0010	negative denormal
_FPCLASS_NZ	0x0020	-0
_FPCLASS_PZ	0x0040	+0
_FPCLASS_PD	0x0080	positive denormal
_FPCLASS_PN	0x0100	positive normal
_FPCLASS_PINF	0x0200	positive infinity

An example in the example section of this chapter will illustrate the use of the <cfloat> standard C++ header file and illustrate how to use many of the functions and masks illustrated in the various tables in this section.

The <cmath> standard C++ Header Syntax

The following listing gives the syntax for using the <cmath> Standard C++ header file:

```
namespace std {#include <math.h> };
```

The <cmath> Standard C++ header is used to include the <math.h> header within the *std* namespace. The <math.h> header file provides a variety of definitions and declarations for the math library.

The definition of _exception structure is found in this header file. This structure is passed to the matherr routine when a floating-point exception is generated.

```
struct _exception {
  int type;         // exception type
  char *name;       // name of function where error occurred
  double arg1;      // first argument
  double arg2;      // second argument
  double retval;    // value returned by function
};
```

Table 18.9 shows six values that can be supplied with the _exception structure.

Table 18.9 Values used in the _exception structure

Name	Value	Description
_DOMAIN	1	argument domain error
_SING	2	argument singularity
_OVERFLOW	3	overflow range error
_UNDERFLOW	4	underflow range error
_TLOSS	5	total loss of precision
_PLOSS	6	partial loss of precision

The math.h header file provides the function prototypes for a wide variety of mathematical operations. The standard math function prototypes are shown in Table 18.10. Most of these functions accept a double as the argument type and return a double.

Table 18.10 Standard math function prototypes

Function Prototypes
int abs(int);
double acos(double);
double asin(double);
double atan(double);
double atan2(double, double);
double cos(double);
double cosh(double);
double exp(double);
double fabs(double);
double fmod(double, double);
long labs(long);
double log(double);
double log10(double);

Table 18.10 Standard math function prototypes *(continued)*

Function Prototypes
double pow(double, double);
double sin(double);
double sinh(double);
double tan(double);
double tanh(double);
double sqrt(double);
double atof(const char *);
double _cabs(struct _complex);
double ceil(double);
double floor(double);
double frexp(double, int *);
double _hypot(double, double);
double _j0(double);
double _j1(double);
double _jn(int, double);
double ldexp(double, int);
int _matherr(struct _exception *);
double modf(double, double *);
double _y0(double);
double _y1(double);
double _yn(int, double);

Many of these standard math function prototypes are also implemented for float and long double arguments, depending on the hardware implementation.

Table 18.11 shows the function prototypes for a MIPS implementation.

Table 18.11 MIPS trigonometric functions

MIPS Function Prototype
float acosf(float);
float asinf(float);
float atanf(float);
float atan2f(float , float);
float cosf(float);
float sinf(float);
float tanf(float);
float coshf(float);
float sinhf(float);
float tanhf(float);
float expf(float);
float logf(float);
float log10f(float);
float modff(float , float*);
float powf(float , float);
float sqrtf(float);
float ceilf(float);
float fabsf(float);
float floorf(float);
float fmodf(float , float);
float hypotf(float, float);

The function prototypes are also implemented for long doubles. Table 18.12 shows this implementation.

Table 18.12 Macros defining long double functions to be their double counterparts

Long-Double Function Prototypes	Implementation
acosl(x)	((long double)acos((double)(x)))
asinl(x)	((long double)asin((double)(x)))
atanl(x)	((long double)atan((double)(x)))
atan2l(x,y)	((long double)atan2((double)(x), (double)(y)))
_cabsl	_cabs
ceill(x)	((long double)ceil((double)(x)))
cosl(x)	((long double)cos((double)(x)))
coshl(x)	((long double)cosh((double)(x)))
expl(x)	((long double)exp((double)(x)))
fabsl(x)	((long double)fabs((double)(x)))
floorl(x)	((long double)floor((double)(x)))
fmodl(x,y)	((long double)fmod((double)(x), (double)(y)))
frexpl(x,y)	((long double)frexp((double)(x), (y)))
_hypotl(x,y)	((long double)_hypot((double)(x), (double)(y)))
ldexpl(x,y)	((long double)ldexp((double)(x), (y)))
logl(x)	((long double)log((double)(x)))
log10l(x)	((long double)log10((double)(x)))
_matherrl	_matherr
modfl(x,y)	((long double)modf((double)(x), (double *)(y)))
powl(x,y)	((long double)pow((double)(x), (double)(y)))
sinl(x)	((long double)sin((double)(x)))
sinhl(x)	((long double)sinh((double)(x)))
sqrtl(x)	((long double)sqrt((double)(x)))
tanl(x)	((long double)tan((double)(x)))
tanhl(x)	((long double)tanh((double)(x)))
long double acosl(long double _X)	{return (acos((double)_X)); }
long double asinl(long double _X)	{return (asin((double)_X)); }
long double atanl(long double _X)	{return (atan((double)_X)); }
long double atan2l(long double _X, long double _Y)	{return (atan2((double)_X, (double)_Y)); }

Table 18.12 Macros defining long double functions to be their double counterparts *(continued)*

Long-Double Function Prototypes	Implementation
long double ceill(long double _X)	{return (ceil((double)_X)); }
long double cosl(long double _X)	{return (cos((double)_X)); }
long double coshl(long double _X)	{return (cosh((double)_X)); }
long double expl(long double _X)	{return (exp((double)_X)); }
long double fabsl(long double _X)	{return (fabs((double)_X)); }
long double floorl(long double _X)	{return (floor((double)_X)); }
long double fmodl(long double _X, long double _Y)	{return (fmod((double)_X, (double)_Y)); }
long double frexpl(long double _X, int *_Y)	{return (frexp((double)_X, _Y)); }
long double ldexpl(long double _X, int _Y)	{return (ldexp((double)_X, _Y)); }
long double logl(long double _X)	{return (log((double)_X)); }
long double log10l(long double _X)	{return (log10((double)_X)); }
long double modfl(long double _X, long double *_Y)	{double _Di, _Df = modf((double)_X, &_Di);
*_Y = (long double)_Di;	return (_Df); }
long double powl(long double _X, long double _Y)	{return (pow((double)_X, (double)_Y)); }
long double sinl(long double _X)	{return (sin((double)_X)); }
long double sinhl(long double _X)	{return (sinh((double)_X)); }
long double sqrtl(long double _X)	{return (sqrt((double)_X)); }

Table 18.12 Macros defining long double functions to be their double counterparts *(continued)*

Long-Double Function Prototypes	Implementation
long double tanl(long double _X)	{return (tan((double)_X)); }
long double tanhl(long double _X)	{return (tanh((double)_X)); }

For this version of the Visual C++ compiler, a long double is the same as double. Additional floating-point function prototypes are shown in Table 18.13.

Table 18.13 Definitions for additional float functions

Float Function Prototypes	Implementation
float ldexpf(float _X, int _Y)	{return ((float)ldexp((double)_X, _Y)); }
float acosf(float _X)	{return ((float)acos((double)_X)); }
float asinf(float _X)	{return ((float)asin((double)_X)); }
float atanf(float _X)	{return ((float)atan((double)_X)); }
float atan2f(float _X, float _Y)	{return ((float)atan2((double)_X, (double)_Y)); }
float ceilf(float _X)	{return ((float)ceil((double)_X)); }
float cosf(float _X)	{return ((float)cos((double)_X)); }
float coshf(float _X)	{return ((float)cosh((double)_X)); }
float expf(float _X)	{return ((float)exp((double)_X)); }
float fabsf(float _X)	{return ((float)fabs((double)_X)); }
float floorf(float _X)	{return ((float)floor((double)_X)); }
float fmodf(float _X, float _Y)	{return ((float)fmod((double)_X, (double)_Y)); }
float logf(float _X)	{return ((float)log((double)_X)); }
float log10f(float _X)	{return ((float)log10((double)_X)); }
float modff(float _X, float *_Y)	{ double _Di, _Df = modf((double)_X, &_Di);
*_Y = (float)_Di;	return ((float)_Df); }
float powf(float _X, float _Y)	{return ((float)pow((double)_X, (double)_Y)); }
float sinf(float _X)	{return ((float)sin((double)_X)); }
float sinhf(float _X)	{return ((float)sinh((double)_X)); }
float sqrtf(float _X)	{return ((float)sqrt((double)_X)); }
float tanf(float _X)	{return ((float)tan((double)_X)); }
float tanhf(float _X)	{return ((float)tanh((double)_X)); }

The math.h header file provides a definition of a _complexl structure that can use _cabsl values.

```
struct _complexl {
  long double x,y;     //real and imaginary parts
} ;
```

The function prototypes for use with this structure are shown in Table 18.14.

Table 18.14 Function prototypes for long double

Function Prototype
long double acosl(long double);
long double asinl(long double);
long double atanl(long double);
long double atan2l(long double, long double);
long double _atold(const char *);
long double _cabsl(struct _complexl);
long double ceill(long double);
long double cosl(long double);
long double coshl(long double);
long double expl(long double);
long double fabsl(long double);
long double floorl(long double);
long double fmodl(long double, long double);
long double frexpl(long double, int *);
long double _hypotl(long double, long double);
long double _j0l(long double);
long double _j1l(long double);
long double _jnl(int, long double);
long double ldexpl(long double, int);
long double logl(long double);
long double log10l(long double);
int _matherrl(struct _exceptionl *);
long double modfl(long double, long double *);
long double powl(long double, long double);

Table 18.14 Function prototypes for long double *(continued)*

Function Prototype
long double sinl(long double);
long double sinhl(long double);
long double sqrtl(long double);
long double tanl(long double);
long double tanhl(long double);
long double _y0l(long double);
long double _y1l(long double);
long double _ynl(int, long double);

The following template is provided in the math.h header file:

```
template<class _Ty> inline
  _Ty _Pow_int(_Ty _X, int _Y)
  {unsigned int _N;
  if (_Y >= 0)
    _N = _Y;
  else
    _N = -_Y;
  for (_Ty _Z = _Ty(1); ; _X *= _X)
    {if ((_N & 1) != 0)
      _Z *= _X;
    if ((_N >>= 1) == 0)
      return (_Y < 0 ? _Ty(1) / _Z : _Z); }}
```

The various function prototypes associated with this template class are shown in Table 18.15.

Table 18.15 Function prototypes associated with the template class

Inline Function Prototype	Return Value
inline long __cdecl abs(long _X)	{return (labs(_X)); }
inline double __cdecl abs(double _X)	{return (fabs(_X)); }
inline double __cdecl pow(double _X, int _Y)	{return (_Pow_int(_X, _Y)); }
inline double __cdecl pow(int _X, int _Y)	{return (_Pow_int(_X, _Y)); }
inline float __cdecl abs(float _X)	{return (fabsf(_X)); }
inline float __cdecl acos(float _X)	{return (acosf(_X)); }
inline float __cdecl asin(float _X)	{return (asinf(_X)); }
inline float __cdecl atan(float _X)	{return (atanf(_X)); }

Table 18.15 Function prototypes associated with the template class *(continued)*

Inline Function Prototype	Return Value
inline float __cdecl atan2(float _Y, float _X)	{return (atan2f(_Y, _X)); }
inline float __cdecl ceil(float _X)	{return (ceilf(_X)); }
inline float __cdecl cos(float _X)	{return (cosf(_X)); }
inline float __cdecl cosh(float _X)	{return (coshf(_X)); }
inline float __cdecl exp(float _X)	{return (expf(_X)); }
inline float __cdecl fabs(float _X)	{return (fabsf(_X)); }
inline float __cdecl floor(float _X)	{return (floorf(_X)); }
inline float __cdecl fmod(float _X, float _Y)	{return (fmodf(_X, _Y)); }
inline float __cdecl frexp(float _X, int * _Y)	{return (frexpf(_X, _Y)); }
inline float __cdecl ldexp(float _X, int _Y)	{return (ldexpf(_X, _Y)); }
inline float __cdecl log(float _X)	{return (logf(_X)); }
inline float __cdecl log10(float _X)	{return (log10f(_X)); }
inline float __cdecl modf(float _X, float * _Y)	{return (modff(_X, _Y)); }
inline float __cdecl pow(float _X, float _Y)	{return (powf(_X, _Y)); }
inline float __cdecl pow(float _X, int _Y)	{return (_Pow_int(_X, _Y)); }
inline float __cdecl sin(float _X)	{return (sinf(_X)); }
inline float __cdecl sinh(float _X)	{return (sinhf(_X)); }
inline float __cdecl sqrt(float _X)	{return (sqrtf(_X)); }
inline float __cdecl tan(float _X)	{return (tanf(_X)); }
inline float __cdecl tanh(float _X)	{return (tanhf(_X)); }
inline long double __cdecl abs(long double _X)	{return (fabsl(_X)); }
inline long double __cdecl acos(long double _X)	{return (acosl(_X)); }
inline long double __cdecl asin(long double _X)	{return (asinl(_X)); }
inline long double __cdecl atan(long double _X)	{return (atanl(_X)); }
inline long double __cdecl atan2(long double _Y, long double _X)	{return (atan2l(_Y, _X)); }
inline long double __cdecl ceil(long double _X)	{return (ceill(_X)); }
inline long double __cdecl cos(long double _X)	{return (cosl(_X)); }
inline long double __cdecl cosh(long double _X)	{return (coshl(_X)); }
inline long double __cdecl exp(long double _X)	{return (expl(_X)); }

Table 18.15 Function prototypes associated with the template class *(continued)*

Inline Function Prototype	Return Value
inline long double __cdecl fabs(long double _X)	{return (fabsl(_X)); }
inline long double __cdecl floor(long double _X)	{return (floorl(_X)); }
inline long double __cdecl fmod(long double _X, long double _Y)	{return (fmodl(_X, _Y)); }
inline long double __cdecl frexp(long double _X, int * _Y)	{return (frexpl(_X, _Y)); }
inline long double __cdecl ldexp(long double _X, int _Y)	{return (ldexpl(_X, _Y)); }
inline long double __cdecl log(long double _X)	{return (logl(_X)); }
inline long double __cdecl log10(long double _X)	{return (log10l(_X)); }
inline long double __cdecl modf(long double _X, long double * _Y)	{return (modfl(_X, _Y)); }
inline long double __cdecl pow(long double _X, long double _Y)	{return (powl(_X, _Y)); }
inline long double __cdecl pow(long double _X, int _Y)	{return (_Pow_int(_X, _Y)); }
inline long double __cdecl sin(long double _X)	{return (sinl(_X)); }
inline long double __cdecl sinh(long double _X)	{return (sinhl(_X)); }
inline long double __cdecl sqrt(long double _X)	{return (sqrtl(_X)); }
inline long double __cdecl tan(long double _X)	{return (tanl(_X)); }
inline long double __cdecl tanh(long double _X)	{return (tanhl(_X)); }

Many of the function prototypes from the math.h header file will be illustrated in the sample code portion of this chapter.

Complex Numbers

Before investigating the <complex> template, a brief review of what complex numbers are is in order. If you have been involved with mathematical, engineering, or physics calculations, you have surely run into complex numbers. Complex numbers result from vectors (no relationship to STL vectors) or, better yet, phasors that have a magnitude and direction and can be described on a x-y coordinate system. The positive and negative x-axis represents the real component of a phasor and the y-axis represents the imaginary component of a phasor. In engineering statics, phasors are often used to represent a force moving in a certain direction. In electrical engineering, phasors are often used to represent voltages and currents and their associated phase angles.

You have three basic ways to represent complex numbers or phasors; polar form, rectangular form or exponential form. For example, imagine a phasor with a magnitude of 20 at an angle of 30 degrees measured counter-clockwise from the positive x-axis.

Polar Form:
In polar form, this phasor could be represented as:
20 /_ 30 deg

Rectangular Form:
In rectangular form, the real component is found using:
20 * cos 30 = 20 * 0.86603 = 17.3205
The imaginary component is
20 * sin 30 = 20 * 0.5 = 10
This phasor could then be presented as:
17.3205 + j10

Exponential Form:
In exponential form, the phasor is represented as:
$20 * e^{j30}$

Because phasors contain both real and imaginary components, they are called complex numbers.

To perform mathematical operations on complex numbers using a computer has always been difficult since most mathematical operators are not overloaded. For example, you cannot add, subtract, multiply, or divide complex numbers without operators overloaded for such purposes or with a template to handle all of that work for you.

Phasors represented in rectangular form are easy to add and subtract. For example:

(20 + j40) - (30 + j20) = -10 +j20
(20 + j40) + (30 + j20) = 50 + j60

Multiplication and division of phasors in rectangular form is not as easy, but not impossible. However, the easiest way to multiply and divide phasors is by working with them in polar form. For example:

(44.72 /_ 63.44 deg) * (36.05 /_ 33.7 deg) = (44.72 * 36.05) /_ (63.44 + 33.7) deg
= 1612.156 /_ 97.14 deg

(20 /_ 50 deg) / (15 /_ 30 deg) = (20 / 15) /_ (50 deg - 30 deg)
= 1.333 /_ 20 deg

As a result of these various forms, conversion from one form to another is typical in most arithmetic operations involving phasors. The calculations can be tedious when using a calculator or computer program that cannot handle complex numbers.

If you would like more information on the use of complex numbers, we recommend any good technical mathematics book, electrical engineering book dealing with ac circuits, or any college physics book.

In the following section, we'll investigate the capabilities of the <complex> template. Then in the sample application section of this chapter, you'll see how the <complex> template can be used in three separate applications.

<complex> Template Syntax

The Standard C++ header <complex> is used to define the template class complex and a large number of supporting template functions. The following listing gives the syntax for the <complex> template:

```
namespace std {
#define __STD_COMPLEX
//    TEMPLATE CLASSES
template<class T>
    class complex;
class "complex<float>;
class "complex<double>;
class "complex<long double>;
//    TEMPLATE FUNCTIONS
template<class T>
    complex<T> operator+(const complex<T>& lhs, const complex<T>& rhs);
template<class T>
    complex<T> operator+(const complex<T>& lhs, const T& rhs);
template<class T>
    complex<T> operator+(const T& lhs, const complex<T>& rhs);
template<class T>
    complex<T> operator-(const complex<T>& lhs, const complex<T>& rhs);
template<class T>
    complex<T> operator-(const complex<T>& lhs, const T& rhs);
template<class T>
    complex<T> operator-(const T& lhs, const complex<T>& rhs);
template<class T>
    complex<T> operator*(const complex<T>& lhs, const complex<T>& rhs);
template<class T>
    complex<T> operator*(const complex<T>& lhs, const T& rhs);
template<class T>
    complex<T> operator*(const T& lhs, const complex<T>& rhs);
template<class T>
```

```
    complex<T> operator/(const complex<T>& lhs, const complex<T>& rhs);
template<class T>
    complex<T> operator/(const complex<T>& lhs, const T& rhs);
template<class T>
    complex<T> operator/(const T& lhs, const complex<T>& rhs);
template<class T>
    complex<T> operator+(const complex<T>& lhs);
template<class T>
    complex<T> operator-(const complex<T>& lhs);
template<class T>
    bool operator==(const complex<T>& lhs, const complex<T>& rhs);
template<class T>
    bool operator==(const complex<T>& lhs, const T& rhs);
template<class T>
    bool operator==(const T& lhs, const complex<T>& rhs);
template<class T>
    bool operator!=(const complex<T>& lhs, const complex<T>& rhs);
template<class T>
    bool operator!=(const complex<T>& lhs, const T& rhs);
template<class T>
    bool operator!=(const T& lhs, const complex<T>& rhs);
template<class E, class Ti, class T>
    basic_istream<E, Ti>& "operator>>(basic_istream<E, Ti>& is,
        complex<T>& x);
template<class E, class T, class U>
    basic_ostream<E, T>& operator<<(basic_ostream<E, T>& os,
        const complex<U>& x);
template<class T>
    T real(const complex<T>& x);
template<class T>
    T imag(const complex<T>& x);
template<class T>
    T abs(const complex<T>& x);
template<class T>
    T arg(const complex<T>& x);
template<class T>
    T norm(const complex<T>& x);
template<class T>
    complex<T> conjg(const complex<T>& x);
template<class T>
    complex<T> polar(const T& rho, const T& theta = 0);
template<class T>
    complex<T> cos(const complex<T>& x);
template<class T>
    complex<T> cosh(const complex<T>& x);
template<class T>
    complex<T> exp(const complex<T>& x);
template<class T>
    complex<T> log(const complex<T>& x);
template<class T>
```

```
    complex<T> log10(const complex<T>& x);
template<class T>
    complex<T> pow(const complex<T>& x, int y);
template<class T>
    complex<T> pow(const complex<T>& x, const T& y);
template<class T>
    complex<T> pow(const complex<T>& x, const complex<T>& y);
template<class T>
    complex<T> pow(const T& x, const complex<T>& y);
template<class T>
    complex<T> sin(const complex<T>& x);
template<class T>
    complex<T> sinh(const complex<T>& x);
template<class T>
    complex<T> sqrt(const complex<T>& x);
    };
```

At the time of this writing, the complex conjugate of a complex number is found by using conj(), not conjg(), as it appears in Microsoft's references.

For this template class, functions that return multiple values will return an imaginary part in the half-open interval given by (-pi, pi].

Table 18.16 lists and describes the template functions for <complex>.

Table 18.16 Template functions for <complex>

Template Functions
`complex<T> operator+(const complex<T>& lhs, const complex<T>& rhs);`
`complex<T> operator+(const complex<T>& lhs, const T& rhs);`
`complex<T> operator+(const T& lhs, const complex<T>& rhs);`
`complex<T> operator-(const complex<T>& lhs, const complex<T>& rhs);`
`complex<T> operator-(const complex<T>& lhs, const T& rhs);`
`complex<T> operator-(const T& lhs, const complex<T>& rhs);`
`complex<T> operator*(const complex<T>& lhs, const complex<T>& rhs);`
`complex<T> operator*(const complex<T>& lhs, const T& rhs);`
`complex<T> operator*(const T& lhs, const complex<T>& rhs);`
`complex<T> operator/(const complex<T>& lhs, const complex<T>& rhs);`
`complex<T> operator/(const complex<T>& lhs, const T& rhs);`

Table 18.16 Template functions for <complex> *(continued)*

Template Functions
complex<T> operator/(const T& lhs, const complex<T>& rhs);
complex<T> operator+(const complex<T>& lhs);
complex<T> operator-(const complex<T>& lhs);
bool operator==(const complex<T>& lhs, const complex<T>& rhs);
bool operator==(const complex<T>& lhs, const T& rhs);
bool operator==(const T& lhs, const complex<T>& rhs);
bool operator!=(const complex<T>& lhs, const complex<T>& rhs);
bool operator!=(const complex<T>& lhs, const T& rhs);
bool operator!=(const T& lhs, const complex<T>& rhs);
basic_istream<E, Ti>& "operator>>(basic_istream<E, Ti>& is, complex<T>& x);
basic_ostream<E, T>& operator<<(basic_ostream<E, T>& os, const complex<U>& x);

The methods in this template class are listed and described in Table 18.17. All the normal operations needed for manipulating complex numbers are provided with this template.

Table 18.17 <complex> template methods

Template Method	Description
template<class T> T abs(const complex<T>& x);	Returns the magnitude of x.
template<class T> T arg(const complex<T>& x);	Returns the phase angle of x.
template<class T> complex<T> conjg(const complex<T>& x);	Returns the conjugate of x. Note: use conj(), at this time, to find the complex conjugate.
template<class T> complex<T> cos(const complex<T>& x);	Returns the cosine of x.
template<class T> complex<T> cosh(const complex<T>& x);	Returns the hyperbolic cosine of x.
template<class T> complex<T> exp(const complex<T>& x);	Returns the exponential of x.

Table 18.17 <complex> template methods *(continued)*

Template Method	Description
template<class T> T imag(const complex<T>& x);	Returns the imaginary part of x.
template<class T> complex<T> log(const complex<T>& x);	Returns the logarithm of x. The branch cuts occur along the negative real axis.
template<class T> complex<T> log10(const complex<T>& x);	Returns the base 10 logarithm of x. The branch cuts occur along the negative real axis.
template<class T> T norm(const complex<T>& x);	Returns the squared magnitude of x.
template<class T> complex<T> polar(const T& rho, const T& theta = 0);	Returns a complex value. The magnitude is rho and the phase angle is theta.
template<class T> complex<T> pow(const complex<T>& x, int y); template<class T> complex<T> pow(const complex<T>& x, const T& y); template<class T> complex<T> pow(const complex<T>& x, const complex<T>& y); template<class T> complex<T> pow(const T& x, const complex<T>& y);	Each function converts both operands to the given return type, and then returns the converted x to the power y. The branch cut for x occurs along the negative real axis.
template<class T> T real(const complex<T>& x);	Returns the real part of x.
template<class T> complex<T> sin(const complex<T>& x);	Returns the imaginary sine of x.
template<class T> complex<T> sinh(const complex<T>& x);	Returns the hyperbolic sine of x.
template<class T> complex<T> sqrt(const complex<T>& x);	Returns the square root of x. The phase angle occurs in the half-open interval (-pi/2, pi/2]. The branch cuts occur along the negative real axis.

The <complex> template class describes an object. This object stores two objects of type T. One object represents the real part of a complex number and the other object the imaginary part of the complex number.

Objects of class T have a public constructor, destructor, copy constructor, and assignment operator. Class T objects can be assigned integer or floating-point values or be **cast** to the desired values. Arithmetic operators are defined for the appropriate floating-point types.

Many of these methods and operators are illustrated in several example programs provided in the sample code section of this chapter, along with a short tutorial on the use of complex numbers.

In the following three sections, you'll see how template class handles three floating-point types: float, double, and long double. For this version of Visual C++, a value of any other type T is **cast** to a double for actual calculations. The return type, a double, is assigned back to the object of type T.

CLASS COMPLEX <FLOAT>

The class complex <float> describes an object that stores two objects of type float. One object represents the real part of a complex number and the second object the imaginary part of the complex number.

```
class complex<float> {
public:
  complex(float re = 0, float im = 0);
  explicit complex(const complex<double>& x);
  explicit complex(const complex<long double>& x);
  // remainder identical to template class complex
};
```

Note that the only difference is in the defined constructors. The first constructor initializes the real part to *re* and the imaginary part *im*. Two final constructors initialize the real part to x.real() and the imaginary part to x.imag().

CLASS COMPLEX <DOUBLE>

The class complex <double> describes an object that stores two objects of type double. One object represents the real part of a complex number and the second object the imaginary part of the complex number.

```
class complex<double> {
public:
  complex(double re = 0, double im = 0);
  complex(const complex<float>& x);
  explicit complex(const complex<long double>& x);
  // remainder identical to template class complex
};
```

Again, the only difference is in the defined constructors. The first constructor initializes the real part to *re* and the imaginary part *im*. Two final constructors initialize the real part to x.real() and the imaginary part to x.imag().

CLASS COMPLEX <LONG DOUBLE>

The class complex <long double> describes an object that stores two objects of type long double. One object represents the real part of a complex number and the second object the imaginary part of the complex number.

```
class complex<long double> {
public:
  complex(long double re = 0, long double im = 0);
  complex(const complex<float>& x);
  complex(const complex<double>& x);
  // remainder identical to the template class complex
};
```

Again, the only difference is in the defined constructors. The first constructor initializes the real part to *re* and the imaginary part *im*. Two final constructors initialize the real part to x.real() and the imaginary part to x.imag().

Sample Code

Several applications are provided in this section to illustrate the use of the <cfloat> and <cmath> standard C++ header files, along with three examples showing the use of the <complex> template.

A <cfloat> Application

The first example application, cfloat1.cpp, uses _controlfp() to alter the output precision by which floating point numbers are stored. The program prints the mathematical results in the system's default precision and then changes the precision to 24-bits, 53-bits, and 64-bits. Finally, the default precision is restored and the results printed, once again, to the screen. Here is the complete listing for this example:

```
// cfloat1.cpp
// Uses <cfloat> by testing _controlfp to output the
control
// word.  The precision is changed from
// the default to 24-bits, then 53-bits, then 64-bits, and
// then back to the default.
// Chris H. Pappas and William H. Murray, 1999

#include <iostream>
#include <cfloat>
```

```
using namespace std;

void main(void)
{
   double a = 0.1;

   // set print precision to 40 digits
   cout.precision(40);

   // default precision
   cout << "default precision: " << hex
        << _controlfp(0,0) << endl;
   cout << "1.1 * 1.1 = " << a * a << endl << endl;

   // change precision to 24 bits
   cout << "24-bit precision: " << hex
        << _controlfp(_PC_24,MCW_PC) << endl;
   cout << "1.1 * 1.1 = " << a * a << endl << endl;

   // change precision to 53 bits
   cout << "53-bit precision: " << hex
        << _controlfp(_PC_53,MCW_PC) << endl;
   cout << "1.1 * 1.1 = " << a * a << endl << endl;

   // change precision to 64 bits
   cout << "64-bit precision: " << hex
        << _controlfp(_PC_64,MCW_PC) << endl;
   cout << "1.1 * 1.1 = " << a * a << endl << endl;

   // reset to default precision
   cout << "reset to default precision: " << hex
        << _controlfp(_CW_DEFAULT,0xfffff) << endl;
   cout << "1.1 * 1.1 = " << a * a << endl;
}
```

The following listing is the output from the program showing how the output precision is affected, for this mathematical result, when the precision is dropped below 53-bits:

```
default precision: 9001f
1.1 * 1.1 = 0.01000000000000000020000

24-bit precision: a001f
1.1 * 1.1 = 0.00999999977648258210000

53-bit precision: 9001f
1.1 * 1.1 = 0.01000000000000000020000

64-bit precision: 8001f
1.1 * 1.1 = 0.01000000000000000020000

reset to default precision: 9001f
1.1 * 1.1 = 0.01000000000000000020000
```

You may want to experiment with _clearfp(), _statusfp(), and _fpreset() and continue your investigation of the <cfloat> standard C++ header file.

A <cmath> Application

The second application, cmath1.cpp, shows how to invoke a number of <cmath> methods in order to calculate a variety of trigonometric values for various angles.

```
// cmath1.cpp
// Uses <cmath> to calculate a variety of trig
// results.  Uses valarray<> to create a number
// of storage locations for data values and
// results.
// Chris H. Pappas and William H. Murray, 1999

#include <iostream>
#include <valarray>
#include <cmath>

using namespace std;

#define ASIZE  5                          // array sizes

void main()
{
  int i;

  // create three valarray<>.
  valarray<double> data_values(ASIZE);    // data
  valarray<double> result_values(ASIZE); //
  valarray<double> temp_array;            // temp return

  // initialize data for data_values array
  data_values[0] = 0.0;          // 0 degrees
  data_values[1] = 0.5235988;    // pi/6 = 30 degrees
  data_values[2] = 0.7853982;    // pi/4 = 45 degrees
  data_values[3] = 1.0471976;    // pi/3 = 60 degrees
  data_values[4] = 1.5707963;    // pi/2 = 90 degrees

  // control printing
  cout.width(6);
  cout.precision(5);

  // table headers
  cout << "funct" << "\t"
       << "0 deg" << "\t"
       << "30 deg" << "\t"
       << "45 deg" << "\t"
       << "60 deg" << "\t"
```

```
    << "90 deg" << endl << endl;

// trigonometric functions
temp_array = sin(data_values);
cout << "sin():" << "\t";
for (i = 0; i < ASIZE; i++)
  cout << temp_array[i] << "\t";
cout << endl;

temp_array = cos(data_values);
cout << "cos():" << "\t";
for (i = 0; i < ASIZE; i++)
  cout << temp_array[i] << "\t";
cout << endl;

temp_array = tan(data_values);
cout << "tan():" << "\t";
for (i = 0; i < ASIZE; i++)
  cout << temp_array[i] << "\t";
cout << endl;


// arc trig functions
temp_array = asin(data_values);
cout << "asin():" << "\t";
for (i = 0; i < ASIZE; i++)
  cout << temp_array[i] << "\t";
cout << endl;

temp_array = acos(data_values);
cout << "acos():" << "\t";
for (i = 0; i < ASIZE; i++)
  cout << temp_array[i] << "\t";
cout << endl;

temp_array = atan(data_values);
cout << "atan():" << "\t";
for (i = 0; i < ASIZE; i++)
  cout << temp_array[i] << "\t";
cout << endl;


// hyperbolic trig functions
temp_array = sinh(data_values);
cout << "sinh():" << "\t";
for (i = 0; i < ASIZE; i++)
  cout << temp_array[i] << "\t";
cout << endl;
```

```
    temp_array = cosh(data_values);
    cout << "cosh():" << "\t";
    for (i = 0; i < ASIZE; i++)
      cout << temp_array[i] << "\t";
    cout << endl;

    temp_array = tanh(data_values);
    cout << "tanh():" << "\t";
    for (i = 0; i < ASIZE; i++)
      cout << temp_array[i] << "\t";
    cout << endl << endl;
}
```

This example uses the normal, arc, and hyperbolic trignometric functions to complete a simple table on the screen. The output for this program reports:

```
funct      0 deg     30 deg     45 deg     60 deg     90 deg

sin():     0         0.5        0.70711    0.86603    1
cos():     1         0.86603    0.70711    0.5        2.6795e-008
tan():     0         0.57735    1          1.7321     3.7321e+007
asin():    0         0.55107    0.90334    -1.#IND    -1.#IND
acos():    1.5708    1.0197     0.66746    -1.#IND    -1.#IND
atan():    0         0.48235    0.66577    0.80845    1.0039
sinh():    0         0.54785    0.86867    1.2494     2.3013
cosh():    1         1.1402     1.3246     1.6003     2.5092
tanh():     0          0.48047     0.65579     0.78071     0.91715
```

If you work in the area of mathematics or engineering you probably already know the trigonometric results for the sin(), cos(), and tan() functions for the angles 0, 30, 45, 60, and 90 degrees. However, you may find the results for the tan() of 90 degrees and the asin() and acos() of 60 and 90 degrees interesting.

The remaining three examples in this chapter deal with complex number applications. Calculations involving complex numbers are frequently made by mathematicians, engineers, and physicists. If complex number calculations do not interest you, perhaps you'll consider the examples from a purely programming prospective.

The First <complex> Application

The first <complex> application, complex1.cpp, shows how to calculate the algebraic sum of three complex numbers. What makes this interesting is that the complex numbers are given in both polar and rectangular forms. However, since the operators are overloaded, no conversions are required for the mathematical operations. Here is the complete source code for this example:

```
// complex1.cpp
// Uses <complex> to calculate x1 + x2 - x3
// of three complex numbers, given in rectangular
// and polar forms.
// Results printed in both rectangular and polar formats.
// Chris H. Pappas and William H. Murray, 1999

#include <iostream>
#include <complex>

using namespace std;

void main()
{
  double pi = 3.14159265359;

  complex<double> x1, x2, x3, z1, z2;

  // phasor one
  x1.real(3.0);                              //3.0 + j4.0
  x1.imag(4.0);
  // phasor two
  double m = 10.0;                           //10 /_45 deg
  double a = 45 * pi / 180;
  x2 = polar(m, a);
  // phasor three
  x3 = polar(6.0, -0.523598776);             //6 /_-30 deg

  // complex arithmetic calculation
  z1 = x1 + x2 - x3;

  // results in rectangular form
  cout << "answer in rectangular format is: "
       << z1 << endl << endl;
  // results in polar form
  cout << "answer in polar format is: "
       << sqrt(norm(z1)) << " at /_ " << arg(z1)
       << " radians (or " << arg(z1)*180.0/pi
       << " degrees)" << endl << endl;
}
```

Remember that all angles must be expressed in radians. Pi radians is equal to 180 degrees, for conversion purposes.

Three phasors are used. The format of each phasor differs slightly to show you just how flexible data entry can be.

```
// phasor one
  x1.real(3.0);                               //3.0 + j4.0
  x1.imag(4.0);
  // phasor two
  double m = 10.0;                            //10 /_45 deg
  double a = 45 * pi / 180;
  x2 = polar(m, a);
  // phasor three
  x3 = polar(6.0, -0.523598776);              //6 /_-30 deg
```

Since the "+" and "-" operators are overloaded, simple arithmetic operations can be achieved without the conversion of data to a particular format.

```
// complex arithmetic calculation
  z1 = x1 + x2 - x3;
```

The cout stream is also overloaded and will print the complex results when any phasor is passed. The default format is rectangular form.

```
// results in rectangular form
  cout << "answer in rectangular format is: "
       << z1 << endl << endl;
```

With just a small amount of work, the results can also be displayed in a polar form by using the following code:

```
  // results in polar form
  cout << "answer in polar format is: "
       << sqrt(norm(z1)) << " at /_ " << arg(z1)
       << " radians (or " << arg(z1)*180.0/pi
       << " degrees)" << endl << endl;
```

The output from this program is simple and straightforward.

```
answer in rectangular format is: (4.87492,14.0711)

answer in polar format is: 14.8916 at /_ 1.23729 radians
                                     (or 70.8914 degrees)
```

The application is fairly simple, but you might want to check the results with your calculator.

The Second <complex> Application

The second <complex> application, complex2.cpp, shows how to use complex numbers to solve a simple series ac circuit problem involving a resistor, capacitor, and inductor. Reactance values for capacitors and inductors are complex quantities determined by the component values and the frequency used in the circuit.

```
// complex2.cpp
// An electrical circuit has a resistance of 8 ohms,
// an inductive reactance of 7 ohms, and a capacitive
// reactance of 13 ohms connected in series.
// Determine the impedance of the circuit and the phase
// angle between the voltage and current.
// Results printed in both rectangular and polar formats.
// Chris H. Pappas and William H. Murray, 1999

#include <iostream>
#include <complex>

using namespace std;

void main()
{
  double pi = 3.14159265359;

  complex<double> x1, x2, x3, z1;

  // phasor one
  x1.real(8.0);          //resistor = 3.0 +j0.0
  // phasor two
  x2.imag(7.0);          //ind react = 0.0 +j7.0
  // phasor three
  x3.imag(-13);          //cap react = 0.0 -j13

  // complex arithmetic calculation
  z1 = x1 + x2 + x3;

  // results in rectangular form
  cout << "answer in rectangular format is: "
       << z1 << endl << endl;
  // results in polar form
  cout << "answer in polar format is: "
       << sqrt(norm(z1)) << " at /_ " << arg(z1)
       << " radians (or " << arg(z1)*180.0/pi
       << " degrees)" << endl << endl;
}
```

You should be able to instantly see that this application does not differ greatly from the first complex number application. Simply stated, three phasors are being added and the results are reported to the screen in both rectangular and polar forms. The output for this application is:

```
answer in rectangular format is: (8,-6)

answer in polar format is: 10 at /_ -0.643501 radians
                              (or -36.8699 degrees)
```

Now you see how easily you can go from a stuffy math problem to a real-world engineering example. We'll bet you can't wait to break out those old engineering books on the bookshelf.

The Third <complex> Application

The third <complex> application, complex3.cpp, is a graphical application that you'll have to build with the Visual C++ AppWizard. Although the details for the use of the AppWizard are beyond the scope of this book, we can give you a few basic instructions.

First, start the Visual C++ compiler and select the New menu item from the File menu. This action will bring up the New dialog box, as shown in Figure 18.1.

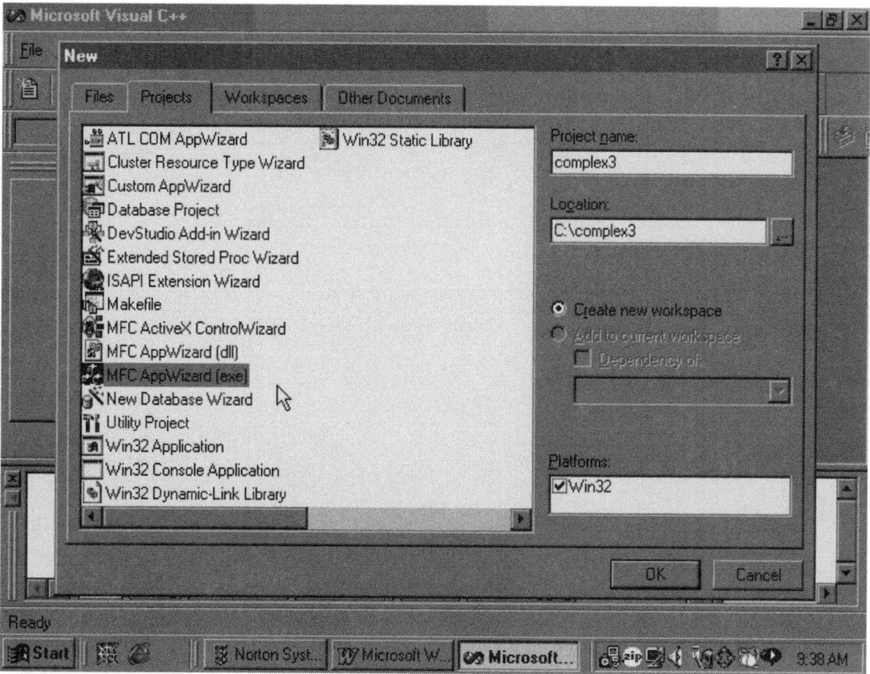

Figure 18.1 *The New dialog box allows you to select the MFC AppWizard(exe)*

To build a MFC application, with the AppWizard, simply follow the on-screen instructions, accepting the suggested defaults along the way.

When the AppWizard has generated the source code and header files for the application, select the complex3View.cpp source code file, as shown in Figure 18.2.

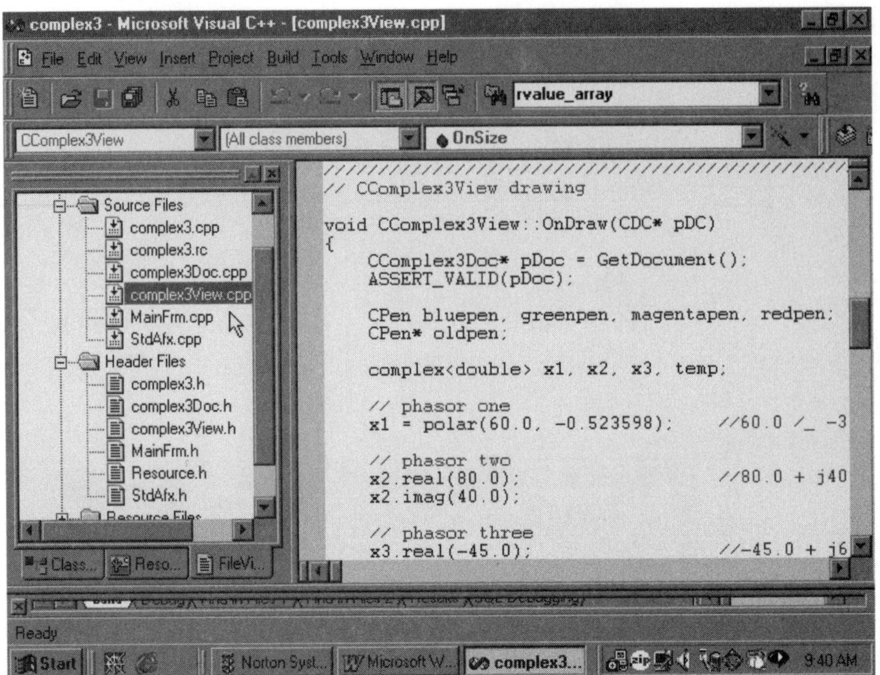

Figure 18.2 *Use the complex3View.cpp source code file to add your Windows drawing code*

Find the OnDraw() method in this files code and add the drawing code shown in a bold font in the following listing:

```
//////////////////////////////////////////////////////////////////////
// CComplex3View drawing

void CComplex3View::OnDraw(CDC* pDC)
{
    CComplex3Doc* pDoc = GetDocument();
    ASSERT_VALID(pDoc);

    CPen bluepen, greenpen, magentapen, redpen;
    CPen* oldpen;

    complex<double> x1, x2, x3, temp;

    // phasor one
    x1 = polar(60.0, -0.523598);    //60.0 /_ -30 deg

    // phasor two
```

```
    x2.real(80.0);                          //80.0 + j40.0
    x2.imag(40.0);

    // phasor three
    x3.real(-45.0);                         //-45.0 + j60.0
    x3.imag(60.0);

    // set mapping modes and viewport
    pDC->SetMapMode(MM_ISOTROPIC);
    pDC->SetWindowExt(250,250);
    pDC->SetViewportExt(m_cxClient,-m_cyClient);
    pDC->SetViewportOrg(m_cxClient/2,m_cyClient/2);

    // draw coordinate axes
    pDC->MoveTo(-120,0);
    pDC->LineTo(120,0);
    pDC->MoveTo(0,-100);
    pDC->LineTo(0,100);

    // draw first phasor with blue pen
    bluepen.CreatePen(PS_DASHDOT,0,RGB(0,0,255));
    oldpen = pDC->SelectObject(&bluepen);
    pDC->MoveTo(0,0);
    pDC->LineTo(real(x1),imag(x1));
    DeleteObject(oldpen);

    temp = x1 + x2;  // add first two phasors

    // draw second phasor with green pen
    greenpen.CreatePen(PS_DASHDOT,0,RGB(0,255,0));
    oldpen = pDC->SelectObject(&greenpen);
    pDC->LineTo(real(temp),imag(temp));
    DeleteObject(oldpen);

    temp += x3;      // add in last phasor

    // draw third phasor with magenta pen
    magentapen.CreatePen(PS_DASHDOT,0,RGB(255,0,255));
    oldpen = pDC->SelectObject(&magentapen);
    pDC->LineTo(real(temp),imag(temp));
    DeleteObject(oldpen);

    // draw sum of phasors with wide red pen
    redpen.CreatePen(PS_SOLID,2,RGB(255,0,0));
    oldpen = pDC->SelectObject(&redpen);
    pDC->LineTo(0,0);
    DeleteObject(oldpen);
}
```

To complete this application, you need a few more steps. First, open the ClassWizard from the Visual C++ compiler's View menu. With all windows set to the values shown in Figure 18.3, you can add a WM_SIZE message handler.

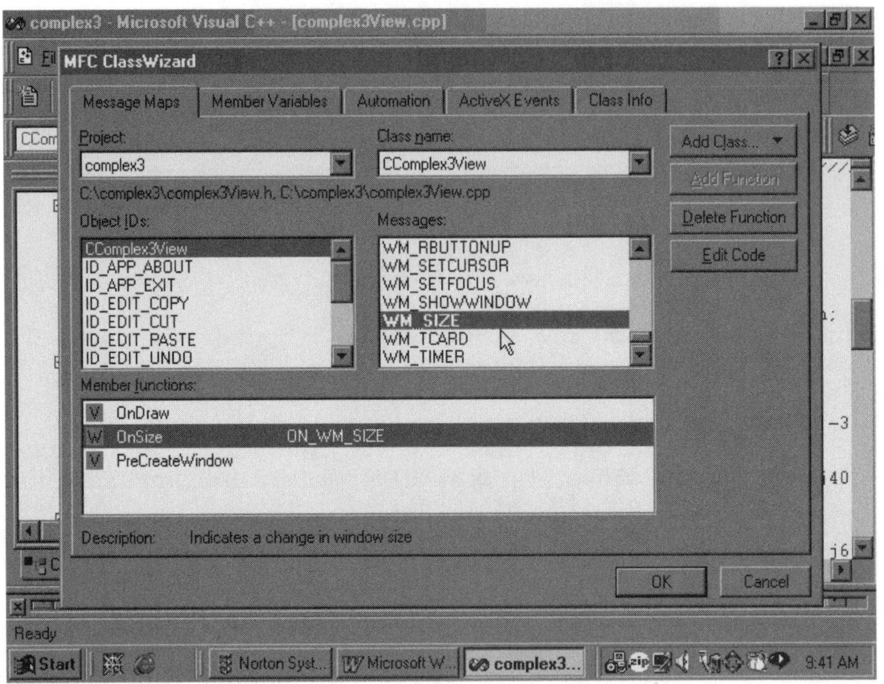

Figure 18.3 *Use the ClassWizard to add a WM_SIZE message handler*

The ClassWizard will add an OnSize() method to the complex3View.cpp source code file, as shown in Figure 18.4.

The code is modified to return information to two member variables, *m_cxClient* and *m_cyClient*, with regards to the size of the window.

```
void CComplex3View::OnSize(UINT nType, int cx, int cy)
{
    CView::OnSize(nType, cx, cy);

    // TODO: Add your message handler code here

    m_cxClient = cx;
    m_cyClient = cy;
}
```

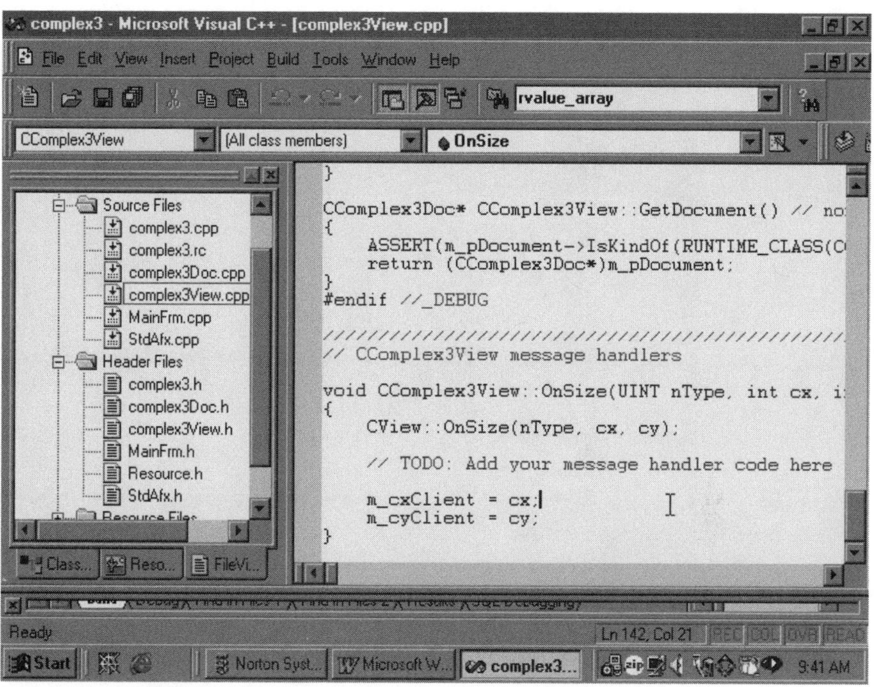

Figure 18.4 *An OnSize() method is added to complex3View.cpp by the ClassWizard.*

To make these variables visible, declare the member variables in the complex3View.h header file, shown in Figure 18.5.

The following listing shows the actual code, in bold, that must be entered in this header file:

```
class CComplex3View : public CView
{
private:   // member variables for resized window
    int m_cxClient;
    int m_cyClient;

protected: // create from serialization only
    CComplex3View();
    DECLARE_DYNCREATE(CComplex3View)

// Attributes
public:
    CComplex3Doc* GetDocument();
      .
      .
      .
```

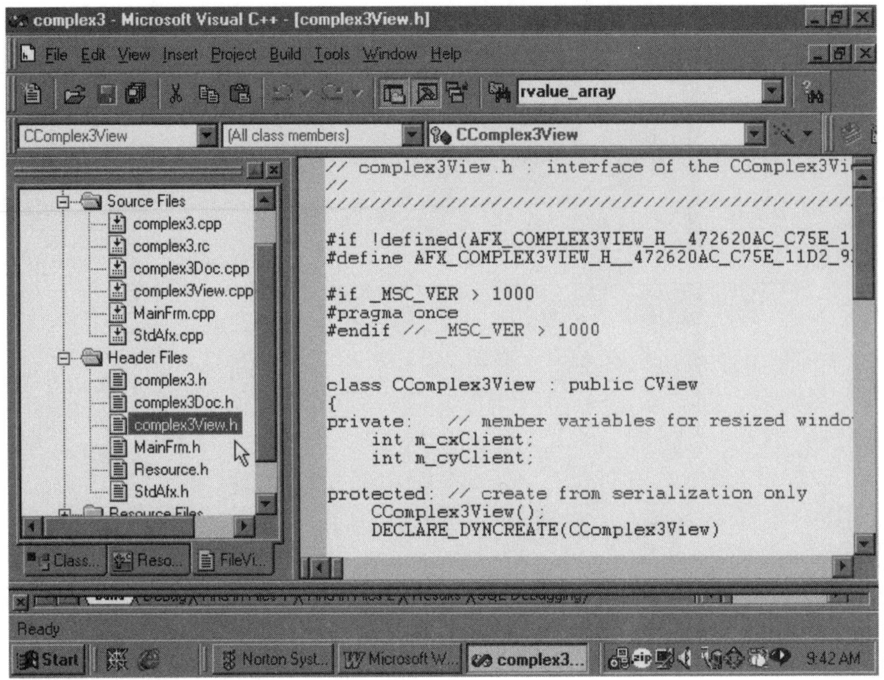

Figure 18.5 *The member variables are declared in the complex3View.h header file*

The only thing left is to compile and execute this application. Figure 18.6 shows the output sent to the window.

The three phasors are shown with dash-dot line segments, and the result of adding the phasors together is shown with a solid wide red line.

We're sure that you'll agree that adding graphing capabilities to complex number arithmetic opens new possibilities to engineering and mathematical calculations.

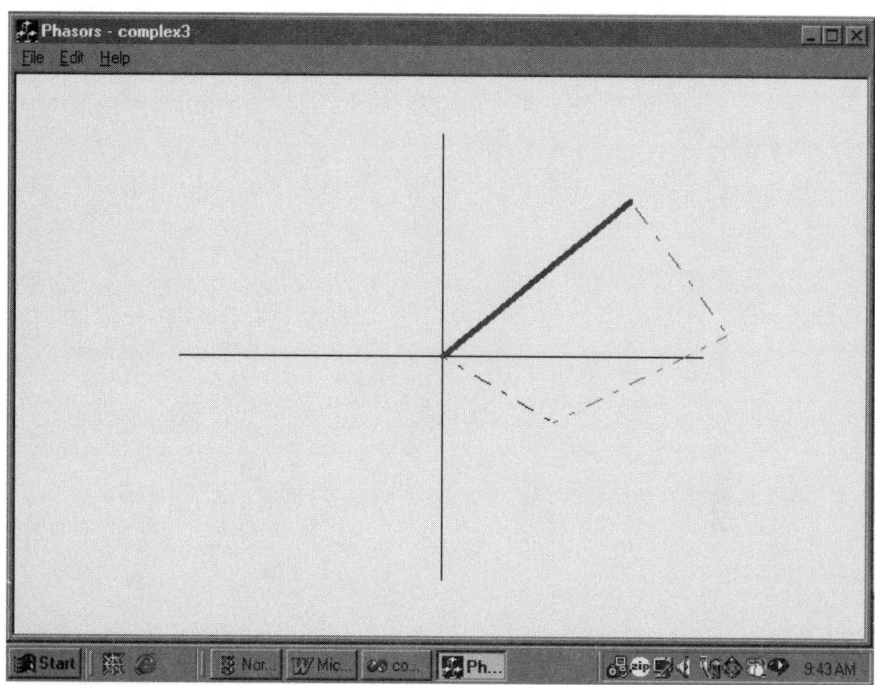

Figure 18.6 *The graphical results of our complex arithmetic drawn in a window.*

Summary

The <cfloat> and <cmath> Standard C++ Headers and <complex> Template Class Standard C++ header files provide powerful new options to the programmer, mathematician, and engineer alike.

The capabilities of the <complex> template added to the MFC Windows environment provides a powerful new tool for viewing the results of complex number calculations.

NINETEEN

The <climits>, <limits>, and <csignal> Standard C++ Headers

This chapter describes <climits>, <limits>, and the <csignal> headers files. The standard header <limits> is used to define the numeric_limits template class. This chapter describes the new ANSI standard header syntax for these headers. We'll also investigate features for implementing the header code and see several working examples for each.

The <climits> Header Syntax

The following listing gives the syntax for using the <climits> standard header file:

```
namespace std {#include <limits.h> };
```

The <climits> standard header is used to include the <limits.h> header within the *std* namespace. The basic purpose of this header file is for testing integer type properties.

The <limits.h> header file provides a number of constants, as shown in Table 19.1, that define maximum and minimum ranges for integers, shorts, and longs.

Table 19.1 Maximum and minimum values for integers, shorts, and longs

Constant	Value	Description
INT_MAX	2147483647	max (signed) int value
INT_MIN	-2147483647 - 1	min (signed) int value
LONG_MAX	2147483647L	max (signed) long value
LONG_MIN	-2147483647L - 1	min (signed) long value
MB_LEN_MAX	2	max. # bytes in multibyte char
SHRT_MAX	32767	max (signed) short value
SHRT_MIN	-32768	min (signed) short value
UINT_MAX	0xffffffff	max unsigned int value
ULONG_MAX	0xffffffffUL	max unsigned long value
USHRT_MAX	0xffff	max unsigned short value

The constants in Table 19.1 can be used by applications to test various properties of integer, short, and long values.

Character Ranges

The <limits.h> header file provides a number of constants for testing character data types. Table 19.2 shows the constants provided for CHAR, SCHAR (signed character), and UCHAR (unsigned character).

Table 19.2 Constants used to test CHAR, SCHAR, and UCHAR types

Constant	Value	Description
CHAR_BIT	8	number of bits in a character
CHAR_MAX	SCHAR_MAX	maximum character value
CHAR_MAX	UCHAR_MAX	same as UCHAR_MAX
CHAR_MIN	SCHAR_MIN	minimum character value
CHAR_MIN	0	value defined as zero
SCHAR_MAX	127	maximum signed character value
SCHAR_MIN	-128	minimum signed character value
UCHAR_MAX	0xff	maximum unsigned character value

The constants in Table 19.2 can be used by applications to test various properties associated with CHAR, SCHAR, and UCHAR data types.

Integer Ranges (8 bits)

Table 19.3 shows the ranges for 8-bit integers as defined in the <limits.h> header file.

Table 19.3 Maximum and minimum ranges for 8-bit integers

Constant	Value	Description
_I8_MAX	127	maximum signed 8-bit value
_I8_MIN	-127 - 1	minimum signed 8-bit value
_UI8_MAX	0xff (255)	maximum unsigned 8-bit value

Table 19.3 includes range values for both signed and unsigned 8-bit integers.

Integer Ranges (16 bits)

Table 19.4 shows the ranges for 16-bit integers as defined in the <limits.h> header file.

Table 19.4 Maximum and minimum ranges for 16-bit integers

Constant	Value	Description
_I16_MAX	32767	maximum signed 16-bit value
_I16_MIN	-32767 - 1	minimum signed 16-bit value
_UI16_MAX	0xffff (65535)	maximum unsigned 16-bit value

Table 19.4 includes range values for both signed and unsigned 16-bit integers.

Integer Ranges (32 bits)

Table 19.5 gives the ranges for 32-bit integers as defined in the <limits.h> header file.

Table 19.5 Maximum and minimum ranges for 32-bit integers

Constant	Value	Description
_I32_MAX	2147483647	maximum signed 32-bit value
_I32_MIN	-2147483647 - 1	minimum signed 32-bit value
_UI32_MAX	0xffffffff (4294967295)	maximum unsigned 32-bit value

Table 19.5 includes range values for both signed and unsigned 32-bit integers.

Integer Ranges (64 bits)

Table 19.6 shows the ranges for 64-bit integers as defined in the <limits.h> header file.

Table 19.6 Maximum and minimum ranges for 64-bit integers

Constant	Value	Description
_I64_MAX	9223372036854775807	maximum signed 64-bit value
_I64_MIN	-9223372036854775807 - 1	minimum signed 64-bit value
_UI64_MAX	0xffffffffffffffff	maximum unsigned 64-bit value

Table 19.6 includes range values for both signed and unsigned 64-bit integers.

Integer Ranges (128 bits)

Table 19.7 shows the ranges for 128-bit integers as defined in the <limits.h> header file.

Table 19.7 Maximum and minimum ranges for 128-bit integers

Constant	Value	Description
_I128_MAX	170141183460469231731687303715884105727	max signed 128-bit value
_I128_MIN	-170141183460469231731687303715884105727 - 1	min signed 128-bit value
_UI128_MAX	0xffffffffffffffffffffffffffffffff	max unsigned 128-bit value

Table 19.7 includes range values for both signed and unsigned 128-bit integers.

POSIX Ranges

The <limits.h> header file defines a group of POSIX constants. POSIX is useful when converting applications from UNIX to Windows. Currently, the Windows NT POSIX subsystem supports only POSIX 1003.1. Microsoft feels that most UNIX applications have already been ported to Win32. The POSIX 1003.1 system is of limited interest, since it does not provide network support and other 1003.2 features.

Table 19-8 gives the POSIX constants and their integer value.

Table 19.8 POSIX constants

POSIX Constant	Integer Value
_POSIX_ARG_MAX	4096
_POSIX_CHILD_MAX	6
_POSIX_LINK_MAX	8
_POSIX_MAX_CANON	255
_POSIX_MAX_INPUT	255
_POSIX_NAME_MAX	14
_POSIX_NGROUPS_MAX	0
_POSIX_OPEN_MAX	16
_POSIX_PATH_MAX	255
_POSIX_PIPE_BUF	512
_POSIX_SSIZE_MAX	32767
_POSIX_STREAM_MAX	8
_POSIX_TZNAME_MAX	3
ARG_MAX	14500
LINK_MAX	1024
MAX_CANON	_POSIX_MAX_CANON
MAX_INPUT	_POSIX_MAX_INPUT
NAME_MAX	255
NGROUPS_MAX	16
OPEN_MAX	32
PATH_MAX	512
PIPE_BUF	_POSIX_PIPE_BUF
SSIZE_MAX	_POSIX_SSIZE_MAX
STREAM_MAX	20
TZNAME_MAX	10

If applications are using the Windows NT POSIX subsystem, they will not have access to all the features available to normal Win32 applications. These limitations include memory-mapped files, networking, and graphics.

The <limits> Header Syntax

The following listing gives the syntax for the <limits> header. This header is used to define the template class `numeric_limits`.

```
namespace std {
  enum float_round_style;
  template<class T>
    class numeric_limits;
};
```

Notice, also, that an enumerated type float_round_style is used. This enumerated type is defined as:

```
 enum float_round_style {
  round_indeterminate = -1,
  round_toward_zero = 0,
  round_to_nearest = 1,
  round_toward_infinity = 2,
  round_toward_neg_infinity = 3
};
```

The enumeration provides several different ways a floating-point value can be rounded to an integer value. Table 19.9 describes each rounding option.

Table 19.9 Rounding methods and descriptions

Rounding Method	Description
round_indeterminate	the rounding method cannot be determined
round_toward_zero	round toward zero
round_to_nearest	round to nearest integer
round_toward_infinity	round away from zero
round_toward_neg_infinity	round toward a more negative integer

The syntax for the template class numeric_limits is shown next. Explicit specializations of this class are used to describe arithmetic properties for scalar types (type T).

```
template<class T>
    class numeric_limits {
public:
    static const bool has_denorm = false;
    static const bool has_denorm_loss = false;
    static const bool has_infinity = false;
    static const bool has_quiet_NaN = false;
    static const bool has_signaling_NaN = false;
```

```
static const bool is_bounded = false;
static const bool is_exact = false;
static const bool is_iec559 = false;
static const bool is_integer = false;
static const bool is_modulo = false;
static const bool is_signed = false;
static const bool is_specialized = false;
static const bool tinyness_before = false;
static const bool traps = false;
static const float_round_style round_style = round_toward_zero;
static const int digits = 0;
static const int digits10 = 0;
static const int max_exponent = 0;
static const int max_exponent10 = 0;
static const int min_exponent = 0;
static const int min_exponent10 = 0;
static const int radix = 0;
static T denorm_min() throw();
static T epsilon() throw();
static T infinity() throw();
static T max() throw();
static T min() throw();
static T quiet_NaN() throw();
static T round_error() throw();
static T signaling_NaN() throw();
};
```

As you examine the listing, notice explicit specializations for the wchar_t, bool, char, signed char, unsigned char, short, unsigned short, int, unsigned int, long, unsigned long, float, double, and long double types. For these specializations, `is_specialized` is true. All other members relevant to the situation have meaningful values.

For arbitrary specializations, the members will not have meaningful values. In these cases, the member object will store a zero (false). Member functions that do not return a meaningful value will return T(0).

has_denorm

This member will store a true for a floating-point type that has denormalized values.

has_denorm_loss

This member will store a true for a type that determines whether a value has lost accuracy because it is delivered as a denormalized result. A denormalized result is too small to be represented as a normalized value. A true will also be returned for a type that is inexact.

has_infinity

This member will store a true for a type that has a representation for positive infinity. It will be true if is_iec559 is true.

has_quiet_NaN

This member will store a true for a type that has a representation for a quiet NaN (not a number). This result will occur for an encoding that does not signal its presence in an expression. It will be true if is_iec559 is true.

has_signaling_NaN

This member will store a true for a type that has a representation for a signaling NaN (not a number). This result will occur for an encoding that signals its presence in an expression by reporting an exception. It will be true if is_iec559 is true.

is_bounded

This member will store a true for a type that has a bounded set of representable values. All predefined types fit into this category.

is_exact

This member will store a true for a type that has exact representations for all its values. All predefined integer types fit into this category. Fixed-point or a rational representation is also considered exact. Floating-point representations are not considered exact.

is_iec559

This member will store a true for a type that has a representation conforming to the IEC 559 standard. The IEC 559, or IEEE 754, standard is an international standard for representing floating-point values.

is_integer

This member will store a true for a type that has an integer representation. All predefined integer types fit this category.

is_modulo

This member will store a true for a type that has a modulo representation. All predefined unsigned integer types fit this category. A modulo representation occurs when results are reduced modulos of some value.

is_signed

This member will store a true for a type that has a signed representation. All predefined floating-point and signed integer types fit this category.

is_specialized

This member will store a true for a type that has an explicit specialization defined for the template class numeric_limits. All scalar types, except pointers, fit this category.

tinyness_before

This member will store a true for a type that determines whether a value is tiny. A tiny value is considered a value too small to represent as a normalized value before rounding.

traps

This member will store a true for a type that generates a signal used to report specific arithmetic exceptions.

round_style

This member will store a value used to describe the various methods for rounding a floating-point value to an integer value.

digits

This member will store the number of radix digits that the type can represent without change. For predefined integer types, this will be the actual number of bits in the number, excluding the sign bit. For floating-point types, this will be the number of digits in the mantissa.

digits10

This member will store the number of decimal digits that the type can represent without change.

max_exponent

This member will store the maximum positive integer such that the type can be represented as a finite value radix raised to that power. It is valid only for floating-point types.

max_exponent10

This member will store the maximum positive integer such that the type can be represented as a finite value 10 raised to that power. It is valid only for floating-point types.

min_exponent

This member will store the minimum negative integer such that the type can be represented as a normalized value radix raised to that power. It is valid only for floating-point types.

min_exponent10

This member will store the minimum negative integer such that the type can represent as a normalized value 10 raised to that power (which is the value `FLT_MIN_10_EXP` for type float). It is meaningful only for floating-point types.

radix

This member will store the base of the representation for the type. A 2 is used for predefined integer types. The base that the exponent is raised to is used for predefined floating-point types.

denorm_min

This function will return the minimum value for the type. This minimum value will be min() if has_denorm is false.

epsilon

This function will return the difference between 1 and the smallest value greater than 1 that can be used to represent the type.

infinity

This function will return the representation of positive infinity for the type. The value returned is valid only if has_infinity is true.

max

This function will return the maximum finite value for the type. Integers will return `INT_MAX` and will float `FLT_MAX`. The value returned is valid only when is_bounded is true.

min

This function will return the minimum normalized value for the type. Integers will return `INT_MIN` and will float `FLT_MIN`. The value returned is valid only when is_bounded is true or when is_signed is false.

quiet_NaN

This function will return a representation of a quiet_NaN for the type. The value returned is valid only when has_quiet_NaN is true.

round_error

This function will return the maximum rounding error for the type.

signaling_NaN

This function will return a representation of a signaling_NaN for the type. The value returned is valid only when has_signaling_NaN is true.

The <csignal> Header Syntax

The standard header <csignal> is used to effectively include the standard header <signal.h> within the *std* namespace

```
namespace std {#include <signal.h>};
```

The purpose of the <signal.h> header is to define signal values and routines. Table 19.10 shows the various signal types and provides a short description.

Table 19.10 Signal types and descriptions

Signal Type	Value	Description
SIGABRT	22	abort call triggered an abnormal termination
SIGBREAK	21	Ctrl-Break sequence
SIGFPE	8	floating-point exception
SIGILL	4	illegal instruction (invalid function image)
SIGINT	2	interrupt
SIGSEGV	11	segment violation
SIGTERM	15	software termination signal from kill

Several signal action codes are also defined. Table 19.11 lists each action code and provides a short description.

Table 19.11 Signal action codes and descriptions

Action Code	Description
SIG_ACK (void (__cdecl *)(int))4	acknowledge
SIG_DFL (void (__cdecl *)(int))0	default signal action
SIG_IGN (void (__cdecl *)(int))1	ignore signal
SIG_SGE (void (__cdecl *)(int))3	signal gets error

The signal error value returned by a signal call on error is defined simply as:

```
SIG_ERR (void (__cdecl *)(int))-1
```

The <signal.h> header file also provides two function prototypes:

```
_CRTIMP void (__cdecl * __cdecl signal(int, void (__cdecl *)(int)))(int);
_CRTIMP int __cdecl raise(int);
```

The function prototypes are described in the following sections.

signal()

The signal() function returns the previous value of *func* associated with the given signal.

```
void ( *signal(int sig,
       void (__cdecl *func)(int sig[, int subcode ])))( int sig );
```

The signal() function allows a process to select a specific way to handle an interrupt signal from the operating system. The *sig* argument is the interrupt to which the signal responds. Table 19.12 shows various arguments for this parameter.

Table 19.12 *sig* parameters

Value	Description
SIGABRT	Abnormal termination
SIGFPE	Floating-point error
SIGILL	Illegal instruction
SIGINT	CTRL+C signal (Not supported by Win32)
SIGSEGV	Illegal storage access
SIGTERM	Termination request

The *func* argument is an address to a signal handler that you must write. It can also be a manifest constant, SIG_DFL or SIG_IGN. If *func* refers to a function's address, it will be installed as the signal handler for the given signal.

Caution should be used when writing signal-handler routines, since they are usually called asynchronously when an interrupt occurs. As a result, the routine may gain control when a run-time operation is incomplete and/or in an unknown state.

raise()

The raise() function sends *sig* to the executing program.

```
int raise( int sig );
```

When a previous call to the signal() function has installed a signal-handling function for *sig*, the raise() function will execute that function. When no handler function exists, the default action associated with the signal value takes place. Table 19.13 lists those possible actions.

Table 19.13 Signal values and descriptions

Value	Description	Default
SIGABRT	abnormal termination	terminates calling program (exit code 3)
SIGFPE	floating-point error	terminates calling program
SIGILL	illegal instruction	terminates calling program
SIGINT	CTRL+C interrupt	terminates calling program
SIGSEGV	illegal storage access	terminates calling program
SIGTERM	termination request sent to application	ignores the signal

The default values listed in Table 19.13 provide an alternative to actually writing signal-handling routines.

Sample Code

In the following sections, sample applications illustrate how to implement several methods from the <limits> standard header.

A Range Application

The first example application, Range.cpp, shows how to obtain numeric ranges for the char, int, long, float, and double data types.

```
//
// Ranges.cpp
// illustrates various type limits
// Chris H. Pappas and William H. Murray, 1999
//

#include <iostream>
#include <limits>

using namespace std;

void main() {

  // characters
  cout << "minimum value for char is " <<
          (int)numeric_limits<char>::min() << endl;
  cout << "maximum value for char is " <<
          (int)numeric_limits<char>::max() <<
          endl << endl;

  // integers
  cout << "minimum value for int is " <<
          numeric_limits<int>::min() << endl;
  cout << "maximum value for int is " <<
          numeric_limits<int>::max() <<
          endl << endl;

  // longs
  cout << "minimum value for long is " <<
          numeric_limits<long>::min() << endl;
  cout << "maximum value for long is " <<
          numeric_limits<long>::max() <<
          endl << endl;

  // floats
  cout << "minimum value for float is " <<
          numeric_limits<float>::min() << endl;
  cout << "maximum value for float is " <<
          numeric_limits<float>::max() <<
```

```
            endl << endl;

    // doubles
    cout << "minimum value for double is " <<
            numeric_limits<double>::min() << endl;
    cout << "maximum value for double is " <<
            numeric_limits<double>::max() <<
            endl << endl;
}
```

The output for this program is obtained by using the min() and max() functions for each data type:

```
minimum value for char is -128
maximum value for char is 127

minimum value for int is -2147483648
maximum value for int is 2147483647

minimum value for long is -2147483648
maximum value for long is 2147483647

minimum value for float is 1.17549e-038
maximum value for float is 3.40282e+038

minimum value for double is 2.22507e-308
maximum value for double is 1.79769e+308
```

In addition to data ranges, radix information can also be obtained, as you'll see in the next example.

The Radix Application

The second application, Radix.cpp, shows how to obtain the radix for various data types.

```
//
// Radix.cpp
// illustrates radix values for numeric types
// Chris H. Pappas and William H. Murray, 1999
//

#include <iostream>
#include <limits>

using namespace std;

void main() {

    // radix for an integer
    cout << "radix for an integer is "  <<
```

```
            numeric_limits<int>::radix <<
            endl << endl;

    // radix for a long
    cout << "radix for a long is "  <<
            numeric_limits<long>::radix <<
            endl << endl;

    // radix for a float
    cout << "radix for a float is "  <<
            numeric_limits<float>::radix <<
            endl << endl;

    // radix for a double
    cout << "radix for a double is "  <<
            numeric_limits<double>::radix <<
            endl << endl;
}
```

The output for this program, implemented on a Pentium computer, should be no surprise:

```
radix for an integer is 2

radix for a long is 2

radix for a float is 2

radix for a double is 2
```

In the next example, we'll see how exponent ranges can be obtained for various numeric types.

The Exponent Application

The third application, Exponent.cpp, shows how to obtain the exponent ranges for various numeric types.

```
//
// Exponent.cpp
// illustrates exponent ranges
// Chris H. Pappas and William H. Murray, 1999
//

#include <iostream>
#include <limits>

using namespace std;

void main() {
```

```
   // float
   cout << "minimum exponent for a float is " <<
           numeric_limits<float>::min_exponent << endl;
   cout << "maximum exponent for a float is " <<
           numeric_limits<float>::max_exponent <<
           endl << endl;

   // double
   cout << "minimum exponent for a double is " <<
           numeric_limits<double>::min_exponent << endl;
   cout << "maximum exponent for a double is " <<
           numeric_limits<double>::max_exponent <<
           endl << endl;

   // base 10
   cout << "minimum exponent in base 10 is " <<
           numeric_limits<float>::min_exponent10 << endl;
   cout << "maximum exponent in base 10 is " <<
           numeric_limits<float>::max_exponent10 <<
           endl << endl;
}
```

Can you anticipate the values returned by this program?

```
minimum exponent for a float is -125
maximum exponent for a float is 128

minimum exponent for a double is -1021
maximum exponent for a double is 1024

minimum exponent in base 10 is -37
maximum exponent in base 10 is 38
```

Now is your time to experiment with other properties described in the numeric_limits template class.

Summary

The <climits> and <limits> standard headers provide an effective means of testing numeric properties. The <csignal> standard file provides a means of testing and writing routines for handling specific error and exception conditions.

T W E N T Y

The <cstdarg>, <cstddef>, and <cstdlib> Standard C++ Headers

This chapter describes <climits>, <limits>, and the <csignal> headers files. The standard header, <limits> is used to define the numeric_limits template class. This chapter describes the new ANSI standard header syntax for these headers. We'll also investigate features for implementing the header code and see several working examples.

The <cstdarg> Header Syntax

The following listing gives the syntax for using the <cstdarg> standard header file:

```
namespace std {#include <stdarg.h> };
```

The <cstdarg> standard header is used to include the <stdarg.h> header within the *std* namespace. This header file is used to define ANSI-style macros for accessing arguments of functions that use a variable number of arguments. As the header file indicates, all Microsoft C compilers for Win32 platforms default to 8-byte alignment.

For Intel hardware platforms, the #defines include:

```
_M_IX86 (Intel)

_INTSIZEOF(n)  ((sizeof(n) + sizeof(int)-1) & ~(sizeof(int)-1))
va_start(ap,v) (ap = (va_list)&v + _INTSIZEOF(v))
va_arg(ap,t)   (*(t *)((ap += _INTSIZEOF(t)) - _INTSIZEOF(t)))
va_end(ap)     (ap = (va_list)0)
```

For MIPS hardware platforms, the #defines include:

```
_M_MRX000  (MIPS)

va_start(ap,v) ap  = (va_list)&v + sizeof(v)
va_end(list)
va_arg(list, mode) ((mode *)(list =                 \
                   (char *) ((((int)list +          \
                   (__builtin_alignof(mode)<=4?3:7)) &  \
                   (__builtin_alignof(mode)<=4?-4:-8))+ \
                   sizeof(mode))))[-1]
```

Set mode to int for char and short types. Set mode to double for float types. Set mode to pointer for array types.

For ALPHA hardware platforms, the #defines include:

```
_M_ALPHA

va_start(list, v) __builtin_va_start(list, v, 1)
va_end(list)
va_arg(list, mode)                                  \
                   ( *(((list).offset +=            \
                  ((int)sizeof(mode) + 7) & -8) ,      \
                  (mode *)((list).a0 + (list).offset - \
                   ((__builtin_isfloat(mode) &&        \
                  (list).offset <= (6 * 8)) ?          \
                   (6 * 8) + 8 : ((int)sizeof(mode)    \
                   + 7) & -8))))
```

These types and definitions should be used when generating code for Alpha platforms. Alpha platforms support two functions used to implement stdarg / varargs. First, the __builtin_va_start() function is used by va_start() to initialize the data structure used to locate the next argument. Then the __builtin_isfloat() function is used by va_arg to select the portion of the home area used for register argument storage. The home area holds up to six integer or floating-point arguments.

For the three Motorola hardware platforms, the #defines include:

```
_M_PPC (Motorola)

_INTSIZEOF(n) ((sizeof(n) + sizeof(int)-1) & ~(sizeof(int)-1))
_ALIGNIT(ap,t) ((((int)(ap))+(sizeof(t)<8?3:7)) &          \
               (sizeof(t)<8?~3:~7))
```

```
va_start(ap,v) (ap = (va_list)&v + _INTSIZEOF(v))
va_arg(ap,t)   (*(t *)((ap = (char *) (_ALIGNIT(ap, t) +  \
                _INTSIZEOF(t))) - _INTSIZEOF(t)) )
va_end(ap)     (ap = (va_list)0)
```

The Microsoft C8 front end is used in the Motorola Merged compiler. Here, return *ap* is adjusted for type *t* in the arglist.

```
_M_M68K  (Motorola)

_INTSIZEOF(n)     ((sizeof(n) + sizeof(int)-1) &      \
                  ~(sizeof(int)-1))

va_start(ap,v)    (ap = (va_list)&v + (sizeof(v) <    \
                  sizeof(int) ? sizeof(v) : _INTSIZEOF(v)))
va_arg(ap,t)      (*(t *)((ap += _INTSIZEOF(t)) - _INTSIZEOF(t)))
va_end(ap)        (ap = (va_list)0)


_M_MPPC  (Motorola)
_INTSIZEOF(n)     ((sizeof(n) + sizeof(int)-1) & ~(sizeof(int)-1))

va_start(ap,v)    (ap = (va_list)&v + _INTSIZEOF(v))
va_arg(ap,t)      (*(t *)((ap += _INTSIZEOF(t)) - _INTSIZEOF(t)))
va_end(ap)        (ap = (va_list)0)
```

For other hardware platforms, the following definitions are recommended. The #defines include:

```
(Other hardware)

_INTSIZEOF(n)     ((sizeof(n) + sizeof(int)-1) & ~(sizeof(int)-1))

va_start(ap,v)    (ap = (va_list)&v + _INTSIZEOF(v))
va_arg(ap,t)      (*(t *)((ap += _INTSIZEOF(t)) - _INTSIZEOF(t)))
va_end(ap)        (ap = (va_list)0)
```

All hardware platforms use va_start(), va_arg(), and va_end(). The only differences exist in the implementation.

The <cstddef> Header Syntax

The following listing gives the syntax for the <cstddef> header. This header is used to include the standard header <stddef.h> within the *std* namespace:

```
namespace std { #include <stddef.h> };
```

The purpose of the <stddef.h> header file is to include definitions and declarations for common constants, types, and variables used in C++ applications. This is a relatively short header file, with some information duplicated in the <cstdlib> standard header.

For example, the definition of NULL appears in both the <stdlib.h> and <stddef.h> header files:

```
#ifndef NULL
  #ifdef  __cplusplus
    #define NULL    0
  #else
    #define NULL ((void *)0)
  #endif
#endif
```

The header file does define a unique macro, offsetof(), as shown:

```
offsetof(s,m) (size_t)&(((s *)0)->m)
```

This macro returns the offset of a member from the beginning of its parent structure. Here, *s* represents the structure name and *m* the member name. The structure name is the name of the parent structure, and the member name is the name in the parent data structure for which the offset is to be found. The offset is returned in bytes.

Implementation-dependent size types are handled with the following portion of code:

```
#ifndef _PTRDIFF_T_DEFINED
  typedef int ptrdiff_t;
#define _PTRDIFF_T_DEFINED
#endif


#ifndef _SIZE_T_DEFINED
  typedef unsigned int size_t;
#define _SIZE_T_DEFINED
#endif


#ifndef _WCHAR_T_DEFINED
  typedef unsigned short wchar_t;
#define _WCHAR_T_DEFINED
#endif


#ifdef  _MT
  _CRTIMP extern unsigned long  __cdecl __threadid(void);
#define _threadid        (__threadid())
  _CRTIMP extern unsigned long  __cdecl __threadhandle(void);
#endif
```

As you examine the <stdlib.h> header file, described in the next section, you'll see some of the contents of <stddef.h> repeated again.

The <cstdlib> Header Syntax

The standard header <cstdlib> is used to effectively include the standard header <stdlib.h> within the *std* namespace:

```
namespace std {#include <stdlib.h>};
```

The purpose of the <cstdlib> standard header file is to allow access to declarations and definitions for commonly used library functions. This header file holds a potpourri of type definitions.

<stdlib.h> typedefs

Several type definitions are of interest. First, _SIZE_T_DEFINED is defined:

```
typedef unsigned int size_t;
```

Then wide character counterpart _WCHAR_T_DEFINED is defined:

```
typedef unsigned short wchar_t;
```

You'll also find the data structure definitions (_DIV_T_DEFINED) used for div_t and ldiv_t operations:

```
typedef struct _div_t {
  int quot;
  int rem;
} div_t;

typedef struct _ldiv_t {
  long quot;
  long rem;
} ldiv_t;
```

Two definitions are provided for the exit() function. Table 20.1 shows both values.

Table 20.1 exit() function defines

Definition	Value
EXIT_FAILURE	1
EXIT_SUCCESS	0

The definition for _ONEXIT_T_DEFINED is defined as:

```
typedef int (__cdecl * _onexit_t)(void);
```

Provisions are made, in this definition, for non-ANSI name compatibility by setting onexit_t equivalent to _onexit_t.

<stdlib.h> #defines

The <stdlib.h> header file holds a number of familiar constant values. Table 20.2 shows constant values associated with the _makepath() and _splitpath() functions.

Table 20.2 _mathpath() and _split_path() constants

Constant	Value	Description
_MAX_DIR	256 32	maximum length of path component, ifndef _MAC maximum length of path component, ifdef _MAC
_MAX_DRIVE	3	maximum length of drive component
_MAX_EXT	256	maximum length of extension component
_MAX_FNAME	256 64	maximum length of file name component, ifndef _MAC maximum length of file name component, ifdef _MAC
_MAX_PATH	260 256	maximum length of full pathname, ifndef _MAC maximum length of full pathname, ifdef _MAC

In a similar manner, the constants used with _set_error_mode() are provided, as shown in Table 20.3:

Table 20.3 _set_error_mode() constants

Constant	Value
_OUT_TO_DEFAULT	0
_OUT_TO_MSGBOX	2
_OUT_TO_STDERR	1
_REPORT_ERRMODE	3

You'll also find the definitions for the __max() and __min() macros.

```
__max(a,b) (((a) > (b)) ? (a) : (b))
__min(a,b) (((a) < (b)) ? (a) : (b))
```

We're sure that you've also wondered where the definitions for a NULL pointer value are located. The following listing shows the definition of NULL as it appears in this header file:

```
#ifndef NULL
  #ifdef __cplusplus
    #define NULL 0
  #else
    #define NULL ((void *)0)
  #endif
#endif
```

The Windows major and minor along with the Operating System version numbers are found in this header file, too.

```
_CRTIMP extern unsigned int _osver;
_CRTIMP extern unsigned int _winver;
_CRTIMP extern unsigned int _winmajor;
_CRTIMP extern unsigned int _winminor;
```

<stdlib.h> Function Prototypes

The following listing gives the various function prototypes found in <stdlib.h>, sorted by the return type. The functions in this listing are void of any specific types and show only return values and parameters.

```
__int64 _atoi64(const char *);
char * _i64toa(__int64, char *, int);
char * _itoa(int, char *, int);
char * _ltoa(long, char *, int);
char * _ui64toa(unsigned __int64, char *, int);
char * _ultoa(unsigned long, char *, int);
char * getenv(const char *);
div_t div(int, int);
double atof(const char *);
double strtod(const char *, char **);
int _set_error_mode(int);
int abs(int);
int atexit(void (*)(void));
int atoi(const char *);
int mblen(const char *, size_t);
int mbtowc(wchar_t *, const char *, size_t);
int rand(void);
int system(const char *);
int wctomb(char *, wchar_t);
ldiv_t ldiv(long, long);
long atol(const char *);
long strtol(const char *, char **, int);
long double _atold(const char *);
long double _strtold(const char *, char **);
long labs(long);
size_t _mbstrlen(const char *s);
size_t mbstowcs(wchar_t *, const char *, size_t);
size_t wcstombs(char *, const wchar_t *, size_t);
unsigned long strtoul(const char *, char **, int);
void abort(void);
void exit(int);
void free(void *);
void qsort(void *, size_t, size_t, int (*), (const void *,
           const void *));
void srand(unsigned int);
void * bsearch(const void *, const void *, size_t, size_t,
```

```
               int (*)(const void *, const void *));
void * calloc(size_t, size_t);
void * malloc(size_t);
void * realloc(void *, size_t);
```

The following listing gives the various wide function prototypes. The functions are sorted by their return type. Again, the functions in this listing are void of any specific types and show only return values and parameters.

```
__int64  _wtoi64(const wchar_t *);
double wcstod(const wchar_t *, wchar_t **);
int  _wsystem(const wchar_t *);
int _wtoi(const wchar_t *);
long  wcstol(const wchar_t *, wchar_t **, int);
long _wtol(const wchar_t *);
unsigned long wcstoul(const wchar_t *, wchar_t **, int);
wchar_t * _i64tow(__int64, wchar_t *, int);
wchar_t * _itow (int, wchar_t *, int);
wchar_t * _ltow (long, wchar_t *, int);
wchar_t * _ui64tow(unsigned __int64, wchar_t *, int);
wchar_t * _ultow (unsigned long, wchar_t *, int);
wchar_t * _wgetenv(const wchar_t *);
```

The following listing gives the various POSIX function prototypes. The functions are sorted by their return type. Again, the functions in this listing are void of any specific types and show only return values and parameters. POSIX is an IEEE standard that defines the language interface between UNIX and application programs.

```
__declspec(noreturn) void _exit(int);
_onexit_t _onexit(_onexit_t);
char * _ecvt(double, int, int *, int *);
char * _fcvt(double, int, int *, int *);
char * _fullpath(char *, const char *, size_t);
char * _gcvt(double, int, char *);
int _putenv(const char *);
int _wputenv(const wchar_t *);
unsigned int _rotl(unsigned int, int);
unsigned int _rotr(unsigned int, int);
unsigned long _lrotl(unsigned long, int);
unsigned long _lrotr(unsigned long, int);
void _exit(int);
void _makepath(char *, const char *, const char *,
              const char *, const char *);
void _searchenv(const char *, const char *, char *);
void _splitpath(const char *, char *, char *, char *, char *);
void _swab(char *, char *, int);
void _wmakepath(wchar_t *, const wchar_t *, const wchar_t *,
               const wchar_t *, const wchar_t *);
void _wperror(const wchar_t *);
void _wsearchenv(const wchar_t *, const wchar_t *, wchar_t *);
```

```
void _wsplitpath(const wchar_t *, wchar_t *, wchar_t *,
                 wchar_t *, wchar_t *);
void perror(const char *);
wchar_t * _wfullpath(wchar_t *, const wchar_t *, size_t);
```

In the next section, you'll see how many of the features described in these header files can be applied to practical applications.

Sample Code

In the following sections, two sample applications illustrate how to access features from the <cstdarg> and <cstdlib> standard headers.

A <cstdarg> Application

The first example application, va.cpp, shows how to obtain the positive sum of numbers by passing a variable number of arguments. This application illustrates the use of va_start(), va_arg(), and va_end().

```
// va.cpp
// Calculating positive sums with the use of
// va_start(), va_arg(), and va_end()
// Chris H. Pappas and William H. Murray, 1999

#include <iostream>
#include <cstdarg>

using namespace std;

int adder(int start, ...);

void main()
{
   cout << "The sum is: " << adder(1,2,3,-1)
        << endl << endl;

   cout << "The sum is: " << adder(1,2,3,4,-1)
        << endl << endl;

   cout << "The sum is: " << adder(1,2,3,4,5,-1)
        << endl << endl;

   cout << "The sum is: " << adder(-1)
        << endl << endl;

   cout << "The sum is: " << adder(10,2,3,-2,-5,-1)
        << endl << endl;
```

```
  cout << "The sum is: " << adder(100,200,300,-1)
       << endl << endl;
}


int adder(int start, ...) {
  int sum=0, i=start;
  va_list mark;

  // variable argument initialized
  va_start(mark,start);

  // sum calculated
  while(i!= -1) {
    sum+=i;
    i=va_arg(mark,int);
  }

  // variable argument reset
  va_end(mark);
  return(sum);
}
```

The output for this program is obtained by using the min() and max() functions for each data type:

```
The sum is: 6

The sum is: 10

The sum is: 15

The sum is: 0

The sum is: 8

The sum is: 600
```

The va_start, va_arg, and va_end macros provide a way to access the arguments to a function when that function uses a variable number of arguments.

The va_start macro sets the argument pointer, *mark*, to the first optional argument in the list of arguments passed to the function. This pointer is of type va_list. The previous parameter argument, *start*, is the name of the parameter that must immediately precede the first optional argument in the argument list.

The va_arg macro retrieves a value of *int* from the location given by the argument pointer and increments *mark* to point to the next argument in the list.

The va_end macro is used after all arguments have been retrieved to set the pointer to NULL, once again.

The <cstdlib> Application

The second application, constants.cpp, shows how to obtain information on the constants used by _makepath() and _splitpath().

```
// constants.cpp
// Reporting _makepath() and _splitpath()
// constants for this hardware implementation.
// Chris H. Pappas and William H. Murray, 1999

#include <iostream>
#include <cstdlib>

using namespace std;

void main()
{
  cout << "The value is: " << _MAX_DIR
       << endl << endl;

  cout << "The value is: " << _MAX_DRIVE
       << endl << endl;

  cout << "The value is: " << _MAX_EXT
       << endl << endl;

  cout << "The value is: " << _MAX_FNAME
       << endl << endl;

  cout << "The value is: " << _MAX_PATH
       << endl << endl;

  cout << "The value is: " << _OUT_TO_DEFAULT
       << endl << endl;

  cout << "The value is: " << _OUT_TO_MSGBOX
       << endl << endl;

  cout << "The value is: " << _OUT_TO_STDERR
       << endl << endl;

  cout << "The value is: " << _REPORT_ERRMODE
       << endl << endl;
}
```

The output for this program matches the information reported in Table 20.2 for this Pentium computer:

```
The value is: 256

The value is: 3

The value is: 256

The value is: 256

The value is: 260

The value is: 0

The value is: 2

The value is: 1

The value is: 3
```

You may now want to experiment with _makepath() and _splitpath() using the information reported by the previous application.

Summary

The <cstdarg>, <cstddef>, and <cstdlib> standard headers provide macros, definitions, declarations, and constants. These include an effective means of defining ANSI-style macros for accessing arguments of functions that use a variable number of arguments, definitions, and declarations for common constants, types, and variables used in C++ applications and that give access to declarations and definitions for commonly used library functions.

TWENTY-ONE

The <cstdio> Standard C++ Header

This chapter describes the <cstdio> header file. The standard header <cstdio> is used for performing input and output operations. This chapter describes the new ANSI standard header syntax for this header. We'll also investigate features for implementing the header code and see several working examples.

The <cstdio> Header Syntax

The following listing gives the syntax for using the <cstdio> standard header file:

```
namespace std {#include <stdio.h> };
```

The <cstdio> standard header is used to include the <stdio.h> header within the *std* namespace. This header provides definitions for functions, macros, structures, and values used by the level 2 standard I/O ANSI/System V routines.

The <stdio.h> header file defines several types that we have worked with in other chapters. For example, you'll find the definitions for int size_t, wchar_t, wint_t, and wctype_t. For alpha hardware, you'll find the following structure and type.

```
typedef struct {
 char *a0;
 int offset;
 } va_list;

typedef char *  va_list;
```

In this structure, *a0* is a pointer to the first homed integer argument. The *offset* member represents the byte offset of the next parameter.

Another structure is provided for cases where _FILE_DEFINED has not been defined:

```
struct _iobuf {
  char *_ptr;
  int   _cnt;
  char *_base;
  int   _flag;
  int   _file;
  int   _charbuf;
  int   _bufsiz;
  char *_tmpfname;
};

typedef struct _iobuf FILE;
```

Numerous constants are also provided for various file operations. The most interesting information in this header, however, is the function prototypes. These function prototypes are discussed in the next section.

Function Prototypes and Macro Definitions

Table 21.1 provides a list of the functions prototyped in the <stdio.h> header file and provides brief descriptions of their use.

Table 21.1 Functions prototyped in <stdio.h>

Return Type	Function	Description
int	_fcloseall(void)	Closes all open streams and returns the total number closed. Will return EOF to indicate an error has occurred.
int	_fgetchar(void)	Reads a character from a stream. Returns the character read as an int or returns EOF to indicate an error or end of file.
int	_flushall(void)	Flushes all streams and clears all buffers. The function writes to the appropriate files using the contents of all buffers associated with open output streams. All buffers that are associated with open input streams are cleared of their contents. All streams remain open after the function is called.
int	_fputchar(int)	Writes a character to stdout. Returns the character written or EOF to indicate an error. This is equivalent to fputc(stdout) and to putchar(). However, _fputchar() is implemented just as a function, instead of a function and macro. This implementation is Microsoft-specific and is not ANSI-compatible.

Table 21.1 Functions prototyped in <stdio.h> *(continued)*

Return Type	Function	Description
int	_getw(FILE *)	Retrieves an integer from a stream. Returns the integer value or EOF. EOF indicates that an error or end of file has occurred. Note: since EOF is a valid integer value, you must use feof() or ferror() to confirm an error condition or valid EOF.
int	_pclose(FILE *)	Waits for a new command processor and then closes the stream on the associated pipe. Returns the exit status of the terminating command processor. A –1 is returned if an error condition exists.
FILE *	_popen(const char *, const char *)	Creates a pipe and executes a command. Returns a stream associated with one end of the created pipe. The remaining pipe end is associated with the spawned command's standard input or output. A NULL is returned for an error condition.
int	_putw(int, FILE *)	Writes an integer to a stream. Returns the value written or EOF. EOF indicates an error, but since it is a valid integer, feeor() must be used for verification.
int	_rmtmp(void)	Removes temporary files in the current directory. Removes only the files created by tmpfile().
int	_setmaxstdio(int)	Sets the maximum for the total number of files that can be simultaneously opened at the stdio() level. Returns *newmax* when successful or a –1 value when not successful.
int	_snprintf(char *, size_t, const char *, ...)	Writes formatted data to a string. Returns the number of bytes stored in first parameter (terminating null character is not counted). When the number of bytes needed exceeds the second parameter, the data will be stored in the buffer indicated by the first parameter with a negative value being returned.
char *	_tempnam(const char *, const char *)	Create temporary file names. The function returns a pointer to the name generated. If the name cannot be created, the function will return NULL.
int	_unlink(const char *)	Deletes a file. The function returns a 0 when successful. A -1 is returned when not successful, and errno() is set to EACCES (a read-only file) or ENOENT (path not found to file).

Table 21.1 Functions prototyped in <stdio.h> *(continued)*

Return Type	Function	Description
int	_vsnprintf(char *, size_t, const char *, va_list)	Writes formatted output using a pointer to a list of arguments. The function returns the number of characters written (not including a terminating null or a negative value when an output error takes place). This function is useful when the number of bytes being written exceeds that specified by the first parameter. When this situation occurs the second parameter holds the number of bytes written and a –1 is returned.
void	clearerr(FILE *)	Resets the error indicator for a stream. This function will reset the error indicator and end-of-file indicator for a stream indicated by the first parameter. Since error indicators are not automatically cleared, once the error indicator for the stream is set, operations on that stream continue to return an error value. Use this function to clear the error indicator.
int	fclose(FILE *)	Closes a stream indicated by the first parameter. The function returns a 0 if the stream can be closed. Returns an EOF when not successful.
int	feof(FILE *)	Use to test for end-of-file on a stream. The function will return a nonzero value after the first read attempt to read past the end of the file. A 0 is returned when the position is not end of file. No error condition is associated with this function.
int	ferror(FILE *)	Tests for an error on a stream. When no error has occurred, a 0 is returned. Otherwise, a nonzero value is returned.
int	fflush(FILE *)	Flushes a stream. The function will return a 0 when the buffer is flushed or in situations where the stream has no buffer or is open for reading only. If EOF is returned, an error has occurred. This may also serve as a warning that data has been lost.
int	fgetc(FILE *)	Reads a character from a stream. The function returns the character read as an int. A EOF is returned to indicate an error or end of file. The function uses feof() or ferror() to discern between an error and an EOF condition.

Table 21.1 Functions prototyped in <stdio.h> *(continued)*

Return Type	Function	Description
`int`	fgetpos(FILE *, fpos_t *)	Gets the file-position indicator for a stream. When successful, the function returns a 0. Otherwise, a nonzero value is returned and errno() is set to EBADF (stream is not a valid file handle or is not accessible) or EINVAL (stream value is not valid).
`char *`	fgets(char *, int, FILE *)	Get a string from a stream. The function returns a string. A NULL value is returned for an error or EOF condition. Use feof() or ferror() to determine whether an error took place.
`FILE *`	fopen(const char *, const char *)	Opens a file. A pointer will be returned to the opened file. A null pointer value is used to indicate an error.
`int`	fprintf(FILE *, const char *, ...)	Prints formatted data to a stream. The function returns the number of bytes written. Returns a negative value to indicate an error.
`int`	fputc(int, FILE *)	Writes a character to a stream. The function returns the character written. A return value of EOF indicates an error.
`int`	fputs(const char *, FILE *)	Writes a string to a stream. The function will return a non-negative value when successful. When an error occurs, the function returns an EOF.
`size_t`	fread(void *, size_t, size_t, FILE *)	Reads data from a stream. Returns the number of items read, which may be less specified by the second parameter if an error occurs or if the end of the file is encountered before reaching the value given by the second parameter. Use feof() or ferror() to discern between a read error and an end-of-file condition. When the second parameter is 0, the function returns 0 and the buffer contents are not changed.
`FILE *`	freopen(const char *, const char *, FILE *)	Reassigns a file pointer. Returns a pointer to the newly opened file. If an error occurs, the file is closed and the function returns a NULL pointer value.
`int`	fscanf(FILE *, const char *, ...)	Reads formatted data from a stream. The function returns the number of fields successfully converted and assigned. This value does not include fields that were read but not assigned. If no fields were assigned, a return value 0 is used. When an error occurs or if the end of the file stream is reached before the first conversion, a return value of EOF is used.

Table 21.1 Functions prototyped in <stdio.h> *(continued)*

Return Type	Function	Description
int	fseek(FILE *, long, int)	Moves the file pointer to a given location. When successful, the functions returns 0. Otherwise, the function returns a nonzero value. If a device cannot seek, the return value is not defined.
int	fsetpos(FILE *, const fpos_t *)	Sets the stream-position indicator. When successful, the function returns a 0. Otherwise, the function returns a nonzero value and sets errno() to EBADF (file is not accessible or the object pointed to by the first parameter is not a valid file handle) or EINVAL (invalid stream value was passed).
long	ftell(FILE *)	Gets the current position of a file pointer. The function returns the current file position. This value may not be the actual physical byte offset for streams opened in text mode, because text mode causes carriage return–linefeed translation. ftell() can be used with fseek() to return correct file locations. When an error occurs, the function returns –1L. errno()will be set to EBADF (the argument is not a valid file-handle value or does not refer to an open file) or EINVAL (invalid argument was passed to the function). If the device is not capable of seeking, the return error is undefined.
size_t	fwrite(const void *, size_t, size_t, FILE *)	Writes data to a stream. Returns the number of items written. This value may be less than that specified by the second parameter if an error occurs. The file-position indicator is invalid when errors occur.
int	getc(FILE *)	Reads a character from a stream. Returns the character read. The function returns an EOF to indicate a read error or end-of-file condition. ferror() or feof() can be used to verify an error or end of file.
int	getchar(void)	Gets a character from stdin. The function returns the character read. For a read error or end-of-file condition, the function returns an EOF. ferror() or feof() can be used to verify an error or end of file.
char *	gets(char *)	Get a line from the stdin stream. Returns the argument when successful. A NULL pointer is used to indicate an error or end-of-file condition. ferror() or feof() can be used to verify an error or end of file.

Table 21.1 Functions prototyped in <stdio.h> *(continued)*

Return Type	Function	Description
void	perror(const char *)	Prints an error message. Function prints an error message to stderr.
int	printf(const char *, ...)	Prints formatted output to the standard output stream. Function returns the number of characters printed. A negative value indicates that an error occurred.
int	putc(int, FILE *)	Writes a character to a stream. The function returns the character written. Returns an EOF to indicate an error or end-of-file condition. ferror() or feof() can be used to verify an error or end of file.
int	putchar(int)	Writes a character to stdout. The function returns the character written. Returns an EOF to indicate an error or end-of-file condition. ferror() or feof() can be used to verify an error or end of file.
int	puts(const char *)	Writes a string to stdout. The function returns a non-negative value when successful. Otherwise, an EOF is returned.
int	remove(const char *)	Deletes a file. Returns a 0 if the file is deleted. On error, returns a –1 and sets errno() to EACCES (path indicates a read-only file) or ENOENT (filename or path was not found or the path is to a directory). This function will also return a -1 if the file is already open.
int	rename(const char *, const char *)	Renames a file or directory. The function returns a 0 when successful. On error, a non-zero value is returned and errno() is set to a specific value: EACCES (file or directory already exists or could not be created) ENOENT (file or path is not found), or EINVAL (name contains invalid characters).
void	rewind(FILE *)	Sets the file pointer to the beginning of a file. The function does not return a value to indicate whether the pointer was moved.
int	scanf(const char *, ...)	Reads formatted data from the standard input stream. Returns the number of fields successfully converted and assigned. The value returned does not include fields that were read but not assigned. A 0 is used to indicate that no fields were assigned. An EOF is returned for an error or if the end-of-file character or the end-of-string character is encountered in the first attempt to read a character.

Table 21.1 Functions prototyped in <stdio.h> *(continued)*

Return Type	Function	Description
void	setbuf(FILE *, char *)	Controls stream buffering. The first parameter is a stream argument that refers to an open file that has not been read or written. If the second parameter is NULL, the stream is unbuffered. If not NULL, the second argument points to a character array of a specified length.
int	setvbuf(FILE *, char *, int, size_t)	Controls stream buffering and buffer size. The function returns 0 when successful. Otherwise, a nonzero value is returned if an illegal type or buffer size is given.
int	sprintf(char *, const char *, ...)	Writes formatted data to a string. Returns the number of bytes stored in the first parameter. This does not count the terminating null character.
int	sscanf(const char *, const char *, ...)	Reads formatted data from a string. Returns the number of fields successfully converted and assigned. The value returned does not include fields that were read but not assigned. A 0 is used to indicate that no fields were assigned. An EOF is used to indicate an error or if the end of the string is reached before the first conversion.
FILE *	tmpfile(void)	Creates a temporary file. Returns a pointer to the stream. If the file cannot be opened, the function returns a NULL pointer. The temporary file is deleted when the file is closed, the program terminates, or when _rmtmp() is called. Temporary files are opened in binary read/write mode.
char *	tmpnam(char *)	Creates temporary file names. Returns a pointer to the file name, unless to create the name is not possible or if the name is not unique. A NULL will be returned under these conditions.
int	ungetc(int, FILE *)	Pushes a character back onto the stream. Returns the character argument given by the first parameter when successful. If the argument cannot be pushed back or if no character has been read, the input stream is unchanged. Under these conditions, an EOF will be returned.

Table 21.1 Functions prototyped in <stdio.h> *(continued)*

Return Type	Function	Description
int	vfprintf(FILE *, const char *, va_list)	Writes formatted output using a pointer to a list of arguments. Returns the number of characters written. This value does not include the terminating null character, or a negative value if an output error occurs.
int	vprintf(const char *, va_list)	Function uses a pointer to an argument list, and then formats and writes the given data to stdout. Otherwise, similar in operation to printf().
int	vsprintf(char *, const char *, va_list)	Function uses a pointer to an argument list, and then formats and writes the given data to memory pointed to by the first parameter. Otherwise, similar in operation to sprintf().

Our intent is not to discuss the parameters for each of these functions, but rather to give you a listing a description of the functions that are available for your use. Your compiler's help facilities will aid in actual implementation of a specific function.

Table 21.2 provides a list of the wide function prototypes and their return types. Each of the wide function prototypes behaves in a manner similar to their counterparts described in Table 21.2.

Table 21.2 Wide function prototypes in <stdio.h>

Return Type	Function
wint_t	_fgetwchar(void)
wint_t	_fputwchar(wint_t)
wchar_t *	_getws(wchar_t *)
int	_putws(const wchar_t *)
int	_snwprintf(wchar_t *, size_t, const wchar_t *, ...)
int	_vsnwprintf(wchar_t *, size_t, const wchar_t *, va_list)
FILE *	_wfdopen(int, const wchar_t *)
FILE *	_wfopen(const wchar_t *, const wchar_t *)
FILE *	_wfreopen(const wchar_t *, const wchar_t *, FILE *)
void	_wperror(const wchar_t *)
FILE *	_wpopen(const wchar_t *, const wchar_t *)

Table 21.2 Wide function prototypes in <stdio.h> *(continued)*

Return Type	Function
int	_wremove(const wchar_t *)
wchar_t *	_wtempnam(const wchar_t *, const wchar_t *)
wchar_t *	_wtmpnam(wchar_t *)
wint_t	fgetwc(FILE *)
wchar_t *	fgetws(wchar_t *, int, FILE *)
wint_t	fputwc(wint_t, FILE *)
int	fputws(const wchar_t *, FILE *)
int	fwprintf(FILE *, const wchar_t *, ...)
int	fwscanf(FILE *, const wchar_t *, ...)
wint_t	getwc(FILE *)
wint_t	getwchar(void)
wint_t	putwc(wint_t, FILE *)
wint_t	putwchar(wint_t)
int	swprintf(wchar_t *, const wchar_t *, ...)
int	swscanf(const wchar_t *, const wchar_t *, ...)
wint_t	ungetwc(wint_t, FILE *)
int	vfwprintf(FILE *, const wchar_t *, va_list)
int	vswprintf(wchar_t *, const wchar_t *, va_list)
int	vwprintf(const wchar_t *, va_list)
int	wprintf(const wchar_t *, ...)
int	wscanf(const wchar_t *, ...)

In Table 21.2, the following relationships hold:

```
getwchar()  =  fgetwc(stdin)
putwchar(_c) = fputwc((_c),stdout)
getwc(_stm) = fgetwc(_stm)
putwc(_c,_stm) = fputwc(_c,_stm)
```

Table 21.3 lists and briefly describes several POSIX function prototypes.

Table 21.3 POSIX function prototypes provided in <stdio.h>

Return Type	Function	Description
`FILE *`	_fdopen(int, const char *)	Associates a stream with a file that was previously opened for low-level I/O. Returns a pointer to the open stream. A NULL pointer value is used to indicate an error.
`FILE *`	_fsopen(const char *, const char *, int)	Opens a stream with file sharing. Returns a pointer to the stream. A NULL pointer value is used to indicate an error.
`int`	_fileno(FILE *)	Gets the file handle associated with a stream. The function will return the file handle. No error return occurs. If the stream, indicated by the first parameter, does not specify an open file, the result of the function call will be not be defined.
`FILE *`	_wfsopen(const wchar_t *, const wchar_t *, int)	Opens a stream with file sharing. Function returns a pointer to the stream. A NULL pointer value is used to indicate an error.

The <stdio.h> header file provides the following macro definitions:

```
#define feof(_stream)         ((_stream)->_flag & _IOEOF)
#define ferror(_stream)       ((_stream)->_flag & _IOERR)
#define _fileno(_stream)      ((_stream)->_file)
#define getc(_stream)         (--(_stream)->_cnt >= 0 \
                               ? 0xff & *(_stream)->_ptr++ \
                               : _filbuf(_stream))
#define putc(_c,_stream)      (--(_stream)->_cnt >= 0 \
                               ? 0xff & (*(_stream)->_ptr++ \
                               = (char)(_c)) : \
                               _flsbuf((_c),(_stream)))
#define getchar()             getc(stdin)
#define putchar(_c)           putc((_c),stdout)
```

The following definitions and types are provided for non-ANSI compatibility:

```
#define SYS_OPEN  _SYS_OPEN

_CRTIMP int __cdecl fcloseall(void);
_CRTIMP FILE * __cdecl fdopen(int, const char *);
_CRTIMP int __cdecl fgetchar(void);
_CRTIMP int __cdecl fileno(FILE *);
_CRTIMP int __cdecl flushall(void);
_CRTIMP int __cdecl fputchar(int);
_CRTIMP int __cdecl getw(FILE *);
_CRTIMP int __cdecl putw(int, FILE *);
_CRTIMP int __cdecl rmtmp(void);
```

```
_CRTIMP char * __cdecl tempnam(const char *, const char *);
_CRTIMP int __cdecl unlink(const char *);
```

In the following section, we'll examine the operation of a few of these common <stdio> functions.

Sample Code

In the following sections, two sample applications illustrate how to access features from the <cstdio> standard header. These examples are adaptations from older Microsoft examples that existed before the standard headers. If you have been programming in C or C++ for any time, we're sure that you are familiar with these popular functions.

An Error-Testing Application

The first example application, clearerr.cpp, shows how to set and clear an error condition using the standard input stream. This application illustrates the use of five functions accessed from the <cstdio> standard header; ferror(), perror(), clearerr(), putc(), and getc().

```
// clearerr.cpp
// Creates an error using the standard input stream.
// Next the error is cleared to prevent subsequent
// reads from failing
// Chris H. Pappas and William H. Murray, 1999

#include <iostream>
#include <cstdio>

using namespace std;

void main()
{
   int c;

   // create an error by writing to standard input.
   putc('c', stdin);

   if(ferror(stdin)) {
     perror("Write the error");
     clearerr(stdin);
   }

   // see whether error cleared by doing a read.
   cout << "Will this input cause an error? ";
   c = getc(stdin);
```

```
   if(ferror(stdin)) {
      perror("read the error");
      clearerr(stdin);
   }
}
```

The output for this program is shown in this listing:

```
Write the error : No error
Will input cause an error?  n
```

You can test the program again by commenting out the call to the clearerr() function. This time you'll see different results.

A File Read/Write Application

The second example application, FileRW.cpp, shows how to write formatted data to a file. The data is then read back from the file using fscanf(). This application illustrates the use of five functions accessed from the <cstdio> standard header: fopen(), fprintf(), fseek(), fscanf(), and fclose().

```
// FileRW.cpp
// Writes formatted data to a file.
// Data is read back from the file using
// fscanf().
// Chris H. Pappas and William H. Murray, 1999

#include <iostream>
#include <cstdio>

using namespace std;

FILE *stream;

void main()
{
  int myint;
  long mylong;
  float myfloat;
  char mystring[27];
  char mychar;

  stream = fopen("test.out", "w+");
  if(stream == NULL)
     cout << "test.out could not be opened\n";
  else {
    fprintf(stream, "%s %d %ld %f%c",
           "abcdefghijklmnopqrstuvwxyz",
           12, 123456789, 1.23456, '#' );

    // put pointer to start of file
```

```
        fseek( stream, 0L, SEEK_SET);

        // read data from file
        fscanf(stream, "%s", mystring);
        fscanf(stream, "%d", &myint);
        fscanf(stream, "%ld", &mylong);
        fscanf(stream, "%f", &myfloat);
        fscanf(stream, "%c", &mychar);

        // print data to screen
        cout << mystring << "\n";
        cout << myint << "\n";
        cout << mylong << "\n";
        cout << myfloat << "\n";
        cout << mychar << "\n";
        cout << endl;

        fclose(stream);
    }
}
```

The output for this program shows that formatted input can be written to and read from a file using a variety of functions including fscanf():

```
abcdefghijklmnopqrstuvwxyz
12
123456789
1.23456
#
```

You may now want to experiment with other functions from the <stdio> made accessible via the <cstdio> standard header file.

Summary

The <cstdio> standard header file allows access to many popular functions provided in the <stdio.h> header file. We've illustrated ten of these functions within the two examples included in this chapter.

T W E N T Y - T W O

The <ctime> Standard C++ Header

This chapter describes the <ctime> header file. The standard header <ctime> is used for performing date and time operations. This chapter describes the new ANSI standard header syntax for this header. We'll also investigate features for implementing the header code and see several working examples.

The <ctime> Header Syntax

The following listing gives the syntax for using the <ctime> standard header file:

```
namespace std {#include <time.h> };
```

The <ctime> standard header is used to include the <time.h> header within the *std* namespace. This header provides definitions for various structures and function prototypes used by date and time routines. The header is ANSI/System-V-compliant.

The <time.h> header file defines several type definitions that you are probably familiar with from your work in C or C++. These include

```
typedef long time_t;
    .
    .
    .
typedef long clock_t;
    .
    .
    .
typedef unsigned int size_t;
```

In addition to these popular type definitions, the <time.h> header defines the NULL pointer value, which we have seen repeated in almost every header file discussed in this book.

A constant, CLOCKS_PER_SEC, is defined in the following manner.

```
#define CLOCKS_PER_SEC  1000
```

Note that the non-ANSI CLK_TCK constant is equivalent to CLOCKS_PER_SEC and is provided for compatibility.

This constant is used by the clock() function. This header file also defines the *tm* structure used by so many date and time functions:

```
struct tm {
  int tm_sec;     /* number of secs after the min - [0,59]  */
  int tm_min;     /* number of mins after the hr - [0,59]   */
  int tm_hour;    /* number of hrs since midnight - [0,23]  */
  int tm_mday;    /* the day of the month - [1,31]          */
  int tm_mon;     /* number of months since Jan - [0,11]    */
  int tm_year;    /* number of yrs since 1900               */
  int tm_wday;    /* number of days since Sun - [0,6]       */
  int tm_yday;    /* number of days since Jan 1 - [0,365]   */
  int tm_isdst;   /* the daylight savings time flag         */
  };
```

Table 22.1 describes external declarations for the global variables used by the ctime() family of routines and found in the <time.h> header file.

Table 22.1 External declarations for global variables

Return Type	Global Variable	Description
Return type	global variable	Description
int	_daylight	non-zero if daylight savings time is used
long	_dstbias	offset for daylight savings time
long	_timezone	difference in seconds between GMT and local time
char *	_tzname[2]	standard/daylight savings time zone names

Specifically, you'll see these variables used by the POSIX _tzset function and macro. Note that the non-ANSI names daylight, timezone, tzname[2], and tzset are also provided for compatibility.

In the following section, we'll investigate the normal function prototypes found in the <time.h> header file.

The <time.h> Function Prototypes

The normal <time.h> function prototypes are described in Table 22.2. We're sure that you are familiar with many of these functions.

Table 22.2 <time.h> function prototypes

Return Type	Function	Description
`char *`	asctime(const struct tm *);	Used to convert a tm time structure to a character string. The function returns a pointer to the resulting character string result. No error return value is provided.
`char *`	ctime(const time_t *);	Used to convert a time value to a string. The data is adjusted for local time zone settings. The function returns a pointer to the resulting character string. If the time value supplied represents a date before January 1, 1970, midnight, UTC, the function will return a NULL.
`clock_t`	clock(void);	Used to calculate the processor time used by the calling process. The function returns the number of clock ticks of elapsed processor time. This value is determined by multiplying the value of the CLOCKS_PER_SEC constant and the amount of time that has elapsed since the start of a process. A -1 is returned if the elapse time cannot be obtained.
`double`	difftime(time_t, time_t);	Used to find the difference between two times, in the format shown. The function returns the elapsed time, in seconds, as a double-precision floating-point number.
`struct tm *`	gmtime(const time_t *);	Used to convert a time value to a *tm* structure. The function returns a pointer to a *tm* structure. The values returned to the structure match the fields for the *tm* structure shown in the previous section. The argument is in UTC instead of local time.

Table 22.2 <time.h> function prototypes *(continued)*

Return Type	Function	Description
struct tm *	localtime(const time_t *);	Used to convert a time value and correct it for the local time zone. The function returns a pointer to a *tm* structure. The values returned to the structure match the fields for the *tm* structure shown in the previous section. Time values before Jan 1, 1970 (midnight), will return a NULL.
time_t	mktime(struct tm *);	Used to convert the local time to a calendar value. The function returns the calendar time encoded as a time_t value. For time values before Jan 1, 1970 (midnight), a -1 cast to a time_t value will be returned.
size_t	strftime(char *, size_t, const char *, const struct tm *);	Used to format a time string. The function returns the number of characters placed in the first parameter. This is true if the number of characters (counting the terminating null) does not exceed that number specified by the second parameter. When the second parameter is exceeded, the function returns a 0 and the first parameter is not valid.
char *	_strdate(char *);	Used to copy a date to a buffer. Returns a pointer to the resulting character string.
char *	_strtime(char *);	Used to copy a time to a buffer. Returns a pointer to the resulting character string.
time_t	time(time_t *);	Used to get the system time. The function returns the time elapsed in seconds. No error return value is provided.

void	tzset(void);
	or
	_tzset(void);
		POSIX function used to set time environment variables. No return type exists. The current setting of the TZ environment variable is assigned to the global variables: _daylight, _timezone, and _tzname.

The following functions are obsolete:

```
unsigned _getsystime(struct tm *);
unsigned _setsystime(struct tm *, unsigned);
```

We recommend that the Win32 API GetLocalTime() and SetLocalTime() functions be used in their place.

Five wide function prototypes are also described in <time.h> and are described in Table 22.3.

Table 22.3 <time.h> wide function prototypes

Return Type	Function	Description
wchar_t *	_wasctime(const struct tm *);	Used to convert a *tm* time structure to a wide character string. The function returns a pointer to the resulting character string result. No error return value is provided.
wchar_t *	_wctime(const time_t *);	Used to convert a time value to a string. The data is adjusted for local time zone settings. The function returns a pointer to the resulting wide character string. If the time value supplied represents a date before January 1, 1970, midnight, UTC, the function will return a NULL.
size_t	wcsftime(wchar_t *, size_t, const wchar_t *, const struct tm *);	Used to format a time string. The function returns the number of wide characters placed in the first parameter. This is true if the number of characters (counting the terminating null) does not exceed that number specified by the second parameter. When the second parameter is exceeded, the function returns a 0 and the first parameter is not valid.
wchar_t *	_wstrdate(wchar_t *);	Used to copy a date to a buffer. Returns a pointer to the resulting wide character string.
wchar_t *	_wstrtime(wchar_t *);	Used to copy a time to a buffer. Returns a pointer to the resulting wide character string.

You'll see many of the functions prototyped in <time.h> illustrated in the sample code section that follows.

Sample Code

In the following sections, five sample applications illustrate how to access features from the <ctime> standard header. Just to add a little spice to the application, let's see what is reported when the date is set to March 23, 2001!

Using the localtime() and asctime() Functions

Many times you need to obtain the time and date in a programming application. The next application returns these values by using the localtime() and asctime() functions.

```
// asctime.cpp
// Application illustrates the use of the localtime()
// and asctime() functions.
// Chris H. Pappas and William H. Murray, 1999

#include <iostream>
#include <ctime>

using namespace std;

void main()
{
  struct tm *time_date_struct_ptr;
  time_t timer;

  time( &timer );
  time_date_struct_ptr = localtime( &timer );

  cout << "The present date and time is: "
       << asctime( time_date_struct_ptr )
       << endl;
}
```

This program formats the time and date information in the manner shown here:

```
The present date and time is: Tue Mar 23 18:29:42 2001
```

Well, no surprises here. The date and time are reported in a satisfactory manner.

Using the asctime() and gmtime() Functions

You can also use other functions to return time and date information. The next application is similar to the last example, except that the gmtime() function is used.

```
// gmtime.cpp
// Application illustrates the use of the gmtime()
// and asctime() functions.
// Chris H. Pappas and William H. Murray, 1999

#include <iostream>
#include <ctime>
```

```
using namespace std;

void main()
{
  struct tm *time_date_struct_ptr;
  time_t timer;

  time( &timer );
  time_date_struct_ptr = gmtime( &timer );

  cout << asctime( time_date_struct_ptr )
       << endl;
}
```

The following date and time information was returned by this program:

```
Tue Mar 23 23:29:52 2001
```

Both of these functions return time and date information in acceptable formats. However, note that this output is a little different from that of the first application.

Using the strftime() Function

The strftime() function provides the greatest formatting flexibility of all the date and time functions. The following application illustrates several formatting options:

```
// strftime.cpp
// Application illustrates the use of the strftime()
// functions.  Watch out for Y2K!
// Chris H. Pappas and William H. Murray, 1999

#include <iostream>
#include <ctime>

using namespace std;

#define MAX_CHARS 80

void main()
{
  struct tm *date_time_struct_ptr;
  time_t timer;

  char conversion_buffer[ MAX_CHARS ];

  time( &timer );
  date_time_struct_ptr = localtime( &timer );

  strftime( conversion_buffer, MAX_CHARS,
```

```
                "It is %X on %A, %x",
                 date_time_struct_ptr );

  cout << conversion_buffer
       << endl << endl;
}
```

Here is a sample of the output for this program:

```
It is 18:30:05 on Tuesday, 03/23/01
```

You may find that the strftime() function is not portable from one system to another. Use it with caution if portability is a consideration, and watch out for that Y2K bug.

Using the ctime() Function

The following application illustrates how to make a call to the ctime() function. This program shows how easily you can obtain date and time information from the system.

```
// ctime.cpp
// Application illustrates the use of the ctime()
// function.
// Chris H. Pappas and William H. Murray, 1999

#include <iostream>
#include <ctime>

using namespace std;

void main()
{
  time_t longtime;

  time( &longtime );
  cout << "The time and date is "
       << ctime( &longtime )
       << endl << endl;
}
```

The output, sent to the screen, would appear in the following format:

```
The time and date is Tue Mar 23 18:30:14 2001
```

The ctime() function reports both date and time in acceptable formats.

Building a Time Delay Routine

Usually, having programs execute as quickly as possible is desirable. However, sometimes, slowing down information makes viewing and understanding easier for the user. The delay_for() function in the following application delays program execution. The delay variable is in seconds. For this application, a five-second delay occurs between each line of output to the screen.

```
// timedelay.cpp
// Application illustrates the use of the several
// functions accessed through <ctime> to build
// a practical time delay application.
// Chris H. Pappas and William H. Murray, 1999

#include <iostream>
#include <ctime>

using namespace std;

#define SECONDS          5
#define NUMBER_OF_TRIES 10

void delay_for( int seconds );

void main()
{
  int loop_control;

  for(loop_control = 0; loop_control < NUMBER_OF_TRIES;
      loop_control ++ ) {
    delay_for( SECONDS );
    cout << "The count is "
         << loop_control << endl;
  }
}

void delay_for( int seconds )
{
  long start, end, ltime;

  start = time( &ltime );
  end = start + seconds;

  while( time(&ltime) < end );
}
```

What other uses might the delay_for() function have? One case might be where the computer is connected to an external data-sensing device, such as a thermocouple or strain gauge. The function could be used to take readings every minute, hour, or day.

```
The count is 0
The count is 1
The count is 2
The count is 3
The count is 4
```

```
The count is 5
The count is 6
The count is 7
The count is 8
The count is 9
```

Remember that a five-second time delay between the printing of each of these lines.

Summary

The <ctime> standard header file allows access to many popular time and date functions provided in the <time.h> header file. The five applications in this chapter illustrate many of these functions.

TWENTY-THREE

The <cwchar> and <cwctype> Standard C++ Header

This chapter describes the <cwchar> and <cwctype> header files. The standard header <cwchar> is used for manipulating wide streams and other types of strings. The standard header <cwctype> is used for classifying wide characters.
This chapter describes the new ANSI standard header syntax for these headers. We'll also investigate features for implementing the header code and see several working examples at the end of this chapter.

The <cwchar> Header Syntax

The following listing gives the syntax for using the <cwchar> standard header file:

```
namespace std {#include <wchar.h> };
```

Again, this header provides the ability for manipulating wide streams and other types of strings. A wide stream handles a file as a sequence of multi-byte characters. A stream will appear similar to a sequence of wide characters within an application. Wide stream conversions can take place with the conversion rules changed by a call to setlocale(). A call to setlocale() changes the LC_CTYPE. Wide streams form their conversion rules when they become wide-oriented. These rules remain in effect even when LC_CTYPE changes.

The only sure way to obtain a file position within a wide stream is to call fgetpos(). Likewise, the only sure way to restore a position is a call to fsetpos().

The <cwchar.h> header file defines macros and function declarations for all wide character-related functions. The macros, functions, and constants, such as those found in <string.h>, that are repeated in <cwchar.h> will not be discussed here.

Interesting <wchar.h> Structures and Constants

The _iobuf structure definition is used by a variety of operations that require the use of a buffer for input/output operations:

```
struct _iobuf {
  char *_ptr;
  int   _cnt;
  char *_base;
  int   _flag;
  int   _file;
  int   _charbuf;
  int   _bufsiz;
  char *_tmpfname;
};
```

The f_wfinddata_t structure is used by functions, such as, _wfindnext(), _wfindnexti64, _wfindfirst, and _wfindfirsti64:

```
struct _wfinddata_t {
  unsigned attrib;
  time_t   time_create;   /* -1 for FAT file systems */
  time_t   time_access;   /* -1 for FAT file systems */
  time_t   time_write;
  _fsize_t size;
  wchar_t  name[260];
};
```

The _wfinddatai64_t structure is used for MAC hardware where _INTEGRAL_MAX_BITS >= 64 occurs in place of _wfinddata_t:

```
struct _wfinddatai64_t {
  unsigned attrib;
  time_t   time_create;   /* -1 for FAT file systems */
  time_t   time_access;   /* -1 for FAT file systems */
  time_t   time_write;
  __int64  size;
  wchar_t  name[260];
};
```

The following three structures are used by _stat, _wstat, _stati64, or _wstati64 to store information on file status:

```
struct _stat {
  _dev_t st_dev;
  _ino_t st_ino;
  unsigned short st_mode;
```

```
  short st_nlink;
  short st_uid;
  short st_gid;
  _dev_t st_rdev;
  _off_t st_size;
  time_t st_atime;
  time_t st_mtime;
  time_t st_ctime;
};
```

The following non_ANSI structure definition is provided for compatibility:

```
struct stat {
  _dev_t st_dev;
  _ino_t st_ino;
  unsigned short st_mode;
  short st_nlink;
  short st_uid;
  short st_gid;
  _dev_t st_rdev;
  _off_t st_size;
  time_t st_atime;
  time_t st_mtime;
  time_t st_ctime;
};
```

The _stati64 structure is used when _INTEGRAL_MAX_BITS >= 64:

```
struct _stati64 {
  _dev_t st_dev;
  _ino_t st_ino;
  unsigned short st_mode;
  short st_nlink;
  short st_uid;
  short st_gid;
  _dev_t st_rdev;
  __int64 st_size;
  time_t st_atime;
  time_t st_mtime;
  time_t st_ctime;
 };
```

You'll also find a number of set bit mask constants for all the possible character types defined in <wchar.h>. Table 23.1 lists and describes these constants.

Table 23.1 Set bit mask constants

Constant	Value	Description
_UPPER	0x1	an upper case letter
_LOWER	0x2	a lower case letter
_DIGIT	0x4	a digit[0-9]
_SPACE	0x8	a tab, carriage return, newline, vertical tab or form feed
_PUNCT	0x10	a punctuation character
_CONTROL	0x20	a control character
_BLANK	0x40	a space char
_HEX	0x80	a hexadecimal digit
_LEADBYTE	0x8000	a multibyte leadbyte
_ALPHA	(0x0100|_UPPER|_LOWER)	an alphabetic character

In the next section, we'll examine a wide range of function prototypes described in the <wchar.h> standard header file.

<wchar> Function Prototypes

The function prototypes contained in <wchar.h> are described in Table 23.2. Here you'll find many wide character function equivalents to function prototypes with which you are already familiar. For example, iswalpha() is the wide character equivalent to isalpha() with which you are also already familiar.

Table 23.2 <wchar.h> function prototypes

Return Type	Function	Description
`int`	iswalpha(wint_t)	Returns true if wint_t represents a wide alphabetic character.
`int`	iswupper(wint_t)	Returns true if wint_t represents a wide uppercase letter.
`int`	iswlower(wint_t)	Returns true if wint_t represents a wide lowercase character.
`int`	iswdigit(wint_t)	Returns true if wint_t represents a wide decimal-digit character.
`int`	iswxdigit(wint_t)	Returns true if wint_t represents a wide hexadecimal digit.

Table 23.2 <wchar.h> function prototypes *(continued)*

Return Type	Function	Description
int	iswspace(wint_t)	Returns true if wint_t represents a wide space character.
int	iswpunct(wint_t)	Returns true if wint_t represents a wide punctuation character.
int	iswalnum(wint_t)	Returns true if wint_t represents a wide alphanumeric character.
int	iswprint(wint_t)	Returns true if wint_t represents a printable character.
int	iswgraph(wint_t)	Returns true if wint_t represents a printable character not including a space.
int	iswcntrl(wint_t)	Returns true if wint_t represents a control character.
int	iswascii(wint_t)	Returns true if wint_t is a particular representation of an ASCII character.
int	isleadbyte(int)	Returns a nonzero value if the argument is the first byte of a multibyte character.
wchar_t	towupper(wchar_t)	Converts character to uppercase and returns the results.
wchar_t	towlower(wchar_t)	Converts character to lowercase and returns the results.
int	iswctype(wint_t, wctype_t)	Function tests first parameter for the property specified by the second parameter. When a match is found, an equivalent wide-character classification routine occurs.
int	_wchdir(const wchar_t *)	Function changes the current working directory. The parameter wchar_t references a wide character string.
wchar_t *	_wgetcwd(wchar_t *, int)	Gets the current working directory. The first parameter indicates the storage location for the path, and the second parameter indicates the maximum length of the path in characters.
wchar_t *	_wgetdcwd(int, wchar_t *, int)	Gets the full path name of current working directory on the given drive. The first parameter specifies the drive, the second parameter indicates the storage location for the path, and the third parameter indicates the maximum length of the path in characters.

Table 23.2 <wchar.h> function prototypes *(continued)*

Return Type	Function	Description
int	_wmkdir(const wchar_t *)	Creates a new directory. The parameter specifies the directory with a wide character string.
int	_wrmdir(const wchar_t *)	Deletes a directory. The parameter specifies the directory with a wide character string.
int	_waccess(const wchar_t *, int)	Function determines file-access permission. The first parameter gives the file or directory path. The second parameter holds the permission setting. Use 00 for this value to check for a file's existence. Use 02 for write permission. Use 04 for read permission and 06 for both read and write permission.
int	_wchmod(const wchar_t *, int)	Used to change the file-permission settings. The first parameter gives the file path. The second parameter holds the permission setting. Use _S_IWRITE for writing permission. Use _S_IREAD for reading permission. Use _S_IREAD | _S_IWRITE for both reading and writing permission.
int	_wcreat(const wchar_t *, int)	Used to create a new file. The first parameter gives the file path. The second parameter holds the permission setting. Use _S_IWRITE for writing permission. Use _S_IREAD for reading permission. Use _S_IREAD | _S_IWRITE for both reading and writing permission.
long	_wfindfirst(wchar_t *, struct _wfinddata_t *)	Used to find information about the first instance of a file name that matches the file specified in the first parameter. The second parameter points to a structure that holds the file information buffer.
int	_wfindnext(long, struct _wfinddata_t *)	Used to find the next name that matches the first parameter in a previous call to _wfindfirst() and then alters the *fileinfo* structure information specified in the second parameter.
int	_wunlink(const wchar_t *)	Delete a file specified in the first parameter.
int	_wrename(const wchar_t *, const wchar_t *)	Renames a file or directory. The first parameter is a pointer to the old file or directory. The second parameter is a pointer to the new file or directory name.

Table 23.2 <wchar.h> function prototypes *(continued)*

Return Type	Function	Description
int	_wopen(const wchar_t *, int, ...)	Opens a file and returns the file handle when successful. An EACCES means that an attempt to open a read-only file for writing occurred. EEXIST means _O_CREAT and _O_EXCL flags are specified, but the file already exists. EINVAL means that an invalid *oflag* or *pmode* argument has been supplied. EMFILE means that no more file handles are available. ENOENT means that the file or path is not found.
int	_wsopen(const wchar_t *, int, int, ...)	Opens a file for sharing. Return values similar to _wopen().
wchar_t *	_wmktemp(wchar_t *)	Used to create a unique file name.
long	_wfindfirsti64(wchar_t *, struct _wfinddatai64_t *)	Used to provide information about the first instance of a file name that matches the file given by the first parameter. The second parameter points to the file information buffer.
int	_wfindnexti64(long, struct _wfinddatai64_t *)	Used to find the next name that matches the first parameter in a previous call to _wfindfirsti64() and then alters the *fileinfo* structure information specified in the second parameter.
wchar_t *	_wsetlocale(int, const wchar_t *)	Used to define the locale. The first parameter specifies the category affected by locale. The second parameter is the locale name.
int	_wexecl(const wchar_t *, const wchar_t *, ...)	Used to load and execute new child processes. The first parameter is the path to the file to be executed. The second parameter points to a list of pointers to parameters.
int	_wexecle(const wchar_t *, const wchar_t *, ...)	Used to load and execute new child processes. The first parameter is the path to the file to be executed. The second parameter points to a list of pointers to parameters. The third parameter points to an array of pointers to environment strings.
int	_wexeclp(const wchar_t *, const wchar_t *, ...)	Used to load and execute new child processes. The first parameter is the path to the file to be executed. The second parameter points to a list of pointers to parameters.

Table 23.2 <wchar.h> function prototypes *(continued)*

Return Type	Function	Description
int	_wexeclpe(const wchar_t *, const wchar_t *, ...)	Used to load and execute new child processes. The first parameter is the path to the file to be executed. The second parameter points to a list of pointers to parameters. The third parameter points to an array of pointers to environment strings.
int	_wexecv(const wchar_t *, const wchar_t * const *)	Used to load and execute new child processes. The first parameter is the path to the file to be executed. The second parameter is to an array of pointers to parameters.
int	_wexecve(const wchar_t *, const wchar_t * const *, const wchar_t * const *)	Used to load and execute new child processes. The first parameter is the path to the file to be executed. The second parameter is an array of pointers to parameters. The third parameter is to an array of pointers to environment settings.
int	_wexecvp(const wchar_t *, const wchar_t * const *)	Used to load and execute new child processes. The first parameter is the path to the file to be executed. The second parameter is to an array of pointers to parameters.
int	_wexecvpe(const wchar_t *, const wchar_t * const *, const wchar_t * const *)	Used to load and execute new child processes. The first parameter is the path to the file to be executed. The second parameter is an array of pointers to parameters. The third parameter is to an array of pointers to environment settings.
int	_wspawnl(int, const wchar_t *, const wchar_t *, ...)	Used to create and execute a new process. The first parameter gives the execution mode for calling the process. The second parameter gives the path of the file to be executed. The third parameter gives a list of pointers to arguments.
int	_wspawnle(int, const wchar_t *, const wchar_t *, ...)	Used to create and execute a new process. The first parameter gives the execution mode for calling the process. The second parameter gives the path of the file to be executed. The third parameter gives a list of pointers to arguments. The fourth parameter is to an array of pointers to environment settings.

Table 23.2 <wchar.h> function prototypes *(continued)*

Return Type	Function	Description
int	_wspawnlp(int, const wchar_t *, const wchar_t *, ...)	Used to create and execute a new process. The first parameter gives the execution mode for calling the process. The second parameter gives the path of the file to be executed. The third parameter gives a list of pointers to arguments.
int	_wspawnlpe(int, const wchar_t *, const wchar_t *, ...)	Used to create and execute a new process. The first parameter gives the execution mode for calling the process. The second parameter gives the path of the file to be executed. The third parameter gives a list of pointers to arguments. The fourth parameter is to an array of pointers to environment settings.
int	_wspawnv(int, const wchar_t *, const wchar_t * const *)	Used to create and execute a new process. The first parameter gives the execution mode for calling the process. The second parameter gives the path of the file to be executed. The third parameter gives an array of pointers to arguments.
int	_wspawnve(int, const wchar_t *, const wchar_t * const *, const wchar_t * const *)	Used to create and execute a new process. The first parameter gives the execution mode for calling the process. The second parameter gives the path of the file to be executed. The third parameter gives an array of pointers to arguments. The fourth parameter gives an array of pointers to environment settings.
int	_wspawnvp(int, const wchar_t *, const wchar_t * const *)	Used to create and execute a new process. The first parameter gives the execution mode for calling the process. The second parameter gives the path of the file to be executed. The third parameter gives an array of pointers to arguments.
int	_wspawnvpe(int, const wchar_t *, const wchar_t * const *, const wchar_t * const *)	Used to create and execute a new process. The first parameter gives the execution mode for calling the process. The second parameter gives the path of the file to be executed. The third parameter gives an array of pointers to arguments. The fourth parameter gives an array of pointers to environment settings.

Table 23.2 <wchar.h> function prototypes *(continued)*

Return Type	Function	Description
int	_wsystem(const wchar_t *)	Used to execute a command. Function passes an argument to the command interpreter. The string is then executed as an operating-system command.

The definitions for many of these wide function prototypes are also defined in this header file. The following listing illustrates how these are achieved using #defines and inline statements:

```
#define iswalpha(_c)  (iswctype(_c,_ALPHA))
#define iswupper(_c)  (iswctype(_c,_UPPER))
#define iswlower(_c)  (iswctype(_c,_LOWER))
#define iswdigit(_c)  (iswctype(_c,_DIGIT))
#define iswxdigit(_c) (iswctype(_c,_HEX))
#define iswspace(_c)  (iswctype(_c,_SPACE))
#define iswpunct(_c)  (iswctype(_c,_PUNCT))
#define iswalnum(_c)  (iswctype(_c,_ALPHA|_DIGIT))
#define iswprint(_c)
(iswctype(_c,_BLANK|_PUNCT|_ALPHA|_DIGIT))
#define iswgraph(_c)  (iswctype(_c,_PUNCT|_ALPHA|_DIGIT))
#define iswcntrl(_c)  (iswctype(_c,_CONTROL))
#define iswascii(_c)  ((unsigned)(_c) < 0x80 )
inline int __cdecl iswalpha(wint_t _C)
  {return (iswctype(_C,_ALPHA));}
inline int __cdecl iswupper(wint_t _C)
  {return (iswctype(_C,_UPPER));}
inline int __cdecl iswlower(wint_t _C)
  {return (iswctype(_C,_LOWER));}
inline int __cdecl iswdigit(wint_t _C)
  {return (iswctype(_C,_DIGIT));}
inline int __cdecl iswxdigit(wint_t _C)
  {return (iswctype(_C,_HEX));}
inline int __cdecl iswspace(wint_t _C)
  {return (iswctype(_C,_SPACE));}
inline int __cdecl iswpunct(wint_t _C)
  {return (iswctype(_C,_PUNCT));}
inline int __cdecl iswalnum(wint_t _C)
  {return (iswctype(_C,_ALPHA|_DIGIT));}
inline int __cdecl iswprint(wint_t _C)
  {return (iswctype(_C,_BLANK|_PUNCT|_ALPHA|_DIGIT));}
inline int __cdecl iswgraph(wint_t _C)
  {return (iswctype(_C,_PUNCT|_ALPHA|_DIGIT));}
inline int __cdecl iswcntrl(wint_t _C)
  {return (iswctype(_C,_CONTROL));}
inline int __cdecl iswascii(wint_t _C)
```

```
  {return ((unsigned)(_C) < 0x80);}
inline int __cdecl isleadbyte(int _C)
  {return (_pctype[(unsigned char)(_C)] & _LEADBYTE);}
```

In the next section we'll see several POSIX function prototypes.

<wchar> POSIX Function Prototypes and More

You'll also find POSIX support included in <wchar.h>. For #ifndef situations, Table 23.3 shows definitions used for returning POSIX status information.

Table 23.3 Definitions used for returning POSIX status information

Definition	Implementation	Non-ANSI Compatibility
_INO_T_DEFINED	unsigned short _ino_t	unsigned short ino_t
_DEV_T_DEFINED	unsigned int _dev_t	unsigned int dev_t
_OFF_T_DEFINED	long _off_t	long off_t
_STAT_DEFINED	none	none
_WSTAT_DEFINED	int _wstat(const wchar_t *, struct _stat *)	none
_INTEGRAL_MAX_BITS >= 64	int _wstati64(const wchar_t *, struct _stati64 *)	none

Many of the POSIX function prototypes have already been described in Chapter 21. They are listed in Table 23.4 for ease of reference.

Table 23.4 POSIX function prototypes

Return Type	POSIX Function Prototype
`wint_t`	_fgetwchar(void);
`wint_t`	_fputwchar(wint_t);
`wchar_t *`	_getws(wchar_t *);
`wchar_t *`	_i64tow(__int64, wchar_t *, int);
`wchar_t *`	_itow (int, wchar_t *, int);
`wchar_t *`	_ltow (long, wchar_t *, int);
`int`	_putws(const wchar_t *);
`int`	_snwprintf(wchar_t *, size_t, const wchar_t *, ...);
`wchar_t *`	_ui64tow(unsigned __int64, wchar_t *, int);
`wchar_t *`	_ultow (unsigned long, wchar_t *, int);
`int`	_vsnwprintf(wchar_t *, size_t, const wchar_t *, va_list);
`FILE *`	_wfdopen(int, const wchar_t *);
`FILE *`	_wfopen(const wchar_t *, const wchar_t *);

Table 23.4 POSIX function prototypes *(continued)*

Return Type	POSIX Function Prototype
FILE *	_wfreopen(const wchar_t *, const wchar_t *, FILE *);
FILE *	_wfsopen(const wchar_t *, const wchar_t *);
FILE *	_wfsopen(const wchar_t *, const wchar_t *, int);
wchar_t *	_wgetenv(const wchar_t *);
void	_wperror(const wchar_t *);
FILE *	_wpopen(const wchar_t *, const wchar_t *);
int	_wremove(const wchar_t *);
int	_wsystem(const wchar_t *);
wchar_t *	_wtempnam(const wchar_t *, const wchar_t *);
wchar_t *	_wtmpnam(wchar_t *);
int	_wtoi(const wchar_t *);
__int64	_wtoi64(const wchar_t *);
long	_wtol(const wchar_t *);
wint_t	fgetwc(FILE *);
wchar_t *	fgetws(wchar_t *, int, FILE *);
wint_t	fputwc(wint_t, FILE *);
int	fputws(const wchar_t *, FILE *);
int	fwprintf(FILE *, const wchar_t *, ...);
int	fwscanf(FILE *, const wchar_t *, ...);
wint_t	getwc(FILE *);
wint_t	getwchar(void);
wint_t	putwc(wint_t, FILE *);
wint_t	putwchar(wint_t);
int	swprintf(wchar_t *, const wchar_t *, ...);
int	swscanf(const wchar_t *, const wchar_t *, ...);
wint_t	ungetwc(wint_t, FILE *);
int	vfwprintf(FILE *, const wchar_t *, va_list);
int	vswprintf(wchar_t *, const wchar_t *, va_list);
int	vwprintf(const wchar_t *, va_list);
double	wcstod(const wchar_t *, wchar_t **);
long	wcstol(const wchar_t *, wchar_t **, int);
unsigned long	wcstoul(const wchar_t *, wchar_t **, int);
int	wprintf(const wchar_t *, ...);
int	wscanf(const wchar_t *, ...);

You'll also find a wide variety of POSIX prototypes described, such as _wcsdup() and _wcsrev(), that have already been described in Chapter 17. These are also described in <string.h>. They will not be listed again.

You'll see several of the functions prototyped in <wchar.h> illustrated in the sample code section of this chapter.

The <cwctype> Header Syntax

The following listing gives the syntax for using the <cwctype> standard header file:

```
namespace std {#include <wctype.h> };
```

This header provides the declarations for wide character functions. The <wctype.h> header file defines types, macros, and function prototypes for all ctype-style wide character functions. These types, macros, and function prototypes are also defined in <wchar.h> and have been described in earlier sections of this chapter.

Sample Code

In this section, we'll use a single application to illustrate the iswalpha(), iswdigit(), iswalnum(), iswascii(), and iswspace() functions.

```
// char1.cpp
// Application illustrates the use of the iswalpha(),
// iswdigit(), iswalnum(), iswascii(), and iswspace()
// functions.
// Chris H. Pappas and William H. Murray, 1999

#include <iostream>
#include <cwchar>

using namespace std;

void main()
{
  wint_t mychar;

  mychar = 't';

  if (iswalpha(mychar))
    cout << "char is an alphabetic character." << endl;
  else
    cout << "char is not an alphabetic character." << endl;
```

```
  if (iswdigit(mychar))
    cout << "char is a decimal digit." << endl;
  else
    cout << "char is not a decimal digit." << endl;

  if (iswalnum(mychar))
    cout << "char is an alphanumeric character." << endl;
  else
    cout << "char is not an alphanumeric character." << endl;

  if (iswascii(mychar))
    cout << "char is an ASCII character." << endl;
  else
    cout << "char is not an ASCII character." << endl;

  if (iswspace(mychar))
    cout << "char is a space." << endl;
  else
    cout << "char is not a space." << endl;

  cout << endl  << endl;
}
```

This program will return the following information when using 't' as the character:

```
char is an alphabetic character.
char is not a decimal digit.
char is an alphanumeric character.
char is an ASCII character.
char is not a space.
```

Now, change the character from a 't' to a ' ' (single space), recompile, and execute to get:

```
char is not an alphabetic character.
char is not a decimal digit.
char is not an alphanumeric character.
char is an ASCII character.
char is a space.
```

Change the character, once again, from a ' ' (single space) to a '5', recompile, and execute to get:

```
char is not an alphabetic character.
char is a decimal digit.
char is an alphanumeric character.
char is an ASCII character.
char is not a space.
```

Well, no surprises here. The functions operate as anticipated.

Summary

The <cwchar> and <cwctype> standard header files provide wide character capabilities for operations on wide characters. Most C programmers are already familiar with their operation from "normal" character equivalents used in most C and C++ programming.

TWENTY-FOUR

The <fstream>, <iostream>, <istream>, <ostream>, <sstream>, <streambuf>, and <strstream> Standard C++ Headers

This chapter describes the <fstream>, <iostream>, <istream>, <ostream>, <sstream>, <streambuf>, and <strstream> header files. These standard header files are used to define template classes that support iostreams operations on sequences stored in external files. The iostreams headers support conversions between text and encoded forms, and input and output to external files.

Basic operations using iostreams require the inclusion of the <iostream> header. Values can then be extracted from cin in order to read standard input or inserted to cout in order to write standard output. Information for reading standard input is found in the basic_istream class. Information for writing standard output is found in the basic_ostream class. The basic_ios class handles format control for both extractions and insertions.

Similar iostreams operations can be applied to files by using <fstream> classes. Conversions between iostreams and objects of the basic_string class use the classes described in <sstream>. In a similar manner, C strings use the classes described in <strstream>.

This chapter describes the new ANSI standard header syntax for these headers. We'll also investigate features for implementing the header code and see several working examples at the end of this chapter.

The <fstream> Header Syntax

The following listing gives the syntax for using the <fstream> standard header file. Note the four template class definitions as you examine this listing:

```
namespace std {
    template<class E, class T = char_traits<E> >
        class basic_filebuf;
    typedef basic_filebuf<char> filebuf;
    typedef basic_filebuf<wchar_t> wfilebuf;
    template<class E, class T = char_traits<E> >
        class basic_ifstream;
    typedef basic_ifstream<char> ifstream;
    typedef basic_ifstream<wchar_t> wifstream;
    template<class E, class T = char_traits<E> >
        class basic_ofstream;
    typedef basic_ofstream<char> ofstream;
    typedef basic_ofstream<wchar_t> wofstream;
    template<class E, class T = char_traits<E> >
        class basic_fstream;
    typedef basic_fstream<char> fstream;
    typedef basic_fstream<wchar_t> wfstream;
    };
```

The iostreams standard header `<fstream>` is used to define template classes that support iostreams operations on sequences stored in external files. In the following sections, we'll examine the syntax used to describe the basic_filebuf, basic_ifstream, basic_ofstream, and basic_fstream classes.

basic_filebuf

The basic_filebuf template class is used to describe a stream buffer that controls the transmission of elements to and from a sequence of elements that are stored in an external file. This template class is used by <fstream>.

```
template <class E, class T = char_traits<E> >
    class basic_filebuf : public basic_streambuf<E, T> {
public:
    basic_filebuf();
    bool is_open() const;
    basic_filebuf *open(const char *s,
        ios_base::openmode mode);
    basic_filebuf *close();
protected:
    virtual pos_type seekoff(off_type off,
        ios_base::seekdir way,
        ios_base::openmode which = ios_base::in |
                                    ios_base::out);
    virtual pos_type seekpos(pos_type pos,
        ios_base::openmode which = ios_base::in |
                                    ios_base::out);
```

```
virtual int_type underflow();
virtual int_type pbackfail(int_type c = T::eof());
virtual int_type overflow(int_type c = T::eof());
virtual int sync();
virtual basic_streambuf<E, T> *setbuf(E *s, streamsize n);
};
```

Here, an object of the class basic_filebuf<E, T> is used to store a file pointer. The file pointer is used to select the FILE object that controls the stream that is associated with an open file. Storage is also provided for pointers to two file conversion facets used by the overflow() and underflow() member functions.

basic_ifstream

The basic_ifstream template class is used to describe an object that controls the extraction of elements and encoded objects from a stream buffer. The stream buffer is of class basic_filebuf<E, T>. The encoded objects use elements of type E with character traits described by the class T. This template class is used by <fstream>:

```
template <class E, class T = char_traits<E> >
    class basic_ifstream : public basic_istream<E, T> {
public:
    explicit basic_ifstream();
    explicit basic_ifstream(const char *s,
        ios_base::openmode mode = ios_base::in);
    basic_filebuf<E, T> *rdbuf() const;
    bool is_open() const;
    void open(const char *s,
        ios_base::openmode mode = ios_base::in);
    void close();
    };
```

The basic_ifstream template class object is used to store an object of class basic_filebuf<E, T>.

basic_ofstream

The basic_ofstream template class is used to describe an object that controls insertion of elements and encoded objects into a stream buffer of class basic_filebuf<E, T>. The encoded objects use elements of type E with character traits described by the class T. This template class is used by <fstream>:

```
template <class E, class T = char_traits<E> >
    class basic_ofstream : public basic_ostream<E, T> {
public:
    explicit basic_ofstream();
    explicit basic_ofstream(const char *s,
        ios_base::openmode mode = ios_base::out |
```

```
                                     ios_base::trunc);
    basic_filebuf<E, T> *rdbuf() const;
    bool is_open() const;
    void open(const char *s,
        ios_base::openmode mode = ios_base::out |
                                  ios_base::trunc);
    void close();
    };
```

The basic_ofstream template class object is used to store an object of class basic_filebuf<E, T>.

basic_fstream

The basic_fstream template class is used to describe an object that controls insertion and extraction of elements and encoded objects using a stream buffer of class nasic_filebuf<E, T>. The encoded objects use elements of type E with character traits described by the class T. This template class is used by <fstream>.

```
template <class E, class T = char_traits<E> >
    class basic_fstream : public basic_iostream<E, T> {
public:
    explicit basic_fstream();
    explicit basic_fstream(const char *s,
        ios_base::openmode mode = ios_base::in | ios_base::out);
    basic_filebuf<E, T> *rdbuf() const;
    bool is_open() const;
    void open(const char *s,
        ios_base::openmode mode = ios_base::in | ios_base::out);
    void close();
    };
```

The basic_fstream template class object is used to store an object of class basic_filebuf<E, T>.

The <iostream> Header Syntax

The following listing gives the syntax for using the <iostream> standard header file. The iostreams standard header `<iostream>` is used to declare objects that control reading and writing to and from standard streams. As you examine the listing, note the use of the **extern** keyword.

```
namespace std {
    extern istream cin;
    extern ostream cout;
    extern ostream cerr;
    extern ostream clog;
```

```
extern wistream wcin;
extern wostream wcout;
extern wostream wcerr;
extern wostream wclog;
};
```

The <iostream> header is usually the only header required for simple input and output (I/O) from C++ applications.

Byte-at-a-time objects include cin, cout, cerr, and clog. Wide character translation objects include wcin, wcout, wcerr, and wclog.

Reading and writing to standard streams before program startup and after program termination is safe, since these objects are constructed before any static objects in the application and are not destroyed until after the destruction of the application's static objects.

The <istream> Header Syntax

The following listing gives the syntax for using the <istream> standard header file. The istreams standard header `<istream>` is used to declare objects that control reading and writing to and from standard streams.

The istream class is used to provide the capability for basic sequential and random-access input. Here, istream objects work in conjunction with a streambuf derived object. The istream class provides formatting, and the streambuf class allows low-level buffered input.

If an appropriate filebuf object is created, istream objects can also be used for sequential disk input:

```
namespace std {
    // Declarations
    template<class E, class T = char_traits<E> >
        class basic_istream;
    typedef basic_istream<char, char_traits<char> > istream;
    typedef basic_istream<wchar_t, char_traits<wchar_t> > wistream;
    template<class E, class T = char_traits<E> >
        class basic_iostream;
    typedef basic_iostream<char, char_traits<char> > iostream;
    typedef basic_iostream<wchar_t, char_traits<wchar_t> > wiostream;
    // Extractors
    template<class E, class T>
        basic_istream<E, T>& "operator>>(basic_istream<E, T> is, E *s);
    template<class E, class T>
        basic_istream<E, T>& "operator>>(basic_istream<E, T> is, E& c);
    template<class T>
        basic_istream<char, T>& "operator>>(basic_istream<char, T> is,
signed char *s);
    template<class T>
        basic_istream<char, T>& "operator>>(basic_istream<char, T> is,
```

```
signed char& c);
    template<class T>
        basic_istream<char, T>& "operator>>(basic_istream<char, T> is,
unsigned char *s);
    template<class T>
        basic_istream<char, T>& "operator>>(basic_istream<char, T> is,
unsigned char& c);
    // Manipulators
    template class<E, T>
        basic_istream<E, T>& ws(basic_istream<E, T> is);
    };
```

The iostreams standard header `<istream>` is included in order to define the template class basic_istream. This class is used to mediate extractions for the iostreams. In a similar manner, the template class basic_iostream is used to mediate insertions and extractions.

basic_istream

The basic_istream template class is used to describe an object that controls extraction of elements and encoded objects from a stream buffer with elements of type E. The encoded objects use elements of type E with character traits described by the class T. This template class is used by <istream>:

```
template <class E, class T = char_traits<E> >
    class basic_istream : virtual public basic_ios<E, T> {
public:
    class sentry;
    explicit basic_istream(basic_streambuf<E, T> *sb);
    virtual ~istream();
    bool ipfx(bool noskip = false);
    void isfx();
    basic_istream& "operator>>(basic_istream& (*pf)(basic_istream&));
    basic_istream& "operator>>(basic_ios<E, T>& (*pf)(basic_ios<E, T>&));
    basic_istream& "operator>>(ios_base<E, T>& (*pf)(ios_base<E, T>&));
    basic_istream& "operator>>(basic_streambuf<E, T> *sb);
    basic_istream& "operator>>(bool& n);
    basic_istream& "operator>>(short& n);
    basic_istream& "operator>>(unsigned short& n);
    basic_istream& "operator>>(int& n);
    basic_istream& "operator>>(unsigned int& n);
    basic_istream& "operator>>(long& n);
    basic_istream& "operator>>(unsigned long& n);
    basic_istream& "operator>>(void *& n);
    basic_istream& "operator>>(float& n);
    basic_istream& "operator>>(double& n);
    basic_istream& "operator>>(long double& n);
    streamsize gcount() const;
    int_type get();
    basic_istream& get(E& c);
```

```
basic_istream& get(E *s, streamsize n);
basic_istream& get(E *s, streamsize n, E delim);
basic_istream& get(basic_streambuf<E, T> *sb);
basic_istream& get(baiic_streambuf<E, T> *sb, E delim);
basic_istream& getline(E *s, streamsize n)E
basic_istream& getline(E *s, streamsize n, E delim);
basic_istream& ignore(streamsize n = 1,
    int_type delim = T::eof());
int_type peek();
basic_istream& read(E *s, streamsize n);
streamsize readsome(E *s, streamsize n);
basic_istream& putback(E c);
basic_istream& unget();
pos_type tellg();
basic_istream& seekg(pos_type pos);
basic_istream& seekg(off_type off, ios_base::seek_dir way);
int sync();
};
```

Member functions that overload "operator>> and are formatted input functions will use code similar to:

```
iostate state = goodbit;
const sentry ok(*this);
if (ok)
    {try
        {used to extract elements and convert
        accumulate flags in state
        store a successful conversion}
    catch (...)
        {if (exceptions() & badbit)
            throw;
        setstate(badbit); }}
setstate(state);
return (*this);
```

Member functions that are unformatted input functions will use code similar to:

```
iostate state = goodbit;
count = 0;
const sentry ok(*this, true);
if (ok)
    {try
        {used to extract elements and deliver
        count extracted elements in count
        accumulate flags in state}
    catch (...)
        {if (rdstate() & badbit)
            throw;
        setstate(badbit); }}
setstate(state);
```

All member functions will call setstate(eofbit) when they encounter an end-of-file while extracting elements.

basic_iostream

The basic_iostream template class is used to describe an object that controls insertions, through the base object basic_ostream<E, T>. Extractions are performed through the base object basic_istream<E, T>. This template class is used by <istream>:

```
template <class E, class T = char_traits<E> >
    class basic_iostream : public basic_istream<E, T>,
        public  basic_ostream<E, T> {
public:
    explicit basic_iostream(basic_streambuf<E, T> *sb);
    virtual ~basic_iostream();
    };
```

The basic_ostream and basic_iostream objects share a common virtual base object, basic_ios<E, T>. The two objects manage a common stream buffer using elements of type E with character traits described by the class T.

The <ostream> Header Syntax

The following listing gives the syntax for using the <ostream> standard header file. The iostreams standard header <ostream> is used to define the template class basic_ostream. This class is used to mediate extractions for the iostreams classes. Note the ten template class definitions as you examine this listing:

```
namespace std {
    template<class E, class T = char_traits<E> >
        class basic_ostream;
    typedef basic_ostream<char, char_traits<char> > ostream;
    typedef basic_ostream<wchar_t,
        char_traits<wchar_t> > wostream;
    // Insertions
    template<class E, class T>
        basic_ostream<E, T>& operator<<(basic_ostream<E, T> os,
        const E *s);
    template<class E, class T>
        basic_ostream<E, T>& operator<<(basic_ostream<E, T> os,
        E c);
    template<class T>
        basic_ostream<char, T>& operator<<(basic_ostream<char, \
        T> os, const signed char *s);
    template<class T>
        basic_ostream<char, T>& operator<<(basic_ostream<char, \
        T> os, signed char c);
```

```
    template<class T>
        basic_ostream<char, T>& operator<<(basic_ostream<char, \
        T> os, const unsigned char *s);
    template<class T>
        basic_ostream<char, T>& operator<<(basic_ostream<char, \
        T> os, unsigned char c);
    // Manipulators
    template class<E, T>
        basic_ostream<E, T>& endl(basic_ostream<E, T> os);
    template class<E, T>
        basic_ostream<E, T>& ends(basic_ostream<E, T> os);
    template class<E, T>
        basic_ostream<E, T>& flush(basic_ostream<E, T> os);
    };
```

This header also defines several related manipulators. In the next section, we'll examine the syntax for basic_ostream.

basic_ostream

The basic_ostream template class is used to describe an object that controls insertion of elements and encoded objects into a stream buffer. The encoded objects use elements of type E with character traits described by the class T. This template class is used by <ostream>:

```
template <class E, class T = char_traits<E> >
    class basic_ostream {
public:
    class sentry;
    explicit basic_ostream(basic_streambuf<E, T> *sb);
    virtual ~ostream();
    bool opfx();
    void osfx();
    basic_ostream& operator<<(basic_ostream& (*pf)(basic_ostream&));
    basic_ostream& operator<<(basic_ios<E, T>& (*pf)(basic_ios<E, T>&));
    basic_ostream& operator<<(ios_base<E, T>& (*pf)(ios_base<E, T>&));
    basic_ostream& operator<<(basic_streambuf<E, T> *sb);
    basic_ostream& operator<<(const char *s);
    basic_ostream& operator<<(char c);
    basic_ostream& operator<<(bool n);
    basic_ostream& operator<<(short n);
    basic_ostream& operator<<(unsigned short n);
    basic_ostream& operator<<(int n);
    basic_ostream& operator<<(unsigned int n);
    basic_ostream& operator<<(long n);
    basic_ostream& operator<<(unsigned long n);
    basic_ostream& operator<<(float n);
    basic_ostream& operator<<(double n);
    basic_ostream& operator<<(long double n);
    basic_ostream& operator<<(void * n);
```

```
basic_ostream& put(E c);
basic_ostream& write(E *s, streamsize n);
basic_ostream& flush();
pos_type tellp();
basic_ostream& seekp(pos_type pos);
basic_ostream& seekp(off_type off, ios_base::seek_dir way);
};
```

Member functions that overload operator<< and are formatted output functions use the following style code:

```
iostate state = goodbit;
const sentry ok(*this);
if (ok)
    {try
        {used to convert and insert elements
        accumulate flags in state}
    catch (...)
        {if (exceptions() & badbit)
            throw;
        setstate(badbit); }}
width(0);    // except for operator<<(E)
setstate(state);
return (*this);
```

Member functions that are unformatted output functions use the following style code:

```
iostate state = goodbit;
const sentry ok(*this);
if (!ok)
    state |= badbit;
else
    {try
        {used to obtain and insert elements
        accumulate flags in state}
    catch (...)
        {if (rdstate() & badbit)
            throw;
        setstate(badbit); }}
setstate(state);
return (*this);
```

All member functions call setstate(badbit) when encountering a failure during the insertion of elements. An object of class basic_ostream<E, T> stores only a virtual public base object of class basic_ios<E, T>.

The <sstream> Header Syntax

The following listing gives the syntax for using the <sstream> standard header file. The iostreams standard header <sstream> is used to define four template classes that support iostreams operations on sequences. The sequences are stored in an allocated array object:

```
namespace std {
    template<class E,
        class T = char_traits<E>,
        class A = allocator<E> >
        class basic_stringbuf;
    typedef basic_stringbuf<char> stringbuf;
    typedef basic_stringbuf<wchar_t> wstringbuf;
    template<class E,
        class T = char_traits<E>,
        class A = allocator<E> >
        class basic_istringstream;
    typedef basic_istringstream<char> istringstream;
    typedef basic_istringstream<wchar_t> wistringstream;
    template<class E,
        class T = char_traits<E>,
        class A = allocator<E> >
        class basic_ostringstream;
    typedef basic_ostringstream<char> ostringstream;
    typedef basic_ostringstream<wchar_t> wostringstream;
    template<class E,
        class T = char_traits<E>,
        class A = allocator<E> >
        class basic_stringstream;
    typedef basic_stringstream<char> stringstream;
    typedef basic_stringstream<wchar_t> wstringstream;
    };
```

The sequences used by this standard header are easily converted to and from objects of the basic_string template class. In the next sections, we'll examine the syntax for basic_stringbuf, basic_istringstream, basic_ostringstream, and basic_stringstream.

basic_stringbuf

The basic_stringbuf template class is used to describe a stream buffer that controls the transmission of elements to and from a sequence of elements stored in an array object. The array object can be allocated, extended, and freed to reflect changes in the sequence. This template class is used by <sstream>:

```
template <class E,
    class T = char_traits<E>,
    class A = allocator<E> >
    class basic_stringbuf {
public:
    basic_stringbuf(ios_base::openmode mode =
        ios_base::in | ios_base::out);
    basic_stringbuf(basic_string<E, T, A>& x,
        ios_base::openmode mode = ios_base::in | ios_base::out);
    basic_string<E, T, A> str() const;
    void str(basic_string<E, T, A>& x);
protected:
    virtual pos_type seekoff(off_type off, ios_base::seekdir way,
        ios_base::openmode mode = ios_base::in | ios_base::out);
    virtual pos_type seekpos(pos_type sp,
        ios_base::openmode mode = ios_base::in | ios_base::out);
    virtual int_type underflow();
    virtual int_type pbackfail(int_type c = T::eof());
    virtual int_type overflow(int_type c = T::eof());
    };
```

Here, an object of class basic_stringbuf<E, T> is used to store a copy of the ios_base::openmode argument as its stringbuf mode. The argument is supplied by the object's constructor. The input buffer is accessible when both mode and ios_base::in are nonzero. The output buffer is accessible when both the mode and ios_base::out are nonzero.

basic_istringstream

The basic_istringstream template class is used to describe an object that controls the extraction of elements and encoded objects from a stream buffer. The stream buffer is of class basic_stringbuf<E, T, A>. The encoded objects use elements of type E with character traits described by the class T and allocated by an allocator of class A. This template class is used by <sstream>:

```
template <class E,
    class T = char_traits<E>,
    class A = allocator<E> >
    class basic_istringstream : public basic_istream<E, T> {
public:
    explicit basic_istringstream(ios_base::openmode mode =
ios_base::in);
    explicit basic_istringstream(const basic_string<E, T, A>& x,
        ios_base::openmode mode = ios_base::in);
    basic_stringbuf<E, T, A> *rdbuf() const;
    basic_string<E, T, A>& str();
    void str(const basic_string<E, T, A>& x);
    };
```

The object is used to store an object of class basic_stringbuf<E, T, A>.

basic_ostringstream

The basic_ostringstream template class is used to describe an object that controls the insertion of elements and encoded objects into a stream buffer. The stream buffer is of class basic_stringbuf<E, T, A>. The encoded objects use elements of type E with character traits described by the class T and allocated by an allocator of class A. This template class is used by <sstream>:

```
template <class E,
    class T = char_traits<E>,
    class A = allocator<E> >
    class basic_ostringstream : public basic_ostream<E, T> {
public:
    explicit basic_ostringstream(ios_base::openmode mode = ios_base::out);
    explicit basic_ostringstream(const basic_string<E, T, A>& x,
        ios_base::openmode mode = ios_base::out);
    basic_stringbuf<E, T, A> *rdbuf() const;
    basic_string<E, T, A>& str();
    void str(const basic_string<E, T, A>& x);
    };
```

The object is used to store an object of class basic_stringbuf<E, T, A>.

basic_stringstream

The basic_stringstream template class is used to describe an object that controls the insertion of elements and encoded objects into a stream buffer. The stream buffer is of class basic_stringbuf<E, T, A>. The encoded objects use elements of type E with character traits described by the class T and allocated by an allocator of class A. This template class is used by <sstream>:

```
template <class E,
    class T = char_traits<E>,
    class A = allocator<E> >
    class basic_stringstream : public basic_iostream<E, T> {
public:
    explicit basic_stringstream(ios_base::openmode mode = ios_base::in
| ios_base::out);
    explicit basic_stringstream(const basic_string<E, T, A>& x,
        ios_base::openmode mode = ios_base::in | ios_base::out);
    basic_stringbuf<E, T, A> *rdbuf() const;
    basic_string<E, T, A>& str();
    void str(const basic_string<E, T, A>& x);
    };
```

This object is used to store an object of class basic_stringbuf<E, T, A>.

The <streambuf> Header Syntax

The following listing gives the syntax for using the <streambuf> standard header file. The iostreams standard header <streambuf> is included in order to define the template class basic_streambuf. This template class is fundamental to the operation of all iostreams classes:

```
namespace std {
    template<class E, class T = char_traits<E> >
        class basic_streambuf;
    typedef basic_streambuf<char, char_traits<char> > streambuf;
    typedef basic_streambuf<wchar_t, char_traits<wchar_t> > wstreambuf;
    };
```

Note that this header file is usually included with the use of other iostreams headers and is usually not directly included.

basic_streambuf

The basic_streambuf template class is used to describe an abstract base class for deriving a stream buffer. The stream buffer is used to control the transmission of elements to and from a representation of a stream. An object of class basic_streambuf<E, T> is used to control a stream using elements of type E with character traits described by the class T. This template class is used by <streambuf>:

```
template <class E, class T = char_traits<E> >
    class basic_streambuf {
public:
    typedef E char_type;
    typedef T traits_type;
    typedef T::int_type int_type;
    typedef T::pos_type pos_type;
    typedef T::off_type off_type;
    virtual ~streambuf();
    locale pubimbue(const locale& loc);
    locale getloc() const;
    basic_streambuf *pubsetbuf(E *s, streamsize n);
    pos_type pubseekoff(off_type off, ios_base::seekdir way,
        ios_base::openmode which = ios_base::in | ios_base::out);
    pos_type pubseekpos(pos_type sp,
        ios_base::openmode which = ios_base::in | ios_base::out);
    int pubsync();
    streamsize in_avail();
    int_type snextc();
    int_type sbumpc();
    int_type sgetc();
    streamsize sgetn(E *s, streamsize n);
    int_type sputbackc(E c);
```

```
    int_type sungetc();
    int_type sputc(E c);
    streamsize sputn(const E *s, streamsize n);
protected:
    basic_streambuf();
    E *eback() const;
    E *gptr() const;
    E *egptr() const;
    void gbump(int n);
    void setg(E *gbeg, E *gnext, E *gend);
    E *pbase() const;
    E *pptr() const;
    E *epptr() const;
    void pbump(int n);
    void setp(E *pbeg, E *pend);
    virtual void imbue(const locale &loc);
    virtual basic_streambuf *setbuf(E *s, streamsize n);
    virtual pos_type seekoff(off_type off, ios_base::seekdir way,
        ios_base::openmode which = ios_base::in | ios_base::out);
    virtual pos_type seekpos(pos_type sp,
        ios_base::openmode which = ios_base::in | ios_base::out);
    virtual int sync();
    virtual int showmanyc();
    virtual streamsize xsgetn(E *s, streamsize n);
    virtual int_type underflow();
    virtual int_type uflow();
    virtual int_type pbackfail(int_type c = T::eof());
    virtual streamsize xsputn(const E *s, streamsize n);
    virtual int_type overflow(int_type c = T::eof());
    };
```

The stream buffer controls two independent streams: one for extractions (input) and one for insertions (output). When a specific representation is used, either or both of these streams may be rendered inaccessible. The stream buffer is used to create a relationship between the two streams so that what is inserted into the output stream using a basic_stringbuf<E, T> object can be extracted later from its input stream.

The public interface of basic_streambuf provides the operations that are common to all stream buffers. The protected interface of basic_streambuf provides the operations needed for a specific representation of a stream in order for it to work. The protected virtual member functions can be used to customize the behavior of a derived stream buffer for a specific representation of a stream. The other protected member functions are used to control copying in and out of any storage supplied to buffer transmissions.

Input buffer functions are described in Table 24.1.

Table 24.1 Input buffer member functions

Member Function	Description
eback()	a pointer that points to the beginning of the buffer
egptr()	a pointer that points just past the end of the buffer
gptr()	a pointer that points to the next element to read

Output buffer functions are described in Table 24.2.

Table 24.2 Output buffer member functions

Member Function	Description
epptr()	a pointer that points just past the end of the buffer
pbase()	a pointer that points to the beginning of the buffer
pptr()	a pointer that points to the next element to write

An object of the class basic_streambuf<E, T> is used to store the pointers described in Tables 24.1 and 24.2. The object also stores a locale object using an object of type locale for use by a derived stream buffer.

The <strstream> Header Syntax

The following listing gives the syntax for using the <strstream> standard header file. The iostream standard header <strstream> is included in order to define four classes that support iostreams operations on sequences stored in an allocated array of objects of type char.

```
namespace std {
    class strstreambuf;
    class istrstream;
    class ostrstream;
    class strstream;
    };
```

The sequences, used by iostreams, can be converted back and forth from C strings.

In the next section, we'll examine sample code that illustrates the use of the previously defined iostream templates and classes.

Sample Code

The three applications presented in this section illustrate basic iostream manipulations.

The first application, insertion.cpp, illustrates the use of the insertion operator. The second application, flush.cpp, shows how flushing the output stream buffer can affect program operation. The third application, strstring.cpp, shows how various flags can be used to format the output stream.

The Insertion Operator

Applications do not have to be complicated to illustrate features of the standard i/o headers. For example, the basic_ostream class shows the insertion overloaded for a variety of types. The little application that follows, insertion.cpp, uses the insertion operator to insert a string into the output stream:

```
// insertion.cpp
// Application illustrates the use of the
// iostream insertion operator.
// Chris H. Pappas and William H. Murray, 1999

#include <string>
#include <iostream>

using namespace std ;

void main()
{
    string str = "Inserted by the insertion operator.";

    cout << str << endl << endl;
}
```

The output from this application is predictable:

```
Inserted by the insertion operator.
```

Well, as simple as this application is, you'll have to admit that it does illustrate the use of the insertion operator in a legitimate application.

The Flush Manipulator

The flush.cpp application illustrates the effect of buffering the output stream. If the program is run, as shown, a 10-second delay will occur between when the first line is printed and the second line.

```
// flush.cpp
// Application illustrates the use of iostream.
// Chris H. Pappas and William H. Murray, 1999
```

```
#include <iostream>
#include <time.h>

using namespace std;

void main()
{
  time_t tm = time(NULL) + 10;

  cout << "Wait for 10 second time delay" << flush;

  while (time(NULL) < tm);

  cout << "\nDelay completed."
       << endl << endl;
}
```

This application works correctly because the output buffer is flushed using the flush manipulator.

Remove the flush manipulator from the application and prepare yourself for a little surprise! That's correct, without flushing, the buffer both lines will be printed after the 10-second delay.

Using <strstream>

The following application, strstring.cpp, illustrates formatting techniques using <iostream> and <strstream>:

```
// strstream.cpp
// Application illustrates the use of advanced
// conversions and formatting using <iostream>
// and <strstream>.
// Chris H. Pappas and William H. Murray, 1999

#include <string>
#include <iostream>
#include <strstream>

using namespace std;

#define INULL_TERMINATOR 1

void row (void);

void main( )
{
  char   c       = 'A',
         psz1[] = "person has a full time job making a ",
         psz2[] = "living today.  Forget free time!";
  int    iln     = 0,
```

```
       ivalue = 2468;
double dPi    = 3.16159265;

char psz_padstring5[5 + INULL_TERMINATOR],
psz_padstring41[41 + INULL_TERMINATOR];

// conversions

// print the character
// notice that << has been overloaded to output char
row( ); // [ 1]
cout << c;

// print the ASCII code for c
row( ); // [ 2]
cout << (int)c;

// print character with ASCII 90
row( ); // [ 3]
cout << (char)90;

// print ivalue as octal value
row( ); // [ 4]
cout << oct << ivalue;

// print lowercase hexadecimal
row( ); // [ 5]
cout << hex << ivalue;

// print uppercase hexadecimal
row( ); // [ 6] cout.setf(ios::uppercase);
cout << hex << ivalue;
cout.unsetf(ios::uppercase);  // turn uppercase off
cout << dec;                  // return to decimal base

// conversions and format options

// minimum width 1
row( ); // [ 7]
cout << c;

// minimum width 5, right-justify
row( ); // [ 8]
ostrstream(psz_padstring5,sizeof(psz_padstring5))
<< "    " << c << ends;
cout << psz_padstring5;

// minimum width 5, left-justify
row( ); // [ 9]
ostrstream(psz_padstring5,sizeof(psz_padstring5))
```

```
<< c << "     " << ends;
cout << psz_padstring5;

// 33 automatically
row( ); // [10]
cout << psz1;

// 31 automatically
row( ); // [11]
cout << psz2;

// minimum 5 overriden, auto
// notice that the width of 5 cannot be overridden!
row( ); // [12]
cout.write(psz1,5);

// minimum width 41, right-justify
// notice how the width of 41 ends with garbage data
row( ); // [13]
cout.write(psz1,41);

// the following is the correct approach
cout << "\n\nCorrected approach:\n";
ostrstream(psz_padstring41,sizeof(psz_padstring41))
     << "       " << psz1 << ends;
row( ); // [14]
cout << psz_padstring41;

// minimum width 41, left-justify
ostrstream(psz_padstring41,sizeof(psz_padstring41))
  << psz2 << "        " << ends;
row( ); // [15]
cout << psz_padstring41;

// default ivalue width
row( ); // [16]
cout << ivalue;

// printf ivalue with + sign
row( ); // [17]
cout.setf(ios::showpos); // don't want row number with +
cout << ivalue;
cout.unsetf(ios::showpos);

// minimum 3 overridden, auto
row( ); // [18]
cout.width(3); // don't want row number padded to width of 3
cout << ivalue;

// minimum width 10, right-justify
```

```
row( ); // [19]
cout.width(10);     // only in effect for first value printed
cout << ivalue;

// minimum width 10, left-justify
row( ); // [20]
cout.width(10);
cout.setf(ios::left);
cout << ivalue;
cout.unsetf(ios::left);

// right-justify with leading 0's
row( ); // [21]
cout.width(10);
cout.fill('0');
cout << ivalue;
cout.fill(' ');

// using default number of digits
row( ); // [22]
cout << dPi;

// minimum width 20, right-justify
row( ); // [23]
cout.width(20);
cout << dPi;

// right-justify with leading 0's
row( ); // [24]
cout.width(20);
cout.fill('0');
cout << dPi;
cout.fill(' ');

// minimum width 20, left-justify
row( ); // [25]
cout.width(20);
cout.setf(ios::left);
cout << dPi;

// left-justify with trailing 0's
row( ); // [26]
cout.width(20);
cout.fill('0');
cout << dPi;
cout.unsetf(ios::left);
cout.fill(' ');

// additional formatting precision
```

```
// minimum width 19, print all 17
row( ); // [27]
cout << psz1;

// prints first 2 chars
row( ); // [28]
cout.write(psz1,2);

// prints 2 chars, right-justify
row( ); // [29]
cout << "                  ";
cout.write(psz1,2);

// prints 2 chars, left-justify
row( ); // [30]
cout.write(psz1,2);

// using printf arguments
row( ); // [31]
cout << "              ";
cout.write(psz1,6);

// width 10, 8 to right of '.'
row( ); // [32]
cout.precision(9);
cout << dPi;

// width 20, 2 to right-justify
row( ); // [33]
cout.width(20);
cout.precision(2);
cout << dPi;

// 4 decimal places, left-justify
row( ); // [34]
cout.precision(4);
cout << dPi;

// 4 decimal places, right-justify
row( ); // [35]
cout.width(20);
cout << dPi;

// width 20, scientific notation
row( ); // [36]
cout.setf(ios::scientific);
cout.width(20);
cout << dPi; cout.unsetf(ios::scientific);

cout << endl  << endl;
```

```
}

void row (void)
{
  static int ln=0;
  cout << "\n[";
  cout.width(2);
  cout << ++ln << "] ";
}
```

The output from this application takes the following form:

```
[ 1] A
[ 2] 65
[ 3] Z
[ 4] 4644
[ 5] 9a4
[ 6] 9a4
[ 7] A
[ 8]        A
[ 9] A
[10] person has a full time job making a
[11] living today.  Forget free time!
[12] perso
[13] person has a full time job making a _ÌÌÌA

Corrected approach:

[14]      person has a full time job making a
[15] living today.  Forget free time!
[16] 2468
[17] +2468
[18] 2468
[19]       2468
[20] 2468
[21] 0000002468
[22] 3.16159
[23]              3.16159
[24] 00000000000003.16159
[25] 3.16159
[26] 3.16159000000000000
[27] person has a full time job making a
[28] pe
[29]                   pe
[30] pe
[31]               person
[32] 3.16159265
[33]                  3.2
[34] 3.162
[35]                3.162
[36]          3.1616e+000
```

This application should give you an idea of how you can manipulate the output stream by setting various formatting flags and so on.

Summary

This chapter has described the <fstream>, <iostream>, <istream>, <ostream>, <sstream>, <streambuf>, and <strstream> header files. These standard header files are used to define template classes that support iostreams operations on sequences stored in external files. The iostreams headers support conversions between text and encoded forms, and input and output to external files.

Three simple applications were used to illustrate various aspects of these standard header files.

T W E N T Y - F I V E

The <ios> and <iosfwd> Standard C++ Headers

This chapter describes the <ios> and <iosfwd> header files. These standard header files are used to define types and functions related to the basic operation of iostreams. Both headers are typically included in applications with the use of other iostreams headers.

This chapter describes the new ANSI standard header syntax for these headers. We'll also investigate features for implementing the header code.

The <ios> Header Syntax

The following listing gives the syntax for using the <ios> standard header file. Note the divisions in the following listing separating template classes and manipulators:

```
namespace std {
    typedef T1 streamoff;
    typedef T2 streamsize;
    class ios_base;
    // TEMPLATE CLASSES
    template <class E, class T = char_traits<E> >
        class basic_ios;
    typedef basic_ios<char, char_traits<char> > ios;
    typedef basic_ios<wchar_t, char_traits<wchar_t> > wios;
    template <class St>
        class fpos;
```

```
typedef fpos<mbstate_t> streampos;
typedef fpos<mbstate_t> wstreampos;
// MANIPULATORS
ios_base& boolalpha(ios_base& str);
ios_base& noboolalpha(ios_base& str);
ios_base& showbase(ios_base& str);
ios_base& noshowbase(ios_base& str);
ios_base& showpoint(ios_base& str);
ios_base& noshowpoint(ios_base& str);
ios_base& showpos(ios_base& str);
ios_base& noshowpos(ios_base& str);
ios_base& skipws(ios_base& str);
ios_base& noskipws(ios_base& str);
ios_base& unitbuf(ios_base& str);
ios_base& nounitbuf(ios_base& str);
ios_base& uppercase(ios_base& str);
ios_base& nouppercase(ios_base& str);
ios_base& internal(ios_base& str);
ios_base& left(ios_base& str);
ios_base& right(ios_base& str);
ios_base& dec(ios_base& str);
ios_base& hex(ios_base& str);
ios_base& oct(ios_base& str);
ios_base& fixed(ios_base& str);
ios_base& scientific(ios_base& str);
};
```

The <ios> standard header contains a group of functions that serve as manipulators. These manipulators are used to alter values stored in its argument object. The argument object is of class ios_base. Manipulators can also perform actions on streams controlled by objects of a type derived from this class. A manipulator can be inserted into an output stream or extracted from an input stream. The various manipulators will be discussed in a later section.

ios_base

The ios_base template class is used to define a stream buffer. This stream buffer is then used to control the transmission of elements to and from a sequence (of elements) stored in an external file. This template class is used by <fstream>:

```
class ios_base {
public:
    class failure;
    typedef T1 fmtflags;
    static const fmtflags boolalpha, dec, fixed, hex, internal,
        left, oct, right, scientific, showbase, showpoint,
        showpos, skipws, unitbuf, uppercase, adjustfield,
        basefield, floatfield;
    typedef T2 iostate;
```

```
    static const iostate badbit, eofbit, failbit, goodbit;
    typedef T3 openmode;
    static const openmode app, ate, binary, in, out, trunc;
    typedef T4 seekdir;
    static const seekdir beg, cur, end;
    typedef T5 event;
    static const event copyfmt_event, erase_event,
        copyfmt_event;
    class Init;
    ios_base& operator=(const ios_base& rhs);
    fmtflags flags() const;
    fmtflags flags(fmtflags fmtfl);
    fmtflags setf(fmtflags fmtfl);
    fmtflags setf(fmtflags fmtfl, fmtflags mask);
    void unsetf(fmtflags mask);
    streamsize precision() const;
    streamsize precision(streamsize prec);
    streamsize width() const;
    stramsize width(streamsize wide);
    locale imbue(const locale& loc);
    locale getloc() const;
    static int xalloc();
    long& iword(int idx);
    void *& pword(int idx);
    typedef void *(event_callback(event ev, ios_base& ios, int idx);
    void register_callback(event_callback pfn, int idx);
    static bool sync_with_stdio(bool sync = true);
protected:
    ios_base();
};
```

Notice, as you examine the listing, that storage and member functions are defined here. These storage and member functions are common to both input and output streams. These input and output streams are not dependent on the template parameters. Objects of the ios_base class store formatting information, as indicated in Table 25.1.

Table 25.1 ios_base formatting information

Object Type	Purpose
iostate	Exception mask.
int	Field width.
int	Display precision.
locale	Locale object.

The ios_base class also uses two extensible arrays. These arrays have elements of type **long** and **void** pointer.

basic_ios

The basic_ios template class is used to describe the storage and member functions that are common to both input and output streams. Specifically, these streams are of the template class basic_istream or basic_ostream. These classes are dependent on the template parameters:

```
template <class E, class T = char_traits<E> >
    class basic_ios : public ios_base {
public:
    typedef E char_type;
    typedef T::int_type int_type;
    typedef T::pos_type pos_type;
    typedef T::off_type off_type;
    explicit basic_ios(basic_streambuf<E, T>* sb);
    virtual ~basic_ios();
    operator void *() const;
    bool operator!() const;
    iostate rdstate() const;
    void clear(iostate state = goodbit);
    void setstate(iostate state);
    bool good() const;
    bool eof() const;
    bool fail() const;
    bool bad() const;
    iostate exceptions() const;
    iostate exceptions(iostate except);
    basic_ios& copyfmt(const basic_ios& rhs);
    E fill() const;
    E fill(E ch);
    basic_ostream<E, T> *tie() const;
    basic_ostream<E, T> *tie(basic_ostream<E, T> *str);
    basic_streambuf<E, T> *rdbuf() const;
    basic_streambuf<E, T> *rdbuf(basic_streambuf<E, T> *sb);
    basic_ios& copyfmt(const basic_ios& rhs);
    locale imbue(const locale& loc);
    E widen(char ch);
    char narrow(E ch, char dflt);
protected:
    basic_ios();
    void init(basic_streambuf<E, T>* sb);
    };
```

Objects of basic_ios<E, T> class are used to control a stream of elements of type E. These elements have character traits described by the T class.

Objects of this class store formatting and stream state information in a base object of type ios_base.

fpos

The fpos template class describes an object that is used to store information required to restore an arbitrary file-position indicator within a stream:

```
template <class St>
    class fpos {
public:
    fpos(St state, fpos_t fposn);
    fpos(streamoff off);
    fpos_t get_fpos_t() const;
    St state() const;
    void state(St state);
    operator streamoff() const;
    streamoff operator-(const fpos<St>& rhs) const;
    fpos<St>& operator+=(streamoff off);
    fpos<St>& operator-=(streamoff off);
    fpos<St> operator+(streamoff off) const;
    fpos<St> operator-(streamoff off) const;
    bool operator==(const fpos<St>& rhs) const;
    bool operator!=(const fpos<St>& rhs) const;
};
```

Objects of fpos<St> class store a byte offset, arbitrary file position, and conversion state. The byte offset is of type streamoff. The arbitrary file position is of type fpos_t. The conversion state is of type mbstate_t.

Manipulators

Table 25.2 lists the manipulators defined in the <ios> standard header and provides a short description for their use.

Table 25.2 <ios> manipulators

Manipulator and Parameters	Operation
`boolalpha(ios_base& str)`	Calls str.setf(ios_base::boolalpha). Returns str.
`noboolalpha(ios_base& str)`	Calls str.unsetf(ios_base::boolalpha). Returns str.
`showbase(ios_base& str)`	Calls str.setf(ios_base::showbase). Returns str.
`noshowbase(ios_base& str)`	Calls str.unsetf(ios_base::showbase). Returns str.
`showpoint(ios_base& str)`	Calls str.setf(ios_base::showpoint), Returns str.
`noshowpoint(ios_base& str)`	Calls str.unsetf(ios_base::showpoint). Returns str.
`showpos(ios_base& str)`	Calls str.setf(ios_base::showpos). Returns str.
`noshowpos(ios_base& str)`	Calls str.unsetf(ios_base:: showp[os). Returns str.
`skipws(ios_base& str)`	Calls str.setf(ios_base:: skipws). Returns str.

Table 25.2 <ios> manipulators *(continued)*

Manipulator and Parameters	Operation
`noskipws(ios_base& str)`	Calls str.unsetf(ios_base:: skipws). Returns str.
`unitbuf(ios_base& str)`	Calls str.setf(ios_base:: unitbuf). Returns str.
`nounitbuf(ios_base& str)`	Calls str.unsetf(ios_base:: unitbuf). Returns str.
`uppercase(ios_base& str)`	Calls str.setf(ios_base:: uppercase). Returns str.
`nouppercase(ios_base& str)`	Calls str.unsetf(ios_base:: uppercase). Returns str.
`internal(ios_base& str)`	Calls str.setf(ios_base:: internal, ios_base:: adjustfield). Returns str.
`left(ios_base& str)`	Calls str.setf(ios_base:: left, ios_base:: adjustfield). Returns str.
`right(ios_base& str)`	Calls str.setf(ios_base:: right, ios_base:: adjustfield). Returns str.
`dec(ios_base& str)`	Calls str.setf(ios_base:: dec, ios_base:: basefield). Returns str.
`hex(ios_base& str)`	Calls str.setf(ios_base:: hex, ios_base:: basefield). Returns str.
`oct(ios_base& str)`	Calls str.setf(ios_base:: oct, ios_base:: basefield). Returns str.
`fixed(ios_base& str)`	Calls str.setf(ios_base:: fixed, ios_base:: floatfield). Returns str.
`scientific(ios_base& str)`	Calls str.setf(ios_base:: scientific, ios_base:: floatfield). Returns str.

You are probably already familiar with the actions of most of the manipulators described in Table 25.2.

The <iosfwd> Header Syntax

The following listing gives the syntax for using the <iosfwd> standard header file. As you examine the listing, notice the division in the listing between template class, char, and wchar_t type definitions:

```
namespace std {
// Type Definitions
typedef T1 streamoff;
typedef T2 streampos;
// Templates
template<class E>
    class char_traits;
class "char_traits<char>;
class "char_traits<wchar_t>;
template<class E, class T = char_traits<E> >
    class basic_ios;
template<class E, class T = char_traits<E> >
    class istreambuf_iterator;
template<class E, class T = char_traits<E> >
```

```
    class ostreambuf_iterator;
template<class E, class T = char_traits<E> >
    class basic_streambuf;
template<class E, class T = char_traits<E> >
    class basic_istream;
template<class E, class T = char_traits<E> >
    class basic_ostream;
template<class E, class T = char_traits<E> >
    class basic_iostream;
template<class E, class T = char_traits<E> >
    class basic_stringbuf;
template<class E, class T = char_traits<E> >
    class basic_istringstream;
template<class E, class T = char_traits<E> >
    class basic_ostringstream;
template<class E, class T = char_traits<E> >
    class basic_stringstream;
template<class E, class T = char_traits<E> >
    class basic_filebuf;
template<class E, class T = char_traits<E> >
    class basic_ifstream;
template<class E, class T = char_traits<E> >
    class basic_ofstream;
template<class E, class T = char_traits<E> >
    class basic_fstream;
// char Type Definitions
typedef basic_ios<char, char_traits<char> > ios;
typedef basic_streambuf<char, char_traits<char> > streambuf;
typedef basic_istream<char, char_traits<char> > istream;
typedef basic_ostream<char, char_traits<char> > ostream;
typedef basic_iostream<char, char_traits<char> > iostream;
typedef basic_stringbuf<char, char_traits<char> > stringbuf;
typedef basic_istringstream<char, char_traits<char> > istringstream;
typedef basic_ostringstream<char, char_traits<char> > ostringstream;
typedef basic_stringstream<char, char_traits<char> > stringstream;
typedef basic_filebuf<char, char_traits<char> > filebuf;
typedef basic_ifstream<char, char_traits<char> > ifstream;
typedef basic_ofstream<char, char_traits<char> > ofstream;
typedef basic_fstream<char, char_traits<char> > fstream;
// wchar_t Type Definitions
typedef basic_ios<wchar_t, char_traits<wchar_t> > wios;
typedef basic_streambuf<wchar_t, char_traits<wchar_t> > wstreambuf;
typedef basic_istream<wchar_t, char_traits<wchar_t> > wistream;
typedef basic_ostream<wchar_t, char_traits<wchar_t> > wostream;
typedef basic_iostream<wchar_t, char_traits<wchar_t> > wiostream;
typedef basic_stringbuf<wchar_t, char_traits<wchar_t> > wstringbuf;
typedef basic_istringstream<wchar_t, char_traits<wchar_t> >
wistringstream;
typedef basic_ostringstream<wchar_t, char_traits<wchar_t> >
wostringstream;
```

```
typedef basic_stringstream<wchar_t, char_traits<wchar_t> >
wstringstream;
typedef basic_filebuf<wchar_t, char_traits<wchar_t> > wfilebuf;
typedef basic_ifstream<wchar_t, char_traits<wchar_t> > wifstream;
typedef basic_ofstream<wchar_t, char_traits<wchar_t> > wofstream;
typedef basic_fstream<wchar_t, char_traits<wchar_t> > wfstream;
};
```

In the following sections, we'll examine the syntax for each of the template classes.

char_traits

The char_traits template class describes various character traits for type E. Here is the code for this class:

```
struct char_traits<E> {
    typedef E char_type;
    typedef T1 int_type;
    typedef T2 pos_type;
    typedef T3 off_type;
    typedef T4 state_type;
    static void assign(E& x, const E& y);
    static E *assign(E *x, size_t n, const E& y);
    static bool eq(const E& x, const E& y);
    static bool lt(const E& x, const E& y);
    static int compare(const E *x, const E *y, size_t n);
    static size_t length(const E *x);
    static E *copy(E *x, const E *y, size_t n);
    static E *move(E *x, const E *y, size_t n);
    static const E *find(const E *x, size_t n, const E& y);
    static E to_char_type(const int_type& ch);
    static int_type to_int_type(const E& c);
    static bool eq_int_type(const int_type& ch1, const int_type& ch2);
    static int_type eof();
    static int_type not_eof(const int_type& ch);
};
```

The information provided by the char_traits template class is used by the basic_string and several iostreams template classes. The basic_ios template class uses the information to manipulate elements of type E. Elements of this type cannot use explicit construction or destruction.

basic_ios

The basic_ios template class was described earlier in this chapter.

istreambuf_iterator

The istreambuf_iterator template class defines an input iterator object. This iterator object is used to extract elements of class E from an input stream buffer. The input stream buffer is accessed through an object that it stores. The object is of type pointer to basic_streambuf<E, T>.

```
template<class E, class T = char_traits<E> >
    class istreambuf_iterator
        : public iterator<input_iterator_tag, T, Dist> {
public:
    typedef E char_type;
    typedef T traits_type;
    typedef T::int_type int_type;
    typedef basic_streambuf<E, T> streambuf_type;

    typedef basic_istream<E, T> istream_type;
    istreambuf_iterator(streambuf_type *sb = 0) throw();
    istreambuf_iterator(istream_type& is) throw();
    const E& operator*() const;
    const E *"operator->();
    istreambuf_iterator& operator++();
    istreambuf_iterator operator++(int);
    bool equal(const istreambuf_iterator& rhs);
};
```

The object of the istreambuf_iterator class can be constructed or incremented with a non-null stored pointer. When this action occurs, the object tries to extract and store an object of type E from the input stream. In cases where the extraction fails, the object in effect replaces the stored pointer with a null pointer.

ostreambuf_iterator

The ostreambuf_iterator template class defines an output iterator object. This output iterator object is used to insert elements of class E into an output stream buffer. The output stream buffer is accessed using an object that it stores. This object is of type pointer to basic_streambuf<E, T>.

```
template<class E, class T = char_traits<E> >
    class ostreambuf_iterator
        : public iterator<output_iterator_tag, void, void>
{
public:
    typedef E char_type;
    typedef T traits_type;
    typedef basic_streambuf<E, T> streambuf_type;
    typedef basic_ostream<E, T> ostream_type;
    ostreambuf_iterator(streambuf_type *sb) throw();
    ostreambuf_iterator(ostream_type& os) throw();
```

```
    ostreambuf_iterator& operator=(E x);
    ostreambuf_iterator& operator*();
    ostreambuf_iterator& operator++();
    T1 operator++(int);
    bool failed() const throw();
};
```

The fact that the ostreambuf_iterator template class is structurally similar to the istreambuf_iterator template class probably comes as no surprise.

basic_streambuf, basic_istream, basic_ostream, basic_iostream, basic_stringbuf, basic_istringstream, basic_ostringstream, basic_stringstream, basic_filebuf, basic_ifstream, basic_ofstream, and basic_fstream

Each of these template classes has been previously described in Chapter 24. Please refer to Chapter 24 to view the syntax and a brief description of each template class.

Sample Code

As you have learned, <ios> serves as the base class for all the input and output stream classes. As such, <ios> is not usually used to construct ios objects nor are classes directly derived from it. Usually, classes are derived from the istream and ostream classes.

Refer to Chapter 24 for three examples involving classes derived from istream and ostream.

Summary

This chapter has described the <ios> and <iosfwd> standard header files. These standard header files are used to define types and functions related to the basic operation of iostreams. You have also learned that both headers are typically included in applications with the use of other iostreams headers.

T W E N T Y - S I X

The <valarray> Standard C++ Header

This chapter describes the <valarray> header file. This standard header file is used to define several classes and template classes that support value-oriented arrays. The valarray template class has several advantages over the vector class.

The <valarray> Header Syntax

The following listing gives the syntax for using the <valarray> standard header file:

```
namespace std {
class slice;
class gslice;

// TEMPLATE CLASSES
template<class T>
    class valarray;
template<class T>
    class slice_array;
template<class T>
    class gslice_array;
template<class T>
    class mask_array;
template<class T>
    class indirect_array;

// TEMPLATE FUNCTIONS
template<class T>
    valarray<T> operator*(const valarray<T>& lhs,
        const valarray<T>& rhs);
template<class T>
    valarray<T> operator*(const valarray<T> lhs,
        const T& rhs);
template<class T>
    valarray<T> operator*(const T& lhs, const valarray<T>& rhs);
template<class T>
    valarray<T> operator/(const valarray<T>& lhs,
        const valarray<T>& rhs);
template<class T>
    valarray<T> operator/(const valarray<T> lhs, const T& rhs);
template<class T>
    valarray<T> operator/(const T& lhs, const valarray<T>& rhs);
template<class T>
    valarray<T> operator%(const valarray<T>& lhs,
        const vararray<T>& rhs);
template<class T>
    valarray<T> operator%(const valarray<T> lhs, const T& rhs);
template<class T>
    valarray<T> operator%(const T& lhs, const valarray<T>& rhs);
template<class T>
    valarray<T> operator+(const valarray<T>& lhs,
        const valarray<T>& rhs);
template<class T>
    valarray<T> operator+(const valarray<T> lhs, const T& rhs);
template<class T>
    valarray<T> operator+(const T& lhs, const valarray<T>& rhs);
template<class T>
    valarray<T> operator-(const valarray<T>& lhs,
        const valarray<T>& rhs);
template<class T>
```

```
    valarray<T> operator-(const valarray<T> lhs, const T& rhs);
template<class T>
    valarray<T> operator-(const T& lhs, const valarray<T>& rhs);
template<class T>
    valarray<T> operator^(const valarray<T>& lhs,
        const valarray<T>& rhs);
template<class T>
    valarray<T> operator^(const valarray<T> lhs, const T& rhs);
template<class T>
    valarray<T> operator^(const T& lhs, const valarray<T>& rhs);
template<class T>
    valarray<T> operator&(const valarray<T>& lhs,
        const valarray<T>& rhs);
template<class T>
    valarray<T> operator&(const valarray<T> lhs, const T& rhs);
template<class T>
    valarray<T> operator&(const T& lhs, const valarray<T>& rhs);
template<class T>
    valarray<T> operator|(const valarray<T>& lhs,
        const valarray<T>& rhs);
template<class T>
    valarray<T> operator|(const valarray<T> lhs, const T& rhs);
template<class T>
    valarray<T> operator|(const T& lhs, const valarray<T>& rhs);
template<class T>
    valarray<T> operator<<(const valarray<T>& lhs,
        const valarray<T>& rhs);
template<class T>
    valarray<T> operator<<(const valarray<T> lhs, const T& rhs);
template<class T>
    valarray<T> operator<<(const T& lhs,
                            const valarray<T>& rhs);
template<class T>
    valarray<T> "operator>>(const valarray<T>& lhs,
        const valarray<T>& rhs);
template<class T>
    valarray<T> "operator>>(const valarray<T> lhs,
                            const T& rhs);
template<class T>
    valarray<T> "operator>>(const T& lhs,
                            const valarray<T>& rhs);
template<class T>
    valarray<bool> operator&&(const valarray<T>& lhs,
        const valarray<T>& rhs);
template<class T>
    valarray<bool> operator&&(const valarray<T> lhs,
                            const T& rhs);
template<class T>
    valarray<bool> operator&&(const T& lhs,
                            const valarray<T>& rhs);
```

```
template<class T>
    valarray<biil> operator||(const valarray<T>& lhs,
        const valarray<T>& rhs);
template<class T>
    valarray<bool> operator||(const valarray<T> lhs,
                              const T& rhs);
template<class T>
    valarray<bool> operator||(const T& lhs,
                              const valarray<T>& rhs);
template<class T>
    valarray<bool> operator==(const valarray<T>& lhs,
        const valarray<T>& rhs);
template<class T>
    valarray<bool> operator==(const valarray<T> lhs,
                              const T& rhs);
template<class T>
    valarray<bool> operator==(const T& lhs,
                              const valarray<T>& rhs);
template<class T>
    valarray<bool> operator!=(const valarray<T>& lhs,
        const valarray<T>& rhs);
template<class T>
    valarray<bool> operator!=(const valarray<T> lhs,
                              const T& rhs);
template<class T>
    valarray<bool> operator!=(const T& lhs,
                              const valarray<T>& rhs);
template<class T>
    valarray<bool> operator<(const valarray<T>& lhs,
        const valarray<T>& rhs);
template<class T>
    valarray<bool> operator<(const valarray<T> lhs,
                             const T& rhs);
template<class T>
    valarray<bool> operator<(const T& lhs,
                             const valarray<T>& rhs);
template<class T>
    valarray<bool> ="operator>=(const valarray<T>& lhs,
        const valarray<T>& rhs);
template<class T>
    valarray<bool> ="operator>=(const valarray<T> lhs,
                                const T& rhs);
template<class T>
    valarray<bool> ="operator>=(const T& lhs,
                                const valarray<T>& rhs);
template<class T>
    valarray<bool> "operator>(const valarray<T>& lhs,
        const valarray<T>& rhs);
template<class T>
    valarray<bool> "operator>(const valarray<T> lhs,
```

```
                               const T& rhs);
template<class T>
    valarray<bool> "operator>(const T& lhs,
                               const valarray<T>& rhs);
template<class T>
    valarray<bool> operator<=(const valarray<T>& lhs,
        const valarray<T>& rhs);
template<class T>
    valarray<bool> operator<=(const valarray<T> lhs,
                               const T& rhs);
template<class T>
    valarray<bool> operator<=(const T& lhs,
                               const valarray<T>& rhs);
template<class T>
    T max(const valarray<T>& x);
template<class T>
    T min(const valarray<T>& x);
template<class T>
    valarray<T> abs(const valarray<T>& x);
template<class T>
    valarray<T> acos(const valarray<T>& x);
template<class T>
    valarray<T> asin(const valarray<T>& x);
template<class T>
    valarray<T> atan(const valarray<T>& x);
template<class T>
    valarray<T> atan2(const valarray<T>& x,
        const valarray<T>& y);
template<class T>
    valarray<T> atan2(const valarray<T> x, const T& y);
template<class T>
    valarray<T> atan2(const T& x, const valarray<T>& y);
template<class T>
    valarray<T> cos(const valarray<T>& x);
template<class T>
    valarray<T> cosh(const valarray<T>& x);
template<class T>
    valarray<T> exp(const valarray<T>& x);
template<class T>
    valarray<T> log(const valarray<T>& x);
template<class T>
    valarray&ttT> log10(const valarray<T>& x);
template<class T>
    valarray<T> pow(const valarray<T>& x,
        const valarray<T>& y);
template<class T>
    valarray<T> pow(const valarray<T> x, const T& y);
template<class T>
    valarray<T> pow(const T& x, const valarray<T>& y);
template<class T>
```

```
    valarray<T> sin(const valarray<T>& x);
template<class T>
    valarray<T> sinh(const valarray<T>& x);
template<class T>
    valarray<T> sqrt(const valarray<T>& x);
template<class T>
    valarray<T> tan(const valarray<T>& x);
template<class T>
    valarray<T> tanh(const valarray<T>& x);
};
```

The <valarray> is used to define the template class valarray and a host of supporting template classes and functions. The template classes include valarray, slice_array, gslice_array, mask_array, and indirect_array. Template functions that return valarray<T> are permitted to return an object of some other type T'. Under these conditions, the function accepts one or more arguments of type valarray<T> and must provide overloads that accept arbitrary combinations of those arguments. Each argument is then replaced with an argument of type T'. As Microsoft so uniquely states, "the only way this substitution can be detected is to go looking for it."

valarray

The valarray template class is used to define an object that controls a varying-length sequence of elements. These elements are of type T:

```
template<class T>
    class valarray {
public:
    typedef T value_type;
    valarray();
    explicit valarray(size_t n);
    valarray(const T& val, size_t n));
    valarray(const T *p, size_t n);
    valarray(const slice_array<T>& sa);
    valarray(const gslice_array<T>& ga);
    valarray(const mask_array<T>& ma);
    valarray(const indirect_array<T>& ia);
    valarray<T>& operator=(const valarray<T>& va);
    valarray<T>& operator=(const T& x);
    valarray<T>& operator=(const slice_array<T>& sa);
    valarray<T>& operator=(const gslice_array<T>& ga);
    valarray<T>& operator=(const mask_array<T>& ma);
    valarray<T>& operator=(const indirect_array<T>& ia);
    T operator[](size_t n) const;
    T& operator[](size_t n);
    valarray<T> operator[](slice sa) const;
    slice_array<T> operator[](slice sa);
    valarray<T> operator[](const gslice& ga) const;
    gslice_array<T> operator[](const gslice& ga);
```

```
    valarray<T> operator[](const valarray<bool>& ba) const;
    mask_array<T> operator[](const valarray<bool>& ba);
    valarray<T> operator[](const valarray<size_t>& xa) const;
    indirect_array<T> operator[](const valarray<size_t>& xa);
    valarray<T> operator+();
    valarray<T> operator-();
    valarray<T> operator~();
    valarray<bool> operator!();
    valarray<T>& operator*=(const valarray<T>& x);
    valarray<T>& operator*=(const T& x);
    valarray<T>& operator/=(const valarray<T>& x);
    valarray<T>& operator/=(const T& x);
    valarray<T>& operator%=(const valarray<T>& x);
    valarray<T>& operator%=(const T& x);
    valarray<T>& operator+=(const valarray<T>& x);
    valarray<T>& operator+=(const T& x);
    valarray<T>& operator-=(const valarray<T>& x);
    valarray<T>& operator-=(const T& x);
    valarray<T>& operator^=(const valarray<T>& x);
    valarray<T>& operator^=(const T& x);
    valarray<T>& operator&=(const valarray<T>& x);
    valarray<T>& operator&=(const T& x);
    valarray<T>& operator|=(const valarray<T>& x);
    valarray<T>& operator|=(const T& x);
    valarray<T>& operator<<=(const valarray<T>& x);
    valarray<T>& operator<<=(const T& x);
    valarray<T>& ="operator>>=(const valarray<T>& x);
    valarray<T>& ="operator>>=(const T& x);
    size_t size() const;
    T sum() const;
    T max() const;
    T min() const;
    valarray<T> shift(int n) const;
    valarray<T> cshift(int n) const;
    valarray<T> apply(T fn(T)) const;
    valarray<T> apply(T fn(const T&)) const;
    void fill(const T& val);
    void free();
    void resize(size_t n, const T& c = T());
};
```

The sequences are stored as an array of T. This storage differs from the vector template class in that it allows arithmetic operations between corresponding elements of valarray<T> objects of the same type and length. You can also overload operator[] so that valarray<T> can be subscripted in a unique manner.

slice_array

The slice_array class is used to define an object that stores a reference to an object x of class valarray<T>. Stored with this object is an object s1 of class slice that is used to describe the sequence of elements to select from the valarray<T> object.

```
template<class T>
    class slice_array {
public:
    typedef T value_type;
    void operator=(const valarray<T> x) const;
    void operator=(const T& x);
    void operator*=(const valarray<T> x) const;
    void operator/=(const valarray<T> x) const;
    void operator%=(const valarray<T> x) const;
    void operator+=(const valarray<T> x) const;
    void operator-=(const valarray<T> x) const;
    void operator^=(const valarray<T> x) const;
    void operator&=(const valarray<T> x) const;
    void operator|=(const valarray<T> x) const;
    void operator<<=(const valarray<T> x) const;
    void ="operator>>=(const valarray<T> x) const;
    void fill();
};
```

You construct a `slice_array<T>` object only by writing an expression of the form x[si]. The member functions of class slice_array then behave like the corresponding function signatures defined for valarray<T>, except that only the sequence of selected elements is affected.

For example: The sequence consists of si.size() elements, where element i becomes the index si.start() + i * si.stride() within x.

```
x[slice(1, 7, 4)]; //selects the following elements
1, 5, 9, 13, 17, 21, 25
```

gslice_array

The gslice_array class is used to define an object that stores a reference to an object x of class calarray<T>. Stored with this object is another object gs of class gslice that is used to describe the sequence of elements to be selected from the valarray<T> object:

```
template<class T>
    class gslice_array {
public:
    typedef T value_type;
    void operator=(const valarray<T> x) const;
    void operator=(const T& x);
    void operator*=(const valarray<T> x) const;
    void operator/=(const valarray<T> x) const;
```

```
    void operator%=(const valarray<T> x) const;
    void operator+=(const valarray<T> x) const;
    void operator-=(const valarray<T> x) const;
    void operator^=(const valarray<T> x) const;
    void operator&=(const valarray<T> x) const;
    void operator|=(const valarray<T> x) const;
    void operator<<=(const valarray<T> x) const;
    void ="operator>>=(const valarray<T> x) const;
    void fill();
};
```

A gslice_array<T> object is created by writing an expression of the form x[gs]. The gslice_array member functions respond like the function signatures for valarray<T>, with only the sequence of selected elements being affected.

For example, a sequence is defined as follows. A vector gs.size(), of length N, is used to construct an index vector calarray<size_t> idx(0, N). In this case, the first element of the sequence has an index k within x given by:

```
k = start;
for (size_t i = 0; i < gs.size()[i]; ++i)
    k += idx[i] * gs.stride()[i];
```

The successor to the index vector value is defined as:

```
for (size_t i = N; 0 < i--; )
    if (++idx[i] < gs.size()[i])
        break;
    else
        idx[i] = 0;
```

So for the following values:

```
const size_t lv[] = {2, 3};
const size_t dv[] = {7, 2};
const valarray<size_t> len(lv, 2), str(dv, 2);

// x[gslice(3, len, str)] selects elements with indices
//   3, 5, 7, 10, 12, 14
```

Can you determine how these values were determined?

mask_array

The mask_array class is used to define an object that stores a reference to an object x of class valarray<T>. Stored along with this object is a class "valarray<bool> that describes the sequence of elements that are to be selected from the valarray<T> object.

```
template<class T>
    class mask_array {
public:
    typedef T value_type;
    void operator=(const valarray<T> x) const;
```

```
    void operator=(const T& x);
    void operator*=(const valarray<T> x) const;
    void operator/=(const valarray<T> x) const;
    void operator%=(const valarray<T> x) const;
    void operator+=(const valarray<T> x) const;
    void operator-=(const valarray<T> x) const;
    void operator^=(const valarray<T> x) const;
    void operator&=(const valarray<T> x) const;
    void operator|=(const valarray<T> x) const;
    void operator<<=(const valarray<T> x) const;
    void ="operator>>=(const valarray<T> x) const;
    void fill();
};
```

The mask_array<T> object is created by writing an expression of the form x[xa]. The member functions of the mask_array object function like the function signatures for valarray<T>, with the exception that only the sequence of specified elements is affected.

For example: A sequence consists of a maximum of ma.size() elements. Elements are included in the sequence only when ma[j] is true. Here, j represents the element(s).

For example:

```
const bool vb[] = {false, true, true, false, false, true};
// x[valarray<bool>(vb, 20)] selects elements with indices
// 1, 2, 5
```

The array consists only of the elements that were true. The other elements in the sequence are not included.

indirect_array

The indirect_array class is used to define an object that stores a reference to an object x of class valarray<T>. This reference is stored along with an object ia of class valarray<size_t>. This object is used to define a sequence of elements that will be selected from the valarray<T> object:

```
template<class T>
    class indirect_array {
public:
    typedef T value_type;
    void operator=(const valarray<T> x) const;
    void operator=(const T& x);
    void operator*=(const valarray<T> x) const;
    void operator/=(const valarray<T> x) const;
    void operator%=(const valarray<T> x) const;
    void operator+=(const valarray<T> x) const;
    void operator-=(const valarray<T> x) const;
    void operator^=(const valarray<T> x) const;
    void operator&=(const valarray<T> x) const;
    void operator|=(const valarray<T> x) const;
    void operator<<=(const valarray<T> x) const;
```

```
    void ="operator>>=(const valarray<T> x) const;
    void fill();
};
```

An indirect_array<T> object is created by writing an expression of the form x[ia]. The member functions of the object behave like the function signatures defined for valarray<T>, with the exception that only the sequence of the selected elements is affected.

For example, assume that a sequence consists of ia.size() elements. In this sequence, element i forms the index ia[i] within x.

So for the following values:

```
const size_t vi[] = {1, 3, 5, 7, 2, 4, 6};


// x[valarray<size_t>(vi, 7)] selects elements with indices
// 1, 3, 5, 7, 2, 4, 6
```

The results of this operation are pretty straightforward.

Sample Code

This section contains three simple applications that illustrate the use of the mask_array template class, + operator, and the indirect_array template class.

The maskarray.cpp Application

This application makes use of the mask_array template class to mask the contents of values stored in a valarray.

```
// maskarray.cpp
// Application illustrates the use of the
// mask_array template class for <valarray>
// Chris H. Pappas and William H. Murray, 1999

#include <iostream>
#include <valarray>

using namespace std ;

#define ORG_ARRAY_SIZE 7

void main()
{
  int i;

  // declare original and new val_arrays
  valarray<double> oval_array(7), nval_array(7);

  // initialize original oval_array
```

```
  for (i = 0; i < ORG_ARRAY_SIZE; i++)
    oval_array[i]= i * i;

  // display original oval_array size
  cout << "original oval_array size is: "
       << oval_array.size() << endl << endl;

  // display values in original oval_array
  cout << "original oval_array values include: "
       << endl << endl;
  for (i = 0; i < oval_array.size(); i++)
    cout << oval_array[i] << "\t";

  cout << endl << endl << endl << endl;


  // prepare a mask
  const bool ba[] = {false, true, true, false,
                     false, true, true};

  // select values into nval_array
  nval_array = oval_array[valarray<bool>(ba,
ORG_ARRAY_SIZE)];


  // display new nval_array size
  cout << "new nval_array size is: "
       << nval_array.size() << endl << endl;

  // display values in new nval_array
  cout << "new nval_array values include: "
       << endl << endl;
  for (i = 0; i < nval_array.size(); i++)
    cout <<  nval_array[i] << "\t";

  cout << endl << endl << endl << endl;
}
```

The output from this application is shown next:

```
original oval_array size is: 7

original oval_array values include:

0    1    4    9    16    25    36



new nval_array size is: 4

new nval_array values include:

1    4    25    36
```

In this example, the original valarray, *oval_array*, is initialized with the squares of the integers from 0 to 6. A mask is prepared that mark the 1, 2, 5, and 6 elements of the array as true. Those results are placed in the new valarray, *nval_array*, and printed to the screen.

The addvalarray.cpp Application

This application makes use of the + operator for adding the contents of two valarrays:

```
// addvalarray.cpp
// Application illustrates the use of the
// + operator for adding values in two valarrays
// Chris H. Pappas and William H. Murray, 1999

#include <iostream>
#include <valarray>

using namespace std ;

#define ORG_ARRAY_SIZE 7

void main()
{
  int i;

  // declare original and new val_arrays
  valarray<double> val_array1(7), val_array2(7),
                   sval_array(7);

  // initialize original val_array1
  for (i = 0; i < ORG_ARRAY_SIZE; i++) {
    val_array1[i] = i * i;
    val_array2[i] = i;
  }

  // display original val_array1 size
  cout << "original val_array1 size is: "
       << val_array1.size() << endl << endl;

  // display values in original val_array1
  cout << "original val_array1 values include: "
       << endl << endl;
  for (i = 0; i < val_array1.size(); i++)
    cout << val_array1[i] << "\t";

  cout << endl << endl << endl << endl;


  // display new val_array2 size
```

```
  cout << "new val_array2 size is: "
       << val_array2.size() << endl << endl;

  // display values in new val_array2
  cout << "new val_array2 values include: "
       << endl << endl;
  for (i = 0; i < val_array2.size(); i++)
    cout <<  val_array2[i] << "\t";

  cout << endl << endl << endl << endl;

  // add values in two valarrays together
  sval_array = val_array1 + val_array2;

  // display the sum
  cout << "sum sval_array size is: "
       << sval_array.size() << endl << endl;

  // display values in sval_array
  cout << "sum sval_array values include: "
       << endl << endl;
  for (i = 0; i < sval_array.size(); i++)
    cout <<  sval_array[i] << "\t";

  cout << endl << endl << endl << endl;
}
```

The output sent to the screen from this application follows:

```
original val_array1 size is: 7

original val_array1 values include:

0	1	4	9	16	25	36



new val_array2 size is: 7

new val_array2 values include:

0	1	2	3	4	5	6



sum sval_array size is: 7

sum sval_array values include:

0	2	6	12	20	30	42
```

In this example, two valarrays are created and initialized. One valarray, *val_array1*, is initialized with the squares of integers from 0 to 6. The second val_array, *val_array2*, is initialized with the integers from 0 to 6.

The following portion of code is used to add the elements of each valarray together using the + operator.

```
// add values in two valarrays together
  sval_array = val_array1 + val_array2;
```

The *sval_array* contains the sums that are eventually printed to the screen.

The indirectarray.cpp Application

This application makes use of the indirect_array template class. It illustrates how to selectively pick elements from a valarray.

```
// indirectarray.cpp
// Application illustrates the use of the
// indirect_array template class for <valarray>
// Chris H. Pappas and William H. Murray, 1999

#include <iostream>
#include <valarray>

using namespace std ;

#define ORG_ARRAY_SIZE 7

void main()
{
  int i;

  // declare original and new val_arrays
  valarray<double> oval_array(7), nval_array(7);

  // initialize original oval_array
  for (i = 0; i < ORG_ARRAY_SIZE; i++)
    oval_array[i]= i * i;

  // display original oval_array size
  cout << "original oval_array size is: "
       << oval_array.size() << endl << endl;

  // display values in original oval_array
  cout << "original oval_array values include: "
       << endl << endl;
  for (i = 0; i < oval_array.size(); i++)
    cout << oval_array[i] << "\t";
```

```
  cout << endl << endl << endl << endl;


  // prepare a mask
  const size_t vi[] = {1, 3, 5, 0, 2, 4, 6};

  // select values into nval_array
  nval_array = oval_array[valarray<size_t>(vi, ORG_ARRAY_SIZE)];


  // display new nval_array size
  cout << "new nval_array size is: "
       << nval_array.size() << endl << endl;

  // display values in new nval_array
  cout << "new nval_array values include: "
       << endl << endl;
  for (i = 0; i < nval_array.size(); i++)
    cout <<  nval_array[i] << "\t";

  cout << endl << endl << endl << endl;
}
```

The output from this application follows:

```
original oval_array size is: 7

original oval_array values include:

0    1    4    9    16    25    36



new nval_array size is: 7

new nval_array values include:

1    9    25    0    4    16    36
```

The output sent to the screen illustrates how various elements of the oval_array are selected. The selection mask is of type size_t.

```
// prepare a mask
  const size_t vi[] = {1, 3, 5, 0, 2, 4, 6};
```

The syntax for making selections and storing them in a valarray named *nval_array* is straightforward.

```
// selects values into nval_array
nval_array = oval_array[valarray<size_t>(vi, ORG_ARRAY_SIZE)];
```

Can you agree that the results shown are correct?

Summary

This chapter has described the <valarray> standard header file. This standard header file provides several classes and template classes that support value-oriented arrays.

You also learned that the valarray template class provides several advantages over the vector template class.

T W E N T Y - S E V E N

The <ciso646>, <clocale>, <csetjump>, and <locale> Standard C++ Headers

This chapter describes the <ciso646>, <clocale>, <csetjump>, and <locale> header files. These standard header files provide iso646 functionality and provide locale support through a large group of template classes and so on.

The <ciso646> Header Syntax

The following listing gives the syntax for using the <ciso646> standard header file.

```
namespace std {#include <iso646.h> };
```

The <ciso646> standard header file is used to include the standard header <iso646.h> within the std namespace.

The <iso646.h> standard header contains eleven #define statements for logical operators that include and, and_eq, bitand, bitor, compl, not, not_eq, or, or_eq, and xor_eq.

The <clocale> Header Syntax

The locale refers to the national and cultural environment in which a system or program is running. The locale defines a number of important items, such as the language used for messages and menus, the sorting order of strings, the keyboard layout, date and time formatting conventions, and so on.

The following listing gives the syntax for using the <clocale> standard header file.

```
namespace std {#include <locale.h> };
```

Include the standard header <clocale> to effectively include the standard header <locale.h> within the std namespace.

This header file defines local categories, as shown in the next listing:

```
#define LC_ALL          0
#define LC_COLLATE      1
#define LC_CTYPE        2
#define LC_MONETARY     3
#define LC_NUMERIC      4
#define LC_TIME         5

#define LC_MIN          LC_ALL
#define LC_MAX          LC_TIME
```

These constants are used by the setlocale() function prototyped in the locale.h header file. Locale conventions can be read or set using the locale convention structure also defined in this header file:

```
struct lconv {
  char *decimal_point;
  char *thousands_sep;
  char *grouping;
  char *int_curr_symbol;
  char *currency_symbol;
  char *mon_decimal_point;
  char *mon_thousands_sep;
  char *mon_grouping;
  char *positive_sign;
  char *negative_sign;
  char int_frac_digits;
  char frac_digits;
  char p_cs_precedes;
  char p_sep_by_space;
  char n_cs_precedes;
  char n_sep_by_space;
  char p_sign_posn;
  char n_sign_posn;
};
```

This structure is used by the localeconv() function prototyped in the locale.h header file. Table 27.1 briefly describes the various structure members.

Table 27.1 lconv structure members and descriptions

Structure Member	Description
*decimal_point	The decimal-point character for non-monetary values.
*thousands_sep	The character used to separate groups of digits to left of decimal point for non-monetary values.
*grouping	The size for groups of digits in non-monetary values.
*int_curr_symbol	The international currency symbol for the locale. The first three characters are derived from the ISO 4217 Codes for the Representation of Currency and Funds standard.
*currency_symbol	The local currency symbol for the locale.
*mon_decimal_point	The decimal-point character to be used with monetary values.
*mon_thousands_sep	The character used to separate groups of digits to left of decimal point for monetary values.
*mon_grouping	The size for groups of digits in monetary values.
*positive_sign	A string used to denote the sign for nonnegative monetary values.
*negative_sign	A string used to denote the sign for negative monetary values.
int_frac_digits	The number of digits to right of decimal point in internationally formatted monetary values.
frac_digits	The number of digits to right of decimal point in internationally formatted monetary values.
p_cs_precedes	When the currency symbol precedes the value for nonnegative formatted monetary values, this is a 1. Otherwise, use a 0.
p_sep_by_space	When the currency symbol is separated by a space from the value for nonnegative formatted monetary values, this is a 1. Otherwise, use a 0.
n_cs_precedes	When the currency symbol precedes the value for a negative formatted monetary quantity, this is a 1. Otherwise, use a 0.
n_sep_by_space	When the currency symbol is separated by space from the value for negative formatted monetary values, this is a 1. Otherwise, use a 0.
p_sign_posn	Provides the position of the positive sign for nonnegative formatted monetary values.
n_sign_posn	Provides the position of the positive sign for negative formatted monetary values.

We mentioned two functions prototypes earlier in this section: setlocale() and localeconv(). Here are the prototypes for these functions:

```
_CRTIMP char * __cdecl setlocale(int, const char *);
_CRTIMP struct lconv * __cdecl localeconv(void);
```

The example section of this chapter will demonstrate uses for these function prototypes.

The <csetjump> Header Syntax

The following listing gives the syntax for using the <csetjump> standard header file:

```
namespace std {#include <setjmp.h> };
```

Include the standard header <csetjump> to effectively include the standard header <setjump.h> within the std namespace.

The setjump.h header file is used to define the machine-dependent buffer used by both setjmp and longjmp, which are used to save and restore the program state and declarations for those routines. The _JUMP_BUFFER structure is machine-dependent. You'll find different versions provided in this header file for Intel, MIPS, Alpha, and PowerPC hardware implementations. The following listing shows the structure used for Intel processors:

```
typedef struct __JUMP_BUFFER {
  unsigned long Ebp;
  unsigned long Ebx;
  unsigned long Edi;
  unsigned long Esi;
  unsigned long Esp;
  unsigned long Eip;
  unsigned long Registration;
  unsigned long TryLevel;
  unsigned long Cookie;
  unsigned long UnwindFunc;
  unsigned long UnwindData[6];
} _JUMP_BUFFER;
```

Two functions prototypes are also provided in this header file:

```
int __cdecl setjmp(jmp_buf);

#if     _MSC_VER >= 1200
_CRTIMP __declspec(noreturn) void __cdecl longjmp(jmp_buf, int);
#else
_CRTIMP void __cdecl longjmp(jmp_buf, int);
#endif
```

The setjmp() function is used to save the current state of the program. The longjmp() function restores the stack environment and execution locale.

The <locale> Header Syntax

The standard header <locale> is used to define a variety of template classes and functions. These classes and functions are used to encapsulate and manipulate locales:

```
namespace std {
    class locale;
    class ctype_base;
    template<class E>
        class ctype;
    class "ctype<char>;
    template<class E>
        class ctype_byname;
    class codecvt_base;
    template<class From, class To, class State>
        class codecvt;
    template<class From, class To, class State>
        class codecvt_byname;
    template<class E, class InIt>
        class num_get;
    template<class E, class OutIt>
        class num_put;
    template<class E>
        class numpunct;
    template<class E>
        class numpunct_byname;
    template<class E>
        class collate;
    template<class E>
        class collate_byname;
    class time_base;
    template<class E, class InIt>
        class time_get;
    template<class E, class InIt>
        class time_get_byname;
    template<class E, class OutIt>
        class time_put;
    template<class E, class OutIt>
        class time_put_byname;
    class money_base;
    template<class E, bool Intl, class InIt>
        class money_get;
    template<class E, bool Intl, class OutIt>
        class money_put;
    template<class E, bool Intl>
        class moneypunct;
    template<class E, bool Intl>
        class moneypunct_byname;
    class messages_base;
```

```
    template<class E>
        class messages;
    template<class E>
        class messages_byname;
//    TEMPLATE FUNCTIONS
    template<class Facet>
        bool has_facet(const locale& loc, const Facet
*fac);
    template<class Facet>
        const Facet& use_facet(const locale& loc,
            const Facet *fac, bool is_std);
    template<class E>
        bool isspace(E c, const locale& loc) const;
    template<class E>
        bool isprint(E c, const locale& loc) const;
    template<class E>
        bool iscntrl(E c, const locale& loc) const;
    template<class E>
        bool isupper(E c, const locale& loc) const;
    template<class E>
        bool islower(E c, const locale& loc) const;
    template<class E>
        bool isalpha(E c, const locale& loc) const;
    template<class E>
        bool isdigit(E c, const locale& loc) const;
    template<class E>
        bool ispunct(E c, const locale& loc) const;
    template<class E>
        bool isxdigit(E c, const locale& loc) const;
    template<class E>
        bool isalnum(E c, const locale& loc) const;
    template<class E>
        bool isgraph(E c, const locale& loc) const;
    template<class E>
        E toupper(E c, const locale& loc) const;
    template<class E>
        E tolower(E c, const locale& loc) const;
};
```

Table 27.2 briefly describes the purpose of each template class.

Table 27.2 Description of <locale> template classes

Class Name	Description
`ctype<char>`	This template class is used to describe an object that serves as a locale facet in order to characterize various properties of a "character" (element) of type *char*.
`codecvt`	This template class is used to describe an object that serves as a locale facet in order to control conversions between a sequence of values of type From and a sequence of values of type To.
`codecvt_base`	This template class is used to describe an enumeration that is common to the template class codecvt.
`codecvt_byname`	This template class is used to describe an object that serves as a locale facet of type codecvt<From, To, State>.
`collate`	This template class is used to describe an object that serves as a locale facet used to control comparisons of sequences of type E.
`collate_byname`	This template class is used to describe an object that serves as a locale facet of type collate<E>.
`ctype`	This template class is used to describe an object that serves as a locale facet to characterize various properties of a "character" (element) of type E.
`ctype_base`	This template class serves as a base class for facets of template class ctype. It defines the enumerated type mask and related constants: alnum, similar to isalnum() alpha, similar to isalpha() cntrl, similar to iscntrl() digit, similar to isdigit() graph, similar to isgraph() lower, similar to islower() print, similar to isprint() punct, similar to ispunct() space, similar to isspace() upper, similar to isupper() xdigit, similar to isxdigit() The constants can be ORed.
`ctype_byname`	This template class is used to describe an object that serves as a locale facet of type ctype<E>.

Table 27.2 Description of <locale> template classes *(continued)*

Class Name	Description
`locale`	This template class is used to describe a locale object that encapsulates a locale. The locale information is presented as a list of facets.
`messages`	This template class is used to describe an object that serves as a locale facet used to characterize properties of a message catalog. The message catalog supplies messages formed as sequences of elements of type E.
`messages_base`	This template class is used to describe a type common to all forms of the template class messages.
`messages_byname`	This template class is used to describe an object that serves as a locale facet of type message<E>.
`money_base`	This template class is used to describe an enumeration and a structure for all forms of template class moneypunct. Here, the enumeration part describes values in elements of the array field contained in the structure pattern. The values include: none, matches zero or more spaces or generates nothing. sign, matches or generates a positive or negative sign. space, matches zero or more spaces or generates a space. symbol, matches or generates a currency symbol. value, matches or generates a monetary value.
`money_get`	This template class is used to describe an object that serves as a locale facet used for conversions of sequences of type E to monetary values.
`money_put`	This template class is used to describe an object that serves as a locale facet for controlling conversions of monetary values to sequences of type E.
`moneypunct`	This template class is used to define an object that serves as a locale facet for describing sequences of type E. These sequences are used to represent a monetary input field or output field.
`moneypunct_byname`	This template class is used to describe an object that serves as a locale facet of type moneypunct<E, Int1>.
`num_get`	This template class is used to describe an object that serves as a locale facet for controlling conversions of sequences of type E to numeric values.
`num_put`	This template class is used to describe an object that serves as a locale facet for controlling conversions of numeric values to sequences of type E.
`numpunct`	This template class is used to describe an object that serves as a locale facet for describing the sequences of type E that are used to represent the input fields or output fields matched or generated by num_get.

Table 27.2 Description of <locale> template classes *(continued)*

Class Name	Description
`numpunct_byname`	This template class is used to describe an object that serves as a locale facet of type numpunct<E>.
`time_base`	This template class functions as a base class for facets of template class time_get. The enumerated type dateorder uses several constants: no_order, used to denote no particular order. dmy, used to denote day, month, and year. mdy, used to denote month, day, and year. ymd, used to denote year, month, and day. ydm, used to denote year, day, and month.
`time_get`	This template class is used to describe an object that serves as a locale facet for controlling conversions of sequences of type E to time values.
`time_get_byname`	This template class is used to describe an object that serves as a locale facet of type time_get<E, InIt>.
`time_put`	This template class is used to describe an object that serves as a locale facet for controlling conversions of time values to sequences of type E.
`time_put_byname`	This template class is used to describe an object that serves as a locale facet of type time_put<E, OutIt>.

Locale facets are referenced in Table 27.2. A facet is a pointer to an object of a class derived from class Facet that has a public object of the following form:

```
static locale::id id;
```

An open-ended set of this type of facet can be defined. You can also create a locale object that specifies an arbitrary number of facets.

The template functions described in this header include those listed and briefly described in Table 27.3. Refer to the <locale> listing for return types and parameters.

Table 27.3 <locale> Template Functions and Descriptions

Template Function	Description
`has_facet()`	Returns true when a locale facet of class Facet is listed within the locale object loc.
`isalnum()`	Returns use_facet<ctype<E> > (loc) is (ctype<E>:: alnum, c).
`isalpha()`	Returns use_facet<ctype<E> > (loc) is (ctype<E>:: alpha, c).

Table 27.3 <locale> Template Functions and Descriptions *(continued)*

Template Function	Description
`iscntrl()`	Returns use_facet<ctype<E> > (loc) is (ctype<E>:: cntrl, c).
`isdigit()`	Returns use_facet<ctype<E> > (loc) is (ctype<E>:: digit, c).
`isgraph()`	Returns use_facet<ctype<E> > (loc) is (ctype<E>:: graph, c).
`islower()`	Returns use_facet<ctype<E> > (loc) is (ctype<E>:: lower, c).
`isprint()`	Returns use_facet<ctype<E> > (loc) is (ctype<E>:: print, c).
`ispunct()`	Returns use_facet<ctype<E> > (loc) is (ctype<E>:: punct, c).
`isspace()`	Returns use_facet<ctype<E> > (loc) is (ctype<E>:: space, c).
`isupper()`	Returns use_facet<ctype<E> > (loc) is (ctype<E>:: upper, c).
`isxdigit()`	Returns use_facet<ctype<E> > (loc) is (ctype<E>:: xdigit, c).
`tolower()`	Returns use_facet<ctype<E> > (loc) tolower(c).
`toupper()`	Returns use_facet<ctype<E> > (loc) to upper(c) .
`use_facet()`	Returns a reference to a locale facet of class Facet that is listed within the locale object loc.

In the next section, we'll examine an example that will highlight material from this chapter.

Sample Code

This section contains a simple application named locale.cpp that will illustrate the use of the <locale> and <ctime> standard headers.

```
// locale.cpp
// Application illustrates the use of <locale>
// and <ctime> standard headers
// Chris H. Pappas and William H. Murray, 1999

#include <iostream>
#include <clocale>
#include <ctime>

using namespace std ;

void main()
{
  time_t timer;
  struct tm *date_time_struct_ptr;
  char conversion_buffer[80];
```

```
// set locale to Italian
setlocale(LC_ALL, "Italian");
time (&timer);
date_time_struct_ptr = gmtime(&timer);

strftime(conversion_buffer, 80, "%X, %A, %x",
         date_time_struct_ptr);

cout << "For Italian locale -> "
     << conversion_buffer << endl << endl;


// set locale to Swiss
setlocale(LC_ALL, "Swiss");
time (&timer);
date_time_struct_ptr = gmtime(&timer);

strftime(conversion_buffer, 80, "%X, %A, %x",
         date_time_struct_ptr);

cout << "For Swiss locale -> "
     << conversion_buffer << endl << endl;


// set locale to French
setlocale(LC_ALL, "French");
time (&timer);
date_time_struct_ptr = gmtime(&timer);

strftime(conversion_buffer, 80, "%X, %A, %x",
         date_time_struct_ptr);

cout << "For French locale -> "
     << conversion_buffer << endl << endl;


// set locale to English
setlocale(LC_ALL, "English");
time (&timer);
date_time_struct_ptr = gmtime(&timer);

strftime(conversion_buffer, 80, "%X, %A, %x",
         date_time_struct_ptr);

cout << "For English locale -> "
     << conversion_buffer << endl << endl;
}
```

We set our clocks ahead to April of 2001 and ran the application. Here is a sample of the output sent to the screen:

```
For Italian locale -> 23.02.42, lunedì, 23/04/01

For Swiss locale -> 23:02:42, Montag, 23.04.01

For French locale -> 23:02:42, lundi, 23/04/01

For English locale -> 11:02:42 PM, Monday, 04/23/01
```

As you can see, the application makes ample use of the setlocale() function. The contant used in each case is LC_ALL. For example:

```
setlocale(LC_ALL, "Swiss");
```

What do you think would happen to the output if the constant was changed to LC_MONETARY, LC_NUMERIC, or LC_TIME?

Summary

This chapter has described the <ciso646>, <clocale>, <csetjump>, and <locale> standard header files. You have learned, through the simple application, that the locale can be changed repeatedly within an application.

INDEX

A

B

D

E

F

K

L

M

N

S

W

Y